Points of View

Readings in American Government and Politics

ELEVENTH EDITION

Edited by

Robert E. DiClerico
Allan S. Hammock
West Virginia University

Boston Burr Ridge, IL Dubuque, IA Madison, WI New York
San Francisco St. Louis Bangkok Bogotá Caracas Kuala Lumpur
Lisbon London Madrid Mexico City Milan Montreal New Delhi
Santiago Seoul Singapore Sydney Taipei Toronto

 **Higher Education**

Published by McGraw-Hill, a business unit of The McGraw-Hill Companies, Inc., 1221 Avenue of the Americas, New York, NY, 10020. Copyright © 2009, 2007, 2004, 2001, 1998, 1995, 1992, 1989, 1986, 1983, 1980 by The McGraw-Hill Companies, Inc. All rights reserved. No part of this publication may be reproduced or distributed in any form or by any means, or stored in a database or retrieval system, without the prior written consent of The McGraw-Hill Companies, Inc., including, but not limited to, in any network or other electronic storage or transmission, or broadcast for distance learning.

Some ancillaries, including electronic and print components, may not be available to customers outside the United States.

This book is printed on acid-free paper.

1 2 3 4 5 6 7 8 9 0 DOC/DOC 0 9 8 7

ISBN: 978-0-07-340390-8
MHID: 0-07-340390-3

Editor-in-chief: *Michael Ryan*
Publisher: *Frank Mortimer*
Sponsoring editor: *Mark Georgiev*
Developmental editor: *Larry Goldberg*
Marketing manager: *Lori DeShazo*
Production editor: *Anne Fuzellier*
Design manager: *Preston Thomas*
Cover Design: *Scott Ratinoff*
Production supervisor: *Tandra Jorgensen*
Production service: *Matrix Productions Inc.*
Composition: *10/12 Palatino by International Typesetting & Composition*
Printing: *45# New Era Matte by R.R. Donnelley/Crawfordsville, IN.*

Library of Congress Cataloging-in-Publication Data

Points of view : readings in American government and politics / [edited by] Robert DiClerico, Allan Hammock.—11th ed.
    p. cm.
  ISBN-13: 978-0-07-340390-8 (alk. paper)
  ISBN-10: 0-07-340390-3 (alk. paper)
  1. United States—Politics and government. I. DiClerico, Robert E.
II. Hammock, Allan S., 1938–
JK21.P59 2009
320.973—dc22
                                            2007041207

The Internet addresses listed in the text were accurate at the time of publication. The inclusion of a Web site does not indicate an endorsement by the authors of McGraw-Hill, and McGraw-Hill does not guarantee the accuracy of the information presented at these sites.

www.mhhe.com

About the Editors

ROBERT E. DiCLERICO is the Eberly Distinguished Professor of Political Science at West Virginia University. An Indiana University (Bloomington) Ph.D. and a Danforth Fellow, he is author of *Voting in America* (2004) and *The American President,* 5th edition (2000); coauthor of *Choosing Our Choices* (2000) and *Few Are Chosen* (1984); and editor of *Political Parties, Campaigns, and Elections* (2000) and *Analyzing the Presidency* (1985).

ALLAN S. HAMMOCK is associate professor and former chairman of the Department of Political Science at West Virginia University. He received his Ph.D. from the University of Virginia and is coauthor of *West Virginia Politics and Government* (1996). He served as chairman of the West Virginia Election Commission from 1983 to 2004.

Contents

Preface

Reflecting the press of current events and editorial judgments, the changes made for the eleventh edition of *Points of View,* though substantial, concentrate primarily on new selections rather than new topics. However, in Chapter 14, on civil liberties, we present a new section on freedom of religion. With respect to new selections, we added a new article on gay marriage in Chapter 3 and a new pair of articles on public opinion in Chapter 4. In Chapter 7, on the general subject of elections, we included one updated and one new article on presidential nominations and two new articles on the Electoral College. Chapter 8 has a new pair of articles on political parties. In Chapter 11, on the presidency, two of the three articles are new, and Chapter 12, on the bureaucracy, contains a new pair of articles.

Our basic goals for the book remain unchanged—namely, to provide students with a manageable number of selections that present readable, succinct, thoughtful, and diverse perspectives across a broad range of issues related to American government.

Acknowledgments

We would like to express our gratitude to a number of individuals who made valuable contributions to this project. A special debt is owed Larry Goldberg, who for this edition, as for the previous one, had primary editorial responsibility and once again did absolutely everything possible to make the editorial process flow smoothly.

We also would like to express our appreciation to sponsoring editor Monica Eckman, who has had overall responsibility for coordinating revisions of the last several editions and as usual did a superb job, and to project manager Aaron Downey, whose guidance throughout the production process was exemplary.

In the course of revising and updating the text, we repeatedly called upon the word-processing skills of administrative associate Lee Ann Greathouse at West Virginia University, who cheerfully responded with unfailing accuracy and in less time than we had any reason to expect.

Finally, we want to express our deep appreciation to the following academicians who carefully read and assessed the previous edition of *Points of View*. Their detailed and constructive suggestions guided several of the changes made for this current revision:

Michael J. Cain, *St. Mary's College of Maryland*

Terri Susan Fine, *University of Central Florida*

James M. Hoefler, *Dickinson College*

James D. King, *University of Wyoming*

Dale S. Kuehne, *Saint Anselm College*

Dante J. Scala, *Saint Anselm College*

Charles R. Shipan, *University of Michigan*

Robert E. DiClerico
Allan S. Hammock
Morgantown, West Virginia

To the Instructor

For some years now, we have jointly taught the introductory course in American government. Each year we perused the crop of existing readers, and although we adopted several different readers over this period, we were not wholly satisfied with any of them. It is our feeling that many of the readers currently on the market suffer from one or more of the following deficiencies: (1) Some contain selections that are difficult for students to comprehend because of the sophistication of the argument, the manner of expression, or both. (2) Many readers do not cover all of the topics typically treated in an introductory American government course. (3) In choosing selections for a given topic, some editors did not always show sufficient concern for how—or whether—one article on a topic relates to other articles on the same topic. (4) Most readers contain too many selections for each topic—indeed, in several cases the number of selections for some topics exceeds ten. Readers are nearly always used in conjunction with a textbook. So to ask students to read a lengthy chapter—jammed with facts—from a textbook and then to read from five to ten selections on the same topic from a reader is to demand that they read more than they can reasonably absorb in a meaningful way. Of course, an instructor need not assign all the selections on a given topic. But this selective approach justifiably disgruntles students who, after purchasing a reader, discover that they may be asked to read only one-half or two-thirds of it.

Instead of continuing to complain about what we considered to be the limitations of existing American government readers, we decided to try our own hand at putting one together. In doing so, we were guided by the following considerations.

Readability

Quite obviously, students will not read dull, difficult articles. We believe that, as well as having something important to say, each of the articles in *Points of View* is clearly written, well organized, and free of needless jargon.

Comprehensiveness

The fifteen chapters of *Points of View* cover all the major topics of concern that are typically treated in the standard introductory course on American government.

Economy of Selections

We decided, generally, to limit the number of selections to two per topic, although we did include three selections on topics in Chapters 5, 7, 10, and 11. The limitation on selections maximizes the likelihood that students will read them. It has been our experience that when students are assigned four, five, or more selections on a given topic, they simply do not read them all. In addition, limiting the selections for each topic increases the likelihood that students will be able to associate an argument with the author who made it.

Juxtaposition

The selections for each topic take *opposing* or *different* points of view on some aspect of the topic. This approach was chosen for three reasons. First, we believe that students' interest is enhanced when one article is played off against the other. Thus, in our view, the "interest" quality of a given article derives not only from its own content but also from its juxtaposition with other articles. Second, we think it is important to sensitize students to the fact that their perspectives on an issue depend on the values that they bring to it. Third, because selections focus on a particular issue related to a given topic, students will achieve greater depth of understanding about that issue. We think our approach is preferable to having five or six selections on a topic, with each selection focusing on a different aspect, and with the result that students are exposed to "a little of this and a little of that"—if they even bother to read all five or six selections.

Although the readers currently available take into account one or, in some instances, several of the considerations identified, we believe that the uniqueness of *Points of View* lies in the fact that we seek to incorporate *all* of them.

Democracy

*A*ny assessment of a society's democratic character is fundamentally determined by what the observer chooses to use as a definition of democracy. Though the concept of democracy has commanded the attention of political thinkers for centuries, the following selections by Howard Zinn and Sidney Hook demonstrate that there continues to be considerable disagreement over its meaning. Each of them has scanned the American scene and reached different conclusions regarding the democratic character of our society. This difference of opinion is explained primarily by the fact that each approaches his evaluation with a different conception of what democracy is.

For Zinn, the definition of democracy includes criteria that bear not only upon how decisions get made but also upon what results from such decisions. Specifically, he argues that such results must lead to a certain level of human welfare within a society. In applying these criteria of human welfare to the United States, he concludes that we fall short of the mark in several areas.

Sidney Hook is willing to acknowledge that democracy might indeed function more smoothly in societies where the conditions of human welfare are high, but he insists that these conditions themselves do not constitute the definition of democracy. Rather, he maintains that democracy is a process—a way of making decisions. Whether such decisions lead to the conditions of human welfare that Zinn prescribes is irrelevant to Hook. The crucial test, according to Hook, is whether the people have the right, by majority rule, to make choices about the quality of their lives—whatever those choices might be.

How Democratic Is America?

Howard Zinn

To give a sensible answer to the question "How democratic is America?" I find it necessary to make three clarifying preliminary statements. First, I want to define "democracy," not conclusively, but operationally, so we can know what we are arguing about or at least what I am talking about. Second, I want to state what my criteria are for measuring the "how" in the question. And third, I think it necessary to issue a warning about how a certain source of bias (although not the only source) is likely to distort our judgments.

Our definition is crucial. This becomes clear if we note how relatively easy is the answer to our question when we define democracy as a set of formal institutions and let it go at that. If we describe as "democratic" a country that has a representative system of government, with universal suffrage, a bill of rights, and party competition for office, it becomes easy to answer the question "how" with the enthusiastic reply, "Very!" . . .

I propose a set of criteria for the description "democratic," which goes beyond formal political institutions, to the quality of life in the society (economic, social, psychological), beyond majority rule to a concern for minorities, and beyond national boundaries to a global view of what is meant by "the people," in that rough, but essentially correct view of democracy as "government of, by, and for the people."

Let me list these criteria quickly, because I will go on to discuss them in some detail later:

1. To what extent can various people in the society participate in those decisions which affect their lives: decisions in the political process and decisions in the economic structure?
2. As a corollary of the above: do people have equal access to the information which they need to make important decisions?
3. Are the members of the society equally protected on matters of life and death—in the most literal sense of that phrase?
4. Is there equality before the law: police, courts, the judicial process—as well as equality *with* the law-enforcing institutions, so as to safeguard equally everyone's person, and his freedom from interference by others, and by the government?

Howard Zinn is emeritus professor of political science at Boston University. This essay was originally published in Robert A. Goldwin, ed., *How Democratic Is America?* (Chicago: Rand McNally, 1971), pp. 39–60. Zinn revised and updated the original for *Points of View* in 1985 and again in 1997.

5. Is there equality in the distribution of available resources: those economic goods necessary for health, life, recreation, leisure, growth?
6. Is there equal access to education, to knowledge and training, so as to enable persons in the society to live their lives as fully as possible, to enlarge their range of possibilities?
7. Is there freedom of expression on all matters, and equally for all, to communicate with other members of the society?
8. Is there freedom for individuality in private life, in sexual relations, family relations, the right of privacy?
9. To minimize regulation: do education and the culture in general foster a spirit of cooperation and amity to sustain the above conditions?
10. As a final safety feature: is there opportunity to protest, to disobey the laws, when the foregoing objectives are being lost—as a way of restoring them? . . .

Two historical facts support my enlarged definition of democracy. One is that the industrialized Western societies have outgrown the original notions which accompanied their early development: that constitutional and procedural tests sufficed for the "democracy" that overthrew the old order; that democracy was quite adequately fulfilled by the Bill of Rights in England at the time of the Glorious Revolution, the Constitution of the United States, and the Declaration of the Rights of Man in France. It came to be acknowledged that the rhetoric of these revolutions was not matched by their real achievements. In other words, the limitations of that "democracy" led to the reformist and radical movements that grew up in the West in the middle and late nineteenth century. The other historical note is that the new revolutions in our century, in Africa, Asia, Latin America, while rejecting either in whole or in part the earlier revolutions, profess a similar democratic aim, but with an even broader rhetoric. . . .

My second preliminary point is on standards. By this I mean that we can judge in several ways the fulfillment of these ten criteria I have listed. We can measure the present against the past, so that if we find that in [2008] we are doing better in these matters than we were doing in 1860 or 1910, the society will get a good grade for its "democracy." I would adjure such an approach because it supports complacency. With such a standard, Russians in 1910 could point with pride to how much progress they had made toward parliamentary democracy; as Russians in 1985 could point to their post-Stalin progress away from the gulag; as Americans could point in 1939 to how far they had come toward solving the problem of economic equality; as Americans in the South could point in 1950 to the progress of the southern African-American. Indeed, the American government has given military aid to brutal regimes in Latin America on the ground that a decrease in the murders by semiofficial death squads is a sign of progress.

Or, we could measure our democracy against other places in the world. Given the high incidence of tyranny in the world, polarization of wealth, and lack of freedom of expression, the United States, even with very serious defects, could declare itself successful. Again, the result is to let us all off easily; some of our most enthusiastic self-congratulation is based on such a standard.

On the other hand, we could measure our democracy against an ideal (even if admittedly unachievable) standard. I would argue for such an approach, because, in what may seem to some a paradox, the ideal standard is the pragmatic one; it affects what we *do*. To grade a student on the basis of an improvement over past performance is justifiable if the intention is to encourage someone discouraged about his ability. But if he is rather pompous about his superiority in relation to other students (and I suggest this is frequently true of Americans evaluating American "democracy"), and if in addition he is a medical student about to graduate into a world ridden with disease, it would be best to judge him by an ideal standard. That might spur him to an improvement fast enough to save lives. . . .

My third preliminary point is a caution based on the obvious fact that we make our appraisals through the prism of our own status in society. This is particularly important in assessing democracy, because if "democracy" refers to the condition of masses of people, and if we as the assessors belong to a number of elites, we will tend (and I am not declaring an inevitability, just warning of a tendency) to see the present situation in America more benignly than it deserves. To be more specific, if democracy requires a keen awareness of the condition of black people, of poor people, of young people, of that majority of the world who are not American—and we are white, prosperous, beyond draft age, and American— then we have a number of pressures tending to dull our sense of inequity. We are, if not doomed to err, likely to err on the side of complacency—and we should try to take this into account in making our judgments.

1. PARTICIPATION IN DECISIONS

We need to recognize first, that whatever decisions are made politically are made by representatives of one sort or another: state legislators, congressmen, senators, and other elected officials, governors and presidents; also by those appointed by elected officials, like Supreme Court justices. These are important decisions, affecting our lives, liberties, and ability to pursue happiness. Congress and the president decide on the tax structure, which affects the distribution of resources. They decide how to spend the monies received; whether or not we go to war; who serves in the armed forces; what behavior is considered a crime; which crimes are prosecuted and which are not. They decide what limitations there should be on our travel, or on our right to speak freely. They decide on the availability of education and health services.

If representation by its very nature is undemocratic, as I would argue, this is an important fact for our evaluation. Representative government is *closer* to democracy than monarchy, and for this reason it has been hailed as one of the great political advances of modern times; yet, it is only a step in the direction of democracy, at its best. It has certain inherent flaws—pointed out by Rousseau in the eighteenth century, Victor Considerant in the nineteenth century, Robert Michels in the beginning of the twentieth century, Hannah Arendt in our own time. No representative can adequately represent another's needs;

the representative tends to become a member of a special elite; he has privileges which weaken his sense of concern at others' grievances; the passions of the troubled lose force (as Madison noted in *The Federalist 10*) as they are filtered through the representative system; the elected official develops an expertise which tends toward its own perpetuation. Leaders develop what Michels called "a mutual insurance contract" against the rest of society. . . .

If only radicals pointed to the inadequacy of the political processes in the United States, we might be suspicious. But established political scientists of a moderate bent talk quite bluntly of the limitations of the voting system in the United States. Robert Dahl, in *A Preface to Democratic Theory*, drawing on the voting studies of American political scientists, concludes that "political activity, at least in the United States, is positively associated to a significant extent with such variables as income, socio-economic status, and education." He says:

> By their propensity for political passivity the poor and uneducated disfran-
> chise themselves. . . . Since they also have less access than the wealthy to the
> organizational, financial, and propaganda resources that weigh so heavily in
> campaigns, elections, legislative, and executive decisions, anything like equal
> control over government policy is triply barred to the members of Madison's
> unpropertied masses. They are barred by their relatively greater inactivity, by
> their relatively limited access to resources, and by Madison's nicely contrived
> system of constitutional checks.[1]

Dahl thinks that our society is essentially democratic, but this is because he expects very little. (His book was written in the 1950s, when lack of commotion in the society might well have persuaded him that no one else expected much more than he did.) Even if democracy were to be superficially defined as "majority rule," the United States would not fulfill that, according to Dahl, who says that "on matters of specific policy, the majority rarely rules."[2] After noting that "the election is the critical technique for insuring that governmental lead-ers will be relatively responsive to nonleaders," he goes on to say that "it is important to notice how little a national election tells us about the preferences of majorities. Strictly speaking, all an election reveals is the first preferences of some citizens among the candidates standing for office."[3] About 45 percent of the potential voters in national elections, and about 60 percent of the voters in local elections do not vote, and this cannot be attributed, Dahl says, simply to indifference. And if, as Dahl points out, "in no large nation state can elections tell us much about the preferences of majorities and minorities," this is "even more true of the interelection period." . . .

Dahl goes on to assert that the election process and interelection activity "are crucial processes for insuring that political leaders will be *somewhat* responsive to the preferences of *some* ordinary citizens."[4] I submit (the empha-sized words are mine) that if an admirer of democracy in America can say no more than this, democracy is not doing very well.

Dahl tells us the election process is one of "two fundamental methods of social control which, operating together, make governmental leaders so respon-sive to nonleaders that the distinction between democracy and dictatorship still makes sense." Since his description of the election process leaves that dubious, let's look at his second requirement for distinguishing democracy: "The other method of social control is continuous political competition among individuals, parties, or both." What it comes down to is "not minority rule but minorities rule."[5]

If it turns out that this—like the election process—also has little democratic content, we will not be left with very much difference—by Dahl's own admission—between "dictatorship" and the "democracy" practiced in the United States. Indeed, there is much evidence on this: the lack of democracy within the major political parties, the vastly disproportionate influence of wealthy groups over poorer ones. What antismoking consumer group in the election year of 1996 could match the five million dollars donated to the Republican Party by the tobacco interests? What ordinary citizen could have the access to President Bill Clinton that a group of bankers had in May of that election year when they were invited to the White House?[6] All of this, and more, supports the idea of a "decline of American pluralism" that Henry Kariel has written about. What Dahl's democracy comes down to is "the steady appeasement of relatively small groups."[7] If these relatively small groups turn out to be the aircraft industry far more than the aged, the space industry far more than the poor, the Pentagon far more than the college youth—what is left of democracy?

Sometimes the elitism of decision-making is defended (by Dahl and by others) on the ground that the elite is enacting decisions passively supported by the mass, whose tolerance is proof of an underlying consensus in society. But Murray Levin's studies in *The Alienated Voter* indicate how much nonparticipation in elections is a result of hopelessness rather than approval. And Robert Wiebe, a historian at Northwestern University, talks of "consensus" becoming a "new stereotype." He approaches the question historically.

> Industrialization arrived so peacefully not because all Americans secretly shared the same values or implicitly willed its success but because its millions of bitter enemies lacked the mentality and the means to organize an effective counterattack.[8]

Wiebe's point is that the passivity of most Americans in the face of elitist decision-making has not been due to acquiescence but to the lack of resources for effective combat, as well as a gulf so wide between the haves and have-nots that there was no ground on which to dispute. Americans neither revolted violently nor reacted at the polls; instead they were subservient, or else worked out their hostilities in personal ways. . . .

Presidential nominations and elections are more democratic than monarchical rule or the procedures of totalitarian states, but they are far from some reasonable expectation of democracy. The two major parties have a monopoly of presidential power, taking turns in the White House. The candidates of minority parties don't have a chance. They do not have access to the financial backing of the major parties, and there is not the semblance of equal attention in the mass media; it is only the two major candidates who have free access to prime time on national television.

More important, both parties almost always agree on the fundamentals of domestic and foreign policy, despite the election-year rhetoric which attempts to find important differences. Both parties arranged for United States intervention in Vietnam in the 1950s and 1960s, and both, when public opinion changed, promised to get out (note the Humphrey-Nixon contest of 1968). In 1984, Democratic candidate Walter Mondale agreed with Republican candidate Ronald Reagan that the United States (which had ten thousand thermonuclear warheads) needed to continue increasing its arms budget, although he asked for a smaller increase than the Republicans. Such a position left Mondale unable to promise representatives of the black community (where unemployment was over 20 percent) that he would spend even a few billion dollars for a jobs program. Meanwhile, Democrats and Republicans in Congress were agreeing on a $297 billion arms bill for the 1985 fiscal year.[9]

I have been talking so far about democracy in the political process. But there is another serious weakness that I will only mention here, although it is of enormous importance: the powerlessness of the American to participate in economic decision-making, which affects his life at every moment. As a consumer, that is, as the person whom the economy is presumably intended to serve, he has virtually nothing to say about what is produced for him. The corporations make what is profitable; the advertising industry persuades him to buy what the corporations produce. He becomes the passive victim of the misallocation of resources, the production of dangerous commodities, the spoiling of his air, water, forests, beaches, cities.

2. ACCESS TO INFORMATION

Adequate information for the electorate is a precondition for any kind of action (whether electoral or demonstrative) to affect national policy. As for the voting process, Berelson, Lazarsfeld, and McPhee tell us (in their book, *Voting*) after extensive empirical research: "One persistent conclusion is that the public is not particularly well informed about the specific issues of the day." . . .

Furthermore, there are certain issues which never even reach the public because they are decided behind the scenes. . . .

Consider the information available to voters on two major kinds of issues. One of them is the tax structure, so bewilderingly complex that the corporation, with its corps of accountants and financial experts, can prime itself for lobbying activities, while the average voter, hardly able to comprehend his own income tax, stands by helplessly as the president, the Office of Management and Budget, and the Congress decide the tax laws. The dominant influences are those of big business, which has the resources both to understand and to act.

Then there is foreign policy. The government leads the citizenry to believe it has special expertise which, if it could only be revealed, would support its position against critics. At the same time, it hides the very information which would reveal its position to be indefensible. The mendacity of the government on the Bay of Pigs operation and the withholding of vital information about the

Tonkin Gulf events are only two examples of the way the average person becomes a victim of government deception.*

In 1990, historian Warren Cohen resigned as adviser to the State Department in its publication of the series *Foreign Relations of the United States*, pointing out that the government was refusing to cover events less than thirty years old. And even what it did publish was not trustworthy. "The United States government is publishing blatantly fraudulent accounts of its activities in Guatemala, Iran, and Southeast Asia in the 1950s" (*World Monitor Magazine*, 1990).

When the United States invaded the tiny island of Grenada in the fall of 1983, no reporters were allowed to observe the invasion, and the American public had little opportunity to get independent verification of the reasons given by the government for the invasion. As a result, President Reagan could glibly tell the nation what even one of his own supporters, journalist George Will, admitted was a lie: that he was invading Grenada to protect the lives of American medical students on the island. He could also claim that documents found on the island indicated plans for a Cuban-Soviet takeover of Grenada; the documents showed no such thing.[10]

Furthermore, the distribution of information to the public is a function of power and wealth. The government itself can color the citizens' understanding of events by its control of news at the source: the presidential press conference, the "leak to the press," the White Papers, the teams of "truth experts" going around the country at the taxpayers' expense. As for private media, the large networks and mass-circulation magazines have the greatest access to the public mind. There is no "equal time" for critics of public policy. . . .

3. EQUAL PROTECTION

Let us go now from the procedural to the substantive, indeed to the most substantive of questions: the right of all people to life itself. Here we find democracy in America tragically inadequate. Not only Locke, one of the leading theorists of the democratic tradition, declared the ultimate right of any person to safeguard his own life when threatened by the government; Hobbes, often looked on as the foe of democratic thought, agreed. Yet, in matters of foreign policy, where the decisions involve life or death for large numbers of Americans, power rests in the hands of the president and a small group of advisers. Despite the constitutional provision that war must be declared by Congress, in reality the President can create situations (as in the Mexican War, as in both world wars) which make inevitable congressional votes for war. And in all post–World War II conflicts (Korea, Vietnam, Iraq) there was no declaration of war by Congress.

It is in connection with this most basic of rights—life itself, the first and most important of those substantive ends which democratic participation is

---

*The Bay of Pigs operation was an unsuccessful, U.S.-backed invasion of Cuba by Cuban exiles in 1961; the Gulf of Tonkin Resolution, passed by Congress in 1965 on the occasion of an alleged attack on U.S. ships by the North Vietnamese, authorized the deployment of thousands of U.S. troops to Vietnam.—*Editors*.

designed to safeguard—that I would assert the need for a global view of democracy. One can at least conceive of a democratic decision for martial sacrifice by those ready to make the sacrifice; a "democratic" war is thus a theoretical possibility. But that presumption of democracy becomes obviously false at the first shot because then *others* are affected who did not decide. . . . Nations making decisions to slaughter their own sons are at least theoretically subject to internal check. The victims on the other side fall without any such chance. For the United States today, this failure of democracy is total; we have the capacity to destroy the world without giving it a chance to murmur a dissent; we did, in fact, destroy a part of southeast Asia on the basis of a unilateral decision made in Washington. There is no more pernicious manifestation of the lack of democracy in America than this single fact.

4. EQUALITY BEFORE THE LAW

Is there equality before the law? At every stage of the judicial process—facing the policeman, appearing in court, being freed on bond, being sentenced by the judge—the poor person is treated worse than the rich, the black treated worse than the white, the politically or personally odd character is treated worse than the orthodox. A defendant's poverty affects his preliminary hearing, his right to bail, the quality of his counsel. The evidence is plentiful in the daily newspapers, which inform us that an African-American boy fleeing the scene of a two-dollar theft may be shot and killed by a pursuing policeman, while a wealthy man who goes to South America after a million-dollar swindle, even if apprehended, need never fear a scratch. The wealthy price-fixer for General Motors, who costs consumers millions, will get ninety days in jail, the burglar of a liquor store will get five years. An African-American youth, or a bearded white youth poorly dressed, has much more chance of being clubbed by a policeman on the street than a well-dressed white man, given the fact that both respond with equal tartness to a question. . . .

Aside from inequality among citizens, there is inequality between the citizen and his government, when they face one another in a court of law. Take the matter of counsel: the well-trained government prosecutor faces the indigent's court-appointed counsel. Four of my students did a study of the City Court of Boston several years ago. They sat in the court for weeks, taking notes, and found that the average time spent by court-appointed counsel with his client, before arguing the case at the bench, was seven minutes.

5. DISTRIBUTION OF RESOURCES

Democracy is devoid of meaning if it does not include equal access to the available resources of the society. In India, democracy might still mean poverty; in the United States, with a Gross National Product of more than $3 trillion a year, democracy should mean that every American, working a short work-week, has adequate food, clothing, shelter, health care, education for himself and his family—in short, the material resources necessary to enjoy life and freedom. Even if only 20 percent of the American population is desperately poor . . . in a country so rich, that is an inexcusable breach of the democratic principle. Even if there is a large, prosperous middle class, there is something grossly unfair in the fact that in 1995 the richest 1 percent of the population owned over 40 percent of the total wealth, a figure that, throughout our history, has rarely been under 33 percent.

Whether you are poor or rich determines the most fundamental facts about your life: whether you are cold in the winter while trying to sleep, whether you suffocate in the summer; whether you live among vermin or rats; whether the smells around you all day are sweet or foul; whether you have adequate medical care; whether you have good teeth; whether you can send your children to college; whether you can go on vacation or have to take an extra job at night; whether you can afford a divorce, or an abortion, or a wife, or another child. . . .

6. ACCESS TO EDUCATION

In a highly industrialized society, education is a crucial determinant of wealth, political power, social status, leisure, and the ability to work in one's chosen field. Educational resources in our society are not equitably distributed. Among high-school graduates of the same IQ levels, a far higher percentage of the well-to-do go on to college than the poor.[11] A mediocre student with money can always go to college. A mediocre student without money may not be able to go, even to a state college, because he may have to work to support his family. Furthermore, the educational resources in the schools—equipment, teachers, etc.—are far superior in the wealthy suburbs than in the poor sections of the city, whether white or black.

7. FREEDOM OF EXPRESSION

Like money, freedom of expression is available to all in America, but in widely varying quantities. The First Amendment formally guarantees freedom of speech, press, assembly, and petition to all—but certain realities of wealth, power, and status stand in the way of the equal distribution of these rights. Anyone can stand on a street corner and talk to ten or a hundred people. But someone with the resources to buy loudspeaker equipment, go through the necessary red tape, and post a bond with the city may hold a meeting downtown and reach a thousand or five thousand people. A person or a corporation with $100,000 can buy time on television and reach 10 million people. A rich person simply has much more freedom of speech than a poor person. The government has much more freedom of expression than a private individual, because the president can command the airwaves when he wishes, and reach 60 million people in one night.

Freedom of the press also is guaranteed to all. But the student selling an underground newspaper on the street with a nude woman on the cover may be arrested by a policeman, while the airport newsstand selling *Playboy* and ten magazines like it will remain safe. Anyone with $10,000 can put out a newspaper to reach a few thousand people. Anyone with $10 million can buy a few newspapers that will reach a few million people. Anyone who is penniless had better have a loud voice; and then he might be arrested for disturbing the peace.

8. FREEDOM FOR INDIVIDUALITY

The right to live one's life, in privacy and freedom, in whatever way one wants, so long as others are not harmed, should be a sacred principle in a democracy. But there are hundreds of laws, varying from state to state, and sometimes joined by federal laws, which regulate the personal lives of people in this country: their marriages, their divorces, their sexual relations. Furthermore, both laws and court decisions protect policemen and the FBI in their use of secret devices which listen in on private conversations, or peer in on private conduct.

9. THE SPIRIT OF COOPERATION

The maintenance of those substantive elements of democracy which I have just sketched, if dependent on a pervasive network of coercion, would cancel out much of the benefit of that democracy. Democracy needs rather to be sustained by a spirit in society, the tone and the values of the culture. I am speaking of something as elusive as a mood, alongside something as hard as law, both of which would have to substitute cooperation tinged with friendly competition for the fierce combat of our business culture. I am speaking of the underlying drive that keeps people going in the society. So long as that drive is for money and power, with no ceiling on either, so long as ruthlessness is built into the rules of the game, democracy does not have a chance. If there is one crucial cause in the failure of American democracy—not the only one, of course, but a fundamental one—it is the drive for corporate profit, and the overwhelming influence of money in every aspect of our daily lives. That is the uncontrolled libido of our society from which the rape of democratic values necessarily follows.

The manifestations are diverse and endless: The drug industry's drive for profit has led to incredible overpricing of drugs for consumers (700 percent markup, for instance, for tablets to arthritic patients). It was disclosed in 1979 that Johns-Manville, the nation's largest asbestos manufacturer, had deliberately withheld from its workers X-ray results that showed they were developing cancer. In 1984, a company making an intrauterine birth control device—the Dalkon Shield—was found by a Minnesota court to have allowed tens of thousands of women to wear this device despite knowing that it was dangerous to their health (*Minneapolis Star and Tribune*, May 18, 1984). In the mid-1990s, it was revealed that tobacco companies had concealed information showing the narcotic nature of cigarettes. All in the interest of maximizing profit.

If these were isolated cases, reported and then eliminated, they could be dismissed as unfortunate blemishes on an otherwise healthy social body. But the major allocations of resources in our society are made on the basis of money profit rather than social use. . . .

. . . News items buttress what I have said. The oil that polluted California's beautiful beaches in the 1960s . . . was produced by a system in which the oil companies' hunger for profit has far more weight than the ordinary person's need to swim in clean water. This is not to be attributed to Republicanism over-riding the concern for the little fellow of the Democratic Party. Profit is master whichever party is in power; it was the liberal Secretary of the Interior Stewart Udall who allowed the dangerous drilling to go on. . . .

In 1984, the suit of several thousand veterans against the Dow Chemical Company, claiming that they and their families had suffered terrible illnesses as a result of exposure in Vietnam to the poisonous chemical Agent Orange, was settled. The Dow corporation avoided the disclosures of thousands of doc-uments in open court by agreeing to pay $180 million to the veterans. One thing seemed clear: The company had known that the defoliant used in Vietnam might be dangerous, but it held back the news, and blamed the government for ordering use of the chemical. The government itself, apparently wanting to shift blame to the corporation, declared publicly that Dow Chemical had been motivated in its actions by greed for profit.

10. OPPORTUNITY TO PROTEST

The first two elements in my list for democracy—decision-making and infor-mation to help make them—are procedural. The next six are substantive, deal-ing with the consequences of such procedures on life, liberty, and the pursuit of happiness. My ninth point, the one I have just discussed, shows how the money motive of our society corrupts both procedures and their consequences by its existence and suggests we need a different motive as a fundamental requisite of a democratic society. The point I am about to discuss is an ultimate requisite for democracy, a safety feature if nothing else—neither procedures nor conse-quences nor motivation—works. It is the right of citizens to break through the impasse of a legal and cultural structure, which sustains inequality, greed, and murder, to initiate processes for change. I am speaking of civil disobedience, which is an essential safeguard even in a successful society, and which is an absolute necessity in a society which is not going well.

If the institutional structure itself bars any change but the most picayune and grievances are serious, it is silly to insist that change must be mediated through the processes of that legal structure. In such a situation, dramatic expressions of protest and challenge are necessary to help change ways of thinking, to build up political power for drastic change. A society that calls itself democratic (whether accurately or not) must, as its ultimate safeguard, allow such acts of disobedience. If the government prohibits them (as we must expect from a government committed to the existent) then the members of a society concerned with democracy must not only defend such acts, but encourage them. Somewhere near the root of democratic thought is the theory of popular sovereignty, declaring that government and laws are instruments for certain ends, and are not to be deified with absolute obedience; they must constantly be checked by the citizenry, and challenged, opposed, even overthrown, if they become threats to fundamental rights.

Any abstract assessment of *when* disobedience is justified is pointless. Proper conclusions depend on empirical evidence about how bad things are at the moment, and how adequate are the institutional mechanisms for correcting them....

One of these is the matter of race. The intolerable position of the African-American, in both North and South, has traditionally been handled with a few muttered apologies and tokens of reform. Then the civil disobedience of militants in the South forced our attention on the most dramatic (southern) manifestations of racism in America. The massive African-American urban uprisings of 1967 and 1968 showed that nothing less than civil disobedience (for riots and uprisings go beyond that) could make the nation see that the race problem is an American—not a southern—problem and that it needs bold, revolutionary action.

As for poverty: It seems clear that the normal mechanisms of congressional pretense and presidential rhetoric are not going to change things very much. Acts of civil disobedience by the poor will be required, at the least, to make middle-class America take notice, to bring national decisions that begin to reallocate wealth.

The war in Vietnam showed that we could not depend on the normal processes of "law and order," of the election process, of letters to the *Times,* to stop a series of especially brutal acts against the Vietnamese and against our own sons. It took a nationwide storm of protest, including thousands of acts of civil disobedience (14,000 people were arrested in one day in 1971 in Washington, D.C.), to help bring the war to an end. The role of draft resistance in affecting Lyndon Johnson's 1968 decision not to escalate the war further is told in the Defense Department secret documents of that period. In the 1980s and 1990s civil disobedience continued, with religious pacifists and others risking prison in order to protest the arms race and the plans for nuclear war.

The great danger for American democracy is not from the protesters. That democracy is too poorly realized for us to consider critics—even rebels—as the chief problem. Its fulfillment requires us all, living in an ossified system which sustains too much killing and too much selfishness, to join the protest.

NOTES

1. Robert A. Dahl, *A Preface to Democratic Theory* (Chicago: University of Chicago Press, 1963), p. 81.
2. Ibid., p. 124.
3. Ibid., p. 125.
4. Ibid., p. 131.
5. Ibid., pp. 131–32.

6. *The New York Times*, January 25, 27, 1997.
7. Dahl, *A Preface to Democratic Theory*, p. 146.
8. Robert Wiebe, "The Confinements of Consensus," *TriQuarterly*, 1966. Copyright by TriQuarterly 1966. All rights reserved.
9. *The New York Times*, September 25, 1984.
10. *The New York Times* reported, November 5, 1983: "There is nothing in the documents, however, that specifically indicates that Cuba and the Soviet Union were on the verge of taking over Grenada, as Administration officials have suggested."
11. See the Carnegie Council on Children study, *Small Futures*, by Richard deLore, 1979.

How Democratic Is America?
A Response to Howard Zinn
Sidney Hook

Charles Peirce, the great American philosopher, once observed that there was such a thing as the "ethics of words." The "ethics of words" are violated whenever ordinary terms are used in an unusual context or arbitrarily identified with another concept for which other terms are in common use. Mr. Zinn is guilty of a systematic violation of the "ethics of words." In consequence, his discussion of "democracy" results in a great many methodological errors as well as inconsistencies. To conserve space, I shall focus on three.

I

First of all, he confuses democracy as a political process with democracy as a political *product* or state of welfare; democracy as a *"free society"* with democracy as a *"good society,"* where good is defined in terms of equality or justice (or both) or

Sidney Hook (1902–1989) was head of the Department of Philosophy at New York University from 1934 to 1969 and a senior research fellow at the Hoover Institution on War, Revolution, and Peace at Stanford University from 1973 to 1989. This essay was originally published in Robert A. Goldwin, ed., *How Democratic Is America?* (Chicago: Rand McNally, 1971), pp. 62–75. Hook revised and updated the original for *Points of View* in 1985.

some other constellation of values. One of the reasons for choosing to live under a democratic political system rather than a nondemocratic system is our belief that it makes possible a better society. That is something that must be empirically established, something denied by critics of democracy from Plato to Santayana. The equality which is relevant to democracy as a *political process* is, in the first instance, political equality with respect to the rights of citizenship. Theoretically, a politically democratic community could vote, wisely or unwisely, to abolish, retain, or establish certain economic inequalities. Theoretically, a benevolent despotism could institute certain kinds of social and even juridical equalities. Historically, the Bismarckian political dictatorship introduced social welfare legislation for the masses at a time when such legislation would have been repudiated by the existing British and American political democracies. Some of Mr. Zinn's proposed reforms could be introduced under a dictatorship or benevolent despotism. Therefore, they are not logically or organically related to democracy.

The second error in Mr. Zinn's approach to democracy is "to measure our democracy against an ideal (even if admittedly unachievable) standard . . . even if utopian . . ." without *defining* the standard. His criteria admittedly are neither necessary nor sufficient for determining the presence of democracy since he himself admits that they are applicable to societies that are not democratic. Further, even if we were to take his criteria as severally defining the presence of democracy—as we might take certain physical and mental traits as constituting a definition of health—he gives no operational test for determining whether or not they have been fulfilled. For example, among the criteria he lists for determining whether a society is democratic is this: "Are the members of the society equally protected on matters of life and death—in the most literal sense of that phrase?" A moment's reflection will show that here—as well as in other cases where Mr. Zinn speaks of equality—it is impossible for all members to be equally protected on matters of life and death—certainly not in a world in which men do the fighting and women give birth to children, where children need *more* protection than adults, and where some risk-seeking adults require and deserve less protection (since resources are not infinite) than others. As Karl Marx realized, "in the most literal sense of that phrase," there cannot be absolute equality even in a classless society. . . .

The only sensible procedure in determining the absence or presence of equality from a democratic perspective is comparative. We must ask whether a culture is more or less democratic in comparison to the past with respect to some *desirable* feature of equality (Zinn ignores the fact that not all equalities are desirable). It is better for some people to be more intelligent and more knowledgeable than others than for all to be unintelligent and ignorant. There never is literally equal access to education, to knowledge and training in any society. The question is: Is there more access today for more people than yesterday, and how can we increase the access tomorrow?

Mr. Zinn refuses to take this approach because, he asserts, "it supports complacency." It does nothing of the sort! On the contrary, it shows that progress is possible, and encourages us to exert our efforts in the same direction if we regard the direction as desirable.

It will be instructive to look at the passage in which Mr. Zinn objects to this sensible comparative approach because it reveals the bias in his approach:

"With such a standard," he writes, "Russia in 1910 could point with pride to how much progress they had made toward parliamentary democracy; as Russians in 1985 could point to their post-Stalin progress away from the gulag; as Americans could point in 1939 to how far they had come in solving the problem of economic equality; as Americans in the South could point in 1950 to the progress of the southern African-American."

a. In 1910 the Russians were indeed moving toward greater progress in local parliamentary institutions. Far from making them complacent, they moved towards more inclusive representative institutions which culminated in elections to the Constituent Assembly in 1918, which was bayoneted out of existence by Lenin and the Communist Party, with a minority party dictatorship established.

b. Only Mr. Zinn would regard the slight diminution in terror from the days of Stalin to the regime of Chernenko as progress toward democracy. Those who observe the ethics of words would normally say that the screws of repression had been slightly relaxed. Mr. Zinn seems unaware that as bad as the terror was under Lenin, it was not as pervasive as it is today.* But no one with any respect for the ethics of words would speak of "the progress of democracy" in the Soviet Union from Lenin to Stalin to Khrushchev to Chernenko. Their regimes were varying degrees of dictatorship and terror.

c. Americans could justifiably say that in 1939 progress had been made in giving workers a greater role, not as Mr. Zinn says in "solving the problem of economic equality" (a meaningless phrase), but in determining the conditions and rewards of work that prevailed in 1929 or previously because the existence of the Wagner Labor Relations Act made collective bargaining the law of the land. They could say this *not* to rest in complacency, but to use the organized force of their trade unions to influence further the political life of the country. And indeed, it was the organized labor movement in 1984 which in effect chose the candidate of the Democratic Party.

d. Americans in the South in 1950 could rightfully speak of the progress of the southern African-American over the days of unrestricted Jim Crow and lynching bees of the past, not to rest in complacency, but to agitate for further progress through the Supreme Court decision of *Brown v. Board of Education in Topeka* and through the Civil Rights Act of Congress. This has not made them complacent, but more resolved to press further to eliminate remaining practices of invidious discrimination.

Even Mr. Zinn should admit that with respect to some of his other criteria this is the only sensible approach. Otherwise we get unhistorical answers, the hallmark of the doctrinaire. He asks—criterion 1—"To what extent can various people in the society participate in those decisions which affect their

---

*These words and subsequent references to the Soviet Union preceded the reforms initiated under Mikhail Gorbachev and continued under Boris Yeltsin and Vladimir Putin.—*Editors.*

lives?" and—criterion 7—"Is there freedom of expression on all matters, and equally for all, to communicate with other members of the society?" Why doesn't Mr. Zinn adopt this sensible comparative approach? Because it would lead him to inquire into the extent to which people are free to participate in decisions that affect their lives *today*, free to express themselves, free to organize, free to protest and dissent today, *in comparison with the past*. It would lead him to the judgment *which he wishes to avoid at all costs*, to wit, that despite the grave problems, gaps, and tasks before us, the United States is more democratic today than it was a hundred years ago, fifty years ago, twenty years ago, five years ago with respect to every one of the criteria he has listed. To recognize this is not an invitation to complacency. On the contrary, it indicates the possibility of broadening, deepening, and using the democratic political process to improve the quality of human life, to modify and redirect social institutions in order to realize on a wider scale the moral commitment of democracy to an equality of concern for all its citizens to achieve their fullest growth as persons. This commitment is to a process, not to a transcendent goal or a fixed, ideal standard.

In a halting, imperfect manner, set back by periods of violence, vigilantism, and xenophobia, the political democratic process in the United States has been used to modify the operation of the economic system. The improvements and reforms won from time to time make the still-existing problems and evils more acute in that people become more aware of them. The more the democratic process extends human freedoms, and the more it introduces justice in social relations and the distribution of wealth, the greater grows the desire for *more* freedom and justice. Historically and psychologically, it is false to assume that reforms breed a spirit of complacency. . . .

The third and perhaps most serious weakness in Mr. Zinn's view is his conception of the nature of the formal political democratic process. It suffers from several related defects. First, it overlooks the central importance of majority rule in the democratic process. Second, it denies in effect that majority rule is possible by defining democracy in such a way that it becomes impossible. . . .

"Representation by its very nature," claims Mr. Zinn, "is undemocratic." This is Rousseauistic nonsense. For it would mean that no democracy—including all societies that Mr. Zinn ever claimed at any time to be democratic—could possibly exist, not even the direct democracies or assemblies of Athens or the New England town meetings. For all such assemblies must elect officials to carry out their will. If no representative (and an official is a representative, too) can adequately represent another's needs, there is no assurance that in the actual details of governance, the selectmen, road commissioners, or other town or assembly officials will, in fact, carry out their directives. No assembly or meeting can sit in continuous session or collectively carry out the common decision. In the nature of the case, officials, like representatives, constitute an elite and their actions *may* reflect their interests more than the interests of the governed. This makes crucial the questions whether and how an elite can be removed, whether the consent on which the rule of the officials or representatives rests is free or coerced, whether a minority can peacefully use these mechanisms, by which freely given consent is registered, to win over or become a majority. The existence of representative assemblies makes democracy difficult, not impossible.

Since Mr. Zinn believes that a majority never has any authority to bind a minority as well as itself by decisions taken after free discussion and debate, he is logically committed to anarchy. Failing to see this, he confuses two fundamentally different things—the meaning or definition of democracy, and its justification.

1. A democratic government is one in which the general direction of policy rests directly or indirectly upon the freely given consent of a majority of the adults governed. Ambiguities and niceties aside, that is what democracy means. It is not anarchy. The absence of a unanimous consensus does not entail the absence of democracy.

2. One may reject on moral or religious or personal grounds a democratic society. Plato, as well as modern totalitarians, contends that a majority of mankind is either too stupid or vicious to be entrusted with self-government, or to be given the power to accept or reject their ruling elites, and that the only viable alternative to democracy is the self-selecting and self-perpetuating elite of "the wise," or "the efficient," or "the holy," or "the strong," depending upon the particular ideology of the totalitarian apologist. The only thing they have in common with democrats is their rejection of anarchy.

3. No intelligent and moral person can make an *absolute* of democracy in the sense that he believes it is always, everywhere, under any conditions, and no matter what its consequences, ethically legitimate. Democracy is obviously not desirable in a head-hunting or cannibalistic society or in an institution of the feeble-minded. But wherever and whenever a principled democrat accepts the political system of democracy, he must accept the binding authority of legislative decisions, reached after the free give-and-take of debate and discussion, as binding upon him whether he is a member of the majority or minority. Otherwise the consequence is incipient or overt anarchy or civil war, the usual preface to despotism or tyranny. Accepting the decision of the majority as binding does not mean that it is final or irreversible. The processes of freely given consent must make it possible for a minority to urge amendment or repeal of any decision of the majority. Under carefully guarded provisions, a democrat may resort to civil disobedience of a properly enacted law in order to bear witness to the depths of his commitment in an effort to *reeducate* his fellow citizens. But in that case he must voluntarily accept punishment for his civil disobedience, and so long as he remains a democrat, voluntarily abandon his violation or noncompliance with law at the point where its consequences threaten to destroy the democratic process and open the floodgates either to the violent disorders of anarchy or to the dictatorship of a despot or a minority political party.

4. That Mr. Zinn is not a democrat but an anarchist in his views is apparent in his contention that not only must a democracy allow or tolerate civil disobedience within limits, but that "members of a society concerned with democracy must not only defend such acts, but encourage them."

On this view, if southern segregationists resort to civil disobedience to negate the long-delayed but eminently just measures adopted by the government to implement the amendments that outlaw slavery, they should be encouraged to do so. On this view, any group that defies any law that violates its conscience—with respect to marriage, taxation, vaccination, abortion, education—should be encouraged to do so. Mr. Zinn, like most anarchists, refuses to generalize the principles behind his action. He fails to see that if all fanatics of causes deemed by them to be morally just were encouraged to resort to civil disobedience, even our imperfect existing political democracy would dissolve in chaos, and that civil disobedience would soon become quite uncivil. He fails to see that *in a democracy the processes of intelligence, not individual conscience, must be supreme.*

II

I turn now to some of the issues that Mr. Zinn declares are substantive. Before doing so I wish to make clear my belief that the most substantive issue of all is the procedural one by which the inescapable differences of interests among men, once a certain moral level of civilization has been reached, are to be negotiated. The belief in the validity of democratic procedures rests upon the conviction that where adult human beings have freedom of access to relevant information, they are, by and large, better judges of their own interests than are those who set themselves up as their betters and rulers, that, to use the homely maxim, those who wear the shoes know best where they pinch and therefore have the right to change their political shoes in the light of their experience. . . .

Looking at the question "How democratic is America?" with respect to the problems of poverty, race, education, etc., we must say "Not democratic enough!", but not for the reasons Mr. Zinn gives. For he seems to believe that the failure to adopt *his* solutions and proposals with respect to foreign policy, slum clearance, pollution, etc., is evidence of the failure of the democratic process itself. He overlooks the crucial difference between the procedural process and the substantive issues. When he writes that democracy is devoid of meaning if it does not include "equal access to the available resources of the society," he is simply abusing language. Assuming such equal access is desirable (which some might question who believe that access to *some* of society's resources—for example, to specialized training or to scarce supplies—should go not equally to all but to the most needful or sometimes to the most qualified), a democracy may or may not legislate such equal access. The crucial question is whether the electorate has the power to make the choice, or to elect those who would carry out the mandate chosen. . . .

When Mr. Zinn goes on to say that "in the United States . . . democracy should mean that every American, working a short work-week, has adequate food, clothing, shelter, health care, . . ." he is not only abusing language, he is revealing the fact that the procedural processes that are essential to the meaning of democracy, in ordinary usage, are not essential to his conception. He is violating the basic ethics of discourse. If democracy "should mean" what Mr. Zinn says it should, then were Huey Long or any other dictator to seize power and introduce a "short work-week" and distribute "adequate food, clothing, shelter, health care" to the masses, Mr. Zinn would have to regard his regime as democratic.

After all, when Hitler came to power and abolished free elections in Germany, he at the same time reduced unemployment, increased the real wages of the German worker, and provided more adequate food, clothing, shelter, and health care than was available under the Weimar Republic. On Zinn's view of what democracy "should mean," this made Hitler's rule more democratic than that of Weimar. . . .

Not surprisingly, Mr. Zinn is a very unreliable guide even in his account of the procedural features of the American political system. In one breath he maintains that not enough information is available to voters to make intelligent choices on major political issues like tax laws. (The voter, of course, does not vote on such laws but for representatives who have taken stands on a number of complex issues.) "The dominant influences are those of big business, which has the resources both to understand and to act." In another breath, he complains that the electorate is at the mercy of the propagandist. "The propagandist does not need to lie; he overwhelms the public with so much information as to lead it to believe that it is all too complicated for anyone but the experts."

Mr. Zinn is certainly hard to please! The American political process is not democratic because the electorate hasn't got enough information. It is also undemocratic because it receives too much information. What would Mr. Zinn have us do so that the public gets just the right amount of information and propaganda? Have the government control the press? Restrict freedom of propaganda? But these are precisely the devices of totalitarian societies. The evils of the press, even when it is free of government control, are many indeed. The great problem is to keep the press free and responsible. And as defective as the press and other public media are today, surely it is an exaggeration to say that with respect to tax laws "the dominant influences are those of big business." If they were, how can we account for the existence of the income tax laws? If the influence of big business on the press is so dominant and the press is so biased, how can we account for the fact that although 92 percent of the press opposed Truman's candidacy in 1948, he was reelected? How can we account for the profound dissatisfaction of Vice President Agnew with the press and other mass media?* And since Mr. Zinn believes that big business dominates our educational system, especially our universities, how can we account for the fact that the universities are the centers of the strongest dissent in the nation to public and national policy, that the National Association of Manufacturers bitterly complained a few years ago that the economics of the free enterprise system was derided, and often not even taught, in most Departments of Economics in the colleges and universities of the nation?

---

*Spiro Agnew, former governor of Maryland and vice president of the United States before being forced to resign in 1973 during the second term of President Richard Nixon, was a frequent and vociferous critic of the "liberal" press.—*Editors.*

Mr. Zinn's exaggerations are really caricatures of complex realities. Far from being controlled by the monolithic American corporate economy, American public opinion is today marked by a greater scope and depth of dissent than at any time in its history, except for the days preceding the Civil War. The voice and the votes of Main Street still count for more in a democratic polity than those of Wall Street. Congress has limited, and can still further limit, the influence of money on the electoral process by federal subsidy and regulations. There are always abuses needing reforms. By failing to take a comparative approach and instead focusing on some absolute utopian standard of perfection, Mr. Zinn gives an exaggerated, tendentious, and fundamentally false picture of the United States. There is hardly a sentence in his essay that is free of some serious flaw in perspective, accuracy, or emphasis. Sometimes they have a comic effect, as when Mr. Zinn talks about the lack of "equal distribution of the right of freedom of expression." What kind of "equal distribution" is he talking about? Of course, a person with more money can talk to more people than one with less, although this does not mean that more persons will listen to him, agree with him, or be influenced by him. But a person with a more eloquent voice or a better brain can reach more people than you or I. What shall we do to insure equal distribution of the right of freedom of expression? Insist on equality of voice volume or pattern, and equality of brain power? More money gives not only greater opportunity to talk to people than less money but the ability to do thousands of things barred to those who have less money. Shall we then decree that all people have the same amount of money all the time and forbid anyone from depriving anyone else of any of his money even by fair means? "The government," writes Mr. Zinn, "has much more freedom of expression than a private individual because the president can command the airwaves when he wishes, and reach 60 million people in one night."

Alas! Mr. Zinn is not joking. Either he wants to bar the president or any public official from using the airwaves or he wants all of us to take turns. One wonders what country Mr. Zinn is living in. Nixon spoke to 60 million people several times, and so did Jimmy Carter. What was the result? More significant than the fact that 60 million people hear the president is that 60 million or more can hear his critics, sometimes right after he speaks, and that no one is compelled to listen.

Mr. Zinn does not understand the basic meaning of equality in a free, open democratic society. Its philosophy does not presuppose that all citizens are physically or intellectually equal or that all are equally gifted in every or any respect. It holds that all enjoy a *moral* equality, and that therefore, as far as is practicable, given finite resources, the institutions of a democratic society should seek to provide an equal opportunity to all its citizens to develop themselves to their full desirable potential.

Of course, we cannot ever provide complete equal opportunity. More and more is enough. For one thing, so long as children have different parents and home environments, they cannot enjoy the same or equal opportunities. Nonetheless, the family has compensating advantages for all that. Let us hope that Mr. Zinn does not wish to wipe out the family to avoid differences in opportunity. Plato believed that the family, as we know it, should be abolished because it did not provide equality of opportunity, and that all children should be brought up by the state.

Belief in the moral equality of men and women does not require that all individuals be treated identically or that equal treatment must be measured or determined by equality of outcome or result. Every citizen should have an equal right to an education, but that does not mean that, regardless of capacity and interest, he or she should have the same amount of schooling beyond the adolescent years, and at the same schools, and take the same course of study. With the increase in national wealth, a good case can be made for an equal right of all citizens to health care or medical treatment. But only a quack or ideological fanatic would insist that therefore all individuals should have the same medical regimen no matter what ails them. This would truly be putting all human beings in the bed of Procrustes.

This conception of moral equality as distinct from Mr. Zinn's notions of equality is perfectly compatible with intelligent recognition of human inequalities and relevant ways of treating their inequalities to further both the individual and common good. Intelligent and loving parents are equally concerned with the welfare of all their children. But precisely because they are, they may provide different specific strategies in health care, education, psychological motivation, and intellectual stimulation to develop the best in all of them. The logic of Mr. Zinn's position—although he seems blissfully unaware of it—leads to the most degrading kind of egalitarian socialism, the kind which Marx and Engels in their early years denounced as "barracks socialism."

It is demonstrable that democracy is healthier and more effective where human beings do not suffer from poverty, unemployment, and disease. It is also demonstrable that to the extent that property gives power, private property in the means of social production gives power over the lives of those who must live by its use, and, therefore, that such property, whether public or private, should be responsible to those who are affected by its operation. Consequently one can argue that political democracy depends not only on the extension of the franchise to all adults, not only on its active exercise, but on programs of social welfare that provide for collective bargaining by free trade unions of workers and employees, unemployment insurance, minimum wages, guaranteed health care, and other social services that are integral to the welfare state. It is demonstrable that although the existing American welfare state provides far more welfare than was ever provided in the past—my own lifetime furnishes graphic evidence of the vast changes—it is still very far from being a genuine welfare state. Political democracy can exist without a welfare state, but it is stronger and better with it.

The basic issue that divides Mr. Zinn from others no less concerned about human welfare, but less fanatical than he, is how a genuine welfare state is to be brought about. My contention is that this can be achieved by the vigorous exercise of the existing democratic process, and that by the same coalition politics through which great gains have been achieved in the past, even greater gains can be won in the future.

For purposes of economy, I focus on the problem of poverty, or since this is a relative term, hunger. If the presence of hunger entails the absence of the democratic political process, then democracy has never existed in the past—which would be an arbitrary use of words. Nonetheless, the existence of hunger is always a threat to the continued existence of the democratic process because of the standing temptation of those who hunger to exchange freedom for the promise of bread. This, of course, is an additional ground to the even weightier moral reasons for gratifying basic human needs.

That fewer people go hungry today in the United States than ever before may show that our democracy is better than it used to be but not that it is as good as it can be. Even the existence of one hungry person is one too many. How then can hunger or the extremes of poverty be abolished? Certainly not by the method Mr. Zinn advises: "Acts of civil disobedience by the poor will be required, at the least, to make middle-class America take notice, to bring national decisions that begin to reallocate wealth."

This is not only a piece of foolish advice, it is dangerously foolish advice. Many national decisions to reallocate wealth have been made through the political process—what else is the system of taxation if not a method of reallocating wealth?—without resort to civil disobedience. Indeed, resort to civil disobedience on this issue is very likely to produce a backlash among those active and influential political groups in the community who are aware that normal political means are available for social and economic reform. The refusal to engage in such normal political processes could easily be exploited by demagogues to portray the movement towards the abolition of hunger and extreme poverty as a movement towards the confiscation and equalization of all wealth.

The simplest and most effective way of abolishing hunger is to act on the truly revolutionary principle, enunciated by the federal government, that it is responsible for maintaining a standard of relief as a minimum beneath which a family will not be permitted to sink. . . .

For reasons that need no elaboration here, the greatest of the problems faced by American democracy today is the race problem. Although tied to the problems of poverty and urban reconstruction, it has independent aspects exacerbated by the legacy of the Civil War and the Reconstruction period.

Next to the American Indians, African-Americans have suffered most from the failure of the democratic political process to extend the rights and privileges of citizenship to those whose labor and suffering have contributed so much to the conquest of the continent. The remarkable gains that have been made by African-Americans in the last twenty years have been primarily through the political process. If the same rate of improvement continues, the year 2000 may see a rough equality established. The growth of African-American suffrage, especially in the South, the increasing sense of responsibility by the white community, despite periodic setbacks resulting from outbursts of violence, opens up a perspective of continuous and cumulative reform. The man and the organization he headed chiefly responsible for the great gains made by African-Americans, Roy Wilkins and the NAACP, were convinced that the democratic political process can be more effectively used to further the integration of African-Americans into our national life than by reliance on any other method. . . .

The only statement in Mr. Zinn's essay that I can wholeheartedly endorse is his assertion that the great danger to American democracy does not come from the phenomena of protest as such. Dissent and protest are integral to the democratic process. The danger comes from certain modes of dissent, from the substitution of violence and threats of violence for the mechanisms of the political process, from the escalation of that violence as the best hope of those who still have grievances against our imperfect American democracy, and from views such as those expressed by Mr. Zinn which downgrade the possibility of peaceful social reform and encourage rebellion. It is safe to predict that large-scale violence by impatient minorities will fail. It is almost as certain that attempts at violence will backfire, that they will create a climate of repression that may reverse the course of social progress and expanded civil liberties of the last generation. . . .

It is when Mr. Zinn is discussing racial problems that his writing ceases to be comic and silly and becomes irresponsible and mischievous. He writes:

> The massive African-American urban uprisings of 1967 and 1968 showed that nothing less than civil disobedience (for riots and uprisings go beyond that) could make the nation see that the race problem is an American—not a southern—problem and that it needs bold, revolutionary action.

First of all, every literate person knows that the race problem is an American problem, not exclusively a southern one. It needs no civil disobedience or "black uprisings" to remind us of that. Second, the massive uprisings of 1967 and 1968 were violent and uncivil, and resulted in needless loss of life and suffering. The Civil Rights Acts, according to Roy Wilkins, then head of the NAACP, were imperiled by them. They were adopted despite, not because, of them. Third, what kind of "revolutionary" action is Mr. Zinn calling for? And by whom? He seems to lack the courage of his confusions. Massive civil disobedience when sustained becomes a form of civil war.

Despite Mr. Zinn and others, violence is more likely to produce reaction than reform. In 1827 a resolution to manumit slaves by purchase (later, Lincoln's preferred solution) was defeated by three votes in the House of Burgesses of the State of Virginia. It was slated to be reintroduced in a subsequent session with excellent prospects of being adopted. Had Virginia adopted it, North Carolina would shortly have followed suit. But before it could be reintroduced, Nat Turner's rebellion broke out. Its violent excesses frightened the South into a complete rejection of a possibility that might have prevented the American Civil War—the fiercest and bloodiest war in human history up to that time, from whose consequences American society is still suffering. Mr. Zinn's intentions are as innocent as those of a child playing with matches.

III

One final word about "the global" dimension of democracy of which Mr. Zinn speaks. Here, too, he speaks sympathetically of actions that would undermine the willingness and capacity of a free society to resist totalitarian aggression.

The principles that should guide a free democratic society in a world where dictatorial regimes seek to impose their rule on other nations were formulated by John Stuart Mill, the great defender of liberty and representative government, more than a century ago:

> To go to war for an idea, if the war is aggressive not defensive, is as criminal as to go to war for territory or revenue, for it is as little justifiable to force our ideas on other people, as to compel them to submit to our will in any other aspect. . . . *The doctrine of non-intervention, to be a legitimate principle of morality, must be accepted by all governments.* The despots must consent to be bound by it as well as the free states. Unless they do, the profession of it by free countries comes but to this miserable issue, that the wrong side may help the wrong side but the right may not help the right side. Intervention to enforce non-intervention is always right, always moral *if not always prudent.* Though it may be a mistake to give freedom (or independence—S.H.) to a people who do not value the boon, it cannot be right to insist that if they do value it, they shall not be hindered from the pursuit of it by foreign coercion (*Fraser's Magazine,* 1859, emphasis mine).

Unfortunately, these principles were disregarded by the United States in 1936 when Hitler and Mussolini sent troops to Spain to help Franco overthrow the legally elected democratic Loyalist regime. The U.S. Congress, at the behest of the administration, adopted a Neutrality Resolution which prevented the democratic government of Spain from purchasing arms here. This compelled the Spanish government to make a deal with Stalin, who not only demanded its entire gold supply but the acceptance of the dread Soviet secret police, the NKVD, to supervise the operations. The main operation of the NKVD in Spain was to engage in a murderous purge of the democratic ranks of anti-Communists which led to the victory of Franco. The story is told in George Orwell's *Homage to Catalonia.* He was on the scene.

The prudence of American intervention in Vietnam may be debatable but there is little doubt that [UN ambassador] Adlai Stevenson, sometimes referred to as the liberal conscience of the nation, correctly stated the American motivation when he said at the UN on the very day of his death: "My hope in Vietnam is that resistance there may establish the fact that changes in Asia are not to be precipitated by outside force. This was the point of the Korean War. This is the point of the conflict in Vietnam."

. . . Mr. Zinn's remarks about Grenada show he is opposed to the liberal principles expressed by J. S. Mill in the passage cited above. His report of the facts about Grenada is as distorted as his account of present-day American democracy. On tiny Grenada, whose government was seized by Communist terrorists, were representatives of every Communist regime in the Kremlin's orbit, Cuban troops, and a Soviet general. I have read the documents captured by the American troops. They conclusively establish that the Communists were preparing the island as part of the Communist strategy of expansion.[1]

It is sad but significant that Mr. Zinn, whose heart bleeds for the poor Asians who suffered in the struggle to prevent the Communist takeover in Southeast Asia, has not a word of protest, not a tear of compassion for the hundreds of thousands tortured, imprisoned, and drowned in flight after the victory of the North Vietnamese "liberators," not to mention the even greater number of victims of the Cambodian and Cuban Communists. . . .

NOTE

1. *The Grenada Papers: The Inside Story of the Grenadian Revolution—and the Making of a Totalitarian State as Told in Captured Documents* (San Francisco: Institute of Contemporary Studies, 1984).

Rebuttal to Sidney Hook

Howard Zinn

Mr. Hook *does* have the courage of his confusions. I have space to point out only a few.

1. He chooses to define democracy as a "process," thus omitting its substance. Lincoln's definition was quite good—"government of, by, and for the people." Mr. Hook pooh-poohs the last part as something that could be done by a despot. My definition, like Lincoln's, requires "of" and "by" as well as "for," process as well as content. Mr. Hook is wild about voting, which can also be allowed by despots. Voting is an improvement over autocracy, but insufficient to make any society democratic. Voting, as Emma Goldman said (true, she was an anarchist), and as Helen Keller agreed (true, she was a socialist), is "our modern fetish." It is Mr. Hook's fetish.

   Mr. Hook's "democracy" is easily satisfied by hypocrisy, by forms and procedures which look good on paper, and behind which the same old injustices go on. Concealed behind the haughty pedant's charge of "methodological errors" is a definition of democracy which is empty of human meaning, a lifeless set of structures and procedures, which our elementary school teachers tried to pawn off on us as democracy—elections, checks and balances, how a bill becomes a law. Of course, we can't have the perfect democracy, and can't avoid representation, but we get closer to democracy when representation is supplemented by the direct action of citizens.

Howard Zinn's rebuttal was written specifically for this volume.

The missing heart, the flowing blood, the life-giving element in democracy is the constant struggle of people inside, around, outside, and despite the ordinary political processes. That means protest, strikes, boycotts, demonstrations, petitions, agitation, education, sometimes the slow buildup of public opinion, sometimes civil disobedience.

2. Mr. Hook seems oblivious of historical experience in the United States. His infatuation with "political process" comes out of ancient textbooks in which presidents and congresses act in the nick of time to save us when we're in trouble. In fact, that political process has never been sufficient to solve any crucial problem of human rights in our country: slavery, corporate despotism, war—all required popular movements to oppose them, movements outside those channels into which Mr. Hook and other apologists for the status quo constantly invite us, so we can get lost. Only when popular movements go into action do the channels themselves suddenly come to life.

The test is in history. When Mr. Hook says African-Americans got their gains "primarily through the political process" he simply does not know what he is talking about. The new consciousness of the rights of African-Americans, the gains made in the past twenty years—were they initiated by the "political process"? That process was dead for one hundred years while five thousand African-Americans were lynched, segregation flourished, and presidents, Congress, and the Supreme Court turned the other cheek. Only when African-Americans took to the streets by the tens of thousands, sat-in, demonstrated, even broke the law, did the "political process" awaken from its long lethargy. Only then did Congress rush to pass civil rights laws, just in time for Mr. Hook to say, cheerily, "You see, the process works."

Another test. Mr. Hook talks about the progress made "because the existence of the Wagner Labor Relations Act made collective bargaining the law of the land." He seems unaware of the wave of strikes in 1933–34 throughout the nation that brought a dead labor relations act to life. Peter Irons, in his prize-winning study, *The New Deal Lawyers*, carefully examines the chronology of 1934, and concludes: "It is likely that the existing National Labor Relations Board would have limped along, unable to enforce its orders, had not the industrial workforce erupted in late April, engulfing the country in virtual class war . . . Roosevelt and the Congress were suddenly jolted into action." Even after the act was passed in 1935, employers resisted it, and it took the sitdown strikes of 1936–37—yes, civil disobedience—to get contracts with General Motors and U.S. Steel.

A third test. The political process was pitifully inept as a handful of decision-makers, telling lies, propelled this country into the ugly war in Vietnam. (Mr. Hook joins them, when he quotes Adlai Stevenson that we were in Vietnam to act against "outside force"; the overwhelming "outside force" in Vietnam was the United States, with 525,000 troops, dropping 7 million tons of bombs on Southeast Asia.) A president elected in 1964 on his promises to keep the peace took us into war; Congress, like sheep, voted the money; the Supreme Court enveloped itself in its black robes and refused to discuss the constitutionality of the war. It took an unprecedented movement of protest to arouse the nation, to send a surge of energy moving through those clogged processes, and finally bring the war to an end.

3. Mr. Hook doesn't understand civil disobedience. He makes the common error of thinking that a supporter of Martin Luther King's civil disobedience must also support that of the Ku Klux Klan. He seems to think that if you believe civil disobedience is sometimes justified, for some causes, you must support civil disobedience done any time, by any group, for any reason. He does not grasp that the principle is not one of absolute civil disobedience; it simply denies absolute obedience. It says we should not be fanatics about "law and order" because sometimes the law supports the disorder of poverty, or racism, or war.

We can certainly distinguish between civil disobedience for good causes and for bad causes. That's what our intelligence is for. Will this lead to "chaos," as Mr. Hook warns? Again, historical experience is instructive: Did the civil disobedience of African-Americans in the sixties lead to chaos? Or the civil disobedience of anti-war protesters in the Vietnam years? Yes, they involved some disorder, as all social change does; they upset the false tranquillity of segregation, they demanded an end to the chaos of war.

4. Mr. Hook thinks he is telling us something new when he says we can't, and sometimes should not, have perfect equality. Of course. But the point of having ideals is not that they can be perfectly achieved, but that they do not let us rest content, as Mr. Hook is, with being somewhat better off today than yesterday. By his standard, we can give just enough more to the poor to appease anger, while keeping the basic injustice of a wealthy society. In a country where some people live in mansions and others in slums, should we congratulate ourselves because the slums now have TV antennas sticking out of the leaky roofs? His prescription for equality would have us clean out the Augean stables with a spoon, and boast of our progress, while comparing us to all the terrible places in the world where they don't even have spoons. Mr. Hook tries to avoid this issue of inequality by confusing inequality in intellect and physique, which obviously can't be helped much, with inequality of wealth, which is intolerably crass in a country as wealthy as ours.

Mr. Hook becomes ludicrous when he tries to deny the crucial importance of wealth in elections and in control of the media. When he says, "The voice and votes of Main Street still count for more in a democratic polity than those of Wall Street," I wonder where he has been. If Main Street counts more than Wall Street, how come congressional cutbacks in social programs in 1981–82 brought the number of people officially defined as poor to its highest level since 1965—25.3 million—while at the same time eight thousand millionaires saved a billion dollars in lowered taxes? And how can we account for this news item of October 16, 1984, in *The New York Times*: "Five of the nation's top dozen military contractors earned profits in the years

1981, 1982, and 1983, but paid no Federal income taxes." Can you name five schoolteachers or five social workers who paid no federal income taxes?

What of the system of justice—has it not always favored Wall Street over Main Street? Compare the punishment given to corporation executives found guilty of robbing billions from consumers by price-fixing with the punishment given to auto thieves and house burglars.

Money talks loudly in this "democratic polity." But, Mr. Hook says, in an absurd defense of the control of the media, you don't have to listen! No, the mother needing medical aid doesn't have to listen, but whether her children live or die may result from the fact that the rich dominate the media, control the elections, and get legislation passed which hurts the poor. A *Boston Globe* dispatch, May 24, 1984:

> Infant mortality, which had been declining steadily in Boston and other cities in the 1970s, shot up suddenly after the Reagan Administration reduced grants for health care for mothers and children and cut back sharply on Medicaid eligibility among poor women and children in 1981, according to new research.

5. As for "the global dimension of democracy," Mr. Hook's simple view of the world as divided between "free society" and "totalitarian aggression" suggests he is still living back in the heroic battles of World War II. We are now in the nuclear age, and that neat division into "free" and "totalitarian" is both factually wrong and dangerous. Yes, the United States is a relatively free society, and the Soviet Union is a shameful corruption of Marx's dreams of freedom.* But the United States has established or supported some of the most brutal totalitarian states in the world: Chile, South Africa, El Salvador, Guatemala, South Korea, the Philippines. Yes, the Soviet Union has committed cruel acts of aggression in Hungary, Czechoslovakia, and especially Afghanistan. But the United States has also, whether by the military or the CIA, committed aggression in Iran, Guatemala, Cuba, and the Dominican Republic, and especially in Vietnam, Laos, and Cambodia.

You cannot draw a line across the globe, as Mr. Hook does, to find good on one side and evil on the other. We get a sense of Mr. Hook's refusal to face the complexities of evil when he passes off the horror of the American invasion of Southeast Asia, which left a million dead, with: "The prudence of American intervention in Vietnam may be debatable." One can hear Mr. Hook's intellectual counterparts in the Soviet Union saying about the invasion of Afghanistan: "Our prudence . . . may be debatable." Such moral blindness will have to be overcome if there is to be movement toward real democracy in the United States, and toward real socialism in the Soviet Union. It is the fanaticism on both sides, justifying war "to defend freedom," or "to defend socialism," or simply, vaguely, "national security," that may yet kill us all. That will leave the issue of "how democratic we are" for archeologists of a future era.

---

*This rebuttal was written prior to the collapse of the Communist regime in the former Soviet Union.—*Editors.*

Rejoinder to Howard Zinn

Sidney Hook

I may have been mistaken about Mr. Zinn's courage. I am not mistaken about his confusion—his persistent confusion of a free or democratic society with a good society as he defines a good society. Zinn has not understood my criticism and therefore not replied to it. Perhaps on rereading it he will grasp the point.

1. Of course, there is no guarantee that the democratic process will yield a good society regardless of how Zinn or anyone else defines it. Democracies, like majorities, may sometimes be wrong or unwise. But if the decision is a result of a free and fair discussion and vote, it is still democratic. If those who lose in the electoral process resort to civil disobedience, democratic government ultimately breaks down. Even though the processes of democracy are slow and cumbersome and sometimes result in unwise action, its functioning Bill of Rights makes it possible to set them right. That is why Churchill observed, "Democracy is the worst of all forms of government except all the others that have been tried," including, we should add, anarchism.

   Zinn dismisses our democratic processes as "a lifeless set of structures and procedures." But it is these very structures and procedures which have enabled us to transform our society from one in which only white men with property voted to one in which all white men voted, then all men, then all men and women. It is these structures and procedures which have extended and protected the right to dissent, even for all sorts of foolishness like Zinn's. They currently protect Mr. Zinn in his academic freedom and post, in his right to utter any criticism of the democratic system under which he lives—a right he would never enjoy in any so-called socialist society in the world today.

   Mr. Zinn gives his case away when he refers to the democratic process, which requires voting in *free* elections, as a "fetish." A fetish is an object of irrational and superstitious devotion which enlightened persons reject. Like Marx, Zinn rejects "the fetishism of commodities." Is he prepared to reject the democratic process, too, if its results do not jibe with *his* conception of the good society?

   How, one wonders, does Zinn know that his conception is inherently more desirable than that of his fellow citizens? The democrat says: *Let us leave this choice to the arbitrament of the democratic process.* Zinn has a shorter way. He labels any conception other than his own as undemocratic; and if it prevails, he urges the masses to take to the streets.

Sidney Hook's rejoinder was written specifically for this volume.

2. The space allotted to me does not permit adequate discussion of the international aspects of the struggle for a free society. (I refer students to my *Philosophy and Public Policy* and *Marxism and Beyond*.) Suffice it to say here that sometimes when the feasible alternatives are limited, the wisest choice between evils is the lesser one. This is the same principle, supported by Zinn, that justified military aid to the Soviet Union when Nazi Germany invaded, although Stalin's regime at the time oppressed many more millions than Hitler's. From the standpoint of the free society, Stalin was the lesser evil then. Today Nazism is destroyed and globally expanding communism has taken its place. If, and only if, we are anywhere confronted by a choice of support between an authoritarian regime and a totalitarian one, the first is the lesser evil. This is not only because the second is far more oppressive of human rights (compare Batista to Castro, Thieu to Hanoi, Syngman Rhee to North Korea, Lon Nol to Pol Pot) but because authoritarian regimes sometimes develop peacefully into democracies (Spain, Portugal, Greece, Argentina) whereas no Communist regime allied to the Kremlin so far has.*

3. Within narrowly prescribed limits, a democracy may tolerate civil disobedience of those who on grounds of conscience violate its laws and willingly accept their punishment. (Cf. the chapter in my *Revolution, Reform and Social Justice*.) But Zinn does not advocate civil disobedience in this sense. He urges what is clearly *uncivil* disobedience like the riotous actions that preceded the Civil Rights Acts from which African-Americans, not white racists, suffered most, and the extensive destruction of property from factory sit-ins. Roy Wilkins, who should know, is my authority for asserting that the Civil Rights Acts were adopted by Congress not because of, but despite, these disorders. The most significant racial progress since 1865 was achieved by *Brown v. Topeka Board of Education* without "the disorders" Zinn recommends—a sly term that covers broken heads, loss of property, and sometimes loss of life, which are no part of civil disobedience.

   Until now, the most charitable thing one could say of Zinn's position is what Cicero once said of another loose thinker: there is no absurdity to which a person will not resort to defend another absurdity. But when Zinn with calculated ambiguity includes "disorders" in the connotation of civil disobedience, *without denouncing violence as no part of it as Gandhi and Martin Luther King did,* he is verging on moral irresponsibility. From the safety of his white suburbs, he is playing with fire.

   Law and order are possible without justice; but Mr. Zinn does not seem to understand that justice is impossible without law and order.

mhhe.com/diclerico11e | **Internet resources**
Visit our Web site at www.mhhe.com/diclerico11e for links and resources relating to Democracy.

---

*Again, this rejoinder was written prior to the breakup of the former Soviet Union.—*Editors.*

chapter 2

The Constitution

*O*f the many books that have been written about the circumstances surrounding the creation of our Constitution, none generated more controversy than Charles Beard's An Economic Interpretation of the Constitution of the United States *(1913). A historian by profession, Beard challenged the belief that our Constitution was fashioned by men of democratic spirit. In what appeared to be a systematic marshaling of evidence, Beard sought to demonstrate (1) that the impetus for a new constitution came from individuals who saw their own economic interests threatened by a growing trend in the population toward greater democracy; (2) that the Founding Fathers themselves were men of considerable "personalty" (i.e., holdings other than real estate), who were concerned not so much with fashioning a democratic constitution as with protecting their own financial interests against the more democratically oriented farming and debtor interests within the society; and (3) that the individuals charged with ratifying the new Constitution also represented primarily the larger economic interests within the society. Although space limitations prevent a full development of Beard's argument here, the portions of his book that follow should provide some feel for both the substance of his argument and his method of investigation.*

Beard's analysis has been subject to repeated scrutiny over the years. The most systematic effort came in 1956 with the publication of Robert Brown's Charles Beard and the Constitution: A Critical Analysis of "An Economic Interpretation of the Constitution." *Arguing that the rigor of Beard's examination was more apparent than real, Brown accuses Beard of citing only the facts that supported his case while ignoring those that did not. Moreover, he contends that even the evidence Beard provided did not warrant the interpretation he gave to it. Brown concludes that the best evidence now available does not support the view that "the Constitution was put over undemocratically in an undemocratic society by personal property."*

An Economic Interpretation of the Constitution of the United States

Charles A. Beard

Suppose it could be shown from the classification of the men who supported and opposed the Constitution that there was no line of property division at all; that is, that men owning substantially the same amounts of the same kinds of property were equally divided on the matter of adoption or rejection—it would then become apparent that the Constitution had no ascertainable relation to economic groups or classes, but was the product of some abstract causes remote from the chief business of life—gaining a livelihood.

Suppose, on the other hand, that substantially all of the merchants, money lenders, security holders, manufacturers, shippers, capitalists, and financiers and their professional associates are to be found on one side in support of the Constitution and that substantially all or the major portion of the opposition came from the nonslaveholding farmers and the debtors—would it not be pretty conclusively demonstrated that our fundamental law was not the product of an abstraction known as "the whole people," but of a group of economic interests which must have expected beneficial results from its adoption? Obviously all the facts here desired cannot be discovered, but the data presented in the following chapters bear out the latter hypothesis, and thus a reasonable presumption in favor of the theory is created.

Of course, it may be shown (and perhaps can be shown) that the farmers and debtors who opposed the Constitution were, in fact, benefited by the general improvement which resulted from its adoption. It may likewise be shown, to take an extreme case, that the English nation derived immense advantages from the Norman Conquest and the orderly administrative processes which were introduced, as it undoubtedly did; nevertheless, it does not follow that the vague thing known as "the advancement of general welfare" or some abstraction known as "justice" was the immediate, guiding purpose of the leaders in either of these great historic changes. The point is, that the direct, impelling motive in both cases was the economic advantages which the beneficiaries

Charles A. Beard (1874–1948) was professor of history and political science at Columbia University and a former president of the American Political Science Association. Reprinted with the permission of Scribner, an imprint of Simon & Schuster Adult Publishing Group, from *An Economic Interpretation of the Constitution of the United States* by Charles A. Beard. Copyright 1935 by The Macmillan Company; copyright renewed © 1963 by William Beard and Mrs. Miriam Beard Vagts.

expected would accrue to themselves first, from their action. Further than this, economic interpretation cannot go. It may be that some larger world process is working through each series of historical events: but ultimate causes lie beyond our horizon. . . .

THE FOUNDING FATHERS: AN ECONOMIC PROFILE

A survey of the economic interests of the members of the Convention presents certain conclusions:

A majority of the members were lawyers by profession.

Most of the members came from towns, on or near the coast, that is, from the regions in which personalty was largely concentrated.

Not one member represented in his immediate personal economic interests the small farming or mechanic classes.

The overwhelming majority of members, at least five-sixths, were immediately, directly, and personally interested in the outcome of their labors at Philadelphia, and were to a greater or less extent economic beneficiaries from the adoption of the Constitution.

1. Public security interests were extensively represented in the Convention. Of the fifty-five members who attended no less than forty appear on the Records of the Treasury Department for sums varying from a few dollars up to more than one hundred thousand dollars. . . .

   It is interesting to note that, with the exception of New York, and possibly Delaware, each state had one or more prominent representatives in the Convention who held more than a negligible amount of securities, and who could therefore speak with feeling and authority on the question of providing in the new Constitution for the full discharge of the public debt. . . .

2. Personalty invested in lands for speculation was represented by at least fourteen members. . . .

3. Personalty in the form of money loaned at interest was represented by at least twenty-four members. . . .

4. Personalty in mercantile, manufacturing, and shipping lines was represented by at least eleven members. . . .

5. Personalty in slaves was represented by at least fifteen members. . . .

It cannot be said, therefore, that the members of the Convention were "disinterested." On the contrary, we are forced to accept the profoundly significant conclusion that they knew through their personal experiences in economic affairs the precise results which the new government that they were setting up was designed to attain. As a group of doctrinaires, like the Frankfort assembly of 1848, they would have failed miserably; but as practical men they were able to build the new government upon the only foundations which could be stable: fundamental economic interests.[1] . . .

RATIFICATION

New York

There can be no question about the predominance of personalty in the contest over the ratification in New York. That state, says Libby, "presents the problem in its simplest form. The entire mass of interior counties . . . were solidly anti-Federal, comprising the agricultural portion of the state, the last settled and the most thinly populated. There were however in this region two Federal cities (not represented in the convention [as such]), Albany in Albany county and Hudson in Columbia county. . . . The Federal area centred about New York city and county: to the southwest lay Richmond county (Staten Island); to the southeast Kings county, and the northeast Westchester county; while still further extending this area, at the northeast lay the divided county of Dutchess, with a vote in the convention of 4 to 2 in favor of the Constitution, and at the southeast were the divided counties of Queens and Suffolk. . . . These radiating strips of territory with New York city as a centre form a unit, in general favorable to the new Constitution; and it is significant of this unity that Dutchess, Queens, and Suffolk counties, broke away from the anti-Federal phalanx and joined the Federalists, securing thereby the adoption of the Constitution."[2]

Unfortunately the exact distribution of personalty in New York and particularly in the wavering districts which went over to the Federalist party cannot be ascertained, for the system of taxation in vogue in New York at the period of the adoption of the Constitution did not require a state record of property.[3] The data which proved so fruitful in Massachusetts are not forthcoming, therefore, in the case of New York; but it seems hardly necessary to demonstrate the fact that New York City was the centre of personalty for the state and stood next to Philadelphia as the great centre of operations in public stock.

This somewhat obvious conclusion is reinforced by the evidence relative to the vote on the legal tender bill which the paper money party pushed through in 1786. Libby's analysis of this vote shows that "no vote was cast against the bill by members of counties north of the county of New York. In the city and county of New York and in Long Island and Staten Island, the combined vote was 9 to 5 against the measure. Comparing this vote with the vote on the ratification in 1788, it will be seen that of the Federal counties 3 voted against paper money and 1 for it; of the divided counties 1 (Suffolk) voted against paper money and 2 (Queens and Dutchess) voted for it. Of the anti-Federal counties none had members voting against paper money. The merchants as a body were opposed to the issue of paper money and the Chamber of Commerce adopted a memorial against the issue."[4]

Public security interests were identified with the sound money party. There were thirty members of the New York constitutional convention who voted in favor of the ratification of the Constitution and of these no less than sixteen were holders of public securities. . . .

South Carolina

South Carolina presents the economic elements in the ratification with the utmost simplicity. There we find two rather sharply marked districts in antagonism over the Constitution. "The rival sections," says Libby, "were the coast or lower district and the upper, or more properly, the middle and upper country. The coast region was the first settled and contained a larger portion of the wealth of the state; its mercantile and commercial interests were important; its church was the Episcopal, supported by the state." This region, it is scarcely necessary to remark, was overwhelmingly in favor of the Constitution. The upper area, against the Constitution, "was a frontier section, the last to receive settlement; its lands were fertile and its mixed population was largely small farmers. . . . There was no established church, each community supported its own church and there was a great variety in the district."[5]

A contemporary writer, R. G. Harper, calls attention to the fact that the lower country, Charleston, Beaufort, and Georgetown, which had 28,694 white inhabitants, and about seven-twelfths of the representation in the state convention, paid £28,081:5:10 taxes in 1794, while the upper country, with 120,902 inhabitants, and five-twelfths of the representation in the convention, paid only £8390:13:3 taxes.[6] The lower districts in favor of the Constitution therefore possessed the wealth of the state and a disproportionate share in the convention—on the basis of the popular distribution of representation.

These divisions of economic interest are indicated by the abstracts of the tax returns for the state in 1794 which show that of £127,337 worth of stock in trade, faculties, etc. listed for taxation in the state, £109,800 worth was in Charleston, city and county—the stronghold of Federalism. Of the valuation of lots in towns and villages to the amount of £656,272 in the state, £549,909 was located in that city and county.[7]

The records of the South Carolina loan office preserved in the Treasury Department at Washington show that the public securities of that state were more largely in the hands of inhabitants than was the case in North Carolina. They also show a heavy concentration in the Charleston district.

At least fourteen of the thirty-one members of the state-ratifying convention from the parishes of St. Philip and Saint Michael, Charleston (all of whom favored ratification) held over $75,000 worth of public securities. . . .

CONCLUSIONS

At the close of this long and arid survey—partaking of the nature of catalogue—it seems worthwhile to bring together the important conclusions for political science which the data presented appear to warrant.

The movement for the Constitution of the United States was originated and carried through principally by four groups of personalty interests which had been adversely affected under the Articles of Confederation: money, public securities, manufactures, and trade and shipping.

The first firm steps toward the formation of the Constitution were taken by a small and active group of men immediately interested through their personal possessions in the outcome of their labors.

No popular vote was taken directly or indirectly on the proposition to call the Convention which drafted the Constitution.

A large propertyless mass was, under the prevailing suffrage qualifications, excluded at the outset from participation (through representatives) in the work of framing the Constitution.

The members of the Philadelphia Convention which drafted the Constitution were, with a few exceptions, immediately, directly, and personally interested in, and derived economic advantages from, the establishment of the new system.

The Constitution was essentially an economic document based upon the concept that the fundamental private rights of property are anterior to government and morally beyond the reach of popular majorities.

The major portion of the members of the Convention are on record as recognizing the claim of property to a special and defensive position in the Constitution.

In the ratification of the Constitution, about three-fourths of the adult males failed to vote on the question, having abstained from the elections at which delegates to the state conventions were chosen, either on account of their indifference or their disfranchisement by property qualifications.

The Constitution was ratified by a vote of probably not more than one-sixth of the adult males.

It is questionable whether a majority of the voters participating in the elections for the state conventions in New York, Massachusetts, New Hampshire, Virginia, and South Carolina, actually approved the ratification of the Constitution.

The leaders who supported the Constitution in the ratifying conventions represented the same economic groups as the members of the Philadelphia Convention; and in a large number of instances they were also directly and personally interested in the outcome of their efforts.

In the ratification, it became manifest that the line of cleavage for and against the Constitution was between substantial personalty interests on the one hand and the small farming and debtor interests on the other.

The Constitution was not created by "the whole people" as the jurists have said; neither was it created by "the states" as southern nullifiers long contended; but it was the work of a consolidated group whose interests knew no state boundaries and were truly national in their scope.

NOTES

1. The fact that a few members of the Convention, who had considerable economic interests at stake, refused to support the Constitution does not invalidate the general conclusions here presented. In the cases of Yates, Lansing, Luther Martin, and Mason, definite economic reasons for their action are forthcoming; but this is a minor detail.

2. O. G. Libby, *Geographical Distribution of the Vote of the Thirteen States on the Federal Constitution*, p. 18. Libby here takes the vote in the New York convention, but that did not precisely represent the popular vote.

3. *State Papers: Finance*, vol. 1, p. 425.

4. Libby, *Geographical Distribution*, p. 59.

5. Ibid., pp. 42–43.

6. "Appius," *To the Citizens of South Carolina* (1794), Library of Congress, Duane Pamphlets, vol. 83.

7. *State Papers: Finance*, vol. 1, p. 462. In 1783 an attempt to establish a bank with $100,000 capital was made in Charleston, S.C., but it failed. "Soon after the adoption of the funding system, three banks were established in Charleston whose capitals in the whole amounted to twenty times the sum proposed in 1783." D. Ramsey, *History of South Carolina* (1858 ed.), vol. 2, p. 106.

Charles Beard and the Constitution
A Critical Analysis

Robert E. Brown

At the end of Chapter XI [of *An Economic Interpretation of the Constitution of the United States*], Beard summarized his findings in fourteen paragraphs under the heading of "Conclusions." Actually, these fourteen conclusions merely add up to the two halves of the Beard thesis. One half, that the Constitution originated with and was carried through by personalty interests—money, public securities, manufactures, and commerce—is to be found in paragraphs two, three, six, seven, eight, twelve, thirteen, and fourteen. The other half—that the Constitution was put over undemocratically in an undemocratic society—is expressed in paragraphs four, five, nine, ten, eleven, and fourteen. The lumping of these conclusions under two general headings makes it easier for the reader to see the broad outlines of the Beard thesis.

Before we examine these two major divisions of the thesis, however, some comment is relevant on the implications contained in the first paragraph. In it

Beard characterized his book as a long and arid survey, something in the nature of a catalogue. Whether this characterization was designed to give his book the appearance of a coldly objective study based on the facts we do not know. If so, nothing could be further from reality. As reviewers pointed out in 1913, and as subsequent developments have demonstrated, the book is anything but an arid catalogue of facts. Its pages are replete with interpretation, sometimes stated, sometimes implied. Our task has been to examine Beard's evidence to see whether it justifies the interpretation which Beard gave it. We have tried to discover whether he used the historical method properly in arriving at his thesis.

If historical method means the gathering of data from primary sources, the critical evaluation of the evidence thus gathered, and the drawing of conclusions consistent with this evidence, then we must conclude that Beard has done great violation to such method in this book. He admitted that the evidence had not been collected which, given the proper use of historical method, should have precluded the writing of the book. Yet he nevertheless proceeded on the assumption that a valid interpretation could be built on secondary writings whose authors had likewise failed to collect the evidence. If we accept Beard's own maxim, "no evidence, no history," and his own admission that the data had never been collected, the answer to whether he used historical method properly is self-evident.

Neither was Beard critical of the evidence which he did use. He was accused in 1913, and one might still suspect him, of using only that evidence which appeared to support his thesis. The amount of realty in the country compared with the personalty, the vote in New York, and the omission of the part of *The Federalist*, No. 10, which did not fit his thesis are only a few examples of the uncritical use of evidence to be found in the book. Sometimes he accepted secondary accounts at face value without checking them with the sources; at other times he allowed unfounded rumors and traditions to color his work.

Finally, the conclusions which he drew were not justified even by the kind of evidence which he used. If we accepted his evidence strictly at face value, it would still not add up to the fact that the Constitution was put over undemocratically in an undemocratic society by personalty. The citing of property qualifications does not prove that a mass of men were disfranchised. And if we accept his figures on property holdings, either we do not know what most of the delegates had in realty and personalty, or we know that realty outnumbered personalty three to one (eighteen to six). Simply showing that a man held public securities is not sufficient to prove that he acted only in terms of his public securities. If we ignore Beard's own generalizations and accept only his evidence, we have to conclude that most of the country, and that even the men who were directly concerned with the Constitution, and especially Washington, were large holders of realty.

Perhaps we can never be completely objective in history, but certainly we can be more objective than Beard was in this book. Naturally, the historian must always be aware of the biases, the subjectivity, the pitfalls that confront him, but this does not mean that he should not make an effort to overcome these obstacles. Whether Beard had his thesis before he had his evidence, as some have said, is a question that each reader must answer for himself. Certain it is that the evidence does not justify the thesis.

So instead of the Beard interpretation that the Constitution was put over undemocratically in an undemocratic society by personal property, the following fourteen paragraphs are offered as a possible interpretation of the Constitution and as suggestions for future research on that document.

1. The movement for the Constitution was originated and carried through by men who had long been important in both economic and political affairs in their respective states. Some of them owned personalty, more of them owned realty, and if their property was adversely affected by conditions under the Articles of Confederation, so also was the property of the bulk of the people in the country, middle-class farmers as well as town artisans.

2. The movement for the Constitution, like most important movements, was undoubtedly started by a small group of men. They were probably interested personally in the outcome of their labors, but the benefits which they expected were not confined to personal property or, for that matter, strictly to things economic. And if their own interests would be enhanced by a new government, similar interests of other men, whether agricultural or commercial, would also be enhanced.

3. Naturally there was no popular vote on the calling of the convention which drafted the Constitution. Election of delegates by state legislatures was the constitutional method under the Articles of Confederation, and had been the method long established in this country. Delegates to the Albany Congress, the Stamp Act Congress, the First Continental Congress, the Second Continental Congress, and subsequent congresses under the Articles were all elected by state legislatures, not by the people. Even the Articles of Confederation had been sanctioned by state legislatures, not by popular vote. This is not to say that the Constitutional Convention should not have been elected directly by the people, but only that such a procedure would have been unusual at the time. Some of the opponents of the Constitution later stressed, without avail, the fact that the Convention had not been directly elected. But at the time the Convention met, the people in general seemed to be about as much concerned over the fact that they had not elected the delegates as the people of this country are now concerned over the fact that they do not elect our delegates to the United Nations.

4. Present evidence seems to indicate that there were no "propertyless masses" who were excluded from the suffrage at the time. Most men were middle-class farmers who owned realty and were qualified voters, and, as the men in the Convention said, mechanics had always voted in the cities. Until credible evidence proves otherwise, we can assume that state legislatures were fairly representative at the time. We cannot condone the fact that a few men were probably disfranchised by prevailing property qualifications, but it makes a great deal of difference to an interpretation of the Constitution whether the disfranchised comprised 95 percent of the adult men or only 5 percent. Figures which give percentages of voters in terms of

the entire population are misleading, since less than 20 percent of the people were adult men. And finally, the voting qualifications favored realty, not personalty.

5. If the members of the Convention were directly interested in the outcome of their work and expected to derive benefits from the establishment of the new system, so also did most of the people of the country. We have many statements to the effect that the people in general expected substantial benefits from the labors of the Convention.

6. The Constitution was not just an economic document, although economic factors were undoubtedly important. Since most of the people were middle class and had private property, practically everybody was interested in the protection of property. A constitution which did not protect property would have been rejected without any question, for the American people had fought the Revolution for the preservation of life, liberty, and property. Many people believed that the Constitution did not go far enough to protect property, and they wrote these views into the amendments to the Constitution. But property was not the only concern of those who wrote and ratified the Constitution, and we would be doing a grave injustice to the political sagacity of the Founding Fathers if we assumed that property or personal gain was their only motive.

7. Naturally the delegates recognized that protection of property was important under government, but they also recognized that personal rights were equally important. In fact, persons and property were usually bracketed together as the chief objects of government protection.

8. If three-fourths of the adult males failed to vote on the election of delegates to ratifying conventions, this fact signified indifference, not disfranchisement. We must not confuse those who could *not* vote with those who *could* vote but failed to exercise their right. Many men at the time bewailed the fact that only a small portion of the voters ever exercised their prerogative. But this in itself should stand as evidence that the conflict over the Constitution was not very bitter, for if these people had felt strongly one way or the other, more of them would have voted.

Even if we deny the evidence which I have presented and insist that American society was undemocratic in 1787, we must still accept the fact that the men who wrote the Constitution believed that they were writing it for a democratic society. They did not hide behind an iron curtain of secrecy and devise the kind of conservative government that they wanted without regard to the views and interests of "the people." More than anything else, they were aware that "the people" would have to ratify what they proposed, and that therefore any government which would be acceptable to the people must of necessity incorporate much of what was customary at the time. The men at Philadelphia were practical politicians, not political theorists. They recognized the multitude of different ideas and interests that had to be reconciled and compromised before a constitution would be acceptable. They were far too practical, and represented far too many clashing interests themselves, to fashion a government weighted in favor of personalty or to believe that the people would adopt such a government.

9. If the Constitution was ratified by a vote of only one-sixth of the adult men, that again demonstrates indifference and not disfranchisement. Of the one-fourth of the adult males who voted, nearly two-thirds favored the Constitution. Present evidence does not permit us to say what the popular vote was except as it was measured by the votes of the ratifying conventions.

10. Until we know what the popular vote was, we cannot say that it is questionable whether a majority of the voters in several states favored the Constitution. Too many delegates were sent uninstructed. Neither can we count the towns which did not send delegates on the side of those opposed to the Constitution. Both items would signify indifference rather than sharp conflict over ratification.

11. The ratifying conventions were elected for the specific purpose of adopting or rejecting the Constitution. The people in general had anywhere from several weeks to several months to decide the question. If they did not like the new government, or if they did not know whether they liked it, they could have voted no and there would have been no Constitution. Naturally the leaders in the ratifying conventions represented the same interests as the members of the Constitutional Convention—mainly realty and some personalty. But they also represented their constituents in these same interests, especially realty.

12. If the conflict over ratification had been between substantial personalty interests on the one hand and small farmers and debtors on the other, there would not have been a constitution. The small farmers comprised such an overwhelming percentage of the voters that they could have rejected the new government without any trouble. Farmers and debtors are not synonymous terms and should not be confused as such. A town-by-town or county-by-county record of the vote would show clearly how the farmers voted.

13. The Constitution was created about as much by the whole people as any government could be which embraced a large area and depended on representation rather than on direct participation. It was also created in part by the states, for as the *Records* show, there was strong state sentiment at the time which had to be appeased by compromise. And it was created by compromising a whole host of interests throughout the country, without which compromises it could never have been adopted.

14. If the intellectual historians are correct, we cannot explain the Constitution without considering the psychological factors also. Men are motivated by what they believe as well as by what they have. Sometimes their actions can be explained on the basis of what they hope to have or hope that their children will have. Madison understood this fact when he said that the universal hope of acquiring property tended to dispose people to look favorably upon property. It is even possible that some men support a given economic system when they themselves have nothing to gain by it. So we

would want to know what the people in 1787 thought of their class status. Did workers and small farmers believe that they were lower class, or did they, as many workers do now, consider themselves middle class? Were the common people trying to eliminate the Washingtons, Adamses, Hamiltons, and Pinckneys, or were they trying to join them?

As did Beard's fourteen conclusions, these fourteen suggestions really add up to two major propositions: the Constitution was adopted in a society which was fundamentally democratic, not undemocratic; and it was adopted by a people who were primarily middle-class property owners, especially farmers who owned realty, not just by the owners of personality. At present these points seem to be justified by the evidence, but if better evidence in the future disproves or modifies them, we must accept that evidence and change our interpretation accordingly.

After this critical analysis, we should at least not begin future research on this period of American history with the illusion that the Beard thesis of the Constitution is valid. If historians insist on accepting the Beard thesis in spite of this analysis, however, they must do so with the full knowledge that their acceptance is founded on "an act of faith," not an analysis of historical method, and that they were indulging in a "noble dream," not history.

mhhe.com/diclerico11e

Internet resources
Visit our Web site at www.mhhe.com/diclerico11e for links and resources relating to the Constitution.

chapter 3

Federalism

Unfunded Mandates

The Tenth Amendment to the U.S. Constitution states: "The powers not delegated to the United States by the Constitution, nor prohibited by it to the States, are reserved to the States respectively, or to the people." Although this brief amendment, containing just slightly more than twenty-five words, seems simple and uncomplicated, it has constituted the basis for one of the more protracted debates in U.S. history—namely, the extent to which the national and state governments may encroach on each other's powers and prerogatives.

A modern manifestation of this debate is to be found in the controversy over "unfunded federal mandates." Unfunded mandates are those laws passed by Congress that require states to carry out national regulations without federal government funding. Examples are the Clean Water Act of 1972, the Americans with Disabilities Act of 1990, the National Voter Registration Act of 1993, and the No Child Left Behind Act of 2001. Although noble in purpose, these acts have frequently been criticized as interfering with the powers and financial responsibilities of the states in violation of the spirit, if not the letter, of the constitutional division of powers between the national government and the states.

In 1995, Congress attempted to curb the number and scope of unfunded mandates by passing the Unfunded Federal Mandates Reform Act. This act required Congress, when passing laws mandating states to carry out federal law, to determine the costs of mandates and to provide sufficient funding for them, or, in the worst-case scenario, to reconsider the desirability of the mandate once costs are known. In the years since the passage of the act, the issue of federal mandates has remained highly contentious, as revealed by the two selections that follow.

In the first, U.S. Representative George Miller, Democrat from California, makes the case for mandates, both funded and unfunded. In a speech on the floor of the House of Representatives at the time the Unfunded Federal Mandates Reform Act was being debated, he argues that mandates, despite their critics, actually improve the quality of life in America and address problems that states have been unable or unwilling to deal with adequately on their own.

In the second selection, U.S. Senator Lamar Alexander, Republican from Tennessee, protests the continued use of mandates to force states into taking actions they would not otherwise favor. According to Senator Alexander, the Unfunded Federal Mandates Reform Act of 1995 simply has not worked the way the original sponsors thought, and Congress should now take steps to ensure that it does, restoring once again the rightful place of the states in the federal system.

Unfunded Mandates
Laws That Bind Us Together
George Miller

Mr. Chairman, [the Federal Unfunded Mandates Reform Act] strikes at the very heart of the body of laws that bind us together as a progressive society, and with the highest standard of living in the world; the body of law that ensures that no matter where you live in this country, you can enjoy clean water: that no matter where you live in this country, local government and the private sector are working every day to improve the air that you breathe, so we no longer have to send our children indoors because it is too smoggy out. We no longer have to tell our senior citizens they cannot go out for a walk because the air quality is too bad, or we cannot drive to work because they do not want the automobiles on the road.

These are the laws that accomplished those successes. These are laws that said "Yes, if you take money from the Federal Government, we are going to put onto you an obligation to educate the handicapped children of this Nation," because before that was the law, the handicapped children of this Nation could not get an education in the public school systems run by the States and localities that we now say are so ready to do the job.

But for that law, tens of thousands of handicapped children, because they have cerebral palsy, because they have Down's syndrome, would not be allowed in our public schools, but that is a Federal mandate. Yes, we pay part of the freight, but this law would say "Unless the Federal Government presents 100 percent of it, no school district would be required to educate that handicapped child. Unless the Federal Government spends 100 percent of the money to clean up the local water supply, the local sewage treatment, the city would have no obligation."

What happens along the Mississippi River in Indiana or Minnesota if they choose, or in Ohio, if they choose not to clean up the municipal sewage because the Federal Government will not pay 100 percent? That means the people in Mississippi and Louisiana have to inherit that sewage.

An unfunded mandate upstream is untreated sewage downstream. What does that mean to the fishermen, to the commercial enterprises, and to the tourist industry in those States? It means they suffer. That is why we have national laws.

George Miller is a Democratic U.S. representative from California. Excerpted from a speech delivered in the U.S. House of Representatives, *Congressional Record,* Proceedings and Debates of the 104th Congress, First Session, House of Representatives, January 19, 1996, vol. 141, No. 11, H355–H356.

When I was a young man you could smell San Francisco Bay before you could see it, but now we require all of the cities, not just the town that I live in, not just the oil industry, not just the chemical industry, but the cities upstream and downstream [to clean up]. Some of them, we had to take them to court to tell them to clean it up. Today San Francisco Bay is a tourist attraction. Commercial fishing is back. People can use it for recreation.

That is what these mandates have done. Yes, we have not paid 100 percent, but we have put billions and billions and billions of dollars into helping local communities make airports safe so they could become international airports, so people would have confidence in going to those cities. We have cleaned up their water and air. We have made it safe to drink. That is what this legislation is an assault on.

Mr. Chairman, the proponents of this legislation would have us believe this is a simple and straightforward initiative: Congress should mandate the States and local governments to do nothing that Congress is not willing to pay for in its entirety.

In fact, this legislation strikes at the very heart of the entire concept on which our Government is based. Government does not have the responsibility to require that those in our societies—private individuals, businesses, and State and local governments—meet certain responsibilities.

Even the drafters of this legislation recognize that some mandates need not be paid for. They are ideologues of convenience. They do not require we pay for compliance with civil rights and disability laws. But they would compel funding for actions relating to public health and safety, protection of the environment, education of children, medical services to our elderly, safeguards to our workers.

And they would require that we pay only when that burden is imposed on entities of government. Private industry, many of which compete with State and local government in the provision of services, is accorded no relief. And those who work for Government, performing exactly the same services as those in the private sector, are potentially denied such basic protections as minimum wages, worker right to know about hazardous substances, and OSHA protections.

Never mind that the same State and local governments to whose aid we are rushing impose precisely the same unfunded mandates on lower levels of government.

So, I think this clearly demonstrates what is going on here: this is not about unfunded mandates: It is about undermining this Nation's environmental, education, health and labor laws, and wrapping the attack in the flag of unfunded mandates.

The last time we tried this deceptive tactic—cutting away at the basic role of Government in the name of cost savings—we tripled the national debt in 8 years.

But let me take issue with the very name of this concept—unfunded mandates. Unfunded? Really?

We have spent tens of billions of dollars helping States and local communities meet these mandates by improving water systems, upgrading drinking water supplies, building and improving transportation systems, improving education programs, and on and on.

Have we funded every mandate fully? No. Should the Federal Government have to pay States and local communities to protect their employees, their environment and their public health and safety? Because let's remember: A lot of them were not protecting those people and those resources before the Federal mandates came along.

No, we haven't funded every dollar. But have we covered 50, 75, 90 percent of the cost of many of these projects? Time and time again.

And have we provided these same State and local governments with hundreds of billions of dollars to build, expand and improve highways, rapid transit and harbors and to respond to disasters—even when there was no Federal responsibility to provide a dollar? Have we provided money to assure that communities are safe from nuclear power plants and hazardous waste sites? Have we provided money to educate the handicapped, to train the jobless, and to house tens of millions of Americans?

I have little doubt that those who champion this legislation fully expect that its passage would have no effect on our willingness to fund their future actions in these areas. They are very wrong. Every State and community should be aware that the appetite of the Congress for funding local projects and programs that fail to meet a Federal standard of quality and protection and performance is going to be very minimal, particularly in light of the coming effort for a balanced budget amendment that would slash Federal spending radically.

So I think we should proceed with some caution here. If the States and local communities don't want the mandates, don't expect the Federal dollars either.

I find it somewhat ironic that in my own State of California, for example, the Governor [Republican Governor Pete Wilson—*Editors*] has failed to come up with his promise of matching funds for the $5 billion in Federal disaster aid following [the] Northridge earthquake. Now he wants more Federal money for earthquake assistance; and he will want more still for the flooding, and he'll probably throw in a few billion dollars' worth of dams and other infrastructure from Federal taxpayers.

Yet he is one of the biggest proponents of this unfunded mandates legislation—and at the same time that he forces unfunded mandates down the throat of every county and city in California.

We see that kind of hypocrisy in the legislation before us today.

In case you didn't read the fine print, this mandate ban neglects to include the dozens of new unfunded Federal mandates contained in the Republicans' Contract With America. Just the mandates in the welfare bill alone could bring the States to their knees. But all those new mandates are exempted, even though none of them have yet been enacted into law. So much for being honest with the American people.

Let's be very clear what this legislation is going to do to some of the most important laws this Congress has passed and has spent billions of dollars helping States and local communities implement.

Safe drinking water. We have upgraded the water supply across this Nation, virtually eliminating disease, contamination and danger. Much of that has been paid for by Federal dollars. Which local community would like to have taken on that task without Federal assistance? Which Americans want to put the future and the consistency of our safe drinking water at risk through this legislation?

Clean water. You used to be able to smell San Francisco Bay before you could see it. You used to need a battery of shots if you stuck your toe in the Potomac River. The sewage and waste water of 80 million Americans from a score of States flows out of the mouth of the Mississippi River, and for years contaminated the commercial fishing areas. A few years before the Clean Water Act was passed, the Cuyahoga River in Cleveland was burning. Want to go back to those days? You tell me which financially strapped city and State will take on that burden without Federal assistance?

Nuclear safety. Should nuclear power plants and generators of radioactive wastes—which exist in every large city and many small ones—be able to ignore Federal safety standards for operations and waste disposal?

Deadbeat parents. We are collecting hundreds of millions of dollars a year from parents who have ignored their financial responsibilities to their children, thanks to Federal law. Should we just abandon that program? . . .

Of course we should examine whether Federal funding of mandates has been adequate. In fact, that process was begun last year. . . .

But let us not . . . pass a deeply flawed, confusing, and deceptive bill . . . that misrepresents not only the need for mandates, but ignores the billions of dollars we have given to States and communities to help meet those mandates.

The Federal Unfunded Mandates Reform Act
"Lost in the Weeds"

Lamar Alexander

. . . March 15, 2005, is the 10th birthday of the Federal Unfunded Mandates Reform Act, affectionately known in Washington, D.C., as UMRA.

UMRA was supposed to stop or slow down the one thing that made me maddest as governor—some congressman coming up with a big idea, passing a law, holding a press conference, bragging about it and then sending the bill back to Tennessee for me and the legislature to pay. And then the next weekend, that same congressman would usually be back in Tennessee making a speech about local control.

Lamar Alexander is a Republican U. S. senator from Tennessee. Excerpted from a speech given by Senator Alexander before the National League of Cities' Congressional City Conference, March 14, 2005.

UMRA was supposed to discourage that—to discourage the imposition of new laws and new rules on state and local governments without paying for them. . . . [I]t was the right policy and a great accomplishment, and it undoubtedly discouraged some action. But it hasn't done nearly as much as we might have hoped.

Just look around you:

- Cities are raising taxes to pay for new EPA storm water run-off rules;
- School boards are still taking money out of one classroom and putting it in another to meet federal requirements for children with disabilities;
- The National Council of State Legislatures has identified $29 billion in federal cost shifts to states in transportation, health care, education, environment, homeland security, election laws and in other areas.
- And just last year . . . in the name of lowering Internet access taxes, Congress tried to take away from state and local officials local control over how to pay for governmental services.

And that's not all.

- The U.S. House of Representatives recently passed legislation that would turn 190 million state drivers' licenses into national ID cards with the states paying most of the cost;
- [In March 2005] governors of both parties met with the president and they asked him how they could reduce the growth of Medicaid spending when federal laws dictate eligibility standards, when federal bureaucrats limit state flexibility and federal courts just say no. . . .

And then the federal courts have piled on—using outdated federal court consent decrees to run Medicaid in Tennessee, to run foster care in Utah, to run transportation in Los Angeles and to decide how to teach English to children in New York City.

During these last 10 years, in my view, about the only part of the federal government that has recognized the importance of strong state and local governments in our federal system is the United States Supreme Court, which has rediscovered that the 10th Amendment to the United States Constitution reserves the states' powers that are not expressly granted to the central government.

So here is what I see is the picture of federalism in Washington, D.C., today—Democrats, still stuck in the New Deal, are reflexively searching for national solutions to local problems; Republicans, having found ourselves in charge, have decided it is more blessed to impose our views rather than to liberate Americans from Washington; and, across America, federal judges have discovered the joys of acting like governors and mayors without having to run for office.

Meanwhile in the states and cities, federal funds make up as much as half of state and local budgets, bringing with them more and more rules that direct and limit what mayors and governors are able to do with revenues raised from state and local taxes.

So as a result, the job of mayor and governor is becoming more and more like the job of university president, which I also used to be: it looks like you're in charge, but you're really not.

That is why to celebrate this 10th birthday of UMRA I propose three steps to give mayors and governors, legislators and local councils more authority to do what they were elected to do.

First, amend UMRA to increase to 60 the number of Senate votes it takes to enact legislation that imposes unfunded federal mandates. . . . For the last 10 years the number has been 50, and it hasn't been used once as a budget point of order. It's a penalty flag that hasn't been thrown.

Second, make it easier for governors and mayors to change or vacate outdated federal court consent decrees and harder for courts and plaintiffs' lawyers to run the government. I have introduced legislation with Senator Mark Pryor of Arkansas and Senator Ben Nelson of Nebraska. They're both Democrats. One was an attorney general of his state, and one was a governor of his state. This legislation would put term limits on consent decrees, shift to plaintiffs the burden of proving that the decrees need to be continued and require that courts draw decrees narrowly with the objective of moving responsibility back into the hands of elected officials as soon as possible.

In Tennessee, for example, we have a governor of the other party who ran to fix what we call our TennCare system; it's our Medicaid system. He's come up with a plan to do it. He's concerned, as I am in looking at it from a distance, that because of the unbridled growth of healthcare spending that we don't have the money for education spending and we need to make some adjustment of that. But he finds himself restricted by four federal court consent decrees entered into by his predecessors over the past 25 years, so he's not able to do what he was elected to do. The people of our state believe that if we have an important policy decision—not a rights decision, but a policy decision—that elected officials ought to be able to make that decision.

Finally, the third thing we should do is to not allow any new federal statute to preempt a local law unless the new federal law specifically states that there is a direct conflict between state and local law.

Now after all this pessimistic talk about ominous trends, let me conclude with an optimistic word about our federal system.

I am optimistic because I believe that excessive centralization of government runs against the grain of what it means to be an American. To ignore that I believe is political dynamite.

Americans do expect Washington, D.C., to take care of war, welfare, social security, health care and debt.

Americans do not want Washington, D.C., running schools, colleges, law enforcement, city parks and most roads. . . .

I recall in October of 1994, Representative Newt Gingrich stood with 300 Republican candidates for Congress on the Capitol steps offering a "Contract With America" promising no more unfunded federal mandates. "If we break our promise," said my fellow Republicans, "throw us out."

Mindful of that promise, new United States Senate Majority Leader Bob Dole in 1995 designated the Federal Unfunded Mandate Reform Act as S.1—the birthday that we celebrate tomorrow, the day of its passage—he made it the first order of business of the new Republican Senate. Senator Dole then campaigned for president across the country pulling a copy of the constitution from his pocket and reading the 10th Amendment to his audiences. . . .

One of the most important reasons to come to Washington to serve is to remind those already here that a plane ticket to Washington doesn't make you any smarter.

That parents and teachers of 50 million students in 15,000 school districts can usually do more to improve a child's education than some national school board can.

That if Washington makes you spend more for Medicaid then you'll probably have less to spend for preschool education—and at least someone elected, who is closer to the problem, needs to decide that issue.

In some countries, which are smaller and in which people are more ethnically alike than we are, it might be possible to have a national school board, a state church and a central government that calls most of the shots.

But we know that doesn't stand a prayer of working in the United States of America. Alexis de Tocqueville in his early writings about America observed that our country works community by community by community. We are so big, we have so many different views, and we come from so many different backgrounds that we need many places to work things out in many different ways. Put too many one-size-fits-all jackets on Americans and this country will explode.

And in America, such an explosion occurs at election time.

That is why most candidates for president run against Washington, D.C.

That is why senators from Washington, D.C., are almost never elected president, and governors from outside Washington, D.C., often are.

That is one reason why Americans elected a Republican Congress in 1994. . . .

So as a good Republican, I am using this birthday celebration of the Unfunded Federal Mandate Act to remind my Republican colleagues that we promised to the American people in 1994: no more unfunded mandates. "If we break our promise, throw us out." I am certain that if we don't remember our promise, our Democratic friends will.

Most of our policy debates in Congress involve conflicting principles of which most of us agree. The principle of federalism should not always be the trump card. There are other important principles to weigh: liberty, equal opportunity, laissez faire, individualism and the rule of law, for example.

But the federalism that the Republican Congress was elected to protect in 1994 has gotten lost in the weeds. It is time to find it and to put it back up front where it belongs. And the first three steps should be to take the Unfunded Mandate Reform Act and increase to 60 the number of votes it takes to enact an unfunded mandate, to put term limits on federal court consent decrees, and to require Congress to specify, announce and admit whenever it decides to preempt a state or local law.

If Congress were to do those three things, then maybe on UMRA's 20th birthday, 10 years from now, we can celebrate an American federal system that has the kind of respect for mayors, governors, legislators and city council members that the founders of this great republic envisioned.

Gay Marriage: A Matter for the States or the Federal Government?

*O*ne of the newest controversies about the proper roles of the federal and state governments in the federal system is sparked by the issue of gay marriage.

Recently, some states, supported in part by court decisions, have acted to permit marriage by gay and lesbian couples. In response, President George W. Bush and an active group of congressional leaders proposed an amendment to the U.S. Constitution allowing marriage only between a man and woman. Marriage has traditionally been a matter handled primarily by the states, although Congress from time to time has legislated in this area, as in the case of polygamy, outlawed by Congress and upheld by the U.S. Supreme Court in 1878. Passage of a constitutional amendment banning gay marriage would effectively remove from the states the power to determine what constitutes marriage.

The selections that follow stake out the pro– and anti–constitutional amendment positions. Adam White, a member of the Federalist Society, a states' rights advocacy group, argues that a constitutional amendment defining marriage is an appropriate exercise of national authority, if only because such an action seems inevitable given the reality of what is happening in the states and in the courts. Judge J. Harvie Wilkinson III, currently serving on the U.S. Court of Appeals for the Fourth Circuit, warns against a rush to ban gay marriage through constitutional amendments. While recognizing both the sanctity of marriage between a man and a woman and the rights of the gay community, Wilkinson argues that constitútional amendments—at either the federal or the state level—are not the way to proceed. According to Wilkinson, constitutions should not be used to restrict rights, nor should the federal government take on by means of constitutional amendment what the states are perfectly capable of doing through ordinary legislation—namely, passing laws that govern marriage and the family in any way that state legislatures may wish.

"States, Right?"
Not in the Gay Marriage Debate
Adam J. White

"The President, who believes so strongly in states' rights in other contexts, should let the states do their jobs and work out their marriage laws before resorting to a constitutional amendment." With those words, the editors of *The New York Times* (Feb. 25, 2004) summed up one prong of the public criticism of the President's proposed Defense of Marriage Amendment.

President Bush is not exactly a poster-boy for "states' rights," but to the extent that he points to Justices Thomas and Scalia as his ideal jurists, the question is a good one: To what extent is a Federal Marriage Amendment compatible with Federalism?

This Federalist's answer, in short: They fit quite well.

The Left seems to have discovered "states' rights" this year, and many point to hypocrisy of those Federalists who do not support a "states' rights" solution to the gay marriage issue.

But "Federalism" is not synonymous with "states rights." Federalism is an ideological commitment to the appropriate division of power between Federal and state governments. Where the Constitution does not pre-ordain the solution, Federalism calls for a pragmatic apportionment of power, not knee-jerk endorsement of "states' rights."

For the marriage question, a Federal solution is not just pragmatically appropriate. It's also inevitable. And, for those who've forgotten, it's *long* been a federal issue.

The baseline form of marriage—be it "one man–one woman," "two people," or "more than one person"—is most pragmatically regulated at the national level. Most obviously, our national legal and financial systems have already integrated marriage into their basic structures. Insurance, tax, federal criminal law (e.g., spousal privilege), and countless other legal/financial matters depend on marriage. Inconsistency among the states severely hampers commerce, a core Federal concern under Federalist principles.

Moreover, the federal government has a strong interest in family structure. The last century's system of social programs (predominantly erected by liberals)

Adam J. White graduated from Harvard Law School in 2004. He served as editorial-page editor of the *Harvard Law Record.* He later clerked for Judge David B. Sentelle at the U.S. Court of Appeals for the District of Columbia and is now an attorney in Washington, D.C. From *The Record*, the independent newspaper of Harvard Law School. Reprinted with the author's permission.

are greatly affected by marital status. Will the federal government's social programs draw lines between similarly situated "marriages" simply because of the
marriage laws of the several States? Will gay couples in Georgia stand pat while
gay couples in California collect Federal benefits? Should they?

Finally, the Federal government has a strong interest in the protection of
children. . . . In a nation where freedom of movement is not only a constitutional value but also an increasing reality for mobile families, how will children
fare when their family's legal structure changes depending on the state in
which they currently move? Custody battles will become all the more ugly
when same-sex "parents" can try to game the system by fleeing the state, kids
in tow. And hospital visitation rights should not vary wildly on the state in
which a family's vacation takes a tragic turn.

The above pragmatic concerns strongly suggest that a federal resolution of
the marriage question is appropriate. But that justification aside, a national
solution strikes this Federalist as a appropriate if only because a national solution seems *inevitable*.

The Federal courts may enforce a national norm on the states. In *Romer* and
*Lawrence** the court has grown increasingly eager to force pro-homosexuality
positions through the states. Justices may have disclaimed gay marriage in
Lawrence, but that is hard to swallow from a legal institution that has grown
bolder every year in taking sides in these culture wars. The logic of *Lawrence*
and *Romer* destroys the foundation of any laws that might preempt someone
making his own decisions about the sweet mystery of sexual life.

The Court has made it increasingly clear that in matters of sexual liberation,
the life of the law is not logic, but experiment. The Court's own doctrines leave it
with no principled opposition to gay marriage (or polygamy, or any other form
of "marriage"). Should we simply assume that they'll suddenly discover
restraint—and, in waiting, allow Liberal states to spend years building up inertia
by handing out thousands of gay-marriage licenses? Those horses won't return
to the barn; to wait for the Courts is to enact gay marriage by default.

Liberals are also lining up to challenge Full Faith and Credit defenses of
states; why else would gay couples flood San Francisco and return home?
Certainly not to watch their marital benefits vanish. They've picked California
as the epicenter, not outer limits, of the gay marriage battle.

The Left has declared national war on marriage. There is no reason why
Federalists should handcuff themselves in a state-by-state resolution in this case.
Given that gay marriage will be decided at the federal level in a manner that will
likely pre-empt states that wish to dissent from gay marriage, this Federalist
sees no shame in fighting back at the federal level. And at least the Right seeks
to do it through an original Constitutional tool—Article V—instead of through
a Court-centered social policy power-grab wholly foreign to the Framers.

---

*In *Romer v. Evans* (1996), the U.S. Supreme Court invalidated a Colorado constitutional amendment prohibiting state and local governments from outlawing discrimination on the basis of sexual
orientation. In *Lawrence v. Texas* (2003), the Supreme Court invalidated a law making same-sex
sodomy a crime.—*Editors.*

Finally, let us not ignore the obvious: the form of marriage—one man and one woman—has long been a federal issue. The basic structure of marriage has never differed from state to state (in 1789, who could have dreamed of "alternative" marriages?), and the federal government has vigorously enforced its notion of marriage on the states before. The Union refused to accept not only Utah, but also Arizona, New Mexico, and Oklahoma, until each renounced polygamy. The federal norm of marriage—one man, one woman—was enforced there. Likewise, the federal courts enforced their colorblind notion of marriage on the states.

Charges of "states' rights" hypocrisy, at least those directed at Federalists, simply don't hold water. "Federalism" only requires deference to states where the Constitution requires it or, where the Constitution is silent, where pragmatism requires—in short, not here. The Left's new fondness for "states' rights" is an amusing development but an empty rallying cry.

Hands Off Constitutions
This Isn't the Way to Ban Same-Sex Marriage
J. Harvie Wilkinson III

The chief casualty in the struggle over same-sex marriage has been the American constitutional tradition. Liberals and conservatives—judges and legislators—bear responsibility for this sad state of affairs.

Twenty states have constitutional amendments banning gay marriages; many more are in the offing. On the ballot this fall [2006] in Virginia and five other states will be proposed constitutional amendments banning gay marriage. Passage of the amendments is all but foreordained, but the first principles of American law will be further endangered.

Judges began the rush to constitutionalize. The Massachusetts Supreme Court concocted a state constitutional right to marry persons of the same sex. The court went on to say that opposing views lacked so much as a rational basis. In other words, centuries of common-law tradition, legislative sanction

J. Harvie Wilkinson III is a judge on the U.S. Court of Appeals for the Fourth Circuit. Reprinted from *The Washington Post*, September 9, 2006, p. A19. Reprinted with the author's permission.

and human experience with marriage as a bond between one man and one woman were deemed by that court unworthy to the point of irrationality.

It would be altogether understandable for Congress and state legislatures to counter this constitutional excess with constitutional responses of their own. Yet it would be the wrong thing to do.

The Framers meant our Constitution to establish a structure of government and to provide individuals certain inalienable rights against the state. They certainly did not envision our Constitution as a place to restrict rights or enact public policies, as the Federal Marriage Amendment does.

Ordinary legislation—not constitutional amendments—should express the community's view that marriage "shall consist only of the union of a man and a woman." To use the Constitution for prescriptions of policy is to shackle future generations that should have the same right as ours to enact policies of their own. To use the Constitution as a forum for even our most favored views strikes a blow of uncommon harshness upon disfavored groups, in this case gay citizens who would never see this country's founding charter as their own.

Let's look in the mirror. Conservatives who eloquently challenged the Equal Rights Amendment and *Roe v. Wade* for federalizing core areas of state law now support an amendment that invites federal courts to frame a federal definition of marriage and the legal incidents thereof.

Proponents of the amendment say that states need protection from activist judges in other jurisdictions, but states already have this protection through the Defense of Marriage Act and public policy defenses allowed under the full faith and credit clause. As a result, a constitutional amendment is at most a backstop for powers that states possess without any congressional action at all. There is no greater need for such a constitutional backstop here than there is for a constitutional amendment bolstering states' authority to pass a sales tax, establish a transportation department or support public education.

The Federal Marriage Amendment has helped spread the constitutional fever to the states. State constitutional bans on same-sex marriages vary considerably in their wording, particularly with respect to civil unions. But most would repose in judges the authority to interpret such ambiguous terms as "domestic union," "similar to marriage," "rights, obligations, privileges and immunities of marriage," "incidents of marriage" and so forth. Thus the irony: Those who wish to curb activist judges are vesting judges with unprecedented interpretative authority whose constitutional nature makes it all but impervious to legislative change.

To constitutionalize matters of family law is to break with state traditions. The major changes in family law in the 19th and 20th centuries, such as the recognition of married women's property rights and the liberalization of divorce, occurred in most states at the statutory level. Even the infamous bans on interracial marriage were adopted nonconstitutionally by 35 states, and by constitutional amendment in only six.

Where is the threat that justifies so radical a break with our constitutional heritage? State courts in Georgia, New York and Washington have recently rejected invitations to follow Massachusetts and find a right to same-sex marriage in their constitutions. The great majority of state court judges—more than

80 percent by some counts—are subject to election in some form and unlikely to overturn state legislatures on so volatile a matter as same-sex marriage. States have numerous tools that enable them to reject objectionable marriages from other jurisdictions—tools that have long been the basis for refusing to recognize marriages involving polygamy, incest, and underage or mentally incompetent parties.

I do not argue that same-sex marriage is a good or desirable phenomenon, only that constitutional bans on same-sex unions carry terrible costs. Partisans see only one side of a profound controversy when in fact there are two. It is not wrong for gay citizens to wish to share fully in the life of this country, to partake of its most basic and sacred institution, and to experience the intimacy, bonding and devotion to another that only an institution such as marriage can bring. To embrace this view one need not believe that sexual infidelities will disappear but only that many gay couples will make good on their vows and lead fuller, richer and more productive lives as a result.

That, however, is hardly the end of the matter. Marriage between male and female is more than a matter of biological complementarity—the union of the two has been thought through the ages to be more mystical and profound than the separate identities of each alone. Without strong family structures, there will be no stable and healthy social order, and alternative marriage structures might weaken the sanction of law and custom necessary for human families to flourish and children to grow. These are no small risks, and present trends are not often more sound than the cumulative wisdom of the centuries.

Is it too much to ask that judges and legislatures acknowledge the difficulty of this debate by leaving it to normal democratic processes? In fact, the more passionate an issue, the less justification there often is for constitutionalizing it. Constitutions tempt those who are way too sure they are right. Certainty is, to be sure, a constant feature of our politics—some certainties endure; others are fated to be supplanted by the certainties of a succeeding age. Neither we nor the Framers can be sure which is which, but the Framers were sure that we should debate our differences in this day's time and arena. It is sad that the state of James Madison and John Marshall will in all likelihood forsake their example of limited constitutionalism this fall. Their message is as clear today as it was at the founding: Leave constitutions alone.

mhhe.com/diclerico11e

Internet resources
Visit our Web site at
www.mhhe.com/diclerico11e for links
and resources relating to Federalism.

chapter 4

Public Opinion

*P*ublic opinion polling has become a mainstay of our daily news diet. Nearly every
*major television news network—CBS, ABC, NBC, CNN, FOX—and every major
newspaper and newsmagazine—*New York Times, Washington Post, Wall Street
Journal, Chicago Tribune, Los Angeles Times, Time, Newsweek, U.S. News and
World Report—*conduct weekly, if not daily polls. Commercial and university-
affiliated polling organizations such as Gallup, Louis Harris, Roper, Zogby, National
Opinion Research Center, and the Survey Research Center at the University of Michigan are busy tapping the American people's opinions on a range of political and social
issues. In a sense, contemporary American politics can be boiled down to "polling and
governing," with an occasional election thrown in to catch large-scale shifts in opinion.*

*The routinization of modern scientific polling has had the effect of legitimizing
polls in the minds of the American people and making polls an acceptable part of everyday political life. Among serious scholars, political commentators, and politicians, however, the reliance on public opinion polls may be viewed as either a blessing or a curse.*

*The selections in this chapter address a serious controversy over polling: Is polling
good or bad for the polity? Pollster Frank Newport presents a strong argument in favor
of polling as a guide to lawmakers who are charged with making decisions about public policy. Newport's thesis that "polls are good" is based on the long-held view that the
collective judgment of the people is likely to be better than the opinion of any smaller
group of governing elites.*

*The distinguished political scientist Robert Weissberg offers a contrary view.
Weissberg presents a wholly unorthodox view of polls, claiming that "surveys cannot
provide useful advice." His reasoning is based on an assessment of two major factors
related to polling: the ignorance of the public and the ignorance of the pollsters. His critique of the modern poll indicates that even though polls are widely conducted and ana-
lyzed, and conclusions are drawn from them, their value and legitimacy are still
matters of some debate.*

Polling Matters

Frank Newport

. . . The single most important reason why polls are so valuable is that they provide us with a way of collecting and collating a distilled, summarized wisdom based on the input of the members of a society. This wisdom can be used as the basis for altering and improving the direction of the societies in which we live.

This is based on the key proposition that *groups of people often have more wisdom among them than does any one person alone.* The collected opinions, observations, and attitudes of all of the individuals in a population provide a distillation of knowledge and insights that is more likely to be sensible and useful than the insights and knowledge of single individuals or small groups of people independently. There is a great deal that can be done with that wisdom—more than just measuring it, studying it, and talking about it. It can be used to help guide a society forward.

In a mass society, polling is the only practical way to bring this knowledge together. The power of polling lies in its ability to harness wisdom and apply it to the problems of governing societies and making decisions about what those societies should do.

This is a pretty radical thesis. It implies that insight, wisdom, and knowledge levels increase with larger and larger numbers of people. This flies in the face of the feelings of many who hold just the opposite thesis: that wisdom and knowledge *decrease* as groups become larger and larger. There is in fact a long history of distrust of the mob or group, with a concomitant reverence accorded the contributions made by individuals and brilliant, single-minded leaders. Here I'm arguing that the views of the mob, as it were, have the potential to be extremely valuable to all concerned, and that the views of individuals or small elites often leave much to be desired.

One of the ways to approach this issue, I think, is to look around us. There is something very natural about the derivation of great value from many discrete actions collected together. It appears as if nature itself operates such that the combined actions of millions of entities in a social system can ultimately work to produce the most adaptive and useful structural patterns and actions for that system. Similarly, while the attitudes of single individuals in human

social systems may seem insignificant in and of themselves, one attitude cou-
pled with another and another and another ultimately brings together a total-
ity of thought that is much more than the sum of its parts. Every person in a
human social system is distinct in many ways and has a different genetic inheritance. In addition, by adulthood, humans have lived through and experienced
life in distinctly different ways, reflecting the results of their *cultural* exposure.
When the results of all of these differences in background and exposure are
brought together, it constitutes the basis for an extraordinarily powerful body
of knowledge. And that knowledge is gathered and processed by polls.

The core principle here is straightforward. The bringing together of *all* of
the experiences and knowledge of a group of individuals allows for a distillation of truth that is more profound than an alternative that involves only the
experience and knowledge of a few. It is my conviction that in many situations
*no individual or small group knows as much about the real world in which problems
originate (and in which they must be solved) as larger groups and populations.* No one
physician knows as much about a disease or treatment as do all physicians
combined, and no one rocket scientist knows as much about the space shuttle
as do all rocket scientists put together.

No single football coach or sportswriter can decide on the best college football team in the nation as fairly as a group of many coaches or sportswriters.
No single corporate purchasing agent's views on the progress of the economy
are as likely to be accurate as are the views of hundreds of purchasing agents
amalgamated together. No central economic authority can determine the value
of companies as efficiently as the actions of millions of stock buyers and sellers
acting individually on the major stock exchanges. No juror is as likely to produce a fair decision in a court case as are twelve jurors with their collectively
combined views. And, in the most general sense, no individual can make as
effective and efficient a decision on the broad direction a society should take as
the collected views of all that society's citizens.

It is this last point that seems to generate the most resistance from observers.
Many well-meaning citizens feel that powerful or smart people—rather than the
public and its collected insights—are in the best position to provide the information and understanding that a society needs to rely on for direction.

Of course, nothing is absolute. There are certainly situations in which individual guidance is exactly what is needed. No one argues that the opinions of a
broad cross section of society can provide the same insights into the treatment of
cancer as can the judgment of trained specialists. No one argues that the views of all
of the people in a society are as valuable in making a decision on the course of a
hurricane as are the insights of meteorological specialists, or that random samples of average citizens can provide meaningful insights into decisions on the
selection of the proper flu vaccine at the beginning of the influenza season.

But the broad principle here is that the thoughts, opinions, and insights of
larger groups of people *in many cases* have the potential to be more valuable
than the thoughts, opinions, insights, or wisdom of just one person or a small
number of people. Or at the least, they add significant value to the decision
making of whoever is in power. . . .

There is no shortage of examples. One of the most contentious issues facing the United States today is health care. Certainly, Harvard professors and legislative committee staffers who focus on health care can have encyclopedic knowledge of health care statistics and the intricacies of how health payment systems work. But these experts may never have set foot in a charity hospital, have probably never had to sit in an emergency waiting room for hours seeking diagnosis and treatment, and have never gone without medical help as a result of not knowing where to go or how to pay for it. Average Americans, on the other hand, have collectively seen it all: hospitals, bad doctors, bureaucracy, HMOs, Medicaid, and ridiculously expensive drugs. Their combined experiences could provide the basis for a textbook of health care wisdom far exceeding that of the experts.

It is thus no surprise that the health care plan proposed by the Clinton administration in the 1990s, guided by experts meeting behind closed doors, failed miserably. What was missing? At least in part, a strong reliance on the wisdom of the people. Hillary Clinton and her task force gave short shrift to the tremendous expertise lodged in the "collected together" insights of the people, and proposed a system that the people were unwilling to accept. Imagine how much better the proposed health care reform system might have been if every aspect of it incorporated comprehensive polling of the people who were expected to live with it, examining how individuals dealt with health care issues in the real world and what they thought might most effectively be changed to make the system work to the greater benefit of all involved. . . .

As I've noted, the use of collective opinions may not apply in all circumstances and is certainly not appropriate as the basis for decision in every situation. The collected wisdom of all of the people in a society isn't of as much value when those in positions of power are making informed decisions about the best way to send astronauts into space, arguing arcane principles of law, deciding on which submarine systems to fund, or revising complex elements and loopholes in the tax code. But many of the major decisions made by those in power don't deal with highly specialized issues. They're concerned with matters quite close to the daily experience of the average person in a society. These include social policies relating to such matters as race relations, welfare and poverty, deciding on the best way to define certain activities as deviant (sexual behavior, alcohol, smoking, drugs, abortion) and imposing sanctions when they occur, the impact of specific economic policies on daily life, and such issues as taxes, health care, and education. The citizens of a society can and do have a great deal of knowledge about these areas of concern. It is my conviction that the average people of a society are able to provide wisdom that has great value when these types of issues and problems are on the policy-making agenda. . . .

DOCTORS, JURIES, AND BUSINESS

Doctors are increasingly figuring out that they simply can't make the best possible and most informed decisions about the diagnosis and treatment for their patients all by themselves—no matter how smart the doctors may be.

There is simply too much to take into account. Physicians are thus relying more and more on the collective wisdom of their colleagues to help guide their decision making. What's called the evidence-based medicine (EBM) movement assumes that any one physician, no matter how well trained, cannot have all of the knowledge at his or her fingertips that is needed to properly diagnose and prescribe treatment for every condition that presents itself. The EBM approach argues that the individual physician should rely on the collective insights of many different experts (and the existing database of research findings) in deciding how to handle any given patient diagnosis and treatment plan. It may be damaging to the doctor's ego to admit that help is needed, but it's ultimately more beneficial to the patient.

   . . . The American jury system assumes that a group of individuals with various backgrounds and experiences will reach a verdict that has a higher probability of being just and fair than would occur if any one person— including even a learned and highly experienced judge—made the decision. Each juror brings a different perspective to bear on a case. Each has different levels of background knowledge. All of these varied skills and differing perspectives help make sure, so the theory goes, that the jury renders a just decision.

   The stock market is a method of pooling thousands of individual perceptions of the value of a business and arriving at an assessment of what that value is. The pricing of a stock through this mechanism is often called a perfect process that takes into account a vast amount of knowledge and input that extends far beyond what would be possible if only a selected subset of stock analysts were called upon to value the stock. . . .

   In one of the most intriguing developments in recent years, new search engines on the World Wide Web operate by analyzing which sites are most frequently used by the individuals who begin a search on a given topic. The assumption behind the algorithms that drive these sites is that the record of the collective actions of a large group of people looking for information on a topic can be the most valuable guide for future individuals seeking information about that same topic. And preference marketing, which is gaining prominence in business circles, attempts to follow the purchase decisions of individuals in order to build a trial that suggests the products or services they might like in the future—based on the collective actions of others with similar interests. . . .

   One of the other reasons collective opinions of a broad group are valuable is the fact that they produce effective decisions. Experts focusing on social issues and policies often come up with programs or laws doomed for failure when they ignore the views of the people potentially affected by such measures. When experts and bureaucrats spin out programs and impose them on a people who don't understand them and don't want them, they simply don't work in the long run. When decision makers and bureaucrats view the opinion of the people upon whom programs must be imposed as irrelevant, the programs have a lower probability of success. . . .

POLLING MATTERS

Even with skilled pollsters and survey scientists, how reasonable is it that public opinion can be increasingly taken into account in governing a country? Even if one accepts the idea that the people of the society should have their opinions used by government and elected representatives on a regular basis, it is of course impossible to enlist the public's help in making each of the thousands of decisions that come up in any given year. Moreover, some of these decisions involve technical issues that are beyond the understanding of the majority of the population. A government large enough to run a major state or a country has a huge range of activity. As a result, it assembles legions of bureaucrats, experts, commissions, and task forces to help in making daily decisions and moving forward. There is no doubt that the citizens—no matter how powerfully one believes in democracy—cannot be involved in all of what goes on. The issue becomes one of how frequently and in how much detail the people of the society can and should be asked for guidance. George Gallup addressed this concern more than sixty years ago:

> There is something tempting about the view that an aristocracy of specialists should lead the people . . . We must agree that most people do not and in the nature of things, cannot have the necessary knowledge to judge the intimate details of policy . . . There are things that cannot be done by public opinion, just as there are things that can only be done by public opinion . . . The ultimate values of politics and economics, the judgments on which public policy is based, do not come from special knowledge or from intelligence alone. They are compounded from the day-to-day experience of the men and women who together make up the society we live in. That is why public opinion polls are important today. Instead of being attempts to sabotage representative government, kidnap the members of Congress, and substitute the taxi driver for the experts in politics, as some critics insist, public opinion research is a necessary and valuable aid to truly representative government. What is evident here is that representatives will be better able to represent if they have an accurate measure of the wishes, aspirations, and needs of different groups within the general public.[1]

Dr. Gallup's point is straightforward: the people of an entity of almost any size can be and should be trusted to provide input into its day-to-day running. The people of a societal entity *can* make decisions on the *overall direction* of the world in which they live. I'm not talking about specific decisions on daily minutiae or choices among involved and technical policy alternatives, but on the broad direction and general policies that their representatives adopt and that ultimately affect them. The people of a society can be trusted to operate as a board of directors, giving insight and input into the broader direction of what the people they elected should do.

If the fundamental idea behind a democracy is recognizing the wisdom in the aggregated experiences of its citizens, then *polling is actually a more efficient way to collect this wisdom than the vote.*

This is a particularly important insight. Our object as citizens is to move the society forward in the best possible fashion. For that purpose we cannot afford to miss out on the opinions of the lazy and those who choose not to participate in voting. Society needs the input of all its citizens. Indeed, some countries take this idea to the extreme and have made voting mandatory. The United States is not yet at that point, and the proportion of the population that votes is now down to 50 percent in some presidential elections, with the proportion lower still in other elections. A "wisdom at any cost" position argues that polls conducted more frequently among all of the people provide valuable input that is missing if the views of voters are all that is taken into account. . . .

All in all, a society can't have it both ways. Either the people are the best source of decisions on how to run the society or they are not. The basic principle of democracy is that the people are ultimately a better source for making decisions on what the collectivity should do than is any other alternative. There are good reasons for the hybrid model we have today, wherein people vote for representatives or experts they put in place to facilitate the society's day-to-day functioning. But leaving the people's opinions out of the picture until the next vote is a way of saying that the people have only limited brainpower and can be trusted only so far. That's wrong. Representatives need to spend more time between elections maximizing the valuable insights derivable from the public they represent. To ignore the wisdom of the people is folly to the extreme.

If the people can be trusted to vote for representatives, they should certainly have their wisdom taken into account after elections as well. Our best path to progress is to commit to the idea that polls can and should be a positive, fundamentally important element of a well-functioning democratic society. The people's voice is wise, and almost always on target, forming what Dr. George Gallup proclaimed as the true pulse of democracy.

NOTE

1. George Gallup and Saul Forbes Rae, *The Pulse of Democracy* (New York: Simon & Schuster, 1940), 266.

Leaders Should Not Follow Opinion Polls

Robert Weissberg

In the space of 50 years, the public opinion poll has evolved from an occasional curiosity to a carefully heeded political force. "Bad poll numbers" can be disastrous. Nobody wants to champion unpopular schemes or seek public office when drawing single-digit name recognition in the latest survey. Even skeptical officials routinely monitor approval ratings lest tumbling figures embolden rivals. Poll-supplied numbers often shape momentous decisions. The Reagan White House spent $1,000,000 a year on polling. Pres. Bill Clinton's legislative agenda on spending the budget surplus, funding Social Security, and other key issues was shaped almost entirely by poll findings. When he discovered that his plan to make parents legally responsible for their children's crimes drew dismal numbers, it was quickly abandoned.

Is such homage to the polls wise? Pollsters certainly think so. They celebrate their accomplishments as promoting democracy, especially defending the "ordinary citizen" against the powerful. Telephone surveys, they maintain, allow once-unheard voices to force government responsiveness. Ordinary citizens seemingly echo pollsters' claims. One 1999 survey found that 80% believed the nation would benefit if leaders heeded poll results. Ninety percent expressed greater confidence in their own reasoning over what leaders believed. Two-thirds agreed with the pollsters that polls served the public interest.

We profoundly disagree—surveys cannot provide useful advice. It is not that numbers lie, analysts are dishonest, or people are secretive over the telephone, although these misrepresentations do occur. The surveys' shortcomings are more serious and, critically, these deficiencies are not curable under present-day conditions, if at all. What garden-variety advice solicitations uncover is generally politically irrelevant, even if respondents are absolutely honest and the highest technical standards are satisfied. The wrong opinions are being collected, and leaders following this guidance only invite trouble. Intuition or personal experiences provide a better course of action.

Let's begin by comparing polling with elections. An obvious point is that elections impose strict participatory standards. Laws about voting stipulate necessary age, citizenship, and residency qualifications plus standards of mental

Robert Weissberg is emeritus professor of political science at the University of Illinois at Urbana. Reprinted with permission from *USA Today* magazine May 2002. Copyright © 2002 by the Society for the Advancement of Education, Inc. All rights reserved.

competence and criminal background for potential voters. Detailed registration requirements guard against fraud. These restrictive provisions are taken seriously, and violators are punished. Imagine an "Everybody welcome, no questions asked" sign on Election Day! Abolishing standards would insult democracy. Who would accept an outcome if illegal immigrants or foreign tourists cast millions of ballots?

The modern poll, by contrast, resembles a "you cannot be turned down" credit card offer. Who knows if the agreeable voice at the other end is really a citizen, over 18, or mentally competent? The interviewer can hardly verify fraudulent claims by checking proof of age, citizenship documents, or any other requirement prior to soliciting opinions. The opposite is possible as well. No doubt, millions of absolutely qualified voters are "disqualified" by interviewers if their English is limited or if they are uneasy about revealing guarded views to strangers.

The vote, unlike the survey response, is private, and this protection is legally guaranteed. The scientific pollster is absolutely correct that small samples can represent entire populations. This is beside the point, though. Random samples of people owning phones are not legally stipulated governing majorities. Governance is only by those legally permitted to participate, however we may draw the lines. It is bizarre to insist that any 1,000 people selected by a random number generator should authoritatively advise government.

The electoral process is also eminently accountable and transparent. Everything about it, from ballot layout to polling place location, must pass official approval. These critical details may be flawed—recall the famous Palm Beach, Fla., butterfly ballot confusion in the 2000 presidential election—but, for better or worse, these features are publicly controllable. If people, acting through elected officials, prefer old-style paper ballots, this can be done. Where disputes arise—again recall the Florida Circus—they are open to public inspection, even lawsuits. In fact, the disgruntled have endlessly petitioned legislatures and judges to act, and it is inconceivable that any U.S. election official would secretly try to gain advantage without risking public reprimand.

The contrast with polling is, again, enormous. Polling (with scant exception) is a private, commercial enterprise. Everything is negotiated between the paying client and the private firm, and is ultimately owned by the client. Zero public scrutiny attends this process, and, should the public peek behind the curtain, it still remains powerless. Pollster integrity is irrelevant: public control is the issue, not professional honesty or expertise. Analysts can make unwelcome results vanish or be quietly manipulated statistically, and everything would pass professional muster. Enraged citizens cannot demand to see the questionnaire or listen in on interviews.

What might happen to pollsters or clients "cooking" the results before passing them off as "the true popular democratic voice"? Absolutely nothing. Envision a Secretary of State who refused public oversight of absentee ballot validation or utilized a mysterious formula to "adjust" the final vote count. The uproar would be deafening, and the courts would instantly (and properly) intervene once a challenge came before them. Pollsters escape even the most minimal public regulation despite their lofty self-anointed public responsibility. Barbers and hairdressers are held to higher standards.

PUBLIC IGNORANCE

A different poll deficiency concerns the quality of this advice. Whether ordinary citizens are sufficiently wise to rule is a complicated subject, but even the most ardent popular sagacity defenders concur that the average person cannot respond intelligently when unexpectedly quizzed on dozens of issues long baffling experts. Learning about Social Security, educational testing, balancing the budgets, and untold other pollster repertory items is no small task, and to expect those suddenly picking up the telephone to be well-prepared is utter fantasy. Thoughtful survey firms should at least provide advance warning so information could be gathered, mail off some balanced background material, or offer on-the-spot tutorials. Alas, this vital service is almost never provided, and if some additional facts are supplied, they are merely gross simplifications of hugely complex issues.

Compounding this lack of preparation is that the questions themselves seldom permit informed respondents to render intelligent advice. By commercial necessity, modern polling must produce instant results by reducing complicated, multifaceted issues to a few crude alternatives. Queries about the military budget typically focus on "increasing/decreasing/or no change" spending choices. No room exists for more-sophisticated respondents who might want to cut some expenditures while expanding others. Nor does this typical question permit well-versed advice that reflects actual conditions—for example, increasing spending provided certain bellicose dictators remain in power, but otherwise seek reductions. Worse, this commonplace format never asks for specific dollar figures. Two people can agree on cutting Pentagon budgets, but one desires a modest $100,000,000 largely symbolic cut while the other prefers lopping off $200,000,000,000. This numerical difference is critical politically, but disappears when the public's "voice" is crudely transmitted via the poll.

What makes the pollsters' celebration of poll-solicited advice especially odd is that they certainly know the public's limitations. Surveys relentlessly confirm public ignorance beyond the most obvious. This is particularly true when wrestling with specific policies, even though these have long been newsworthy. Poll after poll reveals majorities poorly informed about tax rates, entitlement programs, and legislative proposals, although, to be sure, opinions on these topics are readily offered. This pessimistic assessment has less to do with innate cognitive capacity than the irrelevancy of most political debates from daily life. People pay attention to what matters and, for most of them, the topics raised by interviewers can safely be ignored.

POLLSTER IGNORANCE

The poll's inadequacy of providing sound advice is made even worse by poll-ster ignorance. Poll question writers are expert in drafting questionnaires, not the policy at hand. To expect otherwise is unrealistic given commercial survey cost constraints. Not even Gallup could hire learned experts to consult on each of hundreds of questions. The upshot is that the array of permissible answers inevitably reflects the imperfect worldview of a policy amateur, and often an inadequate view at that. If the respondent rejects this imposed framework or these options have little to do with actual government choices, the results—no matter how honest and sincere—are politically meaningless. Irrelevant questions beget beside-the-point answers.

A particularly glaring, though hardly extreme, inappropriateness example comes framed in terms of increasing foreign aid to cut world hunger in half by 2014. The public's response was heartfelt support (83% favored it), and pro-grams to assist children and women were particularly popular. Even though respondents usually expressed reservations about foreign aid, most still wanted sharp increases in national generosity (boosting outlays by a factor of 10, no less!). On its face, then, the poll's message is clear: Washington should be more big-hearted in eliminating overseas famine. What could possibly be ambiguous about this message?

Plenty could be. For one, astute observers of world hunger might argue that the problem is not one of donating food for the famished. A more-daunting quandary may be convincing host governments to permit this humanitarian intervention or supplying the infrastructure necessary to promote self-sufficiency. There are also momentous political problems having little to do with airlifting wheat to famine-stricken regions—for instance, ending wars in which starvation is a military tactic. More telling, such generosity may make matters worse by destroying local agriculture and breeding permanent dependency. How can local farmers compete against free food? Genuine assistance might mean withhold-ing foodstuff while demanding the necessary political and economic reforms to prevent future catastrophes. In other words, the question writer's off-the-top-of-the-head opinions to the contrary, starvation is not really a foreign aid issue, and those who grasp this fact are totally "lost" in this survey.

Our last qualm regarding poll-solicited public counsel concerns the funda-mental disjunction between economic reality and the poll-supplied reality. Simply put, by rejecting economics, polls facilitate fantasy. Consider supermarket shop-ping. Certain absolutely inescapable facts attend this journey. First, acquiring food is not free, so better bring money, but not one's entire fortune, since there are also rent, car payments, etc. Second, though one might covet everything in the aisles, budgetary constraints may mandate picking and choosing—buying expensive T-bone steaks forgoes other essential edibles. Third, each additional item's mar-ginal value must be calculated. Hamburger may be on sale for an incredible 69 cents a pound, but blowing every last nickel on 300 pounds of chopped beef is stupid. Finally, risk and liabilities must be appraised—skip rancid hamburger regardless of its cheap price.

Polls are oblivious to these clear economic limits. When shopping for government policies via the survey, consumers are wonderfully free. When offered government-provided health care, more schools, assistance to senior citizens, and/or cleaner environments, the entire menu is easily purchased. Unlike the prudent shopper, the survey respondent need not fret about costs (and no bill is sent). Nobody is forced to choose among competing benefits, nor are respondents told that buying more and more may mean progressively less value received. When embracing such skyrocketing government spending, nobody remembers that 300 pounds of hamburger can be a liability. To make this gluttony even more pleasurable, dangers are banished from the poll-created universe. Respondents are not told, for example, that Washington's bounteousness toward local education may load more red tape onto already overburdened schools or distort educational objectives. Nor is anybody informed that higher taxes mean less personal choice for acquiring identical benefits. Drug manufacturers should enjoy such freedom from listing potentially dangerous side effects in advertising their panaceas.

This obliviousness to inescapable economics is not a nefarious pollster plot to entice Americans to "buy" dubious government-supplied nostrums. Some analysts may welcome this benevolence given their liberal bents, but ideological bias is hardly the chief culprit. More relevant is that the modern poll, for all of its scientific paraphernalia and claims of exactitude, cannot insert credible economic checks into the standard telephone interview. Like any instrument, the poll can perform only so much. The interviewer is not the IRS, which can compel payment for desired government services. The brief telephone interview is also incapable of permitting respondents to make realistic trade-offs, calculating benefits vs. costs, and including all the other ingredients necessary for sensible decision making. While, in principle, a policy's downside can be explained, this is often impractical given typical respondent attention spans. There is also the quandary of deciding what, exactly, constitute a proposal's genuine risks, no small matter given future uncertainties. All in all, then, to expect sound advice when polling citizens about what government should do is unreasonable.

Our argument has focused on a single aspect of polling—its use to solicit policy advice from ordinary citizens. Even though we believe that this invariably invites foolishness, we are not attacking polls per se. The debate concerns appropriateness. To maintain that the people, as haphazardly defined by a telephone-dialing machine and as interviewed by those beyond public unaccountability, should guide elected officials is nonsense. Moreover, no government, no matter how attentive to public opinion, can possibly satisfy people unencumbered by the most-elementary economic constraints. These poll-formulated solicitations invite bankruptcy. It would be the equivalent of turning the space program over to engineers who disbelieve the laws of physics.

The opinion poll's proper role is assessing public opinion. Opinions differ fundamentally from advice in their standards. Everyone has a valid opinion: not everyone can offer sound advice. If our doctor says that the Beatles were the best rock-and-roll group ever, who can argue, or even insist upon documentation?

It is quite different, however, if one's physician counsels sacrificing chickens to cure pneumonia. The standards for advice are infinitely higher, and, by these tough standards, most Americans are ill-prepared to render expert snap judgments about matters of national significance beyond their expertise. Let us not confuse flattering popular wisdom with gaining something of value.

mhhe.com/diclerico11e

Internet resources
Visit our Web site at www.mhhe.com/diclerico11e for links and resources relating to Public Opinion.

chapter 5

Voting

*D*espite the fact that our population is better educated and faces fewer procedural impediments to voting than ever before, a significant portion of the American electorate does not participate in elections. Indeed, from 1960 through 1996 voting turnout in presidential elections declined some fourteen percentage points, and the turnout figure of just over 49 percent in 1996 was the lowest in seventy-two years. The turnout rate edged up to 51.27 percent in 2000 and, of course, took a considerable jump in 2004— between 5 and 10 percent, depending on how it is calculated. To many observers, however, the turnout rate is still shockingly low. Low voter turnout, it is argued, is just one more sign of a general deterioration in the quality of political life in the United States as citizens increasingly opt out of the political system.

Should we be alarmed by the decline in voting? In the next selections, three distinguished political commentators address this question. First, Martin Wattenberg, professor of political science at the University of California at Irvine, takes a look at the jump in turnout in 2004 and concludes that there really isn't that much to crow about. Turnout, he argues, though improved, is still below what it was at its peak in 1960, and the rate in 2004 is not likely to be any more than a blip in the history of turnout in America. According to Wattenberg, voting turnout is still primarily a function of political interest, and although interest was high in 2004, it might not be so high in 2008 and beyond. Though not optimistic about permanently improving voting turnout, Wattenberg does have one suggestion for improving turnout: Make the election day a national holiday as most other countries do.

In the second selection, Arend Lijphart, a former president of the American Political Science Association, argues that low voter turnout is indeed a serious problem about which citizens ought to be concerned, for the level of voter participation has important implications for the legitimacy of government, as well as its policies. Indeed, so concerned is Lijphart about low voter turnout in the United States that he proposes what some might regard as a radical solution: compulsory voting.

Finally, the political scientist Austin Ranney argues that we need not fear the fact that many persons choose not to vote. Ranney bases his argument on two main propositions. First, because voters and nonvoters do not differ significantly in policy and candidate preferences, no great harm is done to our system of representation if a sizable percentage of people do not vote. Second, nonvoting does not offend any basic democratic principle, for the right not to vote is every bit as precious as the right to vote.

Turnout in the 2004 Presidential Election

Martin P. Wattenberg

One of the major stories of the 2004 presidential election was the increase in voter turnout from 2000. There is no doubt that there was heightened interest in the 2004 campaign and that rates of voter participation increased most everywhere in the United States. All Americans should be pleased with this aspect of the contest between Bush and Kerry. Yet, this good news needs to be tempered once one puts political interest and turnout in 2004 into historical perspective. Journalists who wrote of "unprecedented interest" in the 2004 race for the White House were clearly exaggerating. And anyone who wrote of "record turnout" among voters could only justify such a claim by focusing on the sheer number of voters who cast ballots—not on the percentage of eligible persons. . . .

TURNOUT OF THE VOTING AGE POPULATION IN 2004

The widely reported figure of 122 million voters who participated in the 2004 presidential election was a record-shattering number in terms of raw number of votes, far exceeding the previous mark of 105 million in 2000. Of course, if what is most important in voter turnout is the number of people who vote, then India would win hands down as the world's greatest democracy. One has to take into account the size of the adult population in order to evaluate turnout in any election. Although the American media seemed fascinated with the statistic of 122 million voters, the denominator for calculating turnout was rarely mentioned. The traditionally used measure in the United States, where registration is far from automatic and tens of millions of eligible people do not bother to register, is the Census Bureau's estimate of the voting age population. As of July 2003, the Census estimate of the American population over 18 years of age was 217.8 million. Assuming that the population continued to increase at the recent rate yields an estimate of 221.3 million for voting age population in November 2004. Thus, the turnout rate among Americans who were at least 18 years of age was about 55 percent. Although this represents a 4 percent

Mark P. Wattenberg is professor of political science at the University of California at Irvine. He is the author of *Where Have All the Voters Gone?* and *The Decline of American Political Parties, 1952–1996.* From "Elections: Turnout in the 2004 Presidential Elections," in *Presidential Studies Quarterly,* 35, no. 1 (March). © 2005 Center for the Study of the Presidency. Reprinted by permission of Blackwell Publishing.

increase over turnout of voting age population in 2000, it is exactly equal to the 55 percent turnout the nation experienced in 1992 and well short of the modern high of 63 percent in 1960. . . .

TURNOUT OF THE CITIZEN VOTING AGE POPULATION IN 2004

It should be noted that all of the turnout percentages presented above are based on a denominator that includes everyone over the age of 18 residing in the United States, including non-citizens, felons, and other individuals who are not actually eligible to vote due to a variety of state laws. McDonald and Popkin argue that turnout decline is a "myth" because the voting age population has increasingly contained more people ineligible to vote due to rising immigration and crime rates.[1] Although they have a reasonable point, adjusting the voting age population for non-citizens does not greatly change the pattern since 1960, as displayed in Table 1. When non-citizens are removed from the calculations, one finds that only about 61 percent of people in the non-South voted in 2004 as compared to 71 percent in 1960; in the South a significant increase can again be seen from 41 to 57 percent. It would be hard to see how a change of this magnitude outside the South can be seen as a myth. And taking into account changes in the percentage of the population that is disenfranchised due to felony convictions (currently about 1.6 percent) is scarcely likely to change the pattern noticeably either.

Substantively, it is my view that the fact that non-citizens and convicted felons are not voting is of importance, and that such information should not be ignored by removing them from the national calculations. Many of these people pay taxes and potentially stand to benefit from government programs as well. Whether it is right or wrong to exclude them from voting is not self-evident, as demonstrated by the varying franchise rules that have been applied throughout U.S. political history[2] and which currently are in place around the world.[3] In his last message to Congress, President Clinton recommended restoring voting rights to felons after they have served their sentences, a proposal which was subsequently endorsed by the National Commission on Federal Election Reform.[4] On the citizenship question, many leaders in the Latino community believe that those who are on the road to becoming citizens

TABLE 1 Voter Turnout Rates in 2004 and 1960 by Region

	2004	1960
Voting age population		
Non-South	56	70
South	52	40
Citizen voting age population		
Non-South	61	71
South	57	41

should be allowed to vote.[5] And in any event, non-citizens are counted in the Census, which means that apportionment of political districts includes them. (In fact, there are districts in the Los Angeles area where the majority of adults are resident aliens. These people are probably receiving de facto representation, even though they can't vote for the people who represent their interests.) In sum, we need to take into account that such people are not voting today, just as the fact that people who were effectively disenfranchised by Jim Crow laws was taken into account in 1960.

STATE PATTERNS OF VOTER TURNOUT

. . . Turnout rates of citizens varied quite widely from state to state in 2004, with a difference of nearly 30 percent between the states with the highest and lowest percentages. Yet, a common pattern is evident among high-, medium-, and low-turnout states alike—namely that the percentage of citizens participating in choosing the president increased from 2000 to 2004. The only clear source of variation is that turnout tended to go up the most in the battleground states, where the candidates focused the vast majority of their time and resources in the final week of the 2004 campaign. In the eleven battleground states (shown in italics in Table 2) the mean increase in turnout was 6.6 percent. In contrast, the typical increase in voter participation in the other states was just 4.2 percent. Thus, greater interest in the presidential campaign nationwide can be estimated to have pushed turnout up about 4 percent. And in the relatively few places where there was extraordinary activity to get out the vote, the rate of increased participation was even greater.

The importance of intense political competition in getting people out to vote can also be seen in the instance of one hard-fought Senate campaign. The race between Democratic Senate leader Tom Daschle and Republican challenger John Thune in South Dakota probably attracted more attention than any other statewide race in 2004. Interestingly, turnout in South Dakota went up 10 percent over the state's 2000 rate, more than any other state. Given that there was never any doubt that Bush would win South Dakota's electoral votes, it is readily apparent that the major force in driving turnout up must have been the heated Senate contest. In fact, South Dakota was the only state in 2004 that recorded more votes for a statewide race (391,092 votes for the Senate contest) than for the presidency (388,156 votes).[6]

Another factor that almost certainly accounts for some of the increase in turnout in 2004 involves technological improvements in voting machines in many states. Because not every state reports the number of people who actually cast ballots, analysts are forced to rely on the total number of votes cast for president as the numerator in calculating turnout. But as the nation learned during the 2000 Florida recount controversy, not everyone who votes has a presidential choice recorded, either because they fail to mark a choice or because of technical problems with their votes. A national study by Caltech and MIT estimated that this percentage was approximately 2.3 percent of all voters in 2000.[7] As a

TABLE 2 Turnout of Citizens of Voting Age by State in 2004, and Changes from 2000 and 1960

State	Turnout of Citizens in 2004	Change from 2000	Change from 1960
Minnesota	77	+5	−1
Wisconsin	74	+6	0
Maine	72	+4	−1
Oregon	71	+6	−2
New Hampshire	70	+6	−10
Iowa	69	+5	−8
Alaska	69	0	+24
South Dakota	68	+10	−10
Colorado	67	+7	−3
Michigan	66	+7	−8
Ohio	66	+10	−5
North Dakota	65	+4	−14
Vermont	65	0	−9
Washington	65	+4	−8
Massachusetts	65	+4	−13
Missouri	64	+6	−8
Florida	64	+7	+14
Montana	64	+2	−7
Wyoming	63	+2	−10
Delaware	63	+5	−10
Connecticut	63	+2	−15
Pennsylvania	62	+7	−9
Nebraska	62	+4	−9
Maryland	62	+7	+4
New Jersey	62	+6	−11
Kansas	61	+5	−9
Idaho	60	+4	−20
Virginia	60	+5	+27
Illinois	60	+4	−17
Louisiana	59	+4	+14
Kentucky	57	+4	0
California	57	+5	−10
New Mexico	57	+7	−5
North Carolina	57	+5	+4
New York	57	0	−12
Rhode Island	56	−1	−21
Oklahoma	56	+6	−7
Tennessee	56	+7	+6
Alabama	56	+5	+25
D.C.	56	+2	—
Utah	55	+4	−20
Arizona	55	+7	+1
Nevada	54	+6	−5
Indiana	54	+4	−23
Mississippi	54	+5	+29
West Virginia	53	+7	−25
Georgia	53	+7	+24
Texas	52	+5	+10
Arkansas	52	+3	+11
South Carolina	52	+5	+22
Hawaii	48	+4	−4

Note: States in *italics* were battleground states in the final week of the 2004 campaign.

result of the Florida fiasco, a number of states undertook major efforts to reduce the percentage of lost votes. These efforts appear to have succeeded splendidly.

Florida itself decertified punch-card machines, which were widely blamed for the high rate of invalid votes in Palm Beach, Miami-Dade, and Broward Counties in 2000. As a result of improved voting machinery between 2000 and 2004, the proportion of invalid votes for president fell from 6.4 to 0.5 percent in Palm Beach, from 4.4 to 0.5 percent in Miami-Dade, and from 2.5 to 0.4 percent in Broward. These numbers clearly played a part in boosting the proportion of Florida's citizens casting a vote for president from 57 percent in 2000 to 64 percent in 2004.

Similarly, Georgia took action to adopt touch-screen voting throughout the state after its secretary of state reported that 3.5 percent of Georgians who showed up at the polls in 2000 had no valid choice for president. Invalid votes were particularly a problem in large counties using punch-card equipment such as Fulton and DeKalb, which had rates of invalid votes of 6.3 and 3.7 percent, respectively; in 2004, both counties reported undervotes were reduced to a mere 0.3 percent. As was the case in Florida, Georgia also experienced a turnout increase, of 7 percent from 2000 to 2004. But unlike Florida, Georgia was never considered to be anything but a Bush state and an easy Senate pickup for the GOP, thereby making it a particularly clear case of turnout being driven up by more efficient voting machinery.

It might be thought that the introduction of punch-card machines in the 1960s played a role in the fall of turnout rates that became apparent soon afterward. However, *The American Voter* estimated in 1960 that 2 percent of votes cast were invalid[8]—a percentage virtually identical to the MIT/Caltech study conducted just after the 2000 election. Thus, if anything, technological changes in vote recording have probably had a favorable impact on turnout rates between 1960 and 2004.

Nevertheless, as can be seen in the right-hand column of Table 2, many non-southern states still have a long way to go to get their rate of citizen turnout up to what it was in 1960. Declines of 15 percentage points or more are found in seven states, and another nine states have experienced declines of at least 10 percentage points. These state-level data demonstrate just how serious the waning of turnout is in some parts of the United States, even with the increase in participation rates from 2000 to 2004. Notably, a fairly steep decline in turnout is quite evident in some of the states that permit Election Day registration, such as Idaho and Wyoming, as well as North Dakota, which does not require registration at all. And those who believe that the decline of turnout is overblown due to the increase of non-citizens in recent years should particularly note that these numbers reflect citizens only.

CONCLUSION: THE START OF A RECOVERY OR JUST A BLIP?

Although the increase in turnout rates from 2000 to 2004 is surely good news, the prospects for this being the start of an extended upward trend are less sanguine. The prospects for interest in the 2008 campaign even equaling that of

2004 are not so good. One only has to briefly reflect on the extraordinary events from the disputed outcome of the 2000 race, to the tragedy of September 11th, to the invasions of Afghanistan and Iraq to realize that the period leading up to Election Day 2004 was no ordinary time. As the old Chinese curse goes: "May you live in interesting times." Were this level of interest in presidential campaigns to be continued through 2008 it would probably not be a good sign for the United States.

Like the substantial increase in turnout which occurred between 1988 and 1992, this most recent increase may well prove to be just a short-lived blip. It is noteworthy that turnout fell off sharply after 1992 even though the newly elected president worked with the Congress to take historic action to make voter registration easier. The National Voter Registration Act of 1993 (widely known as the "Motor Voter Act") succeeded in increasing the percentage of the public that was registered to vote, but this positive development was more than offset by declining interest in the subsequent two presidential elections. Unlike the situation in 1992, in the aftermath of the 2004 campaign the president and the Congress show no apparent interest in further legislation to boost America's still anemic rate of voter turnout.

The lack of momentum in Congress for legislation that might increase turnout is not due to a lack of good ideas on this subject. After the 2000 election, the National Commission on Federal Electoral Reform led by former Presidents Ford and Carter recommended that Congress make Election Day a national holiday—a proposal that was also endorsed by President Clinton. Based on data collected shortly after the 2004 election, there is good reason to suspect that turnout would have been even higher had Election Day been a holiday. A post-election survey by Harvard's Vanishing Voter project found that 24 percent of non-voters said that they didn't vote because they were so busy they didn't have time to go to the polls. Of course, some of these people just used time pressures as an easy excuse, but it does seem reasonable in today's busy world that many of them would have voted had they had the day off from work or school. According to the Pew Center's post-election poll, 42 percent of voters who went to the polls on Election Day 2004 had to wait in line. Of these voters who faced lines, over 40 percent reported waiting at least half an hour. It does not take much of a leap of faith to infer that some people may have been discouraged by the prospect of waiting in long lines on a workday.

To those who question whether an Election Day holiday would really make a positive difference, I would simply ask them to consider whether they would recommend that Iraq or Afghanistan hold their elections on Tuesday like we do. It is doubtful that any American elections expert would recommend that these countries emulate our example in this respect. So if Americans wouldn't recommend Tuesday elections to other countries, why should the United States continue this practice? By joining the modern world and voting on a leisure day, it is likely that American turnout would increase.

NOTES

1. Michael P. McDonald and Samuel L. Popkin, "The Myth of the Vanishing Voter," *American Political Science Review* 95(2001): 963–74.
2. See Alexander Keyssar, *The Right to Vote: The Contested History of Democracy in the United States* (New York: Basic Books, 2000).
3. See André Blais, Louis Massicotte, and Antoine Yoshinaka, "Deciding Who Has the Right to Vote: A Comparative Analysis of Election Laws," *Electoral Studies* 20(2001): 41–62.
4. See President William Jefferson Clinton, "The Unfinished Work of Building One America," Message to Congress, January 15, 2001; and the National Commission on Federal Election Reform, "To Assure Pride and Confidence in the Electoral Process," August 2001.
5. See Louis DeSipio, *Counting on the Latino Vote: Latinos as a New Electorate* (Charlottesville, VA: University of Virginia Press, 1996), 131.
6. South Dakota is the exception that proves the rule, however. When a variety of indicators of competitiveness of Senate and gubernatorial elections were tested in a multivariate model predicting turnout change, they consistently failed to show any significant impact.
7. The Caltech/MIT Voting Project, "Residual Votes Attributable to Technology: An Assessment of the Reliability of Existing Voting Equipment," Version 2, March 30, 2001, p. 7.
8. Angus Campbell, Philip E. Converse, Warren E. Miller, and Donald E. Stokes, *The American Voter* (Chicago: University of Chicago Press, 1960), 95.

Compulsory Voting Is the Best Way to Keep Democracy Strong

Arend Lijphart

Voting is the commonest and most basic way of participating in a democracy, but far too many citizens do not exercise their right to vote, especially in the United States. In the 1988 and 1992 Presidential elections, the turnout of registered voters was only 50 and 55 percent, respectively, and in the midterm Congressional elections in 1990 and 1994, it was only 33 and 36 percent. Four years later, the turnout in the Presidential election was 49 percent, while for the 1998 off-year Congressional election it was 36 percent.*

This is a serious problem for two reasons. One is democratic legitimacy: Can a government that has gained power in a low-turnout election really claim to be a representative government? For instance, some Americans questioned President Clinton's mandate because he received only 43 percent of the votes cast and because only 55 percent of those registered to vote actually did so—which meant that he received the support of fewer than 25 percent of all eligible voters in 1992. The other, even more serious problem is that low turnout almost inevitably means that certain groups vote in greater numbers than other groups and hence gain disproportionate influence on the government and its policies.

The only way to solve these problems is to maximize turnout. It may not be realistic to expect everyone to vote, but a turnout of, say, 90 percent is a feasible goal, as the experience of quite a few democracies shows.

On the basis of studies ranging from the 1920s work of Harold F. Gosnell at the University of Chicago to the 1990s research of Robert W. Jackman of the University of California at Davis and Mark N. Franklin of the University of Houston, we know a great deal about the institutional mechanisms that can increase turnout. They include voter-friendly registration procedures; voting on the weekend instead of during the week; easy access to absentee ballots; proportional representation, with multiple lawmakers representing electoral districts instead of the current U.S. system of winner-takes-all elections; and scheduling as many elections as possible—national, state, and local—on the same day.

Arend Lijphart is professor of political science at the University of California at San Diego and a former president of the American Political Science Association. From "Compulsory Voting Is the Best Way to Keep Democracy Strong," in *The Chronicle of Higher Education* (October 18, 1996), B3–4. Reprinted by permission.

*The 2000 presidential election turnout was 51.2 percent; the 2002 congressional election turnout was 39.3 percent; the 2004 presidential election turnout was 60.7 percent.—*Editors.*

The evidence suggests that using all of these measures together can produce a voter turnout of around 90 percent. But adopting all of them is a tall order. Only a handful of states have even managed to introduce the minor reform of allowing citizens to register to vote on the same day as the election.

Fortunately, one other reform, by itself, can maximize turnout as effectively as all of the other methods combined: compulsory voting. In Australia, Belgium, Brazil, Greece, Italy, Venezuela, and several other Latin American democracies, mandatory voting has produced near-universal voter turnout.

It is somewhat surprising that making voting compulsory is so effective, because the penalties for failing to vote are typically minor, usually involving a fine roughly equal to that for a parking violation. Moreover, enforcement tends to be very lax; because of the large numbers of people involved, compulsory voting simply cannot be strictly enforced. (Parking rules tend to be enforced much more strictly.)

For instance, with 10 million eligible voters in Australia, even a typical turnout of 95 percent means that half a million people did not vote, and it obviously is not practical to issue such a large number of fines. Australia is actually among the strictest enforcers of compulsory voting, but even there, only about 4 percent of nonvoters end up having to pay the small fines. In Belgium, fewer than one-fourth of 1 percent of nonvoters are fined.

Mandatory-voting requirements produce large turnouts, however, even though a government technically cannot compel an actual vote. A government can require citizens to show up at the polls, or even to accept a ballot and then drop it into the ballot box, but it cannot require its citizens to cast a valid vote; secret ballots mean that nobody can be prevented from casting an invalid or blank one.

It is worth emphasizing why low voter turnout is such a serious problem for democracies—one that deserves our attention. Low turnout typically means that privileged citizens (those with better education and greater wealth) vote in significantly larger numbers than less-privileged citizens. This introduces a systematic bias in favor of well-off citizens, because, as the old adage has it, "If you don't vote, you don't count." The already-privileged citizens who vote are further rewarded with government policies favoring their interests.

The socio-economic bias in voter turnout is an especially strong pattern in the United States, where turnout is extremely low. In Presidential elections from 1952 to 1988, turnout among the college-educated was 26 percentage points higher than that among the population as a whole; the turnout for people without a high-school diploma was 16 percentage points lower. Unless turnout is very high—about 90 percent—socio-economic biases in voting tend to be a major problem. For instance, low and unequal voter turnout is a major reason why politicians find it so much easier to reduce government aid to the poor than to cut entitlement programs that chiefly benefit the middle class.

The low levels of voter turnout in the United States are often contrasted with turnouts as high as 95 percent in a few other countries. But when we measure turnout in other democracies in the way we usually measure it in the

United States—as a percentage of the *voting-age population*, rather than as a percentage of *the registered electorate*—we find very few countries with turnouts above 90 percent, and most of those nations have compulsory voting. According to a study by G. Bingham Powell of the University of Rochester, half of the world's democracies have turnout levels below about 75 percent of the voting-age population. This half includes most of the larger democracies; not only the United States, but also Britain, France, Japan, and India, none of which require citizens to vote.

Even these figures cast turnouts in a deceptively favorable light, because they measure voting in what political scientists call first-order elections—that is, national-level parliamentary or presidential elections. But the vast majority of elections are second-order elections—for lesser posts—which attract less attention from citizens and lower turnouts. In the United States, only Presidential elections produce turnouts of more than 50 percent of the voting-age population; turnout in midterm Congressional elections has been only about 35 percent in recent years, and in local elections is closer to 25 percent.

Low turnout is typical for second-order elections in other countries, too. For local elections in Britain, it is only about 40 percent. Even in Australia, it is only about 35 percent, because voting at the local level is not mandatory, as it is for national elections. In the 1994 elections for the European Parliament, another example of a second-order contest, the average turnout in the 12 nations of the European Union was 58 percent. The power of mandatory voting is highlighted by the fact that when it is applied to local elections—as it is in all nations with compulsory voting except Australia—turnout levels are almost the same as those for presidential and parliamentary contests.

It is time that we paid more attention to the issue of voter turnout, because the already low levels of voting in many countries around the world are declining even more. In the United States, voting in Presidential elections has fallen to 50 to 55 percent of the voting-age population in the 1980s and '90s, from 60 to 65 percent during the 1950s and '60s. . . .

The biggest advantage of compulsory voting is that, by enhancing voter turnout, it equalizes participation and removes much of the bias against less-privileged citizens. It also has two other significant advantages. One is that mandatory voting can reduce the role of money in politics, since it does away with the need for candidates and political parties to spend large sums on getting voters to the polls. Second, it reduces the incentives for negative advertising.

As the political scientists Stephen Ansolabehere of the Massachusetts Institute of Technology and Shanto Iyengar of the University of California at Los Angeles have shown in *Going Negative: How Attack Ads Shrink and Polarize the Electorate* (Free Press, 1995), attack ads work—indeed, they work all too well. They are effective not because they persuade people to vote for the candidate making the attack and *against* the candidate attacked in the ads, but because they raise enough doubts in voters' minds that they decide not to vote at all. So the candidate making the attack has lowered his or her opponent's total vote.

Moreover, attack ads breed general distrust of politicians and cynicism about politics and government. Under mandatory voting, it would be so much harder for attack ads to depress turnout that I believe they would no longer be worth the effort.

The main objection to compulsory voting is that it violates the individual's freedom—the freedom not to vote. This was the main reason it was abolished in the Netherlands in 1970, for example. It is unlikely, however, that the Dutch would have made this decision had they foreseen the disastrous plunge in their voter turnouts, from about 90 percent in all elections to only 50 percent and 36 percent, respectively, in the most recent elections for provincial offices and for seats in the European Parliament.

In any case, the individual-freedom argument is extremely weak, because—as I've noted—compulsory voting does not actually require a citizen to cast a valid ballot. Besides, mandatory voting entails an extremely small decrease in freedom compared with many other, more onerous tasks that democracies require their citizens to perform, such as serving on juries, paying taxes, and serving in the military.

Some scholars argue that U.S. courts might rule compulsory voting unconstitutional because it restricts individual freedom. Richard L. Hasen, of the Chicago-Kent College of Law at the Illinois Institute of Technology, . . . has argued, in "Voting Without Law?" (*University of Pennsylvania Law Review*, May 1996), that the only plausible ground for such a ruling would be the First Amendment's guarantee of freedom of speech. But the Supreme Court has explicitly rejected the notion that voting can be regarded as a form of speech. For instance, in 1992, in *Burdick* v. *Takushi*, the Court upheld Hawaii's ban on write-in votes, ruling against a voter's claim that the ban deprived him of the right to cast a protest vote for Donald Duck. The Court said an election is about choosing representatives, not about expressing oneself. Of course, even if mandatory voting were to be found unconstitutional, a constitutional amendment permitting it could be adopted—a difficult, but not impossible, prospect.

Probably the most important practical obstacle to compulsory voting in countries that do not have it is the opposition of conservative parties, like the Republican Party in the United States. High turnout is clearly not in their partisan self-interest, because unequal turnout favors privileged voters, who tend to be conservative. But conservative parties generally were also opposed to universal suffrage, which eventually was accepted by all democracies, because it was recognized to be a basic democratic principle. Compulsory voting should be seen as an extension of universal suffrage—which we now all take for granted.

Nonvoting Is Not a Social Disease

Austin Ranney

In 1980 only 53 percent of the voting-age population in the United States voted for president, and in 1982 only 38 percent voted for members of the House.* As the statistics are usually presented, this rate is, on the average, from 10 to 40 points lower than in the democratic nations of Western Europe, Scandinavia, and the British Commonwealth—although such numbers involve major technical problems of which we should be aware.[1] We also know that the level of voter participation has [declined] since the early 1960s.

All forms of *in*voluntary nonvoting—caused by either legal or extralegal impediments—are violations of the most basic principles of democracy and fairness. Clearly it is a bad thing if citizens who want to vote are prevented from doing so by law or intimidation. But what about *voluntary* nonvoters—the 30 percent or so of our adult citizens who *could* vote if they were willing to make the (usually minimal) effort, but who rarely or never do so? What does it matter if millions of Americans who could vote choose not to?

We should begin by acknowledging that suffrage and voting laws, extralegal force, and intimidation account for almost none of the nonvoting. A number of constitutional amendments, acts of Congress, and court decisions since the 1870s—particularly since the mid-1960s—have outlawed all legal and extralegal denial of the franchise to African-Americans, women, Hispanics, people over the age of 18, and other groups formerly excluded. Moreover, since the mid-1960s most states have changed their registration and voting laws to make casting ballots a good deal easier. Many states, to be sure, still demand a somewhat greater effort to register than is required by other democratic countries. But the best estimates are that even if we made our voting procedures as undemanding as those in other democracies, we would raise our average turnouts by only nine or so percentage points. That would still leave our voter participation level well below that of all but a handful of the world's democracies, and far below what many people think is the proper level for a healthy democracy.

Austin Ranney (1920–2000) was emeritus professor of political science at the University of California at Berkeley and a former president of the American Political Science Association. This selection was adapted from a paper delivered to the ABC/Harvard Symposium on Voter Participation on October 1, 1983. From Austin Ranney, "Nonvoting Is Not a Social Disease," *Public Opinion* (October/November 1983), pp. 16–19. Reprinted with permission of The American Enterprise Institute for Public Policy Research, Washington, D.C.

*The 2000 presidential election turnout was 51.2 percent; the 2002 congressional election turnout was 39.3 percent; the 2004 presidential election turnout was 60.7 percent.—*Editors.*

Throughout our history, but especially in recent years, many American scholars, public officials, journalists, civic reformers, and other people of good will have pondered our low level of voting participation and have produced a multitude of studies, articles, books, pamphlets, manifestoes, and speeches stating their conclusions. On one point they agree: All start from the premise that voluntary, as well as involuntary, nonvoting is a bad thing for the country and seek ways to discourage it. Yet, despite the critical importance of the question, few ask *why* voluntary nonvoting is a bad thing.

Voluntary nonvoting's bad name stems from one or a combination of three types of arguments or assumptions. Let us consider these arguments in turn.

WHAT HARM DOES IT DO?

One of the most often-heard charges against nonvoting is that it produces unrepresentative bodies of public officials. After all, the argument runs, if most of the middle-class WASPs vote and most of the African-Americans, Hispanics, and poor people do not, then there will be significantly lower proportions of African-Americans, Hispanics, and poor people in public office than in the general population. Why is that bad? For two reasons. First, it makes the public officials, in political theorist Hanna Pitkin's term, "descriptively unrepresentative." And while not everyone would argue that the interests of African-Americans are best represented by African-American officials, the interests of women by women officials, and so on, many people believe that the policy preferences of the underrepresented groups will get short shrift from the government. Second, this not only harms the underrepresented groups but weakens the whole polity, for the underrepresented are likely to feel that the government cares nothing for them and they owe no loyalty to it. Hence it contributes greatly to the underclasses' feelings of alienation from the system and to the lawlessness that grows from such alienation.

This argument seems plausible enough, but a number of empirical studies comparing voters with nonvoters do not support it. They find that the distributions of policy preferences among nonvoters are approximately the same as those among voters, and therefore the pressures on public officials by constituents for certain policies and against others are about the same as they would be if everyone, WASPs and minorities, voted at the same rate.

Moreover, other studies have shown that the level of cynicism about the government's honesty, competence, and responsiveness is about the same among nonvoters as among voters, and an increased level of nonvoting does not signify an increased level of alienation or lawlessness. We can carry the argument a step further by asking if levels of civic virtue are clearly higher and levels of lawlessness lower in Venezuela (94 percent average voting turnout), Austria (94 percent), and Italy (93 percent) than in the United States (58 percent), Switzerland (64 percent), and Canada (76 percent). If the answer is no, as surely it is, then at least we have to conclude that there is no clear or strong relationship between high levels of voting turnout and high levels of civic virtue.

Another argument concerns future danger rather than present harm to the Republic. Journalist Arthur Hadley asserts that our great and growing number of "refrainers" (his term for voluntary nonvoters) constitutes a major threat to the future stability of our political system. In his words:

> These growing numbers of refrainers hang over the democratic process like a bomb, ready to explode and change the course of our history as they have twice in our past. . . . Both times in our history when there have been large numbers of refrainers, sudden radical shifts of power have occurred. As long as the present gigantic mass of refrainers sits outside of our political system, neither we nor our allies can be certain of even the normally uncertain future. This is why creating voters, bringing the refrainers to the booth, is important.

Hadley's argument assumes that if millions of the present nonvoters suddenly voted in some future election, they would vote for persons, parties, and policies radically different from those chosen by the regular voters. He asserts that that is what happened in 1828 and again in 1932, and it could happen again any time. Of course, some might feel that a sudden rush to the polls that produces another Andrew Jackson or Franklin Roosevelt is something to be longed for, not feared, but in any case his assumption is highly dubious. We have already noted that the policy preferences of nonvoters do not differ greatly from those of voters, and much the same is true of their candidate preferences. For example, a leading study of the 1980 presidential election found that the five lowest voting groups were African-Americans, Hispanics, whites with family incomes below $5,000 a year, whites with less than high school educations, and working-class white Catholics. The study concluded that if all five groups had voted at the same rate as the electorate as a whole, they would have added only about one-and-a-half percentage points to Carter's share of the vote, and Reagan would still have been elected with a considerable margin. So Hadley's fear seems, at the least, highly exaggerated.

WHAT SOCIAL SICKNESS DOES NONVOTING MANIFEST?

Some writers take the position that, while a high level of voluntary nonvoting may not in itself do harm to the nation's well-being, it is certainly a symptom of poor civic health. Perhaps they take their inspiration from Pericles, who, in his great funeral oration on the dead of Marathon, said:

> . . . Our ordinary citizens, though occupied with the pursuits of industry, are still fair judges of public matters; for, unlike any other nation, regarding him who takes no part in these duties not as unambitious but as useless. . . .

One who holds a 20th-century version of that view is likely to believe that our present level of voluntary nonvoting is a clear sign that millions of Americans are civically useless—that they are too lazy, too obsessed with their own selfish affairs and interests, and too indifferent to the welfare of their country and the quality of their government to make even the minimum effort required to vote. A modern Pericles might ask, How can such a nation hope to defend itself in war and advance the public welfare in peace? Are not the lassitude and indifference manifested by our high level of nonvoting the root cause of our country's declining military strength and economic productivity as well as the growing corruption and bungling of our government?

Perhaps so, perhaps not. Yet the recent studies of nonvoters have shown that they do not differ significantly from voters in the proportions who believe that citizens have a civic duty to vote or in the proportions who believe that ordinary people have a real say in what government does. It may be that nonvoters are significantly less patriotic citizens, poorer soldiers, and less productive workers than voters, but there is no evidence to support such charges. And do we accept the proposition that the much higher turnout rates for the Austrians, the French, and the Irish show that they are significantly better on any or all of these counts than the Americans? If not, then clearly there is no compelling reason to believe that a high level of nonvoting is, by itself, a symptom of sickness in American society.

WHAT BASIC PRINCIPLES DOES IT OFFEND?

I have asked friends and colleagues whether they think that the high level of voluntary nonvoting in America really matters. Almost all of them believe that it does, and when I ask them why they usually reply not so much in terms of some harm it does or some social illness it manifests but rather in terms of their conviction that the United States of America is or should be a democracy, and that a high level of voluntary nonvoting offends some basic principles of democracy.

Their reasoning goes something like this: The essential principle of democratic government is government by the people, government that derives its "just powers from the consent of the governed." The basic institution for ensuring truly democratic government is the regular holding of free elections at which the legitimate authority of public officials to govern is renewed or terminated by the sovereign people. Accordingly, the right to vote is the basic right of every citizen in a democracy, and the exercise of that right is the most basic duty of every democratic citizen.

Many have made this argument. For example, in 1963 President John F. Kennedy appointed an 11-member Commission on Registration and Voting Participation. Its report, delivered after his death, began:

> Voting in the United States is the fundamental act of self-government. It provides the citizen in our free society the right to make a judgment, to state a choice, to participate in the running of his government. . . . The ballot box is the medium for the expression of the consent of the governed.

In the same vein the British political philosopher Sir Isaiah Berlin declares, "Participation in self-government is, like justice, a basic human requirement, *an end in itself.*"

If these views are correct, then any nominal citizen of a democracy who does not exercise this basic right and fulfill this basic duty is not a full citizen, and the larger the proportion of such less-than-full citizens in a polity that aspires to democracy, the greater the gap between the polity's low realities and democracy's high ideals.

Not everyone feels this way, of course. The late Senator Sam Ervin, for example, argues:

> I'm not going to shed any real or political or crocodile tears if people don't care enough to vote. I don't believe in making it easy for apathetic, lazy people. I'd be extremely happy if nobody in the United States voted except for the people who thought about the issues and made up their own minds and wanted to vote. No one else who votes is going to contribute anything but statistics, and I don't care that much for statistics.

The issues between these two positions are posed most starkly when we consider proposals for compulsory voting. After all, if we are truly convinced that voluntary nonvoting is a violation of basic democratic principles, and a major social ill, then why not follow the lead of Australia, Belgium, Italy, and Venezuela and enact laws *requiring* people to vote and penalizing them if they do not?

The logic seems faultless, and yet most people I know, including me, are against compulsory voting laws for the United States. All of us want to eradicate all vestiges of involuntary nonvoting, and many are disturbed by the high level of voluntary nonvoting. Yet many of us also feel that the right to abstain is just as precious as the right to vote, and the idea of legally compelling all citizens to vote whether they want to or not is at least as disturbing as the large numbers of Americans who now and in the future probably will not vote without some compulsion.

THE BRIGHT SIDE

In the light of the foregoing considerations, then, how much should we worry about the high level of voluntary nonvoting in our country? At the end of his magisterial survey of voting turnout in different democratic nations, Ivor Crewe asks this question and answers, "There are . . . reason[s] for not worrying—too much."

I agree. While we Americans can and probably should liberalize our registration and voting laws and mount register-and-vote drives sponsored by political parties, civic organizations, schools of government, and broadcasting companies, the most we can realistically hope for from such efforts is a modest increase of 10 or so percentage points in our average turnouts. As a college professor and political activist for 40 years, I can testify that even the best reasoned and most attractively presented exhortations to people to behave like good democratic citizens can have only limited effects on their behavior, and most get-out-the-vote drives by well-intentioned civic groups in the past have had disappointingly modest results.

An even more powerful reason not to worry, in my judgment, is that we are likely to see a major increase in our voting turnouts to, say, the 70 or 80 percent levels, only if most of the people in our major nonvoting groups—African-Americans,

Hispanics, and poor people—come to believe that voting is a powerful instrument for getting the government to do what they want it to do. The . . . register-and-vote drives by the NAACP and other African-American-mobilization organizations have already had significant success in getting formerly inactive African-American citizens to the polls. . . . Organizations like the Southern Voter Registration Education Project have had some success with Hispanic nonvoters in Texas and New Mexico and may have more. Jesse Helms and Jerry Falwell may also have success in their . . . efforts to urge more conservatives to register and vote. But hard evidence that voting brings real benefits, not exhortations to be good citizens, will be the basis of whatever success any of these groups enjoy.

If we Americans stamp out the last vestiges of institutions and practices that produce *in*voluntary nonvoting, and if we liberalize our registration and voting laws and procedures to make voting here as easy as it is in other democracies, and if the group-mobilization movements succeed, then perhaps our level of voting participation may become much more like that of Canada or Great Britain. (It is unlikely ever to match the levels in the countries with compulsory voting or even those in West Germany or the Scandinavian countries.)

But even if that does not happen, we need not fear that our low voting turnouts are doing any serious harm to our politics or our country, or that they deprive us of the right to call ourselves a democracy.

NOTE

1. European and American measures of voting and nonvoting differ significantly. In all countries the numerator for the formula is the total number of votes cast in national elections. In most countries the denominator is the total number of persons on the electoral rolls—that is, people we would call "registered voters"—which includes almost all people legally eligible to vote. In the United States, on the other hand, the denominator is the "voting-age population," which is the estimate by the Bureau of the Census of the number of people in the country who are 18 or older at the time of the election. That figure, unlike its European counterpart, includes aliens and inmates of prisons and mental hospitals as well as persons not registered to vote. One eminent election analyst, Richard M. Scammon, estimates that if voting turnout in the United States were computed by the same formula as that used for European countries, our average figures would rise by 8 to 10 percentage points, a level that would exceed Switzerland's and closely approach those of Canada, Ireland, Japan, and the United Kingdom.

 **mhhe.com/**diclerico11e

Internet resources
Visit our Web site at
www.mhhe.com/diclerico11e for links and
resources relating to Voting.

 chapter 6

Campaigns and the Media

*P*robably nothing has so revolutionized American politics as the emergence of television as the principal means of communicating with voters. What used to be the experience of only a few people—hearing and seeing a candidate at a campaign rally, for example—is now an experience shared by many millions of Americans. Because television enables political candidates to be seen and heard in every living room of the country, it is no wonder that politicians devote so much time and resources to producing television advertisements and other political programming.

The advent of TV advertising also has led to shorter and shorter campaign spots, in which candidates in thirty-second or shorter sound and picture bites bash their opponents or attempt to communicate key word messages to the sometimes uninformed, unsuspecting, and undecided voters. These political advertisements are most often referred to as "negative ads," though exactly what constitutes a negative ad is often in dispute.

The thirty-second or less campaign TV spots, particularly those deemed "negative," are roundly criticized by "good government" advocates. Critics claim that such ads do not simply present a negative view of specific candidates for office, but also damage the political system itself. Such a view is taken by the author of the first selection in this chapter—Fred Wertheimer—who argues that the effect of negative ads is to breed public distrust of the political process. According to Wertheimer, the damage done by negative ads makes it very difficult to govern in a world increasingly beset with public cynicism and distrust, that cynicism being fed by negative campaigning. To remedy this, Wertheimer suggests a number of reforms to make the sponsors of negative ads more accountable.

Defenders of TV spots, however, argue that political ads, be they negative or not, actually are highly beneficial. Such a point of view is presented by the authors of the second selection—Stephen Bates and Edwin Diamond. While recognizing that TV spots have their negative aspects, Bates and Diamond are not convinced that such spots are as bad as critics allege. Indeed, they see such ads as contributing greatly to political "discourse," leaving voters better informed than would otherwise be the case. To Bates and Diamond, then, reforming TV campaign spots is like trying to remove politics from campaigns. They argue that TV is simply the modern medium of politics, and they insist that it cannot and should not be "turned off" for the sake of satisfying critics.

TV Ad Wars
How to Cut Advertising Costs in Political Campaigns
Fred Wertheimer

[Television,] like the colossus of the ancient world, stands astride our political system, demanding
tribute from every candidate for major public office, incumbent or challenger. Its appetite
is insatiable, and its impact is unique.
—SENATOR EDWARD KENNEDY, SENATE COMMITTEE ON
COMMERCE, HEARINGS, 92ND CONGRESS, 1971

. . . Television advertising is the principal means by which candidates publicly define for the voters their opponents and themselves and the government in which they serve or hope to serve. Television advertising is characterized in the public's mind by one word: negative.

Every two years during the fall, and much earlier in presidential election years, a focused, intense, negative message goes out to the American people over the airwaves about how bad the candidates are, how dangerous their ideas are, how their programs don't work, how problems cannot be solved. Obviously, discussing and disagreeing with your opponent's record and views is a normal and necessary part of our political process. It is a key part of informing and educating voters on the choice they have to make. However, our political TV ad campaigns go far beyond traditional comparative advertising.

Although many candidates have some positive things to say in their TV ads, these messages are overwhelmed by the negative attack ads that set the tone and dominate the debate. Because television appeals to our emotions and magnifies and intensifies what it communicates, the impact of the negative message is much more powerful and damaging on television than if the same message were being communicated through print.

Most politicians and their media handlers focus their TV advertising exclusively on one goal: winning on election day. If winning on election day means undermining your own credibility or damaging your ability to govern or breeding public distrust and cynicism or turning large segments of the public away from voting, so be it. Thus we end up with the perverse result that many

Fred Wertheimer is president of Democracy 21 and served as president of Common Cause from 1981 to 1995. "TV Ad Wars: How to Cut Advertising Costs in Political Campaigns," by Fred Wertheimer from *The Harvard International Journal of Press/Politics* 2 (Summer 1997), pp. 93–101. © 1997. Permission conveyed through Copyright Clearance Center, Inc.

politicians use TV advertising in their campaigns in ways that ultimately do as much damage to their own credibility as they do to their opponents'.

Regardless of what politicians may believe about negative advertising "working" in their campaigns, it certainly does not work when it comes to doing their jobs and serving the American people as effective and credible representatives. As Stephen Ansolabehere and Shanto Iyengar find in their book, *Going Negative*, "Negative advertising demoralizes the electorate . . . eats away at the individual's sense of civic duty . . . and contribute[s] to the general antipathy towards politicians and parties and the high rates of disapproval and distrust of political institutions" (1996).

Although the candidates bear the principal responsibility for this happening, we cannot underestimate how important the role played by media consultants is in bringing about these enormously damaging results. As a result of the perceived need for consultant expertise to design and produce TV ad campaigns, many candidates abdicate much of the power to define themselves and their opponents to their media consultants. The media consultants have only one objective—winning the election—and this is often equated with negative attack ads. The carnage that is left after the election is over and it is time to govern is someone else's problem.

Media consultants, furthermore, normally receive as part of their fee a percentage of the amount spent to purchase TV advertising time for the campaign, such as 15 percent. This can involve hundreds of thousands of dollars—sometimes even millions of dollars—in fees. It also means that media consultants have a strong personal economic incentive to spend as much money as they can to conduct the negative TV ad campaigns they devise.

Although the thirty-second negative ad has a preeminent role in U.S. politics today, it hasn't always been this way, in terms of either the length or the content of our political ads. During the first twenty years of presidential ads, for example, sixty-second spots were the dominant form of TV advertising. In the 1970s, ads of four minutes and twenty seconds played the dominant role, and starting in the 1980s, the thirty-second spot became dominant in presidential campaigns. Presidential ads also went through a transition, over time, from positive to negative. According to one study, for example, from 1960 to 1988, ads in presidential campaigns were 72 percent positive and 29 percent negative. In 1992, 63 percent of Bill Clinton's ads and 56 percent of George Bush's ads were negative, representing a high-water mark, as of that time, in negative ad emphasis in a presidential campaign (Kaid and Holtz-Bacha, 1995).

A PROPOSED SOLUTION

A number of proposals have been offered to challenge and break out of the grip of the thirty-second negative attack ad. The most radical proposal would bar all political advertising on TV. Other proposals include requiring that candidates appear on screen the whole time in their campaign TV ads, that whenever a negative charge is made in a campaign TV ad that it be made on screen by the candidate, that all campaign TV ads be five minutes or more in length, and that candidates take greater personal responsibility for their campaign ads.

The issues and choices involved here are very difficult. On the one hand, there is great value to our political process and our democracy in moving away from the political culture embedded in the thirty-second attack ad. On the other hand, regulating, through mandatory requirements, the use and content of political ads raises fundamental First Amendment and policy concerns regarding the ability of citizens to exercise free speech in presenting their candidacies to the American people.

Although TV ad campaigns are causing deep problems for our political system today, it is also important to keep in mind how valuable communicating on TV can be. TV campaign ads allow candidates to communicate their views to mass audiences and to do so unfiltered by any intermediaries, such as the media. Ansolabehere and Iyengar point out the real problem: "It's not the pervasiveness of broadcast advertising that spawns public cynicism; it is instead the tone of the advertising campaign. If campaigns were to become more positive, people would be less embittered about politics as usual and more willing to vote" (1996).

Congress should require that candidates appear on screen at the end of their political ads and state they are responsible for the ads. This would provide clearer public accountability for candidates regarding the messages they present to voters on TV. By having to take personal responsibility for their ads, visually, candidates may become less interested in and less likely to run the kinds of negative attack ads that are common practice today.

Congress should also require TV stations to provide a designated amount of free TV time to political parties for use either by their candidates for their campaigns or by party officials to present party views. The free TV time to the parties could be conditioned on the candidates and party officials appearing on screen to present their messages. Broadcasters could be provided financial relief for this free TV time through tax credits or deductions. (Most democracies provide free TV time for campaigns, and since most of these countries involve parliamentary systems, the free time is given to the political parties.) This would strengthen the role of political parties, providing them with new clean campaign resources to use to support their candidates or present their views. It would also provide the parties with the opportunity to focus new resources on underfinanced challengers, to the extent the parties are willing to assist them as opposed to their incumbent candidates.

CONCLUSION

There *are* ways to reduce the financial and social costs of TV advertising in U.S. campaigns. The policy changes proposed here would greatly reduce the current financial costs to federal candidates of communicating through TV. The changes would also challenge the basic premise that currently drives TV political ad campaigns. Through a combination of incentives and requirements, they would help move us away from the thirty-second negative attack ad without intruding on the candidates' First Amendment free-speech rights.

Changing the culture of American political campaigns is no easy task, needless to say. Citizens, however, are rightly fed up with the current system. The stakes involved here for our politics, our governance, and our country are enormous. Now is the time to begin changing our TV ways.

REFERENCES

Ansolabehere, Stephen, and Shanto Iyengar. 1996. *Going Negative: How Political Advertisements Shrink and Polarize the Electorate.* New York: Free Press.
Kaid, Lynda Lee, and Christiana Holtz-Bacha, eds. 1995. *Political Advertising in Western Democracies: Parties and Candidates on Television.* London: Sage.

Damned Spots
A Defense of Thirty-Second Campaign Ads
Stephen Bates and Edwin Diamond

. . . [E]veryone denounc[es] 30-second spots as demeaning, manipulative, and responsible for all that's wrong with American politics. David Broder, the mandarin of the op-ed page, admits he's "a crank on the subject." Otherwise staunch First Amendment champions, including *Washington Monthly* and, yes, *The New Republic*, want Congress to restrict the content of political ads. In fact, such commercials are good for the campaign, the voter, and the republic.

To cite the most common complaints:

1. ***TV Spots Make Campaigns Too Expensive.*** The problem is nearly as old as television itself. William Benton, an ad-agency founder and a U.S. senator from Connecticut, talked of the "terrifying" cost of TV back in 1952. Campaign spending has risen sharply since then, and television advertising has contributed disproportionately. Whereas total political spending,

Stephen Bates is a literary editor of *The Wilson Quarterly.* Edwin Diamond is professor of journalism at New York University and a media columnist for *The New Yorker* magazine. From "Damned Spots," *New Republic* (September 7 and 14, 1992), pp. 14–18. Reprinted by permission of the New Republic, © 1992, The New Republic, LLC.

adjusted for inflation, has tripled since 1952, the amount spent on television has increased at least fivefold. In some races, nine out of ten campaign dollars go to TV.

The important question is what candidates get in return. Quite a lot: a dollar spent on TV advertising may reach as many voters as $3 worth of newspaper ads or $50 worth of direct mail. Banning spots would probably *increase* campaign spending, by diverting candidates to less efficient forms of communication. In addition, spots reach supporters, opponents, and fence-sitters alike. This mass auditing imposes a measure of accountability that other media, particularly direct mail, lack.

2. *A Candidate Can't Say Anything Substantive in 30 Seconds.*   Referring to sound bites as well as spots, Michael Dukakis* sourly concluded that the 1988 campaign was about "phraseology," not ideology. But a lot can be said in thirty seconds. John Lindsay's 1972 presidential campaign broadcast a 30-second spot in Florida that gave the candidate's positions on, among other issues, gun control (for), abortion rights (for), and school prayer (against). Lindsay's media manager, David Garth, later joked that the spot "probably lost the entire population of Florida."

A candidate can even make his point in 10 seconds. In California's 1992 Republican primary for U.S. Senate, one spot said simply: "I'm Bruce Herschensohn. My opponent, Tom Campbell, was the only Republican congressman opposing the 1990 anti-crime bill. He's liberal and wrong." Campbell replied in kind: "Bruce Herschensohn is lying, Tom Campbell voted to extend the death penalty to twenty-seven crimes, and was named Legislator of the Year by the California Fraternal Order of Police."

Though hardly encyclopedic, these spots reveal something about the candidates' priorities. They assert facts that can be checked and conclusions that can be challenged. If nothing else, they improve on what may have been the first ten-second spot, broadcast in 1954: "Minnesota needs a wide-awake governor! Vote for Orville Freeman and bring wide-awake action to Minnesota's problems!"

Brief ads do have one shortcoming. In 30 seconds, a candidate cannot hope to answer a half-true attack spot. In Bush's [Willie Horton] "revolving door" prison ad of 1988,† for instance, the voice-over says that Dukakis "gave weekend furloughs to first-degree murderers not eligible for parole," while the text on the screen tells viewers that "268 escaped" and "many are still at large." But as reporters discovered, only 4 of the 268 escapees were first-degree murderers, and only three escapees—none of them a murderer—were still at large. The Willie Horton example was an aberration.

*Dukakis was the 1988 Democratic candidate for president.—*Editors.*

†The "revolving door" ad became associated with convicted murderer Willie Horton, who, under a Massachusetts furlough program, was released from prison in 1986 for forty-eight hours but never returned. He subsequently assaulted and raped a woman in Maryland, for which he was convicted and sentenced to prison in 1987.—*Editors.*

This point might have been hard for the Dukakis team to convey in 30 seconds. What kept them from responding to Hortonism, however, was not the constraints of brevity; it was their decision to try to get public attention off the furlough program—a subject that, even without the Bush campaign's factual finagling, was bound to cost them votes. No sensible candidate will defend himself by saying he's only half as bad as his opponent charges.

Just as short spots aren't invariably shallow, long telecasts aren't invariably thoughtful. The 1960 John F. Kennedy campaign aired a two-minute spot with a bouncy jingle; it conveyed youth and vitality, but scarcely any information (except for a musical reference to Kennedy's Catholicism: "Can you deny to any man/The right he's guaranteed/To be elected president/No matter what his creed?"). As Ross Perot demonstrated, a candidate determined to be evasive can do so in a 30-second spot or in a two-hour live Q&A session.

3. *Political Ads Are Responsible for the Low-Down-and-Dirty State of Political Discourse.* According to Arthur Schlesinger Jr., television is "draining content out of campaigns." But that assertion romanticizes the past. In the 1890s James Bryce, a Briton, decried American political campaigns in 1990s terms. Campaigns devote less attention to issues, he fretted, than to "questions of personal fitness," such as any "irregularity" in the candidate's relations with women. These issueless campaigns diminish the "confidence of the country in the honor of its public men."

Sleazy ads hardly raise the level of political discourse, but they aren't the superweapon that critics claim. "When a client of ours is attacked," boasts Democratic consultant Bob Squier, "the people of that state are going to get some kind of response the next day." These responses are invariably revealing. In a 1988 Dukakis ad, the candidate watches a TV set showing a Bush ad. "I'm fed up with it," Dukakis says. "Never seen anything like it in twenty-five years of public life—George Bush's negative television ads, distorting my record. . . ." But instead of presenting a sharp reply, Dukakis only turns off the set—a metaphor for his entire campaign.

4. *TV Ads Keep the Potatoes on the Couch.* Barely half of eligible citizens voted in 1988, the lowest turnout in 40 years.* In fact, turnout has declined steadily since 1960. During the same period campaign-TV expenditures have tripled in constant dollars. Many of the TV dollars have been diverted from doorbell pushing, rallies, and other activities that involve citizens in politics. And, according to critics, simplistic, unfair spots discourage people from voting.

It is nearly impossible to untangle the factors that influence voter turnout. Some consultants, like Republican Eddie Mahe, argue that the decline in voting is a passing consequence of demographics. In the 1960s and 1970s the baby-boom generation reached voting age and lowered voting figures (so did the 26th Amendment, which changed the voting age

*Turnout in 1996 was even lower: 49 percent.—*Editors.*

from 21 to 18). No surprises there: Turnout is traditionally lower among the young. So, as the boomer generation ages, turnout will increase.

As for how spots affect turnout in particular elections, the evidence goes both ways. In the 1990 race for U.S. Senate in North Carolina, early polls showed blue-collar whites inclined to stay home. But many of them turned out to vote for Jesse Helms after his anti-quotas spot received heavy air play and news coverage.

Are spots, then, blameless for the parlous state of voter participation? Well, no. Even if they don't cloud the mind, they may in some sense sap the political will. To the extent that spots resemble lifestyle commercials—It's Miller Time, It's Morning in America—they may be taken no more seriously than other TV advertising. This is especially so when no other campaign is visible to the viewer. Today's political rally, as Democratic consultant Robert Shrum has said, consists of three people around the TV set.

But the doomsayers' solution—to try to divorce politics from TV—won't work. Since the 1950s the voting classes have increasingly stayed home to be entertained, a trend encouraged by demographics (the suburban migration), by new at-home options (cable, VCRs), and at least partly by fear (crime in the streets). Banning political spots, as some cranks in the press and Congress would do, wouldn't bring voters outdoors. It would deprive the couch-potato/citizen of a sometimes abused but ultimately unmatched source of electoral information. As Dukakis discovered, melodramatically turning off the TV resolves nothing.

mhhe.com/diclerico11e

Internet resources
Visit our Web site at
www.mhhe.com/diclerico11e for links and
resources relating to Campaigns and the Media.

chapter 7

Elections

Nominations

In the "old days," before 1972, the crucially important decisions about who would be the presidential nominees of our national political parties were made by party "bosses" in "smoke-filled rooms." Presidential candidates, if they entered any primaries at all, did so only to convince the party bosses of their vote-getting ability. Primaries were typically not an important consideration in winning the nomination, in part because there were not very many of them, and in part because most were "beauty contests"—that is, primaries in which voters were able to express a presidential preference but the results had no impact on how a state's delegates to the national party conventions were allocated. Most of the delegates were chosen in caucuses (similar to the Iowa caucus) or else were appointed, and the party bosses controlled both methods.

In the 1970s, reform movements that opened up the presidential nominating process to greater participation swept both parties. The caucus method of selecting delegates was made more democratic and less subject to manipulation by the party bosses, and the number of delegates who could be appointed by the party bosses was greatly reduced. Although the reformers did not require that states select their delegates by primary, more and more states began to switch to this method. To the extent that primaries provided an opportunity for more participation by the party rank and file, they were seen as consistent with the spirit of the reform movement. In addition, states saw a greater economic payoff by switching to the primary, since it seemed to attract more media attention than the caucus and it required a greater expenditure of funds by the candidates. Although a number of states continue to select their delegates by caucus— Iowa being the most notable example—the nominating process is now dominated by primaries.

How well does this seemingly more open and democratic nominating process work? Not very, according to Robert E. DiClerico in the first selection. As he sees it, the way we choose nominees for the most important political office in the world does a disservice to the candidates, the voters, and the political parties. John Armor and Larry Sabato, the authors of the second and third selections, while not disputing DiClerico's general assessment, differ on how to correct what's wrong. Armor favors getting rid of all the primaries and caucuses and replacing them with a single-day national primary. This change, he believes, would be fairer to the candidates and the voters and would invigorate the political parties.

Sabato argues that the political parties simply will not make the tough decisions required to make the nominating process more fair and efficient, that Congress lacks the authority to step in, and that even if Congress could step in, it wouldn't. Accordingly, Sabato calls for drastic action—namely, a constitutional amendment mandating a Regional Lottery Plan. This plan, he says, would shorten the nominating process, preserve an element of personal campaigning, generate excitement, encourage citizen involvement in all parts of the country, and give many more states the potential to influence the outcome.

Choosing Our Choices 2004
Robert E. DiClerico

In July and September of 2004 Republicans and Democrats convened in separate gatherings to nominate the individuals who would lead their parties into the 2004 general election campaign. As has been true for some time now, these national conventions were more coronation than deliberation, the decision on presidential nominees having been determined several months earlier in a series of contests dominated by primaries, with a small sprinkling of caucuses.

Our presidential nominating process, unique among the democracies of the world, is also the most crucial stage in the presidential selection process, structuring as it does the choices we will face on election day. This point was not lost on William "Boss" Tweed, the notorious leader of Tammany Hall, who was fond of reminding his compatriots, "I don't care who does the electin', so long as I do the nominatin'."

The only party with a contested nomination in 2004, the Democrats settled on their nominee with remarkable alacrity. Indeed, it was in a mid-March speech to supporters in Charleston, West Virginia, that John Kerry proclaimed he now had won the Democratic nomination—this coming on the evening of his Illinois primary victory and just seven weeks after the opening contest in Iowa. Unfortunately, neither Democrats in West Virginia nor any of the other seventeen states and territories with contests yet to be held played any role in deciding the matter.

Actually, the Democratic Party nomination was for all practical purposes decided back in January, following John Kerry's decisive victories in Iowa and New Hampshire, both of which provided him with a head of steam nearly impossible to stop. The Iowa win suddenly propelled him from a stagnating third-place standing in the New Hampshire polls into first place, and his commanding finish in the Granite State made him the poll leader in all seven of the states coming a week later—states in which he had scarcely campaigned.[1] By the time Super Tuesday was concluded on March 2, the most John Edwards had been able to manage was a single victory in his native state, Howard Dean, a first-place showing in his home state, and Wesley Clark a narrow win in a state to which he had directed a disproportionate share of his time and money.

Robert E. DiClerico is Eberly Distinguished Professor of Teaching and professor of political science at West Virginia University. An earlier version of this article appeared in *Arts & Sciences* (Eberly College of Arts and Sciences, West Virginia University, Summer 2004), pp. 23–25, and in the 10th edition of *Points of View* (2007). The text was updated for the 11th edition.

The failure to win in both Iowa and New Hampshire appears to doom a presidential candidacy, unless one of those states' own officeholders carries the day, in which case the results are largely discounted as when Iowa Senator Tom Harkin won his state's Democratic caucus in 1992. If you win or exceed expectations in Iowa or New Hampshire, your candidacy is advanced to the next round. Victories in both, however, generate a bandwagon effect that appears unstoppable, as Jimmy Carter demonstrated in 1976 and John Kerry in 2004. The ability of these two opening contests to decide who will be the nominee—and, more often, who will not be—has caused more and more states to move their contests up to the front end of the nominating process lest they be left out of the action completely.[2] The net effect of this "front-loading," which has been steadily increasing in the last four presidential elections, has been to accelerate the decision on a presidential nominee.[3] Thus, whereas Jimmy Carter and Gerald Ford (1976) did not accumulate enough delegates to win until July and August, respectively, Bill Clinton and Robert Dole (1996) and G. W. Bush and Al Gore (2000) did so by March.

The slingshot effect of Iowa and New Hampshire was particularly robust in 2004 because the Democratic Party quite by design allowed states to hold their contests as early as one week after the Granite State. The motives behind configuring the primary calendar in this way were, first, to deny Republican primaries the monopoly on media coverage such as they enjoyed in 2000, when the Democrats did not allow contests to be scheduled until five weeks after New Hampshire, and second, to settle on a nominee quickly, thereby minimizing internal divisions and sending the party into the general election united.[4]

Although an accelerated decision might be good for party unity, it is not entirely clear that this rush to judgment, and the prominent role of Iowa and New Hampshire in it, are best for the voters and the political system. We are, after all, nominating individuals for the most consequential political office in the world. Those who seek it deserve to be tested longer in the rough and tumble of the primary process, and the public deserves more time to take their measure, particularly since most voters don't even start to focus on the candidates until the primaries begin. A Pew Research Center poll, for example, found that late in September of 2003, with the informal campaign under way and one presidential debate already having been held, only 39 percent of Americans could name *one* of the ten announced candidates![5] And just three days before the 2004 Super Tuesday primaries, the National Annenberg Election Survey reported that two-thirds of registered voters felt they lacked enough information to make a choice.[6]

Much was made of the high turnout in the 2004 primaries, but, in fact, only New Hampshire set a record. According to the Committee for the Study of the American Electorate, the overall turnout for all primaries held through Super Tuesday was the lowest *ever* for a contested Democratic nomination race.[7] This should occasion no great surprise, for many voters, concluding that the die had been cast after Kerry's victories in the first few contests, were no doubt less motivated to get out and vote. Nor is it at all surprising that the states holding contests subsequent to John Kerry's March victory announcement had an average turnout of just 9.5 percent.[8] An accelerated nomination decision may be good for party unity but not for participation by the party rank and file.

As the presidential nominating process has grown shorter, the general election campaign has become longer—a development not without consequence. Presidential nominees in the out-party must now scramble to stay in the news, since they no longer enjoy the automatic and free media attention that comes with coverage of the primaries. Moreover, if candidates choose to finance their nomination campaigns with matching public funds, they must abide by the spending limits that come with them. Consequently, they are likely to find themselves, as Robert Dole did in 1996, strapped for funds to tide them over from the end of March until the conventions, their money having been spent at the front end of an increasingly front-loaded primary process. The incumbent president, meanwhile, assuming he faces no serious challenge to his renomination, has an abundant supply of funds (whether public or privately raised) and command of the microphone, both of which he can now direct at his opponent as Bill Clinton did to Republican nominee Robert Dole in 1996 and George W. Bush to John Kerry in 2004. It is largely for this reason that both John Kerry and Howard Dean declined to accept public funding of their nomination campaigns, fearing that the mandated spending limits ($43 million in 2004) would leave them with no money to answer the pounding directed at them by the incumbent during what is now a much longer postnomination period.

The 2004 presidential race, incidentally, marked the first time since groundbreaking campaign finance reform was enacted (1974) that at least one candidate in each party declined public financing of his nomination campaign. The decisions by George W. Bush and John Kerry to raise their money exclusively from private sources no doubt provided Bush with an unprecedented war chest ($170 million) with which to go after his opponent in the postnomination period, and Kerry with some ability to respond. But for anyone concerned about the influence of money in elections, their turndown of public funding was not a welcome development.

Finally, it is not readily apparent why Iowa and New Hampshire should enjoy the privileged position of leading off the race for the presidency, thereby shaping the dynamics of what follows. They are relatively small states and send modest numbers of delegates to their national conventions. Nor is there any reason to believe their voters are more discerning than the inhabitants of the other forty-eight states and D.C. For the Democrats especially, New Hampshire seems an inappropriate choice as the first primary, for it has few urban areas, low union membership, and scarcely any blacks or Hispanics within its borders. Defenders argue that the relatively small size of Iowa and New Hampshire allows the less known and moneyed to compete more effectively, while also affording voters the opportunity to observe candidates "up close and personal." True enough, but other states (e.g., Vermont, Connecticut, Maryland, West Virginia, South Carolina) could serve this purpose equally well.

There has been no shortage of proposals on how to improve the way we nominate presidential candidates, including a national primary, a system of rotating regional primaries, and primary waves beginning with the smallest states and gradually working up to the most populated states. Whether any of these proposals gains traction remains to be seen.

The Democrats, however, did decide to make one far more limited change to their primary/caucus calendar for the 2008 presidential race. In response to charges that Iowa and New Hampshire were not fully reflective of the constituencies that make up the Democratic Party, the Nevada caucus was placed five days after the opening Iowa caucus (January 14) and the South Carolina primary one week after the first primary in New Hampshire (January 22). Nevada has a significant Hispanic population and South Carolina a substantial number of African Americans, and both are strongly Democratic voting groups.

The front-loading problem, meanwhile, continues unabated. As of this writing California, New York, and New Jersey have moved their primaries forward to February 5, joining nine other state contests on that date. Florida, Illinois, and Colorado are thinking about doing so as well. Thus, should a candidate emerge from the opening contests with a clear lead, as Kerry did in 2004, that crucially important momentum would have the potential to influence an even greater number of contests as the campaign turns to the Super Tuesday of February 5. And a favorable result for the leader on that day would effectively decide the race for the nomination—all within a matter of *three* weeks.

The further compression of contests at the front of the presidential nominating process in 2008 is scarcely a heartening development, for it may leave us with candidates insufficiently tested, voters who are inadequately informed, and nominees whom their parties may come to regret.

NOTES

1. *Roll Call,* February 5, 2004, p. 6.
2. William G. Mayer and Andrew E. Busch, *The Front-Loading Problem in Presidential Nominations* (Washington, D.C.: Brookings Institution, 2004), p. 7.
3. Ibid., p. 50.
4. James A. Barnes, "Democrats Compressing the 2004 Calendar," *National Journal,* December 1, 2001, p. 3699.
5. Dana Milbank, "Lost in Cyberspace: Playing Catch-up @ Meetup," *Washington Post,* September 28, 2003, p. A5.
6. *New York Times,* March 3, 2004, p. A16.
7. *New York Times,* March 10, 2004, p. A17; *Washington Post,* March 10, 2004, p. A46.
8. Primary turnout figures were kindly supplied to the author by Curtis B. Gans, director of the Committee for the Study of the American Electorate.

The National Primary
An Excellent Idea
John Armor

TIME TO TALK ABOUT THE 2008 ELECTION

. . . A gentleman named James Talley happened to tell me about a letter he had published in *USA Today* in January. I told him there was a story there, and I'd write it. Here are his first two paragraphs:

"The time has come for this archaic process we call election primary—a long drawn out process state by state—to be abolished and replaced by a true national primary. The year 2004 should be the last year for this old system.

"In our present ancient process by the time the first three or four states have voted, and the news media have declared the trends and the effective result, the party moguls have the stage set for their guy or gal. This disenfranchises the voters. Every registered American citizen deserves the opportunity to enter the voting booth and to express a choice totally uninfluenced by exit polls and media rhetoric."

And Jim went on to suggest a date for this national primary: the Tuesday nearest to the 4th of July. In 2008 that would be July 1.

In any proposal for major change in a long-established system, a necessary question is "How can this be accomplished?" It's like the story about belling the cat. The mice might be in total agreement that a bell on the cat would be a safety measure. But the question immediately arises as to who will get that bell on that cat. There are two theoretical ways to accomplish what Jim suggests. One method would never succeed for pragmatic political reasons. But the other one could work, if properly approached, so it's doable. And we can talk about whether it makes sense.

If you look over the history of national political conventions, beginning with the Anti-Masonic and National Republican Conventions in Baltimore in 1831, most of them have been reasonably exciting and have had actual tasks to perform. They have either chosen nominees in contested elections, or written platforms on contested issues.

John Armor is a graduate of Yale University and Maryland Law School. He has argued First Amendment cases before the U.S. Supreme Court for more than 30 years. This opinion piece was first published on Chronwatch.com.

In the span of American history, 2004 was an exceptionally dull year for conventions. Both candidates were known months in advance of their conventions. (I'm speaking here of the only parties with a chance to win in this year, the Republicans and the Democrats.) Both campaigns controlled their conventions— who would speak, what they would speak about, what the party platforms would say.

Whenever one party has a one-term occupant in the White House, its convention is almost guaranteed to be "thoroughly scripted." That's because no incumbent president has ever been denied renomination if he sought that. Yes, I see your hands waving. No, Lyndon Johnson was not defeated for renomination. He was not even defeated in New Hampshire by Gene McCarthy. McCarthy did run nearly even with Johnson, and demonstrated Johnson's vulnerability. Johnson then announced that he would not run again. The result was the 1968 Chicago Convention, one of the most violent and fractious in history.

Presidential nominations now begin with the Iowa Caucuses, followed by the New Hampshire Primary. Both states defend their turf by threatening to move their caucuses or primaries to an even earlier date, if any other state proposes a law to move its primary into January. Even though these two small states are hardly typical of the United States as a whole, the press and pundits put great stock by the candidates who win in those states, plus a small number of the others who "did better than expected."

So almost anyone who wants to be president has to spend at least a year prior to the election year preparing for a solid showing in Iowa and New Hampshire. Unless that changes, 2008 will be a repeat of 2004. Everyone seeking the presidency will be at it for two years, and as citizens our TVs will be cluttered with both the ads and the sound bites from all those people for two years.

Then as the process continues, it's possible that one candidate will outlast the others and force them out of the race (I'm not referring to the "tick" candidates like Al Sharpton and Dennis Kucinich, who burrowed in and claimed to be still in the race after it was over). When the contests on both sides are over early in the year, as now, states with later primary dates find themselves spending serious money to conduct meaningless primaries in which no one campaigns and few people vote.

There are two ways to defang the early overemphasis on Iowa and New Hampshire. One appears in the U.S. Constitution. Article I, Section 4, of the Constitution gives the control of election laws first to the "State Legislatures," but then adds, "Congress may at any time by Law alter such regulations. . ." So if Congress decided that a national primary was desirable, it could pass a law and require that result. This is theory only. The leaders of Congress have all grown up in the current system of nominations. They know how to play this game, not the new game which would result with this change. Discount to zero the chance that Congress would act on this idea before 2008.

Fortunately, that does not foreclose the change. What if two-thirds of the state legislatures decided that a national primary was a good idea? What if those legislators agreed that July 1, 2008, was a good time to conduct this primary and did so by law?

First, the excessive focus on Iowa and New Hampshire would disappear. Every candidate would justly say that for anyone to win a majority of the delegates to his/her convention, that must include a strong win in many states on July 1. The primaries on other dates could not, mathematically, foreclose the nominations at the conventions.

The first obvious result is that all states holding their primaries on July 1, 2008, would be guaranteed to have contested and relevant elections. All candidates would have an incentive to go to all such states—in person, on TV, by Internet—because all such voting would matter.

The second obvious factor is this: It would be far less likely for any one candidate to take a mathematical majority in the July 1 Primary. All candidates would be "in the race" through July 1. None of them would be likely to be "scraped off," like Indiana Jones falling from the outside of a speeding German truck. It isn't just the press focus on the horse race aspects, but the federal election law's provisions concerning federal matching funds, that destroys candidacies early under the present process.

It's more likely that a national primary would produce just leading candidates for the Republican and Democratic nominations, rather than absolute winners. It's common sense that the leading candidates would negotiate with the trailing candidates that they generally agreed with. Perhaps that would result in a committed majority (and ticket) in either or both parties before their 2008 conventions.

But there's a far greater chance under this process than under the present one, that there would NOT be a final, mathematical victory in either or both of the Republican and Democratic Conventions in 2008 as there was in 2004. Are there public benefits to this difference?

Some Democrats are already having buyer's remorse about their selection of John Kerry in 2004. The wrong time to find out about major defects in your candidate for president is after your party has selected that person. The whole point of primary elections is to test candidates against each other, including a comparison of their defects as well as their assets.

If the proposed National Primary did not produce nominees for both parties, that would guarantee that the public and press review of the candidates continued until the conventions. That would allow a maximum opportunity for sound decisions on nominees and minimum risk of buyer's remorse. "Marry in haste, repent in leisure," is attributed to Ben Franklin. Committing to a candidate is a form of political marriage. The observation applies, though Franklin may have borrowed it.

Another public advantage concerns issues. If the candidates are not buttoned up before the conventions, then the issues and party platforms are probably not buttoned up either. When was the last time you recall seeing a debate on any platform point at a convention? And yet, choosing between policy choices on subjects from war and peace to social security is the very essence of modern American politics.

Why should the presidential nominating process continue to be rigged the way it is today, so that the conversations Americans routinely have around water coolers and at kitchen tables are prevented at the party conventions? A National Primary offers the best chance of conventions that have real work to do—candidates to choose, issues to decide.

And if the conventions offer more than pre-scripted content, the press is more likely to offer more coverage. Danger attracts the press. Would anyone cover NASCAR races if there was a written guarantee in advance of no car crashes? Think of the plot theory behind all movies and television shows. If there's no conflict, there's no story.

Of course, the purpose of the leading candidates is always to go over the top. Close out debate on issues. Line up supporting speakers, and conduct a unified convention. But what's good for the individual candidate isn't necessarily healthy for either the whole party, or the whole nation.

The Regional Lottery Plan
America's Missing Constitutional Link

Larry J. Sabato

. . . In so many respects, today's political system is broken, and there is currently no reasonable prospect of fixing it. Our schedule of presidential primaries and caucuses is a front-loaded mess, and the Congress, the parties, and the states refuse seriously to tackle its reform. The Democrats are currently tinkering at the edges of reform, just as the Republicans attempted to do in prior years, but little will come of it because of the powerful interests with heavy investments in the status quo. . . .

Imagine that a convention of clowns met to design an amusing, crazy-quilt schedule to nominate presidential candidates. The resulting system would probably look much as ours does today. The incoherent organization of primaries and caucuses, and the candidates' mad-dash attempts to move around the map, would be funny if the goal—electing the leader of the free world—weren't so serious. . . .

Few want to go back to the bad old days when party "bosses" chose presidential candidates in smoke-filled rooms. (Yes, the bosses did well by selecting

Larry J. Sabato is professor of political science at the University of Virginia. Excerpted from "America's Missing Constitutional Link," *The Virginia Quarterly Review*, Summer 2006, pp. 149–161. Reprinted with author's permission.

nominees such as Franklin Roosevelt, but they also picked the disastrous Warren G. Harding.) Primaries and caucuses are now fundamental to our conception of popular democracy in presidential selection. But there is such a thing as too much popular democracy, if it is hopelessly disorganized. . . .

Without a constitutional answer, there is simply no remedy to a situation that deteriorates every four years. Try as they might, the political parties cannot orchestrate a fix. In the end, they can only punish a recalcitrant Iowa and New Hampshire in minor ways, perhaps by cutting the size of their convention delegations or giving the delegates bad hotels and poor seating at the party conclaves. And that assumes the national parties have the will to do anything. After all, Iowa and New Hampshire are in catbird seats since both are now swing states in the November 2008 presidential election, and their collective twelve electoral votes can easily be the difference between victory and defeat in this closely divided era.

In addition, Congress arguably has no effective power to intervene in a state-based, party-centered nominating process, and even if the courts held that it did, Congress would be highly unlikely to step into that briar patch. The senators and representatives from Iowa and New Hampshire would be willing to do anything to stop reform, quite possibly with assistance from colleagues who would see their own presidential ambitions at stake. A senator who becomes a hero in Iowa and New Hampshire for saving the caucus and primary would be halfway to a presidential nomination! And realizing this, most or all of the senators with presidential aspirations would jump to back the Iowa/New Hampshire status quo—and it's a rare senator who doesn't get up in the morning and see a president in the mirror.

No, the only possible, comprehensive answer is a constitutional one. In the twenty-first century we the people need to do what the Founders didn't even consider doing in their pre-party, pre-popular-democracy age. The guiding principle should be one that all citizens, in theory, can readily embrace: Every state and region ought to have essentially an equal chance, over time, to influence the outcome of the parties' presidential nominations, and thus the selection of presidents. Why should two small, heavily white, disproportionately rural states have a hammerlock on the making of the president? Together, Iowa and New Hampshire are a mere 1.4 percent of the US population, and about 40 percent of their residents are rural—double the national proportion. Their average population of African Americans *and* Hispanics/Latinos is 3.6 percent, while the nation as a whole is 24.6 percent minority. Even if one assumes, incorrectly, that the two states are somehow representative of their Northeast and Midwest regions, the South and West (containing 55 percent of the country's people) are left entirely out of the critical opening window of presidential selection. . . .

There have been dozens of proposals to revamp the primary scheme, though none has been offered as a constitutional fix. Clearly, that is because the Constitution currently ignores the politics of the system almost entirely and because a constitutional insertion—virtually written in stone—would have to be as fair and foolproof as possible. Submitted for your consideration is the Regional Lottery Plan, which this author has tinkered with for many years in his ivory tower.

THE REGIONAL LOTTERY PLAN FOR THE NEW CONSTITUTION

The Congress should be constitutionally required to designate four regions of contiguous states (with contiguity waved for Alaska and Hawaii, and any other stray territories that might one day become states). The regions would surely look something like the ones on the [accompanying] map . . . , with natural boundaries denoting the Northeast, South, Midwest, and West. These regions have about the same number of states: Northeast (twelve states plus DC), South (thirteen states), Midwest (twelve states), West (thirteen states). All of the states in each region will hold their nominating events in successive months, beginning in April and ending in July. The two major-party conventions would follow in August. This schedule, all by itself, would cut three months off the too-long process currently prevailing in presidential years.

The presidential nominating system would still be state-based, so each state would be free to choose any date it wished within the region's month, and further, it would be free, as currently, to choose either the primary or the caucus method of selecting delegates. Of course, it is possible that all the states in a region will try to front-load their contests on the first possible day, but that actually makes little sense, except perhaps for the first region in the series. Even in that first region, a state may have more influence coming later in the month, perhaps standing alone on a particular day—a situation that will encourage presidential candidates to spend time and money in the stand-alone state. After all, the postprimary headlines will belong solely to the candidate who wins that stand-alone state. If there are ten states on a particular day, the headlines as well as the candidates' time and money will be split ten ways. Note, too, that the regional system concentrates the candidates within a single region for a month. They will have a better opportunity to get to know the problems and peoples of the region and its states, and the geographic proximity of the campaigning will cut down on the wear and tear on the candidates, to some degree anyway.

But how would the order of the regions be determined? In many cases, there would still be a bonus in going first. The establishment of a US Election Lottery, to be held on New Year's Day of the presidential election year, is the answer that yields fairness and adds an element of excitement to the beginning of a presidential year. One of the nation's famous lottery machines with the pop-up Ping-Pong balls will finally find a purpose beyond bestowing untold riches on people who can't handle it. Four color-coded balls, each representing one of the regions, will be loaded into the machine, and in short order—the length of a TV lottery drawing—the regional primary order will be set. Since none of the candidates would know in advance where the political season would begin, part of the permanent presidential campaign would be dismantled. Even a very wealthy candidate wouldn't waste the money necessary to organize all fifty states in advance, and the four-year-long homesteading in Iowa and New Hampshire would be gone forever. Much more importantly, the law of averages would give every state and each region, over time, the precious opportunity of going first.

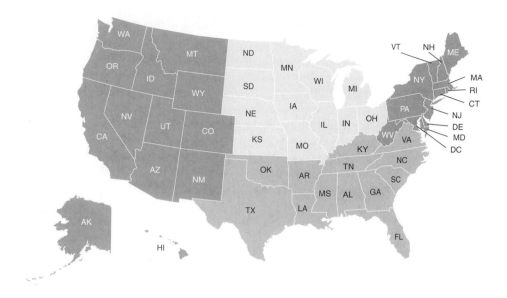

The new constitutional provisions would repeal the nonexistent *right to go first* that Iowa and New Hampshire have appropriated for themselves.

Another benefit of the Regional Lottery Plan would be the reasonable spacing between contests, potentially allowing candidates to recover from setbacks in one region and to regroup for the next set of contests. Today's front-loading nearly ensures that the entire competition for the party nominations is over within a few weeks, whereas under the lottery plan, regional pride and loyalties might demand that the race continue through two or three, and maybe all four, sections of the nation. The press and voters in each region would certainly agree on this critical matter, demanding their fair share of attention.

In order to enhance its effectiveness, one additional element should be added to the lottery plan. Even though the four regions have their usefulness as voting divisions, the United States is a continental country, and each region is still large and expensive for any candidate's travel and advertising. Personal campaigning would be diminished, compared to what now happens in Iowa and New Hampshire. Therefore, it would be appropriate to add a second lottery on January 1. The names of all states with four or fewer members of the US House of Representatives (at present, twenty states) would be placed in a lottery machine, and two balls would be selected; I exclude the island territories, which are far-flung and irrelevant to the November presidential outcome, since they have no electoral votes. The District of Columbia, with three electoral votes, *should* be included, however, and this would mean twenty-one jurisdictions would have a chance to be selected in the second lottery. The two small states (or DC) with relatively low populations would precede the regional contests and be held on or about March 15—at least two full weeks before the initial contests would begin in the first region. These two states would be free to stage a primary or a caucus, and the candidates would be free to participate in one, both, or neither. As a practical matter, most candidates would choose both, unless a prominent candidate hailed from one of the leadoff states. Traditionally, a home candidate is deferred to and nearly unopposed for the state's delegate votes. Of course, the other party can still have a full-fledged fight in the state's primary or caucus.

No doubt, all the candidates would rush to these leadoff states right after the lottery on January 1, and they would have two and a half months to campaign. But there would again be no permanent, four-year campaigns there, and personalized, one-to-one campaigning would be a large part of the effort. In other words, the two states would offer all the advantages of Iowa and New Hampshire, *without having to always be Iowa and New Hampshire*. Additionally, the guarantee of at least two weeks of decompression after the leadoff states gives voters in the first region a chance to evaluate the results and reevaluate the winners—and possibly to make different choices. The present eight-day window between the Iowa caucus and the New Hampshire primary often creates unstoppable, unthinking momentum for the winner of Iowa, and a double winner of Iowa and New Hampshire is practically crowned the party's presidential nominee before any of the other forty-eight states have their say. Under the new plan, this would no longer be likely given the non-front-loaded, rationally spaced, regional primary system.

In sum, the Regional Lottery Plan will achieve simultaneously many good things for a selection process that currently makes little sense. The election campaign will be shortened and focused, a relief both to candidates and to voters. All regions and states will get an opportunity to have a substantial impact on the making of the presidential nominees. A rational, nicely arranged schedule will build excitement and citizen involvement everywhere in the country, without sacrificing the personalized scrutiny of candidates for which Iowa and New Hampshire have become justly known. And all of this can *only* come about by putting politics in its proper place—in the American Constitution.

The Electoral College

No feature of the U.S. Constitution has been the subject of more constitutional amendments than the Electoral College. The primary impetus behind these proposals has been to correct what is widely regarded as the fundamental flaw of the Electoral College: the possibility that candidates with fewer popular votes than their opponents can be elected president. This outcome has been visited upon the United States three times (excluding the 1824 election decided by the House). The most recent "misfiring" of the Electoral College occurred in the 2000 presidential election, in which Vice President Al Gore outran George W. Bush by more than half a million votes nationwide, while losing to Bush by five votes (271–266) in the Electoral College. That outcome renewed the debate.

In the first selection, John R. Koza proposes a solution that has been adopted by the state of Maryland and is being seriously considered in several other states. According to Koza, his plan would ensure that the winner of the national popular vote would be elected president, and it would do so without having to change the Constitution. He argues, moreover, that this change would at long last make all votes count equally in presidential elections and compel candidates to campaign nationwide, rather than ignoring most of the states as they do now.

Political scientist Robert Weissberg, author of the second selection, is dismissive of Koza's proposed cure for the ills of the Electoral College, objecting to the means of achieving it as well as to the plan itself. As to means, he insists that a constitutional amendment, not state law, is the appropriate mechanism for making such a sweeping change. As for the plan, he warns that its adoption could have unpredictable consequences, including disagreements on how to define a "majority," endless delays in determining a winner, loss of accountability, and the overturning of state popular majorities.

A State-Based Plan for Electing the President by National Popular Vote

John R. Koza

In elections for President of the United States, every person's vote should be equally important, regardless of the state in which the vote is cast. The presidential candidate who receives the most popular votes throughout the country should win that office. The current system does not satisfy these principles.

The major shortcoming of the current system is that the voters in two-thirds of the states are ignored by presidential campaigns. Because all of a state's electoral votes are awarded to the candidate winning the state, neither presidential candidate bothers to poll, visit, organize, or advertise in a state that is heavily predisposed toward one political party or the other. Instead, candidates concentrate their attention on a handful of closely divided battleground states, where active campaigning can swing an iffy bloc of electoral votes.

In 2004, candidates concentrated over two-thirds of their advertising and campaign visits in a mere five closely divided "battleground" states, and over 99 percent of their advertising in just 16 states. Seven of the nation's 11 most populous states (including California), 12 of the 13 least populous states, and most of the other states are mere spectators in presidential elections.

It isn't a matter of whether babies in California and 33 other spectator states get kissed by traveling presidential candidates, but that the candidates concentrate their policy attention on issues of concern to the voters of the battleground states, while ignoring issues of concern to voters in two-thirds of the states. Thus, Iowa's ethanol regularly receives outsized attention in presidential campaigns, whereas California's issues do not. Issues that are ignored during a presidential campaign generally continue to be ignored during the entire life of an Administration, because the incumbent's reelection depends on the battleground states, not the spectator states.

A second shortcoming of the current system is that a candidate can win the Presidency without winning the most popular votes nationwide. The winning candidate did not receive the most popular votes nationwide in 1824, 1876, 1888, and 2000. In the past six decades, there have been six presidential elections in

John R. Koza is a consulting professor in the Department of Medicine and the Department of Engineering at Stanford University. He is coauthor of *Every Vote Equal: A State-Based Plan for Electing the President by National Popular Vote* (National Popular Vote Press, 2006). This article may be accessed at http://rangevoting.org/kozaarticle.html. Reprinted with the author's permission.

which a shift of a relatively small number of votes in one or two states would have elected a presidential candidate who lost the popular vote nationwide. A shift of 60,000 votes in Ohio in 2004 would have given the Presidency to John Kerry, even though President Bush had a 3,500,000-vote lead nationwide.

The United States can have nationwide popular election of the President if states amend their state election laws to make the Electoral College reflect the voters' nationwide choice—instead of the voters' state-by-state choices. The California Legislature has just passed legislation to this effect (originally sponsored by Tom Umberg, John Laird, and Merv Dymally). Governor Schwarzenegger has until September 30 to act on this bill.

Under [The National Popular Vote bill], each state would award its electoral votes to the presidential candidate receiving the most votes in all 50 states and the District of Columbia. The bill would only come into effect when identical legislation is enacted by states representing a majority of the people of the country (that is, states possessing a majority of 270 of the 538 electoral votes). These identical state laws would guarantee that the presidential candidate with the most votes nationwide would receive enough electoral votes to win the Presidency. This proposed state-level approach (called an interstate compact) offers a politically practical and constitutional way to achieve what 70 percent of the people have long wanted—nationwide popular election of the President.

Although it is sometimes argued that least populous states benefit from the current system, a national popular vote for President would be especially advantageous to the small states. Twelve of the 13 smallest states are not politically competitive in presidential elections. These states together have 11 million people. In comparison, Ohio has 11 million people and 20 electoral votes. Because of the two-vote bonus that all states receive in the Electoral College, these 12 small states together possess a seemingly impressive 40 electoral votes—twice Ohio's. However, the winner-take-all rule makes Ohio the center of attention in presidential campaigns, while the noncompetitive small states receive almost no polling, visits, advertising, organizing, or policy attention. A national popular vote for President would make the small states' 11 million people as important as Ohio's 11 million.

Some believe that the Republican Party benefits from the small states. However, in the past five presidential elections, six of the smallest states regularly voted Republican (Alaska, Idaho, Montana, Wyoming, North Dakota, and South Dakota); six regularly voted Democratic (Rhode Island, Delaware, Hawaii, Vermont, Maine, and D.C.); and New Hampshire has been a battleground. Even though Kerry lost the popular vote in the 13 smallest states by 2.5 million to 2.7 million, Kerry won 25 electoral votes to Bush's 19—hardly a Republican advantage.

Some speculate that candidates would only pay attention to big cities under a nationwide vote. Contrary evidence comes from the way presidential candidates presently campaign inside the closely divided battleground states, such as Ohio or Florida. Because every vote is equal inside battleground states, presidential candidates avidly seek out voters in small, medium, and large towns. The big cities do not receive all the attention, and Cleveland and Miami certainly do not control the outcome. Indeed, suburbs and rural areas account for about three-quarters of the voters in these states as well as nationally. Similarly, national advertisers do not write off a state merely because a competitor has a 10 percent edge in sales. The leading company does not abandon a state merely because it already has a lead. Instead, both go after every single possible customer.

Under the National Popular Vote bill, neither Democrats nor Republicans could afford to ignore the concerns and interests of voters in California and the numerous other spectator states. States should take advantage of the power they possess under the Constitution and reform the Electoral College so that it reflects the will of the voters on a nationwide basis.

Arnold: Terminate This Gimmick

Robert Weissberg

One of these years an entrepreneurial political junkie will endow the "Wondrous Civic Reforms Gone Awry" museum. It would fill a city block, offer a glitzy gift shop, and have numerous special exhibits, for example, "Today's Cure Is Tomorrow's Villain" (e.g., the poll tax, disenfranchising felons, the long ballot), "It Sounded Perfect at the Time" (e.g., paperless electronic voting, term limits, the FCC's equal-time provision, same-day registration), and "The Cure Is Worse Than the Disease" (e.g., campaign finance reform to reduce electioneering costs, endless primaries, eviscerating political parties). Should it be enacted, Koza's proposal for direct presidential election by having state legislatures reverse their states' popular vote will warrant an exhibit hall. Potential visitors might be forewarned that displays "may be unsuitable for the faint-hearted."

All proposals for reform entail a vision of an allegedly defective status quo. Koza claims that in the United States every vote should be of equal importance regardless of one's residence, and that our current presidential voting arrangement, sadly, fails this requirement. This is a normative—an "ought"—proposition derived from some hazy democratic theory, and as a political dictate it enjoys no

Robert Weissberg is a policy advisor to the Heartland Institute and emeritus professor of political science at the University of Illinois at Urbana-Champaign. This article was written specifically for this edition of *Points of View*.

special legal or historical standing. It is just *his* personal opinion. Many would reasonably insist that inequality remains part of the federal system. This prescription is not any different from other lofty "democratic" essentials—i.e., voters should be informed, elections should be fair, politicians should be honest, and newspapers should be unbiased, among dozens of possibilities. The Founders rejected majority rule as the overarching governance principle (e.g., the structure of the U.S. Senate and numerous super-majority requirements in our Constitution), and to argue that strict uniformity of voter influence somehow defines democracy betrays a simplistic—if naive—grasp of democracy.

More important, this equality can be accomplished via a constitutional amendment if Congress and the states deem it wise, and other than some post-2000 presidential election grumbling, scant support exists for a majority popular vote rule system. The constitutional route—not stealthy politicking in a few accommodating legislatures—is the appropriate pathway. Altering our electoral structure via amendment has been executed on several occasions—the 12th, 15th, 17th, 18th, 22nd, 23rd, 24th, and 26th Amendments all revised our election process—so it is bizarre to insist that constitutional mechanisms are too clumsy or that some pressing national emergency requires immediate action. Besides, reform via the Constitution would permit a full and careful *national* debate, something unlikely to occur with just-below-the radar state legislative measures. If indeed, as Koza claims, 70 percent of the public truly wants direct presidential election, one can only wonder why artful panderers fail to exploit this demand for selfish career gains.

What about Koza's argument that unequal Electoral College votes, compounded by the winner-takes-all system (save in two states), means that voters in two-thirds of states are "ignored" by today's presidential candidates? Koza, for example, speaks of candidates personally fawning over Iowa's voters by pledging to step up ethanol production, surely an economic benefit to a corn-producing state. But, since tax subsidies apply regardless of where corn grows, voters everywhere potentially benefiting from ethanol probably follow these "local" appeals. A vigorous pro-environmental address in media-rich downtown Manhattan may, in fact, be more carefully heeded in Alaska and other wilderness areas, and this is exactly the intent.

More generally, today's highly nationalized mass media make "kissing babies" localism obsolete even though it lingers as part of our civic folklore. "Pressing the flesh" now largely consists of network news accounts of candidates shaking a few hands. Like William McKinley, who conducted his 1896 presidential campaign entirely from his front porch, a modern candidate can reach every citizen, everywhere, without leaving home, and with clever marketing, this can be as folksy "personal" as New York Mayor Fiorello La Guardia reading the funny pages over WNYC radio during the city's newspaper strike. Think of You Tube and other modern "personal" interactive tactics. As for the quaint notion that it is "good" for presidential candidates to visit every state, this is electoral suicide. Richard Nixon in 1960, honoring his promise to do exactly that, flew to Alaska on election eve while John F. Kennedy rallied the troops in key, oft-visited battleground states, and these votes were decisive.

An adviser who suggested this frenzied course would soon be fired—this is a "Go duck hunting among the geese" strategy.

Even if a system rewarded showering attention on voters in every state, this is a recipe for personal exhaustion (if not delirium), huge expense, and pointlessly building organizations to facilitate this manic activity. Sensible grumbling already exists about the "permanent campaign," and a candidate who "personally paid attention to everyone, not just those in key states" (Koza) could do little else other than campaign 24/7. How expensive hyper-*physical* activity (not just broadcasting commercials nationally) enriches "democracy" is uncertain though it will surely enrich consultants, local media, and others feeding off what will be America's first billion-dollar election. Never-ending helter-skelter campaigning will also fatigue the electorate, so that by the time Election Day arrives, voters will be comatose. After several such sleep-inducing marathons, reformers will doubtless propose *limiting* electioneering to a British-style six weeks to sustain excitement and thereby heighten turnout and this, in turn, would necessitate concentrating on only a few key states.

As for the "flaw" of a president elected by pluralities or even losing the popular vote, this is nothing more than rounding up the usual suspects to damn the Electoral College. Elections, like football games, are fought under existing rules, and altering these rules retrospectively will *always* produce different outcomes. To claim that Gore "really" won in 2000 is the equivalent of asserting that one's football team "really" won, despite scoring fewer points, since they outgained their opponents in total yards or some other irrelevant statistic.

Consider the possible legitimacy of this "interstate compact" end-run around the Constitution. A plethora of election systems exist among today's certifiable democratic regimes, from sundry proportional representational (PR) formulas to far simpler single-member district, first-past-the-post American-style arrangements. These survive if judged legitimate—legally valid and psychologically accepted—by the populace. Substantial change thus imposes heavy burdens since participants must grasp the mechanics and, critically, accept the "new" outcome as "fair." This is not as straightforward as it might appear. Americans might be uncomfortable with a European PR list system that precludes selecting individual candidates. Europeans, on the other hand, often belittle our antiquated free-for-all system.

This interstate compact scheme opens the door to nonstop confusion, litigation, and outcomes reflecting unanticipated events. All of these undermine legitimacy, no small cost given that the present system (admitted warts and all) does yield accepted outcomes. Consider what appears to be self-evident: Who won the popular vote? Suppose, as is often the case, that the "victorious" presidential candidate receives less than an absolute majority, thanks to several small parties (1948, 1968, 1992, 1996, and 2000, for instance). Further assume, as was certainly true in 2000, that voters for these third parties might "reasonably" be understood to favor one of the two candidates lacking the absolute majority—i.e., Nader voters generally preferring Gore over Bush. Do state legislatures award their states' Electoral College votes to the statistical winner though he or she lacks a clear majority, or do they become savvy mind readers and choose electors for the "real" winner who may trail the statistical winner by a few votes?

Needless to say, the partisan composition of the state legislature, not some fixed, agreed upon in advance clear-cut rules, may be decisive. Perhaps second choices should be elicited at voting time or, absent that possibility, dubious public opinion polls regarding ideological proximity may suffice in such situations. Circumstances could easily resemble what transpired in 2000 when the courts wrestled with sundry interpretative questions (e.g., should "double voting" be invalidated even though the voter's intention was obvious), though now under the Koza plan battles are to be fought in multiple state legislatures, largely in secret, with all the predictable horse-trading. Much depends on arcane provisions imbedded in these interstate compacts, and consequently the electorate's "final decision" may be unknown for months as armies of lawyers swarm across thirty or more legislatures. Challenges may entail not only disputing interpretations of "majority winner" but taking the entire interstate compact system into court, perhaps arguing that by reversing their states' popular vote outcomes, state legislatures are violating the 14th Amendment's equal protection of the laws. Who knows? The final result might be victory by clever litigation, hardly a "democratic" triumph.

And what legislatures bestow, they can revoke. The presidential election is not concluded when TV pundits declare the winner; rather, only when the Senate president says so some two months later is the tally official (Article II, section 1). What if a state changes its mind in the interim? For example, what if a Republican-dominated state legislature decides to honor its state's popular majority by revoking the compact so as to give the GOP candidate a victory? That is, rules are altered *after* the game seems over, and this would be legal! This reversal could also be executed by unaccountable state or federal judges, and the prospect of this gamesmanship can add troubling uncertainty to a process whose legitimacy requires ironclad rules. This would be government by judiciary, not popular rule.

Moreover, as would be true for any direct election scheme, quarrels over the precise vote count would plague thousands of jurisdictions, not just, say, a suspicious Florida or Ohio county. This, in turn, would encourage prior partisan scrutiny of literally tens of thousands of polling places to stop fraud or shield one's own cheating. Yet again, the acrimony that plagued Florida during 2000 may now become standard and generate bitter charges of "stolen" elections.

But leave aside for the moment likely months of inconclusiveness and the possible need for an interim president. How is the public, long acquainted with Ye Olde Dumb-as-Rocks Electoral College system, to react to states reversing popular majorities in the name of some murky "fairness"? Imagine a Democratic candidate winning a huge majority in California only to see the state's Electoral College votes awarded to the GOP candidate who wins the national popular vote? No doubt, hoards of professors will have to be mobilized to explain that this "restores true democracy" to American politics. A few unsophisticated Californian Democrats might reasonably ask why they voted in the first place since it made no difference. This concoction has just too many moving parts to satisfy those accustomed to the old system.

Now for the bottom line. This supposed "reform," like nearly all reforms, artfully disguises a partisan agenda. I suspect, though I cannot prove, that Democrats champion this restructuring since they anticipate—perhaps thanks to Hispanic immigration—a swelling of future supporters in states where they already dominate, e.g., California, New York, New Jersey, Illinois. But since the present arrangement counts only victory in a state and disregards margin, these "extra" Democratic votes are wasted. The ideal would be to transfer these "surplus" Blue votes to Red states and turn the tide there, but since this is legally impossible, the surplus can be made "to count" in these Red states via interstate compacts. In other words, half a million extra California Democratic votes "wipes out" smaller GOP victories in a dozen or more less populous Red states.

Over and above all the problems we have elicited, this is an uncertain ploy. Such schemes often backfire as circumstances shift and often produce next year's problem to be reformed. We can only advise the California governor (and others contemplating this measure) to just say "no." Or as the Terminator would put it, "*Hasta la vista*, Baby."

mhhe.com/diclerico11e

Internet resources
Visit our Web site at www.mhhe.com/diclerico11e for links and resources relating to Elections.

chapter 8

Political Parties

O*ver the course of our nation's history, the political process has periodically experienced the equivalent of a political earthquake, whereby the reigning majority party in the electorate is replaced by a newly dominant party. This party then runs with the ball until finally losing its appeal and the other party returns to power. Referred to as "political realignments," such events occurred in 1800, 1828, 1896, and 1932, suggesting to some that they were likely to happen every thirty-two to thirty-six years.*

The Republican Party has dominated politics in America for roughly a dozen years, controlling the foreign and domestic agendas of the country since 1995. Moreover, at the conclusion of President George W. Bush's second term in 2008, the Republican Party will have held the White House for twenty-eight out of the last forty years. Thus, it is not an overstatement to suggest that the nation's politics have been controlled, though not exclusively so, by the Republican Party for more than a quarter of a century.

The continuation of Republican Party domination of politics may now be in doubt, however. Reaction to the Iraq War has caused major divisions within the electorate, and the popularity of President George W. Bush declined precipitously in the second term. Moreover, the Democratic Party emerged victorious in the 2006 midterm elections, capturing control of both houses of Congress as well as increasing the number of governorships and statehouses controlled by Democrats. All of those circumstances raise the question: Is the Republican Party era drawing to a close?

In the following two selections, political commentators Ross Douthat, John Judis, and Ruy Teixeira assess what the future holds for the two parties. Douthat, of The Atlantic *magazine, speculates that although George W. Bush will be leaving office, his legacy may be sufficiently robust to blunt a major Democratic realignment. According to Douthat, Bush's moralism in foreign and domestic policy has so permeated the base of the Republican Party, and indeed a sizable portion of the entire nation as well, that it will continue and perhaps be strengthened in years to come, especially in the absence of the unpopular George Bush himself.*

John Judis and Ruy Teixeira, writing in the magazine The American Prospect, *see a different future. Building on their 2002 book,* The Emerging Democratic Majority, *they argue that the 2006 election provides even further evidence of a shift in America's politics from the conservative, right-based Republican Party to center-left politics represented by the Democrats. Judis and Teixeira base their conclusion partially on demographics—the emergence in the electorate of women, working professionals, and minorities, especially Latinos, as major groups tending to vote Democratic—and on shifts in public opinion on some major issues, including the Iraq War, the economy, national security, and social issues such as abortion and the role of religion in public life. The outcome of the election of 2008 will, no doubt, go a long way toward confirming the extent to which the United States is experiencing yet another political realignment.*

It's His Party
Bush Republicanism Is Here to Stay

Ross Douthat

It's become fashionable to draw comparisons between George W. Bush's sins and those of Richard Nixon, and for good reason. Both presidents are likely to be remembered as polarizing figures who left the country more divided than they found it. Both were accused of wartime deceptions; both also lost their way in disastrous second terms. And both men's blunders, as Jonathan Rauch argued in [*The Atlantic*] last fall ("Unwinding Bush," October 2006), are the sort that could take decades to undo.

Bush may resemble his disgraced predecessor in another way as well. When Nixon left office, his attempt to create a conservative majority by drawing blue-collar voters into the GOP through appeals to patriotism and law-and-order seemed to have been killed off by Watergate. As it turned out, however, the working-class conservatism he summoned up has continued to dominate American politics, shaping the campaigns of Ronald Reagan and the second Bush himself.

Since the Republicans' stinging defeat in the 2006 midterm elections, Bush's distinctive ideological cocktail—social conservatism and an accommodation with big government at home, and a moralistic interventionism abroad—has similarly been derided by many as political poison. The various ingredients of "Bushism," it's been argued, have alienated fiscal hawks and foreign-policy realists, Catholics and libertarians—in short, everyone but the party's evangelical base.

But someone must have forgotten to tell the GOP presidential field. If you consider how the nation's most ambitious Republicans are positioning themselves for 2008, Bushism looks like it could have surprising staying power.

All of the prominent candidates, for instance, champion fiscal restraint, but none are likely to revive the small-government conservatism that Bush deliberately abandoned. John McCain may be a vehement foe of pork, but on issues ranging from campaign finance to education, he has shown little aversion to expanding the scope of federal power. Mitt Romney is best known for having delivered universal health care to Massachusetts, the bluest state in the union.

Ross Douthat is an associate editor of *The Atlantic* magazine. Reprinted from "It's His Party," *The Atlantic*, March 2007, pp. 21–22. Reprinted with permission of the author.

And Sam Brownback has supported nearly every one of Bush's big-government gambits, from the faith-based initiative to the costly prescription-drug entitlement. Newt Gingrich might seem a plausible advocate for small government—except that his recent manifesto, *Winning the Future*, includes more spending proposals than specific budget cuts.

The Bush-imitating pattern also holds in foreign policy. McCain talks tougher than Bush about Iran; Gingrich waxes eloquent about a third world war; Rudy Giuliani takes a maximalist view of the war on terrorism, casting it as a decades-long struggle that dates to Munich in 1972. Save for Brownback, all of the major contenders backed Bush's call for a "surge" of troops into Iraq—and Brownback has been more aggressive and moralistic than Bush on humanitarian issues like Darfur.

And although Brownback is the only candidate in the field so far with Bush's personal connection to the party's religious conservatives, everyone—even McCain, even Giuliani—is actively courting them. This is partly because without evangelical Christians, there would essentially *be* no Republican Party anymore: Evangelicals provided more votes to the Republicans in 2006's midterms than African Americans and union members combined gave to the Democrats. Their influence within the party more or less requires that primary candidates endorse Bush-style moralism, not only on gay marriage and abortion but in foreign policy as well—which means continued support for Israel, a continued drift toward confrontation with Iran, and further ventures in conservative humanitarianism, along the lines of Bush's AIDS-in-Africa initiative.

But the Republican candidates have another reason for giving Bushism a second act: It has more potential to appeal to the broad electorate than other visions of where the GOP should go from here. The enduring popularity of the welfare state makes big-government conservatism far more palatable to voters than the government-cutting purism that Bush's right-wing critics hope to revive. (In the long run, the country may be forced to choose between keeping spending high and keeping taxes low; in the short term, though, the deficits Bush has run up are not the public's first priority.) Similarly, although the Iraq War is likely to be an albatross for the Republican Party for years to come, the rest of Bush's national-security vision—from opposing Iran to pushing domestic measures like the PATRIOT Act—could still command widespread support.

On "values" issues, the picture is more complicated. There's no question that the GOP alienated moderate voters in episodes such as the Terri Schiavo case. On the other hand, opposition to gay marriage and abortion are usually political winners for the Republicans (although this could change as tolerance for homosexuality spreads, or if *Roe v. Wade* is overturned). And the GOP benefits significantly from being cast as the party of religious faith. Despite six years of liberal panic over the specter of a U.S. theocracy, only 29 percent of the public thinks that religion has too much influence in American politics, and almost 80 percent believes that the courts have gone too far in purging religion from the public square. Keeping the party's socially conservative base happy without losing the country's religious middle is a challenge, but Bush met it successfully across three election cycles.

It's those elections, ultimately, that are the most important reason Bushism is likely to endure, at least as a pole star for Republican strategy: the strong showing in 2000, when nearly every economic indicator suggested a landslide for Al Gore; the sweeping win in 2002—an off-year election, when the sitting president's party historically loses seats; and the victory over John Kerry in 2004, despite plummeting public support for the Iraq War. While journalists and historians debate where Bush went wrong, Republicans are likely to spend the next decade trying to imitate his successes.

It's possible, of course, that the deep unpopularity of the Iraq War could drag the rest of Bushism down with it, as could the fiscal mess created by the administration's tax cuts. But predictions of the conservative majority's demise are premature. Bush-style conservatism probably won't create a thirty-year Republican realignment, as Karl Rove once hoped, but it has the potential to at least keep the GOP politically competitive.

The perpetuation of Bushism would likely mean that some of today's most acrimonious debates will persist—the culture-war shouting matches, for instance, or the growing "Who lost Iraq?" controversy. And it would probably mean that neither party will grapple seriously with the country's fiscal imbalance, at least until the entitlement crunch puts their backs against the wall.

But a continuation of Bushism might also create areas of bipartisan consensus. For instance, evangelicals and liberal internationalists might come together on the use of force for humanitarian ends overseas. Big-government conservatives and populist liberals might agree on the need to address the financial insecurity of working-class families. Indeed, as in the Nixon era, it's possible that what has made the last six years so polarizing isn't the president's ideology but the president himself—his tongue-tied speeches and lack of interest in policy detail, his mix of incompetence and abrasive self-assurance, his cronyism and disdain for compromise. Once Bush has been ushered offstage, a Republican Party fashioned in his image could actually help unite the country, as Bush-the-candidate famously promised to do, rather than divide it.

Back to the Future
The Re-emergence of the Emerging Democratic Majority
John B. Judis and Ruy Teixeira

As conservative Republicans tell the tale, the 2006 election was merely a referendum on the Bush administration's incompetence in Iraq and New Orleans and on the Republican congressional scandals. . . .

We take a different view: that this election signals the end of a fleeting Republican revival, prompted by the Bush administration's response to the September 11 terrorist attacks, and the return to political and demographic trends that were leading to a Democratic and center-left majority in the United States. In 2006 the turn to the Democrats went well beyond those offices directly concerned with the war in Iraq or affected by congressional scandals. While Democrats picked up 30 House seats and six Senate seats, they also won six governorships, netted 321 state legislative seats, and recaptured legislative chambers in eight states. That's the kind of sweep that Republicans enjoyed in 1994, which led to Republican control of Congress and of the nation's statehouses for the remainder of the decade.

Just as important as these victories is *who* voted for Democrats in 2006. With few exceptions, the groups were exactly those that had begun trending Democratic in the 1990s and had contributed to Al Gore's popular-vote victory over George W. Bush in 2000. These groups, which we described in our 2002 book, *The Emerging Democratic Majority*, included women, professionals, and minorities. But in 2006 they also included two groups our book slighted or ignored altogether: younger voters (those born after 1977) and independents. These voters can generally be expected to continue backing Democrats.

Finally, the 2006 election represented a shift in American politics, away from the right and toward the center-left, on a range of issues that go well beyond the Iraq war, corruption, and competence. Voters in 2006 returned to viewpoints on the economy and society that inclined them, even leaving aside the war, to favor Democrats over conservative Republicans. To understand how this could happen, and happen so suddenly, one has to appreciate the peculiar impact that September 11 had on what had been an emerging Democratic

John B. Judis is a senior editor of *The New Republic*, and Ruy Teixeira is a senior fellow at the Century Foundation and the Center for American Progress. They are coauthors of *The Emerging Democratic Majority* (2002). From "Back to the Future: The Re-Emergence of the Emerging Democratic Majority," *The American Prospect*, July/August 2007, pp. 12–18. Reprinted with permission of John Judis.

majority, and how, once the impact of that event dissipated, the earlier trends reasserted themselves with a vengeance.

I. THE DEMOCRATIC EQUATION

In the 1990s the Democrats displayed the outlines of a new majority that would be different from the older, New Deal majority. The older majority had been based on the "Solid South," blue-collar workers, ethnics, and rural voters; the new would combine women voters, professionals, and minorities, primarily in the North, Midwest, and far West, with close to an even split of the traditional white working-class vote in those regions. Some of the groups making up the new majority were recent converts; others had gone from the edges to the center of the coalition.

- **Women:** Throughout the 1960s, women voters had been disproportionately Republican; but in 1980 (partly in reaction to the Republican identification with the religious right) single, working, and college-educated women began voting disproportionately Democratic. In the 2000 congressional elections, for instance, single women backed Democrats by 63 percent to 35 percent.
- **Professionals:** Professionals, who are, roughly speaking, college-educated producers of services and ideas, used to be the most staunchly Republican of all occupational groups. In the 1960 presidential election, they backed Richard Nixon by 61 percent to 38 percent. But in the 1980s these voters— now chiefly working for large corporations and bureaucracies rather than on their own, and heavily influenced by the environmental, civil-rights, and feminist movements—began to vote Democratic. In the four elections from 1988 to 2000, they backed Democrats by an average of 52 percent to 40 percent.
- **Minorities:** Latinos had been voting Democratic since the New Deal, and blacks since the 1960s; but in the 1990s they were joined by Asian-American voters. In the congressional race in 2000, minorities, who now made up about 19 percent of electorate, backed Democrats by 75 percent to 23 percent.

These groups have different, and sometimes conflicting, political outlooks. Professionals, for instance, are generally skeptical of large government spending programs, which minorities are inclined to support. They also are leery of tax increases, even those aimed at the wealthy. College-educated and single women often fervently back abortion rights and gay rights, both of which many black and Hispanic voters oppose. But in national elections, and in state elections in the Northeast and far West, the socially liberal and fiscally moderate views of the professionals have generally taken precedence. These "new Democratic" or "moderate" politics were at the heart of Democratic victories in the 1990s.

In states like California and New Jersey, these three overlapping and burgeoning groups, rather than the white working class, dominate the electorate. In California, for example, the white working class constitutes only 38 percent of voters. But in many Midwestern and Southern states, white working-class (non-college-educated) voters still dominate. In those states, the Democratic coalition is a sometimes-combustible mixture of old and new, including adherents of social liberalism and of New Deal and fair-trade economics. As long-term economic trends toward a postindustrial economy grow stronger, the white working class, in these states, and nationally, will shrink at the expense of professionals and minorities. But the Democrats have needed and will continue to need significant levels of white working-class support to supplement the newer parts of their coalition. Right now, Democrats need to win between 45 percent and 48 percent of the white working-class vote to carry states like Missouri, Ohio, or Pennsylvania, a little higher for Iowa, and higher still for West Virginia or Kentucky. (In presidential elections, a 43 percent to 44 percent share of the white working-class vote is adequate to win a national majority.) Democrats seemed to be moving in this direction during the late 1990s.

II. DISTRACTION AND DE-ARRANGEMENT

Bush's initial success in waging the war on terror disrupted these trends toward the Democratic majority. American politics became dominated by concerns over national security, an issue on which Republicans had enjoyed voters' confidence since 1980. Some voters who might have supported Democrats were distracted from economic or social concerns that had favored Democrats. They ignored Republicans' religious intolerance and indifference to environmental pollution, rewarding Republicans instead for their presumed success in the war on terror. In 2004 George W. Bush won victories in swing states like Ohio, Iowa, and Florida largely because of these voters' defection. Chief among the defectors were white working-class women voters. In 2000 Bush had won these voters by 7 percent. In 2004 he won them by 18 percent. That year a plurality of these voters identified terrorism and security over the economy and jobs or the war in Iraq as their most important issue.

But there was also evidence of another psychological process, which might be called "de-arrangement." The focus on the war on terror not only distracted erstwhile Democrats and independents but appeared to transform, or de-arrange, their political worldview. They temporarily became more sympathetic to a whole range of conservative assumptions and approaches. In the past, voters had trusted Democrats to manage the economy, and in 2002 that preference should have been strongly reinforced by a recession that occurred on Bush's watch. Instead, voters in that election believed by 41 percent to 37 percent that Republicans were "more likely to make sure the country is prosperous." Recessions could also be expected to reinforce populist perceptions of the economy, but in 2002 the percentage of voters who believed that "the rich just get richer while the poor get poorer" hit its lowest level in 15 years. Most interestingly, opposition to abortion also followed the same curve. The percentage of voters who believed that abortion should be "illegal in all circumstances" (based on Gallup Poll annual averages) rose from 17 percent, in 2000, to 20 percent, in 2002, and was still at 19 percent in 2004.

In 2002 Republican strategists had an easy time making the case for their superiority as the party of national security and putting this issue at the forefront of voters' concerns. In 2004 it was more difficult. Voters had to be convinced that the war in Iraq was part of the war on terror and that whatever setbacks the United States had encountered there should be viewed in the context of overall Republican success in keeping al-Qaeda at bay. Those voters who bought this argument tended to vote Republican; those who had become convinced that the war in Iraq was itself a distraction from the war on terror—and a costly blunder—primarily voted Democratic. These tended to be more-educated voters. In 2004, for instance, college-educated women, who had favored Republicans by 50 percent to 48 percent in the 2002 congressional elections, favored Democrats by 54 percent to 44 percent. Postgraduate voters supported Republicans by a margin of 51 percent to 45 percent in 2002; they backed Democrats by a margin of 52 percent to 46 percent in 2004.

By the 2006 election, many more voters had become disillusioned with the Republicans as the party of national security. They now drew a distinction between the war in Iraq and the war on terror, and they saw the disaster in Iraq overshadowing any success in the war on terror. Others came to doubt the administration's overall ability to protect Americans' national security—either from terrorists or natural disasters. As this change in perception took place, the foundations for the Republican majorities in 2002 and 2004 crumbled. What one sees in the 2006 election is not simply a revolt against the administration's conduct of the war but a return to the political perceptions of the two parties that was inclining the electorate before September 2001 toward a Democratic majority. Voters didn't simply reject the administration for its conduct of the war; angered by its conduct of the war, they reembraced a center-left worldview on a whole range of issues. The electorate of 2006 was like the electorate of 2000—only more so.

Voters returned to a more traditionally liberal view of the economy. Even though the economy is in better shape now than it was in 2002, proportionately more voters now believe that the rich are getting richer and the poor are getting poorer. The gap between those who believe this and those who don't has widened by 16 percentage points. More of today's voters believe it is the responsibility of government to take care of those who can't take care of themselves. That gap has widened by 15 points.

The same results have showed up even in opinions about social issues. The average annual percentage of those believing abortion should be illegal dropped from 19 percent in 2004 to 15 percent in 2006, and the percentage believing it should be legal in "all circumstances" rose from 24 percent to 30 percent. Indeed, the outburst of religiosity that began a decade ago and sustained the Republican Party in the South and the prairie states seems to be abating. A 2007 study from the Pew Research Center reports "a reversal of the increased religiosity observed in the mid-1990s," along with greater tolerance among white evangelical Protestants toward homosexuals and working women. The Pew study finds, for instance, that among white evangelical Protestants, the percentage of those who completely disagree that "women should return to their traditional roles" has risen from 28 percent in 1997 to 42 percent today. That spells trouble for a conservative Republicanism rooted in religious conservatism.

As might be expected, the shift in worldview is reflected in identification with the parties themselves. In Pew surveys conducted in 2002, Republicans and Democrats each commanded the allegiance of 43 percent of the public. But five years later, 50 percent identified with or leaned toward the Democrats, and only 35 percent identified with or leaned toward the Republicans. A 15-percentage-point gap has opened up between the parties. The change is equally dramatic when one looks at specific groups in the electorate.

III. THE DEMOCRATIC MAJORITY

In the 2006 election, all the groups that had been part of the emerging Democratic majority in the late 1990s came roaring back into the fold. College-educated women backed Democrats by 57 percent to 42 percent. Single women backed Democrats by 66 percent to 33 percent. And the key swing group among women voters shifted. White working-class women, who had voted Republican by 57 percent to 42 percent in 2004, backed them by only 52 percent to 47 percent in 2006—a 10-point shift. This movement away from the GOP included a stunning 26-point shift by white working-class women with annual household incomes between $30,000 and $50,000, who went from pro-Republican (60 percent to 39 percent) in 2004 to pro-Democratic (52 percent to 47 percent) in 2006. Post-graduate voters, who are typically professionals, also moved decisively into the Democratic column. In 2002 these voters had backed Republican congressional candidates by 51 percent to 45 percent. In 2006 they backed Democrats by 58 percent to 41 percent.

Minority voters also increased their support for Democratic candidates, largely due to a shift among Hispanics. Hispanics had backed congressional Democrats in 2004 by 59 percent to 40 percent, but in 2006 they supported them by 69 percent to 30 percent. This partly represented a reaction to Republican anti-immigration politics, but it also reflected a shift back to the kind of support that Democrats had enjoyed among Hispanics in the late 1980s and 1990s.

Moreover, each of these groups will likely increase its share of the electorate over the years. Minorities made up 15 percent of the electorate in 1990; they are 21 percent today and are expected to be 25 percent in 2015. Their weight will be much higher in key states like California, Florida, and Texas. In 1970 single women made up 38 percent of adult women; today they are a majority. College-educated women have more than tripled as a percentage of women 25 and older since then, going from 8 percent to 27 percent. Professionals were 7 percent of the workforce in the 1950s; they are 17 percent today and are expected to be 19 percent in 2015. Insofar as they vote at the highest rate of any occupational group, they likely make up a quarter or so of the electorate in many Northeast and far West states.

In 2006 Democrats were able to supplement these votes with sufficient support from the white working class. Democrats had gotten only 39 percent of this vote in the 2004 congressional elections; in 2006 Democrats got 44 percent of the vote, which was enough to give them a solid majority in Congress. Democrats' success among these voters helped the party to pick up three house seats in

Indiana (where the white working class makes up 66 percent of the voting electorate); two seats in Iowa (where it makes up 72 percent); a Senate seat in
Montana (which is 68 percent white working-class); and a Senate seat, a House
seat, and the governorship in Ohio (which is 62 percent white working-class).
By 2015 the white working class is expected to fall from 52 percent to 47 percent
of the U.S. electorate; but it will remain a critically important group nationally
and in many elections in the Midwest and South.

In most of these states, white working-class voters returned to the Democratic
fold because of disillusionment with Bush's foreign policy—and because of a
stagnant economy. While Democrats enjoyed significant gains among noncollege
whites earning between $50,000 and $75,000 annually, they made their most dramatic gains among white working-class voters making between $30,000 to
$50,000. In the 2004 congressional elections, these voters had favored Republicans
by 60 percent to 38 percent; in 2006 they divided their vote equally between
Democrats and Republicans. That's a 22-point shift.

IV. MILLENNIALS AND INDIES

The Democratic majority in 2006 was also bolstered by support from voters ages
18 to 29. Almost all of these voters fall into the category that pollsters call "millennials" or "Generation Y" (those born after 1977). In contrast to the previous generation, dubbed "Generation X" (those born between 1965 and 1977), they prefer
Democrats over Republicans and the center-left over the center-right. According to
a 2006 Pew survey, 48 percent of 18- to 25-year-old millennials identify themselves
as Democrats, and only 35 percent identify themselves as Republicans. In 2006,
18- to-29-year-olds voted for Democratic congressional candidates by 60 percent to
38 percent. By contrast, 55 percent of 18- to 25-year-old Generation Xers had identified themselves as Republicans in the early 1990s. Political generations don't often
change their allegiance. The New Deal generation sustained a Democratic majority
for decades; Generation X has remained a bulwark of the Republican vote; and the
millennials can be expected to bolster a new Democratic majority.

Clearly, different political experiences have shaped these two generations.
Generation X grew up during the Carter and Reagan years, which were marked
by Democratic failure and Republican success. The millennials grew up in
years of the Clinton boom and Bush's disastrous failure in Iraq. Their political
outlook most clearly resembles that of postindustrial professionals: socially liberal, in favor of government regulation of business, more secular, and less
inclined than any other generation to accept the Republican identification with
the religious right. In a 2006 Pew survey, 20 percent of 18- to 25-year-olds
reported they had no religion or were atheist or agnostic, compared with just
11 percent among those over 25.

The other group that has come to make up the Democratic majority is political independents. These voters, who identify themselves to pollsters and public
opinion surveys as "independents," represent an ideology rather than a social
group, but they overlap with some Democratic constituencies and also set limits
on the politics of a Democratic majority. According to the American National

Election Studies, they make up about 38 percent of the potential electorate and 33 percent of actual voters. States with the highest proportions of independents are concentrated in the Northeast, upper Midwest, and far West (including Alaska and Hawaii), plus several mountain states (Colorado, Idaho, Montana) and North Dakota. Interestingly, there is considerable overlap between these states and states where Ross Perot polled more than 20 percent in 1992.

Many independents are professionals, and there are striking similarities between independents' and professionals' attitudes, especially their respect for science and their support for social liberalism. In New Jersey, for example, independent voters support gay marriage at about the same level as Democrats do, while Republicans are solidly opposed. But independents tend to be moderate on economic policy, more skeptical than Democrats that large government programs can be effective, and resistant to tax increases. They are particularly wary of "special interests" in Washington (including the parties themselves) and often favor reforms in lobbying and campaign finance. In the Mountain States, they have a pronounced libertarian streak, both on social and economic issues. Many of them favor the right to an abortion *and* a handgun.

In the 1990s, independents began to lean Democratic in presidential elections. They moved back into the Republican column temporarily in 2000—perhaps because of the Clinton scandals. In 2002 they also backed Republicans in the congressional elections, but they have now scurried back to the Democratic Party. In 2006 they favored Democratic congressional candidates by 57 percent to 39 percent, far and away the largest margin that independents have given Democrats since the inception of exit polls.

In the 2006 congressional elections, libertarian-leaning independents played a decisive role in Democratic victories in prairie and non-Pacific western states. In the Montana Senate race, independents voted 59 percent to 35 percent for Democrat Jon Tester against incumbent Conrad Burns, who had been linked to the Jack Abramoff scandal. In Arizona they strongly backed Gov. Janet Napolitano and even Democratic Senate challenger Jim Pederson, who lost to incumbent Jon Kyl. In Minnesota, where onetime Perot backer Jesse Ventura was elected governor in 1998 on the Reform Party ticket, independents backed Democratic Senate candidate Amy Klobuchar over conservative Republican Mark Kennedy by 63 percent to 28 percent. Independents also played a role in Democratic House pickups in Colorado, Kansas, Connecticut, and New Hampshire (where 44 percent of voters identify themselves as independents).

But it would be a mistake to identify independents as part of the Democratic base. The new Democratic coalition is center-left; independents are more toward the center, especially on fiscal and economic issues, than Democratic identifiers are. In California, independents backed moderate Republican Gov. Arnold Schwarzenegger in November 2006 by virtually the same margin they had given John Kerry over George W. Bush in 2004. Democrats will continue to attract independents—and independents will make up a significant ideological segment of the Democratic majority—so long as Democrats don't forget the "center" part of center-left and so long as Republicans remain on the right, especially on social issues.

V. GEOGRAPHY OF THE DEMOCRATIC MAJORITY

Politics in America is organized around states, and the new Democratic majority can also be seen as a bloc of states and regions that regularly vote Democratic or are, at least, open to Democratic candidates. In 2006 Democrats consolidated their hold on the Northeast, strengthened their position in the Midwest, and made inroads in Southern border states (including Florida) and in the prairies and the non-Pacific West. In the Northeast, Democrats picked up three governorships, two Senate seats, 11 House seats, and 156 state legislative seats. In the Midwest, Democrats picked up one governorship, two Senate seats, nine House seats, and 106 state legislative seats (which translated into a gain of six state legislative chambers). In the non-Pacific West, where Democrats had done poorly in the past, they won a Senate seat in Montana, a governorship and a House seat in Colorado, and two House seats in Arizona.

The Deep South remains strongly Republican. In 2006 Democrats made no net gains across the five contiguous states of Louisiana (which, in the wake of Hurricane Katrina's depopulation, can be expected to become more Republican), Mississippi, Alabama, Georgia, and South Carolina. But Democrats picked up one Senate seat, six House seats, one governorship, and 31 state legislative seats in the other Southern states. Democrats are competitive in Virginia, North Carolina, Tennessee, Kentucky, and Florida. They have the upper hand in Arkansas and West Virginia, where the latest Gallup party-identification data give them stunning advantages of 26 and 24 points, respectively.

In Florida Democrats picked up two U.S. House seats, six Florida House seats, and the position of state chief financial officer. Democratic Sen. Bill Nelson easily won reelection. And opinion polls indicate that Florida's electorate is moving back toward the center. From 2004 to 2006, the percentage of Floridians identifying themselves as "conservative" dropped from 31 percent to 27 percent, while the percentage of those identifying as "middle-of-the-road" or "liberal" rose from 35 percent to 42 percent.

No state or region is as uniformly in one party's camp as the old Solid South used to be. Democrats, for instance, have a 74-to-46 majority in the Mississippi state House, and Maine has two Republican senators. However, the Democrats can generally count on winning a majority of races in the Northeast (from Maine to Maryland), in Pennsylvania and across the upper Midwest (including Illinois), and on the Pacific Coast (except Alaska). That's a total of 248 electoral votes. Republicans can count on the Deep South, Kentucky, Tennessee, Texas, Oklahoma, Utah, Idaho, Wyoming, Alaska, Kansas, Nebraska, and the Dakotas. That's a total of only 154 electoral votes. The parties are more evenly matched in every other state, including formerly Republican states such as Colorado, Arizona, Montana, Virginia, and even Indiana. In these states, Democrats' success will depend on the skill and representativeness of their candidates and on the issues that most concern the electorate at election time.

Democrats also have an important base in large postindustrial metropolitan areas—what we have called ideopolises. These are large areas that merge suburb and city, and that specialize in producing services and ideas. They often generate a distinctive culture of arty boutiques, restaurants, cafés, and book-stores, and they take their political cues from the professionals who live there. The white working class in places like greater Portland or Seattle doesn't vote dramatically differently from the professionals whose culture dominates these areas. And the culture of the ideopolises is spreading to such smaller cities in the heartland, such as Omaha, which now sports an "Old Market District" (similar to Denver's Lower Downtown) and a Democratic mayor.

During the dot-com bust of 2000–2001, many of the ideopolises lost popula-tion, but, according to demographer William Frey, they are bouncing back. "It's a tale of two kinds of cities," Frey told *The New York Times* in April. "Growing and 'new economy' metros that have rebounded from early decade woes, and large coastal and Rust Belt metros where high housing costs or diminishing employment prospects propel continued outmigration. . . . Among the former are a series of high-tech-driven centers like Austin, San Francisco, San Jose, Seattle, Salt Lake City, Boise, Raleigh and Atlanta, where growth slowdowns were reversed or modest growth has accelerated."

The Democratic percentage of the Senate vote in these ideopolises expanded from 52 percent in 2002 to 58 percent in 2006. Democratic House pickups in areas like suburban Denver, suburban Philadelphia, Connecticut, and southern Florida were powered by ideopolis coalitions where professionals and minorities take a leading role. Jim Webb's Senate victory in Virginia was largely due to his mar-gin in Northern Virginia's high-tech suburbs. Democrats also made headway in districts that aren't yet ideopolises but contain significant towns and cities devoted to the production of ideas of services. Democrats now control two House seats in Kansas: one includes the University of Kansas and the high-tech suburbs of Kansas City, and the other includes Kansas State University. In Iowa, Republican Rep. Jim Leach was defeated in a district that includes the University of Iowa. In southern Indiana, the district where Baron Hill defeated a Republican incumbent includes the University of Indiana.

The Democrats also did well in medium size, older industrial cities in the Midwest, reflecting their increased support among the white working class. In Ohio, Democratic Senate candidate Sherrod Brown picked up 60 percent of the vote in midsize metro areas like Akron, Canton, Dayton, Toledo, and Youngstown. In Indiana, Democrats carried the House vote 62 percent to 38 percent in the Evansville area—an area that Bush carried 61 percent to 38 percent in 2004. And in Iowa, Democrats got 54 percent of the House vote and 57 percent of the governor-ship vote in the Davenport area.

VI. WINNING THE WHITE HOUSE

This new Democratic majority should result in Democrats maintaining control of Congress for most of the next 12 to 16 years. But it won't necessarily result in Democrats consistently winning the White House. To win elections, a Democratic candidate for Congress or governor has to maintain the support of the party's base while reaching a sufficient percentage of the swing voters in a given state or dis-trict. In Ohio, Iowa, or Indiana, that can mean appealing to white working-class voters in small towns. In Colorado, Arizona, or Montana, that can mean appealing to libertarian independents. In these local and state elections, Democrats can run candidates who reflect the special political mix of their state or congressional district. For example, in Ohio last year, Democrats ran a gubernatorial candidate who opposed gun control and a Senate candidate who campaigned against free trade. In Colorado, Democrats ran a gubernatorial candidate who opposed abortion and gun control. In Pennsylvania, Democrats ran a Senate candidate who was pro-life who appealed to working-class Catholics. And in every one of these cases, the Democratic candidate was elected.

But in presidential elections, parties don't have the luxury of appealing to individual states and regions. A candidate can't favor gun control in New Jersey but oppose it in West Virginia, or be pro-choice in California but pro-life in Indiana or Kentucky. To win national elections, Democrats have to win not only their base in the Northeast, the upper Midwest, and the far West, but also swing states such as Ohio, Colorado, Florida, Nevada, and Missouri, each of which contains large numbers of voters who might be uncomfortable with a platform that would appeal to a voter in Massachusetts or California. That puts a premium on the political skill and background of the presidential candidate.

Since 1964 the only Democrats who have won the presidency are white Protestant males from the South who appeared to be moderates rather than liberals and whom white working-class voters could envision as "one of us." Candidates from the Northeast or upper Midwest have been trounced, in part, because they were unable to bridge the political and cultural divide between the Democratic base and the swing voters in the Midwest and border South. As the Democrats prepare for the 2008 election, their two leading candidates are Sens. Hillary Clinton and Barack Obama. Clinton, who is seen by voters as a Northeastern cultural liberal, will also probably face resistance from some white working-class males because she is a woman. Obama, a black man from Chicago, will also likely be seen as a cultural liberal; in addition, he could be at a disadvantage among many white voters in the South, lower Midwest, and interior West because of his race.

None of this suggests that the Democrats can't win the White House. Indeed, they will enter presidential elections with a slight advantage because of the tilt in the country toward the political center. But whether they can win will depend on how well they can maintain the Democratic base while reaching out to swing voters, and on the strength of the opposition. Republicans, obviously, will face problems of their own in placating their conservative Christian and pro-business base while reaching out to suburban professionals and the white working class in the North and West. . . .

mhhe.com/diclerico11e

Internet resources
Visit our Web site at
www.mhhe.com/diclerico11e for links and
resources relating to Political Parties.

chapter 9

Interest Groups

At the time the new Constitution was being debated in 1789, James Madison, the "Father of the Constitution," argued in the Federalist Papers (No. 10) that one of the advantages of the proposed new government was that it would allow for the "control of factions" (in modern-day language, "interest groups"). He argues that "Factions," derived as they were mostly from economic interests, had tended to advance their own interests to the detriment of the common interest. It was Madison's idea that the best way to deal with these factions was to incorporate them into the operations of the government, but in such a way as to minimize the possibility of any single faction exercising excessive power. Hence, the new Constitution provided for separation of powers, checks and balances, divided government, staggered elections, overlapping terms of office, and a scheme of governance that emphasized competition for power and influence among an array of interest groups and actors.

Since Madison's day, two views have emerged as to who actually has power in America. The first, the "power elite" view, holds that power is concentrated in the hands of a relatively few corporate elites, specifically, those holding positions in the nation's major corporations. These economically powerful individuals, according to the theory, control what happens not only in the economy but also in government.

The second view, closer to Madison's original idea, is that power is shared, checked, and dispersed among multiple interests and political actors, all of whom compete with each other. According to this "pluralist" perspective, no interest gets all that it might want, but all interests (and by inference the general public) get some of what they want.

The selections in this chapter speak to these divergent views on who exercises power in America. In the first, G. William Domhoff advances the argument that power in America rests in the hands of the economically powerful. According to Domhoff there is indeed a ruling class in America consisting of a group of wealthy individuals, drawn from the upper classes, who control the economy and, in turn, because of their great economic power, determine what the government does or does not do. In the end, according to Domhoff, working-class America is largely left out of the mix as corporate America gets its way.

In the second selection, Jeff Birnbaum, a Washington Post reporter and longtime observer of lobbyists in Washington, contends that the "power elite" view is a popular myth. He argues that power in Washington depends not on the actions of a corporate few, but on the steady mobilization of interests over time. This places Birnbaum in the "pluralist" camp, but it is pluralism with a twist—namely, that those policy interests in Washington that are able to get their issues on the agenda for consideration by the nation's political leaders are those with a well-organized, well-financed, enduring, and persistent campaign to persuade the government to do what they want. To Birnbaum, that is the key to their success.

134

Power in America
Who Has the Power?

G. William Domhoff

Who has predominant power in the United States? The short answer, from 1776 to the present, is: Those who have the money have the power. George Washington was one of the biggest landowners of his day; presidents in the late 19th century were close to the railroad interests; for George W. Bush, it is oil and other natural resources, agribusiness, and finance. But to be more exact, those who own income-producing property—corporations, real estate, and agribusinesses—set the rules within which policy battles are waged.

While this may seem simple and/or obvious, the reasons behind it are complex. They involve an understanding of social classes, the role of experts, the two-party system, and the history of the country. . . . In terms of the big world-historical picture . . . money rules in America because there are no rival networks that grew up over a long and complex history:

- No big church, as in many countries in Europe
- No big government, as it took to survive as a nation-state in Europe
- No big military until after 1940 (which is not very long ago) to threaten to take over the government

So, the only power network of any consequence in the history of the United States has been the economic one, which under capitalism generates a business-owning class that hires workers and a working class, along with small businesses and skilled artisans who are self-employed, and a relatively small number of independent professionals like physicians. . . .

Domination by the few does not mean complete control, but rather the ability to set the terms under which other groups and classes must operate. Highly trained professionals with an interest in environmental and consumer issues have been able to couple their technical information and their understanding of the legislative process with timely publicity to win governmental restrictions on some corporate practices. Wage and salary workers, when they are organized or disruptive, sometimes have been able to gain concessions on wages, hours, and working conditions.

G. William Domhoff is a research professor at the University of Santa Clara. This essay was originally published online at http://sociology.ucsc.edu/whorulesamerica/power/who.html. Reprinted with permission.

Most of all, there is free speech and the right to vote. While voting does not necessarily make government responsive to the will of the majority, under certain circumstances the electorate has been able to place restraints on the actions of the wealthy elites, or to decide which elites will have the greatest influence on policy. This is especially a possibility when there are disagreements within the higher circles of wealth and influence. . . .

POWER AND POWER INDICATORS

. . . By "power" I mean "the capacity of some persons to produce intended and foreseen effects on others" (Wrong, 1995). This is a very general definition that allows for the many forms of power that can be changed from one to another, such as economic power, political power, military power, ideological power, and intellectual power (i.e., knowledge, expertise). . . .

There are three primary indicators of power, which can be summarized as (1) who benefits? (2) who governs? and (3) who wins? In every society there are experiences and material objects that are highly valued. If it is assumed that everyone in the society would like to have as great a share as possible of these experiences and objects, then the distribution of values in that society can be utilized as a power indicator. Those who benefit the most, by inference, are powerful. In American society, wealth and well-being are highly valued. People seek to own property, earn high incomes, to have interesting and safe jobs, and to live long and healthy lives. All of these "values" are unequally distributed, and all may be utilized as power indicators.

Power also can be inferred from studies of who occupies important institutional positions and takes part in important decision-making groups. If a group or class is highly over-represented in relation to its proportion of the population, it can be inferred that the group is powerful. If, for example, a group makes up 10% of the population but has 50% of the seats in the main governing institutions, then it has five times more people in governing positions than would be expected by chance, and there is thus reason to believe that the group is a powerful one.

There are many policy issues over which groups or classes disagree. In the United States different policies are suggested by opposing groups in such "issue-areas" as foreign policy, taxation, welfare, and the environment. Power can be inferred from these issue conflicts by determining who successfully initiates, modifies, or vetoes policy alternatives. . . .

THE SOCIAL UPPER CLASS

One good starting point for the study of power in the United States, and the one I have preferred as a sociologist (especially in the 1960s and 1970s, when there was far less readily available information than there is now) is a careful consideration of the small social upper class at the top of the wealth, income, and status ladders. . . .

The upper class probably makes up only a few tenths of 1% of the population. For research purposes, I use the conservative estimate that it includes 0.5% to 1% of the population for determining the over-representation of its members in corporations, nonprofit organizations, and the government. Members of the upper class live in exclusive suburban neighborhoods, expensive downtown co-ops, and large country estates. They often have faraway summer and winter homes as well. They attend a system of private schools that extends from pre-school to the university level; the best known of these schools are the "day" and "boarding" prep schools that take the place of public high schools in the education of most upper-class teenagers. Adult members of the upper class socialize in expensive country clubs, downtown luncheon clubs, hunting clubs, and garden clubs. Young women of the upper class are "introduced" to high society each year through an elaborate series of debutante teas, parties, and balls. Women of the upper class gain experience as "volunteers" through a nationwide organization known as the Junior League, and then go on to serve as directors of cultural organizations, family service associations, and hospitals (see Kendall, 2002, for a good account of women of the upper class by a sociologist who was also a participant in upper-class organizations). . . .

For research purposes, the important thing about these social institutions is that they provide us with a starting point for systematic studies of power. For example, these class "indicators" allow us to determine which economic and political leaders are and are not members of the upper class. Put another way, class indicators allow us to trace members of the upper class into the economic, political, and ideological power systems of the society. . . .

Cautions aside, there is no doubt that there is a nationwide upper class in the United States with its own distinctive social institutions, lifestyle, and outlook. There is also no doubt that most of these people are active in business or the professions, and that all of them are very wealthy. Their great wealth is obvious, of course, from the large sums that it takes to maintain their homes and their style of life, but systematic studies also show that the wealthiest families are part of the social institutions of the upper class. Combining our studies with findings by economists on the wealth and income distributions, it is possible to say that the upper class, comprising 0.5% to 1% of the population, owns 35–40% of all privately held wealth in the United States and receives 12–15% of total yearly income. In short, the upper class scores very high on the "who benefits" power indicator.

The wealth and income of members of the upper class certainly imply that the upper class is powerful, but they do not demonstrate how power operates. It is therefore necessary to turn to studies of the economy to gain further understanding of the American power structure.

THE CORPORATE COMMUNITY

Major economic power in the United States is concentrated in an organizational and legal form known as the corporation, and has been since the last several decades of the 19th century. No one doubts that individual corporations have great power in the society at large. For example, they can hire and fire workers, decide where to invest their resources, and use their income in a variety of tax-deductible ways to influence schools, charities, and governments. The argument begins over whether the large corporations are united enough to exert a common social power, and then moves to the question of whether they are still controlled by members of the upper class.

The unity of the corporations can be demonstrated in a number of ways. They share a common interest in making profits. They are often owned by the same families or financial institutions. Their executives have very similar educational and work experiences. It is also important for their sense of unity that corporate leaders see themselves as sharing common opponents in organized labor, environmentalists, consumer advocates, and government officials. A sense of togetherness is created as well by their use of the same few legal, accounting, and consulting firms.

However, the best way to demonstrate the unity among corporations is through the study of what are called "interlocking directors," meaning those individuals who sit on two or more of the boards of directors that are in charge of the overall direction of the corporation. Boards of directors usually include major owners, top executives from similar corporations or corporations located in the same area, financial and legal advisors, and the three or four officers who run the corporation on a daily basis. Several studies show that those 15–20% of corporate directors who sit on two or more boards, who are called the "inner circle" of the corporate directorate, unite 80–90% of the largest corporations in the United States into a *well-connected "corporate community."* . . .

. . . More generally, members of the upper class own roughly half of all corporate stock. Then too, upper-class control of corporations can be seen in its over-representation on boards of directors. Several past studies show that members of the upper class sit on boards far more than would be expected by chance. They are especially likely to be part of the "inner circle" that has two or more directorships. According to the "who governs" power indicator, the upper class still controls the corporate community. Thus, we can conclude that the upper class is rooted in the ownership and control of the corporations that comprise the corporate community. We can say that members of the upper class are for the most part a "corporate rich" who continue to be involved in the business world as investors, venture capitalists, bankers, corporate lawyers, and top executives.

True enough, there are many top corporate executives who did not grow up in the upper class. Most CEOs of major corporations do not come from the upper class. However, they are gradually socialized into the upper class and its values as they move up the corporate ladder; indeed, they are advanced on the basis of their ability to fulfill upper-class goals of corporate expansion and profitability. In return, these rising managers are given the opportunity to buy corporate stock at below-market prices, paid very high salaries, and given other "perks" that make it possible for them to join the upper class economically as well as socially. The end result is a strengthening of the power of the upper class, not a diminution of it.

HOW GOVERNMENT POLICY IS SHAPED
FROM OUTSIDE GOVERNMENT

The upper class and the closely related corporate community do not stand alone at the top of the power structure. They are supplemented by a wide range of nonprofit organizations that play an important role in framing debates over public policy and in shaping public opinion. . . .

Upper-class and corporate dominance of the major nonprofit organizations can be seen in their founding by wealthy members of the upper class and in their reliance on large corporations for their funding. However, dominance is once again most readily demonstrated through studies of boards of directors, which have ultimate control of the organizations, including the ability to hire and fire top executives. These studies show that (1) members of the upper class are greatly over-represented on the boards of these organizations, and (2) that non-profit organizations share a large number of directors in common with the corporate community, particularly directors who are part of the "inner circle." In effect, most large nonprofit organizations are part of the corporate community.

All the organizations in the nonprofit sector have a hand in creating the framework of the society in one way or another, and hence in helping to shape the political climate. The cultural and civic organizations set the standard for what is beautiful, important, and "classy." The elite universities play a big part in determining what is important to teach, learn, and research, and they train most of the professionals and experts in the country. However, it is the foundations, think tanks, and policy-discussion organizations that have the most direct and important influences. Their ideas, criticisms, and policy suggestions go out to the general public through a wide array of avenues, including pamphlets, books, local discussion groups, mass media, and not least, the public relations departments of major corporations. . . .

Tax-free foundations receive their money from wealthy families and corporations. Their primary purpose is to provide money for education, research, and policy discussion. They thus have the power to encourage those ideas and researchers they find compatible with their values and goals, and to withhold funds from others. . . .

The role of the think tanks is to suggest new policies to deal with the problems facing the economy and government. Using money from wealthy donors, corporations, and foundations, think tanks hire the experts produced by the graduate departments of the elite universities. The ideas and proposals developed by the experts are disseminated through pamphlets, books, articles in major magazines and newspapers, and, most importantly, through the participation of the experts themselves in the various forums provided by the policy-discussion organizations.

The policy-discussion organizations are the hub of the policy-planning network. They bring together wealthy individuals, corporate executives, experts, and government officials for lectures, forums, meetings, and group discussions of issues that range from the local to the international, and from the economic

to the political to the cultural. New ideas are tried out in weekly or monthly discussion groups, and differences of opinion are aired and compromised. . . .

The many discussion groups that take place within the several policy-
discussion organizations have several functions that do not readily meet the
eye. . . . First, these organizations help to familiarize busy corporate leaders
with policy options outside the purview of their day-to-day business concerns.
This gives these executives the ability to influence public opinion through the
mass media and other outlets, to argue with and influence experts, and to
accept appointments for government service. Second, the policy-discussion
organizations give members of the upper class and corporate community the
opportunity to see which of their colleagues seem to be the best natural leaders
through watching them in the give and take of the discussion groups. . . .

Third, these organizations legitimate their participants to the media and interested public as knowledgeable leaders who deserve to be tapped for public service
because they have used their free time to acquaint themselves with the issues in
nonpartisan forums. The organizations thereby help make wealthy individuals and
corporate executives into "national leaders" and "statesmen." Finally, these organizations provide a forum wherein members of the upper class and corporate community can come to know policy experts. This gives them a pool of people from
which they can draw advisors if they are asked to serve in government. It also gives
them a basis for recommending experts to politicians for government service. . . .

THE POWER ELITE

Now that the upper class, corporate community, and policy-planning network
have been defined and described, it is possible to discuss the leadership group
that I call the "power elite." I define the power elite as the leadership group of
the upper class. It consists of active-working members of the upper class and
high-level employees in profit and nonprofit institutions controlled by members of the upper class through stock ownership, financial support, or involvement on the board of directors. . . .

Conversely, not all those involved in the power elite are members of the
upper class. They are sons and daughters of the middle class, and occasionally,
the blue-collar working class, who do well at any one of several hundred private and state universities, and then go to grad school, MBA school, or law
school at one of a handful of elite universities—e.g., Harvard, Yale, Princeton,
Columbia, MIT, Johns Hopkins, University of Chicago, and Stanford. From
there they go to work for a major corporation, law firm, foundation, think tank,
or university, and slowly work their way to the top. . . .

THE POWER ELITE AND GOVERNMENT

Members of the power elite directly involve themselves in the federal government through three basic processes, each of which has a slightly different
role in ensuring "access" to the White House, Congress, and specific agencies,

departments, and committees in the executive branch. Although some of the same people are involved in all three processes, most leaders specialize in one or two of the three processes. These three processes are:

1. The special-interest process, through which specific families, corporations, and industrial sectors are able to realize their narrow and short-run interests on taxes, subsidies, and regulation in their dealings with congressional committees, regulatory bodies, and executive departments;
2. The policy-making process, through which the policies developed in the policy-planning network described earlier are brought to the White House and Congress;
3. The candidate selection process, through which members of the power elite influence electoral campaigns by means of campaign donations to political candidates.

Power elite domination of the federal government can be seen most directly in the workings of the corporate lobbyists, backroom super-lawyers, and industry-wide trade associations that represent the interests of specific corporations or business sectors. This special-interest process is based in varying combinations of information, gifts, insider dealing, friendship, and, not least, promises of lucrative private jobs in the future for compliant government officials. This is the aspect of business-government relations described by journalists and social scientists in their case studies. While these studies show that the special interests usually get their way, the conflict that sometimes erupts within this process, occasionally pitting one corporate sector against another, reinforces the image of widely shared and fragmented power in America, including the image of a divided corporate community. Moreover, there are some defeats suffered by the corporate rich in the special-interest process. For example, laws that improved auto safety standards were passed over automobile industry objections in the 1970s, as were standards of water cleanliness opposed by the paper and chemical industries.

Policies of concern to the corporate community as a whole are not the province of the special-interest process. Instead, such policies come from the network of foundations, think tanks, and policy-discussion organizations discussed in an earlier section. The plans developed in the organizations of the policy-planning network reach the federal government in a variety of ways. On the most general level, their reports, news releases, and interviews are read by elected officials and their staffs, either in pamphlet form or in summary articles in the *Washington Post, New York Times*, and *Wall Street Journal*. Members of the policy-planning network also testify before congressional committees and subcommittees that are writing legislation or preparing budget proposals. More directly, leaders from these organizations are regular members of the dozens of little-known committees that advise specific departments of the executive branch on general policies, making them in effect unpaid temporary members of the government. They are also very prominent on the extremely important presidential commissions that are appointed to make recommendations on a wide range of issues from foreign policy to highway construction.

They also serve on the *little-known federal advisory committees* that are part of just about every department of the executive branch.

Finally, and crucially, they are appointed to government positions with a frequency far beyond what would be expected by chance. Several different studies show that top cabinet positions in both Republican and Democratic administrations are held by members of the upper class and corporate executives who are leaders in policy-discussion organizations.

The general picture that emerges from the findings on the over-representation of members of the power elite in appointed governmental positions is that the highest levels of the executive branch are interlocked constantly with the upper class and corporate community through the movement of executives and lawyers in and out of government. Although the same person is not in governmental and corporate positions at the same time, there is enough continuity for the relationship to be described as one of "revolving interlocks." Corporate leaders resign their numerous directorships in profit and nonprofit organizations to serve in government for two or three years, then return to the corporate community or policy-planning network. . . .

As important as the special-interest and policy-planning processes are for the power elite, they could not operate successfully if there were not sympathetic, business-oriented elected officials in government. That leads us to the third process through which members of the power elite dominate the federal government, the candidate-selection process. It operates through the two major political parties. . . .

Contrary to what many believe, . . . American political parties are not very responsive to voter preferences. Their candidates are fairly free to say one thing to get elected and to do another once in office. This contributes to confusion and apathy in the electorate. It leads to campaigns where there are no "issues" except "images" and "personalities" even when polls show that voters are extremely concerned about certain policy issues. You don't raise unnecessary issues during a campaign, one successful presidential candidate once said.

It is precisely because the candidate-selection process is so personalized, and therefore dependent on name recognition, images, and emotional symbolism, that it can be in good part dominated by members of the power elite through the relatively simple and direct means of large campaign contributions. Playing the role of donors and money raisers, the same people who direct corporations and take part in the policy-planning network have a crucial place in the careers of most politicians who advance beyond the local level or state legislatures in states with large populations. Their support is especially important in party primaries, where money is an even larger factor than in general elections.

The two-party system therefore results in elected officials who are relatively issueless and willing to go along with the policies advocated by those members of the power elite who work in the special-interest and policy-planning processes. They are motivated by personal ambition far more than they are by political conviction. . . .

In summary, the special-interest process, policy-planning process, and campaign finance make it possible for the power elite to win far more often than it loses on the policy issues that come before the federal government. The power elite is also greatly over-represented in appointed positions, presidential blue-ribbon commissions, and advisory committees within the government. In terms of both the "who wins" and "who governs" power indicators, the power elite dominates the federal government.

However, this domination does not mean control on each and every issue, or lack of opposition, and it does not rest upon government involvement alone. Involvement in government is only the final and most visible aspect of power elite domination, which has its roots in the class structure, the nature of the economy, and the functioning of the policy-planning network. If government officials did not have to wait on corporate leaders to decide where and when they will invest, and if government officials were not further limited by the acceptance of the current economic arrangements by the large majority of the population, then power elite involvement in elections and government would count for a lot less than it does under present conditions.

REFERENCES

Kendall, D. (2002). *The Power of Good Deeds: Privileged Women and the Social Reproduction of Class.* Lanham, MD: Rowman and Littlefield.

Wrong, D. (1995). *Power: Its Forms, Bases, and Uses* (2nd ed.). New Brunswick: Transaction Publishers.

The Forces That Set the Agenda
Jeffrey H. Birnbaum

In the grand scheme of things, Social Security isn't the nation's biggest fiscal problem. That's not my view. That's the assessment of Douglas Holtz-Eakin, a Bush political appointee before he became head of the nonpartisan Congressional Budget Office, who says that looming financial calamities in Medicare and Medicaid are larger and more immediate worries in a strictly budgetary sense.

Jeffrey Birnbaum is a *Washington Post* reporter whose K Street Confidential column on the intersection of business and politics appears on alternate Mondays in the Business section of the *Post.* He has four books on Washington, including *The Money Men: The Real Story of Fund-raising's Influence on Political Power in America* (Crown, 2000). Reprinted from: *The Washington Post,* April 24, 2005, pp. B1, B5. © 2005, *The Washington Post.* Reprinted with permission.

As economic calamities go, more significant crises confront the states, which are responsible for our kids' education; the nation's hospitals, which bear the brunt of an overburdened health care system; and international institutions, which have to deal with famine, poverty and HIV/AIDS.

With all these pressing woes, how did Social Security, Terri Schiavo's end-of-life fight and judicial nominations make it to the top of the Washington agenda? [It was] not merely because the White House or the party in power [wanted] them to be there. [It was] because deep-rooted, well-heeled organizations [had] been targeting those issues for years. What seems like serendipity to the public—why *is* Congress talking about trial lawyers again?—is more often the result of an interest group's advance work combining with the right circumstances to send an issue hurtling into the limelight.

Like it or not, we increasingly live in a stage-managed democracy where highly orchestrated interests filter our priorities. These groups don't have absolute power, of course. In the nation's capital, home to 30,000 registered lobbyists, hundreds of politicians, thousands of journalists and untold numbers of entrenched bureaucrats, no one's in charge. But long-established entities like the AARP, the Family Research Council and the U.S. Chamber of Commerce mold our collective thinking and regularly dictate the language and tenor of our civic debates.

This notion runs counter to an abiding myth—that political leaders actually lead. That's true sometimes, of course, but more often than not, the ideas and movements that get on the government's to-do list come from the broad middle and not from the top.

A case in point: More than a decade ago, the National Federation of Independent Business, the country's premier small-business lobby, began to methodically contact its half-million members by phone and mail to categorize them by political leanings and their willingness to contact federal lawmakers. The lobby group trained its most eager members at local seminars and sent staffers door-to-door during elections in critical congressional districts. Regular "grass-roots" outpourings from this made-to-order machine vaulted NFIB-championed issues onto center stage—especially when the Republicans it favored took control of the White House and Congress. In particular, the inheritance tax (which NFIB loyalists redubbed the "death tax" for marketing purposes) was repealed (temporarily so far, but Congress is now considering whether to make the repeal permanent). This was the organization's No. 1 priority.

The process is a lot like surfing. Interest groups float along, waiting for the perfect wave of public sentiment or official fiat to carry their issues to victory. They can't create the wave, but they can be ready for the moment when it comes. The key is to be prepared for that moment: Not every issue has an organization with the wealth and staying power to be in that position. Those that do have a shot at winning.

"Lobbying is subtle and complicated," says John W. Kingdon, a professor emeritus of political science at the University of Michigan who studies interest groups. But the most important attribute of a successful lobbying campaign, he says, is persistence—something that only entrenched organizations possess.

"It takes a sustained organization, mobilized followers and an immense amount of power to get onto a legislative agenda," agrees Theodore J. Lowi, a professor of government at Cornell University.

In many ways, interest groups have replaced political parties as the real influence brokers. Candidates for office rely on these groups for campaign cash, for campaign workers and, increasingly, for campaign issues—all of which had once been the domain of the Republican and Democratic national committees.

Republican ground troops come from such diverse groups as the NFIB, the U.S. Chamber of Commerce, the Family Research Council and the National Rifle Association. Democratic soldiers are recruited from places like labor unions, the trial bar and Moveon.org. "The standard distinction between interest groups and parties used to be that parties were committed to winning elections and that pressure groups let elections happen and then tried to influence the people who got elected," Lowi said. "Now interest groups through their PACs and a variety of other methods are very much involved in the pre-policy arena."

Such involvement has become a prime factor in agenda-setting. Take Social Security. Few federal programs attract as much scrutiny. AARP, the nation's largest lobbying organization, is dedicated to keeping Social Security alive and well, as are groups such as the National Committee to Preserve Social Security and Medicare. The reason: Large portions of their membership depend on Social Security checks to survive in old age. AARP has taught a million and a half of its 35 million members how to hammer elected officials by mail, phone and in person, primarily about Social Security.

But AARP has learned that it needs to be careful what it wishes for. Its obsession with the issue has made Social Security a front-of-the-mind topic and, therefore, a perennial contender to shoot to Washington's upper tier. Ideological opponents of the current Social Security system have also been active, raising the issue's profile even higher. Free market think tanks such as the Cato Institute and anti-tax-increase lobbies have been churning out position papers for a quarter-century promoting partial privatization of Social Security as a way to undercut what they see as "big government." One appreciator of that work: George W. Bush.

So when the president went looking for a problem to solve that could guarantee him a lasting legacy—and, perhaps, realign party domination—he went for that old chestnut Social Security. He also embraced a proposal that AARP dislikes—the creation of private accounts. That notion has fallen flat largely because of more than $15 million worth of AARP advertising against it. When the process moves to another phase and compromises are explored, AARP is likely to become an important negotiator and perhaps the key indicator of whether the effort will succeed or fail.

The same high-stakes maneuvering couldn't have happened with, say, Medicaid, the health care program for the poor, even though it's in more dire financial straits. Medicaid doesn't have similarly situated citizens' groups beating the bushes on its behalf. So while saving Social Security is the watchword of the day, Medicaid's fate will be to languish and occasionally fend off budget cuts until its finances reach an emergency.

Terri Schiavo is another example of interest-group politics at work. The 41-year-old brain-damaged woman was in many ways not out of the ordinary. She was one of thousands of people whose families annually struggle with the question of when a relative's life has ended. But skilled marketers on the well-established, pro-life side of the abortion debate seized on her situation. The National Right to Life Committee, Operation Rescue, Priests for Life, the Family Research Council and others set up Web sites, held news conferences and raised lots of money for lawyers and for themselves.

Their pleas touched a chord with millions of Americans and made Schiavo's plight a cause celebre. The omnipresence of her situation in direct-mail communications from those groups and on talk radio made her synonymous with the battle over life and death issues of all kinds—from the womb to the grave. By the time Schiavo's parents had finally exhausted their legal options and her feeding tube was about to be removed permanently, the public policy pump had been thoroughly primed. Republican leaders sympathetic to the cause brought Congress back for an extraordinary weekend session. Only later did it appear, based on various polls, that the majority of Americans did not see Schiavo's case the way the Republican leadership did.

As a result, the starvation of a solitary middle-class woman in Florida riveted government for a couple of weeks while similar—and more severe—situations went almost unnoticed. Mass starvation in Sudan, for instance, was a legislative footnote by comparison. Why? It's not only that Sudan is far away and hard to solve. Help for the Sudan catastrophe lacks the backing of as many obsessively focused and widely dispersed interest groups.

The brewing battle in the Senate over a mere seven judicial nominees is another telling example. Groups on the political left and right are making the coming confrontation seem like World War III. (Witness the use of the word "nuclear" to describe the Republicans' effort to force a vote.) In fact, the debate is a warm-up for the more consequential conflict over filling the next Supreme Court vacancy as well as a stand-in for other divisive issues, such as gay rights, abortion rights and affirmative action.

Why such tumult and passion? Organizations with wide and long-standing interest have been on the prowl for supporters on these matters for years. On the anti-Bush side are the Alliance for Justice, the Leadership Conference on Civil Rights and People for the American Way, which was instrumental in derailing Robert Bork's nomination to the Supreme Court in 1987. The president's allies include groups such as the Committee for Justice, Focus on the Family, the Federalist Society, Americans for Tax Reform and Freedom Works, which have not only raised millions for the purpose but coordinate their activities in conference calls among their leaders.

In an odd way, all this attention to Washington ways is heartening. The common view is that elites run the show and sheep-like citizens allow them to. In fact, organized interests able to motivate blocs of voters really can make a difference, as long as they can stick around for a while.

Unfortunately, not every vital issue has a group or groups that are clever or rich enough to generate unrelenting support from back home. That leaves out of the mix too many people with worthy woes: the unemployed, the uninsured, the unaligned.

There's probably an opportunity there for yet another powerful interest.

Internet resources
Visit our Web site at
www.mhhe.com/diclerico11e for links and
resources relating to Interest Groups.

c h a p t e r   1 0

Congress

Representation: Redistricting

The Constitution requires that membership in the U.S. House of Representatives be apportioned on the basis of population every ten years. As a matter of law and practice, state legislatures have the responsibility of redrawing congressional districts after apportionment has been completed. Historically, the drawing of district lines has been a very political process, often involving partisanship, racial politics, regional interests, and intraparty factionalism.

In recent years, redistricting has taken on a whole new dimension as political parties have sought to consolidate their power. In an effort to protect partisan interests, many state legislatures have redrawn districts so as to render them noncompetitive. Indeed, it is estimated that today 90 percent or more of congressional districts are "safe districts," meaning that one party or the other is almost guaranteed election.

The lack of competitive districts, and thus of competitive elections, has become such a problem that one current and one former member of the House of Representatives— a Democrat and a Republican—suggest in the first selection that reform of the process is essential for the health of our democracy. According to these congressmen, Earl Blumenauer and Jim Leach, it is time to take the redistricting process out of state legislatures and turn it over to special commissions in the states.

Reform efforts to the contrary, Bill Bishop, the author of the second selection, argues that any reform might be doomed from the very beginning because it is not the redistricting process that is at fault. According to Bishop, no amount of tinkering with the current system will be able to overcome what is happening demographically in America—namely, that people are simply choosing to live with like-minded people, thereby making any attempt to reform redistricting meaningless.

Redistricting
A Bipartisan Sport

Earl Blumenauer and Jim Leach

Congressional redistricting is about as interesting as someone else's genealogy. But occasionally the subject produces headlines, as it did in [2003] when Democratic members of the Texas Legislature fled to Oklahoma to avoid creating a quorum to address the issue. Their desperate maneuver failed. . . .

Despite the public perception that the drawing of legislative maps is an insider's game of no particular relevance, the health of American democracy hinges on how state officials approach the issue. If competitive elections matter—and to much of the world they are what America stands for—then redistricting also matters.

Using redistricting to gain advantage over one's opponents has been going on almost since America was founded. "Gerrymandering," the term to describe the process of creating strangely shaped legislative districts, dates back to 1812 or so, when Elbridge Gerry devised a legislative map in Massachusetts to benefit his political party's interests.

The courts have occasionally waded into this legislative thicket, principally to protect the one-person, one-vote principle but also to ensure compliance with the Voting Rights Act. But redistricting simply for partisan advantage—so long as it doesn't result in less minority representation and isn't too geographically egregious—is not generally considered grounds for court interference.

It is, however, a matter of profound importance to our system of government. A few partisans should not be allowed to manipulate the landscape of state and national politics by legislative line-drawing. But that's exactly what has happened.

Gerrymandering has become a bipartisan pastime. California Democrats produced a plan that turned a closely divided Congressional delegation (22–21) into a 28–17 Democratic advantage after the 1980 reapportionment. After the 1990 reapportionment, Georgia Republicans were able to turn a 9–1 disadvantage into an eventual 8–3 majority. In fact, Republican control of the House, won in 1994 for the first time in 40 years, was probably due more to shrewd redistricting than to the much-publicized "Contract with America."

In the wake of the 2000 census, candidates for governor and even obscure state legislators who would have a hand in drawing new legislative boundaries

Earl Blumenaur, is a Democratic representative from Oregon, and Jim Leach is a former Republican representative from Iowa. From *The New York Times,* July 8, 2003, p. A27.

received unprecedented attention. In an unusual role reversal, some members of Congress even contributed money to state campaigns and hired their own lobbyists to represent their interests in state capitols.

The effort paid off. In big states that Republicans came to control, they were able to make gains. In Michigan, incumbent Democrats were forced into races against each other. In Pennsylvania, Democratic-leaning districts were eliminated altogether. And though the 2000 presidential election made clear that Florida is evenly divided on party preferences, it sends 18 Republicans to Congress and only 7 Democrats.

Democrats, meanwhile, did their own manipulating where they could, picking up seats in Georgia, North Carolina and Maryland. . . .

More than either political party, however, the real winners in the redistricting games are incumbents. Nationwide, in 2002 only eight incumbents were defeated in the general election—and four of those lost to other incumbents. On average . . . Congressional incumbents won with more than two-thirds of the vote.

One response to all this, of course, could be indifference. Political manipulation is to be expected. . . .

But the consequences of entrenched incumbency should concern us all. Without meaningful competition in 90 percent of all races in the House, representatives become less accountable to voters and citizens lose interest in democracy.

More subtle consequences also unfold. When control of Congress rests on the results of those 20 to 30 races that are potentially competitive, the political dialogue in these campaigns, and legislative strategies in the House, become skewed. The few competitive races become playgrounds for power brokers who specialize in expensive, divisive and manipulative campaign techniques.

In Washington, legislative initiatives are frequently distorted in an effort to keep the vulnerable few in the political cross hairs. Bills on issues like farm policy or free trade are often framed to force members to choose between constituencies—farmers and unions, for example. Bills on health care may force members to choose between doctors and lawyers.

There is also a profound problem that is not subtle at all. Primary elections in districts that are overwhelmingly Republican produce candidates generally to the right of the average Republican, while more liberal Democrats usually emerge from primaries in districts that are overwhelmingly Democratic. The political center—where most Americans are most comfortable—gets the least representation in Congress.

In short, the current system produces a House that is both more liberal and more conservative than the country at large. Members are less inclined to talk and cooperate, much less compromise. The legislative agenda is shaped more to energize the political base than to advance the common good.

It doesn't have to be this way. Iowa, which has about 1 percent of the United States population and only five representatives in the House, saw as many competitive races in the last election as California, New York and Illinois combined. (For the record, those three states account for 101 seats in the House.) Iowa is so competitive largely because it has an independent redistricting commission that is prohibited from considering where incumbents live when it draws new legislative maps.

What works for Iowa could work for the nation. The formula for avoiding inequities, undue partisan advantage and political dysfunction is the creation of independent redistricting commissions. Arizona recently followed Iowa's example, and such a commission has been proposed in Texas.

These commissions offer the best hope for taking partisanship out of the redistricting process. The public should insist that candidates for governor and state legislatures favor the development of strong nonpartisan redistricting plans.

Competitive elections are essential to the American system of government. Just as antitrust laws are necessary for a strong economy, so redistricting reform is critical for a healthy democracy.

You Can't Compete with Voters' Feet

Bill Bishop

When not a single California congressional or state legislative seat changed political party in last year's election, Republican Gov. Arnold Schwarzenegger reacted with his signature bluntness. "What kind of democracy is that?" he demanded. Blaming the lack of competitiveness in all the races on state legislators who in 2000 created voting districts guaranteed to preserve their own seats and their respective parties' dominance, Schwarzenegger has proposed taking control of redistricting away from partisan politicians and entrusting it to a panel of retired judges.

On the virtues of this plan, the unconventional governor has a lot of conventional company. Many see independent redistricting, free from the possibility of gerrymandering—the practice of drawing a voting district to one party's advantage—as the route to resurrecting competitive elections and resuscitating democracy.

But the paucity of competitive elections isn't simply something created by diabolical legislators or nerdy mapmakers. It has been, in large measure, an inside job, the result of citizens who, given the choice, would prefer to live among

Bill Bishop is a reporter with the *Austin American-Statesman* (Texas), where a version of this article previously appeared. Reprinted with permission.

those most like themselves. Taking redistricting away from the politicians may do something about the appearance of partisanship in the legislature, but it can't change the actual partisanship that resides in our communities.

Schwarzenegger has a point, of course. Most legislative races *aren't* competitive. In U.S. House races in 2004, only seven of 401 incumbents lost. Only 22 races were decided by a margin of less than 10 percentage points.

But when the early-19th-century Massachusetts politician Elbridge Gerry redrew a state Senate seat to his party's advantage in a shape that looked like a salamander—thus enshrining the "gerrymander" forevermore—was he contributing to the demise of democracy in the 21st century? Several political scientists who study congressional elections don't think so.

Alan Abramowitz, a professor of political science at Emory University in Atlanta, measured the "competitiveness" of congressional districts in a recent study. He used presidential election returns to get a sense of whether congressional districts vote more Republican or Democratic than the nation as a whole. Abramowitz found that over the past 30 years, there have been fewer and fewer districts where Republicans and Democrats are evenly mixed. But redistricting doesn't seem to be the cause.

Abramowitz reasoned that if partisan redistricting were causing the decline in competitive House races, then there should be a jump in non-competitive districts—defined as districts that are 10 percentage points more Republican or Democratic than the nation as a whole—right after legislative redistricting, which by law must occur after the new census every 10 years. But Abramowitz found no discernible increase after the new districts were drawn. Instead, districts grew most lopsided *in between* redistricting years. So other factors must be at work.

Yes, legislatures can still gerrymander to get rid of incumbents. The Texas legislature did that in 2003, under House Majority Leader Tom DeLay's tutelage, when it drew congressional districts in a way that led to the defeat of four incumbent Democrats last November. But Abramowitz contends that the unusual mid-decade redistricting simply recognized the growing partisanship in Texas.

"I keep hearing Democrats saying that Republicans basically stole those seats by redistricting again," said Abramowitz, who describes himself as a liberal Democrat. "The fact is, that's a minor issue. The underlying reality is that states like Texas and Georgia have been trending Republican. Sooner or later, more likely sooner, that was going to translate into a Republican takeover of the congressional delegation."

This is also true nationally. More people are choosing where to live based on demographic factors that now align with a political party. In effect, voters themselves are largely responsible for tipping the balance in many districts by moving to where they can find neighbors of like mind.

Vanderbilt University professor Bruce Oppenheimer has a simple way of testing whether gerrymandering is increasing partisanship in congressional districts. He recently studied the seven states that have only one representative in the House—Alaska, Delaware, Montana, North and South Dakota, Vermont and Wyoming—to compare their behavior in the 1960 and 2000 presidential elections. Since their borders are unchanging, whatever has happened in the past four decades can't be the result of redistricting.

The national vote in both the 1960 and 2000 presidential elections was evenly split.

But over the 40 years between those two elections, these seven single-district states grew more partisan than the average congressional district. In 1960, the winning candidate for president (whether Republican or Democrat) in these seven states received an average 53.1 percent of the vote. In 2000, however, the winning candidate received an average 62.9 percent of the vote.

"A lot of this has to do with self-selection," Oppenheimer said. "Democrats tend to live next to Democrats. Republicans tend to live next to Republicans."

That is indeed happening. Last year, I helped prepare a series of articles for my newspaper showing that from 1976 to 2004, most U.S. counties became increasingly lopsided politically. The paper's statistical consultant, former University of Texas sociologist Robert Cushing, found that by 2004, in one of the closest elections in U.S. history, nearly half of the country's voters lived in communities where the winning presidential candidate had won by at least a 20 percentage point margin. Over seven presidential elections, Cushing's measurements of Republican and Democratic residential segregation increased by 50 percent.

Another reason why incumbents are winning at increasing rates is that oldest of political advantages: money. Regardless of party, incumbents are raising far more money than opponents, even in districts where Republicans and Democrats live in a near electoral balance, said Abramowitz. From the early 1990s to 2002, the median spending by incumbents in these competitive districts increased from $596,000 to $910,000. Median spending by challengers in these same districts fell from $229,000 to $198,000.

During the 1970s, Abramowitz found, winning congressional candidates spent 69 percent of the amount spent by all candidates in their races. From 1998 through 2002, however, the winning candidates accounted for an average of 82 percent of the total campaign spending.

So if money and demography are mostly to blame for less competitive elections, then what good would it do to turn redistricting over to some retired judges, as Schwarzenegger has suggested? Not much, probably. In most states, regions have become so resolutely partisan that it would be nearly impossible to draw competitive districts, says Nathaniel Persily, a University of Pennsylvania law professor who has worked on redistricting cases in New York, California, Georgia and Maryland.

"That's been my experience every time I've been drawn into these redistricting cases," Persily said. "It's incredibly difficult to draw competitive districts. The only way you can do it is to turn cities into pizzas, where you have districts that go from the inner cities out into the suburbs."

Or barber poles. In the San Francisco area, Schwarzenegger's nonpartisan panels would have to draw legislative districts in stripes connecting the Democratic coast to the Republican inland, says Abramowitz.

This would require some new thinking. The opposite of the gerrymandered district is a compact legislative region encompassing a community of interest. That's the goal of most redistricting reforms. But as communities themselves become politically like-minded, these good government definitions may have to be abandoned in pursuit of competitiveness. Creating competitive districts in the age of political segregation, in short, might require more cunning than that of an Elbridge Gerry—or an action hero turned governor—and more shapes than the simple salamander.

Representation: Legislative Role

The three selections in this section are illustrative of a long-standing debate among political theorists and elected officials alike: Whose views should prevail on a given issue—the constituents' or the representatives'? In the first selection, taken from an early debate in the General Assembly of Virginia, the argument is made that legislators are obliged to act as instructed delegates—*that is, they must vote in accordance with the will of their constituents. In the second selection, Massachusetts senator and future president John F. Kennedy, writing in 1956, argues that legislators should act as* trustees, *voting according to their own consciences, regardless of whether their choices reflect the sentiments of their constituents. Finally, George Galloway, a former staff assistant in Congress, contends that on some occasions legislators must follow public opinion, but on others they are obliged to vote according to their consciences. This view, which combines both the delegate and the trustee approach, is characterized as the* politico *role.*

The Legislator as Delegate

General Assembly of Virginia

There can be no doubt that the scheme of a representative republic was derived to our forefathers from the constitution of the English House of Commons; and that that branch of the English government . . . was in its origin, and in theory always has been, purely republican. It is certain, too, that the statesmen of America, in assuming that as the model of our own institutions, designed to adopt it here in its purest form, and with its strictest republican tenets and principles. It becomes, therefore, an inquiry of yet greater utility than curiosity, to ascertain the sound doctrines of the constitution of the English House of Commons in regard to this right of the constituent to instruct the representative. For the position may safely be assumed that the wise and virtuous men who framed our constitutions deigned, that, in the United States, the constituent should have at least as much, if not a great deal more, influence over the representative than was known to have existed from time immemorial in England. Let us then interrogate the history of the British nation; let us consult the opinions of their wise men.

Instances abound in parliamentary history of formal instructions from the constituent to the representative, of which . . . the following may suffice: In 1640, the knights of the shire for Dorset and Kent informed the commons *that they had in charge from their constituents* seven articles of grievances, which they accordingly laid before the House, where they were received and acted on. In the 33rd year of Charles II, the citizens of London instructed their members to insist on the bill for excluding the Duke of York (afterward King James II) from the succession to the throne; and their representative said "that his *duty* to his electors *obliged* him to vote the bill." At a subsequent election, in 1681, in many places, formal instructions were given to the members returned, to insist on the same exclusion bill; we know, from history, how uniformly and faithfully those instructions were obeyed. . . . In 1741, the citizens of London instructed their members to vote against standing armies, excise laws, the septennial bill, and a long train of evil measures, already felt, or anticipated; and expressly affirm their right of instruction—"We think it" (say they) "our *duty*, as it is *our undoubted right*, to acquaint you, with *what we desire and expect from you, in discharge*

From Commonwealth of Virginia, General Assembly, *Journal of the Senate*, 1812, pp. 82–89. In some instances, spelling and punctuation have been altered from the original in order to achieve greater clarity.

of the great trust we repose in you, and what we take to be *your duty as our repre-sentative,* etc." In the same year, instructions of a similar character were sent from all parts of England. In 1742, the cities of London, Bristol, Edinburgh, York, and many others, instructed their members in parliament to seek redress against certain individuals suspected to have betrayed and deserted the cause of the people. . . .

Instances also are on record of the deliberate formal knowledgement of the right of instruction by the House of Commons itself, especially in old times. Thus the commons hesitated to grant supplies to King Edward III *till they had the consent of their constituents,* and desired that a new parliament might be summoned, which might be *prepared with authority from their constituents.* . . .

"Instructions" (says a member of the House of Commons) "ought to be *followed implicitly,*" after the member has respectfully given his constituents *his* opinion of them: *"Far be it from me to oppose my judgment to that of 6000 of my fellow citizens."* "The practice" (says another) "of consulting our constituents was good. I wish it was continued. *We can discharge our duty no better, than in the direction of those who sent us hither. What the people choose is right, because they choose it."* . . .

Without referring to the minor political authors . . . who have maintained these positions (quoted from one of them)—"that the people have a right to instruct their representatives; that no man ought to be chosen that will not receive instructions; that the people understand enough of the interests of the country to give general instructions; that it was the custom formerly to instruct all the members; and the nature of deputation shows that the custom was well grounded"—it is proper to mention that the great constitutional lawyer Coke . . . says, "It is the *custom of parliament,* when any new device is moved for on the king's behalf, for his aid and the like, that the commons may answer, *they dare not agree to it without conference with their counties."* And Sydney . . . maintains "that members derive their power from those that choose them; that those who give power do not give an unreserved power; that many members, in all ages, and sometimes the whole body of the commons have refused to vote until they consulted with those who sent them; that the houses have often adjourned to give them time to do so and if this were done more frequently, or if cities, towns and counties had on some occasions given instructions to their deputies, matters would probably have gone better in parliament than they have done." . . . The celebrated Edmund Burke, a man, it must be admitted, of profound knowledge, deep foresight, and transcendent abilities, disobeyed the instructions of his constituents; yet, by placing his excuse on the ground that the instructions were but the clamour of the day, he seems to admit the authority of instructions soberly and deliberately given; for he agrees, "he ought to look to their opinions" (which he explains to mean their permanent settled opinions) "but not the flash of the day"; and he says elsewhere, that he could not bear to show himself "a representative, whose face did not reflect the face of his constituents—a face that did not joy in their joys and sorrow in their sorrows." It is remarkable that, notwithstanding a most splendid display of warm and touching eloquence, the people of Bristol would not reelect Mr. Burke, for this very offense of disobeying instructions. . . .

It appears, therefore, that the right of the constituent to instruct the representative, is firmly established in England, on the broad basis of the nature of representation. The existence of that right, there, has been demonstrated by the only practicable evidence, by which the principles of an unwritten constitution can be ascertained—history and precedent.

To view the subject upon principle, the right of the constituent to instruct the representative, seems to result, clearly and conclusively, from the very nature of the representative system. Through means of that noble institution, the largest nation may, almost as conveniently as the smallest, enjoy all the advantages of a government by the people, without any of the evils of democracy— precipitation, confusion, turbulence, distraction from the ordinary and useful pursuits of industry. And it is only to avoid those and the like mischiefs, that representation is substituted for the direct suffrage of the people in the office of legislation. The representative, therefore, must in the nature of things, represent his own particular constituents only. He must, indeed, look to the general good of the nation, but he must look also, and especially to the interests of his particular constituents as concerned in the commonweal; because the general good is but the aggregate of individual happiness. He must legislate for the whole nation; but laws are expressions of the general will; and the general will is only the result of individual wills fairly collected and compared. In order . . . to express the general will . . . it is plain that the representative must express the will and speak the opinions of the constituents that depute him.

It cannot be pretended that a representative is to be the organ of his own will alone; for then, he would be so far despotic. *He must be the organ of others—* of whom? Not of the nation, for the nation deputes him not; but of his constituents, who alone know, alone have trusted, and can alone displace him. And if it be his province and his duty, in general, to express the will of his constituents, to the best of his knowledge, without being particularly informed thereof, it seems impossible to contend that he is not bound to do so when he is so especially informed and instructed.

The right of the constituent to instruct the representative, therefore, is an essential principle of the representative system. It may be remarked that wherever representation has been introduced, however unfavorable the circumstances under which it existed, however short its duration, however unimportant its functions, however dimly understood, the right of instruction has always been regarded as inseparably incidental to it. . . .

A representative has indeed a wide field of discretion left to him; and great is the confidence reposed in his integrity, fidelity, wisdom, zeal; but neither is the field of discretion boundless, nor the extent of confidence infinite; and the very discretion allowed him, and the very confidence he enjoys, is grounded on the supposition that he is charged with the will, acquainted with the opinions, and devoted to the interests of his constituents. . . .

Various objections have been urged to this claim of the constituent, of a right to instruct the representative, on which it may be proper to bestow some attention.

The first objection that comes to be considered . . . is grounded on the supposed impossibility of fairly ascertaining the sense of the constituent body. The *impossibility* is denied. It may often be a matter of great *difficulty;* but then the duty of obedience resolves itself into a question, not of principle, but of fact: whether the right of instruction has been exercised or not. The representative cannot be bound by an instruction that is not given; but that is no objection to the obligation of an instruction *actually given.* . . .

It has been urged that the representatives are not bound to obey the instructions of their constituents because the constituents do not hear the debates, and therefore, cannot be supposed judges of the matter to be voted. If this objection has force enough to defeat the right of instruction, it ought to take away, also, the right of rejecting the representative at the subsequent election. For it might be equally urged on that occasion, as against the right of instruction, that the people heard not the debate that enlightened the representative's mind—the reasons that convinced his judgment and governed his conduct. . . . In other words, the principle that mankind is competent to self-government should be renounced. The truth is, that our institutions suppose that although the representative ought to be, and generally will be, selected for superior virtue and intelligence, yet a greater mass of wisdom and virtue still reside in the constituent body than the utmost portion allotted to any individual. . . .

Finally, it has been objected, that the instructions of the constituent are not obligatory on the representative because the obligation insisted on is fortified with no sanction—the representative cannot be punished for his disobedience, and his vote is valid notwithstanding his disobedience. It is true that there is no mode of legal punishment provided for this . . . default of duty and that the act of disobedience will not invalidate the vote. It is true, too, that a representative may perversely advocate a measure which he knows to be ruinous to his country; and that neither his vote will be invalidated by his depravity, nor can he be punished by law for his crime, heinous as it surely is. But it does not follow that the one representative is *not bound to obey the instructions* of his constituents any more than that the other is not bound to obey the dictates of his conscience. Both duties stand upon the same foundation, with almost all the great political and moral obligations. The noblest duties of man are without any legal sanction: the great mass of social duties . . . , our duties to our parents, to our children, to our wives, to our families, to our neighbor, to our country, our duties to God, are, for the most part, without legal sanction, yet surely not without the strongest obligation. The duty of the *representative* to obey the instructions of the *constituent* body cannot be placed on higher ground.

Such are the opinions of the General Assembly of Virginia, on the subject of this great right of instruction, and such the general reasons on which those opinions are founded. . . .

The Legislator as Trustee

John F. Kennedy

The primary responsibility of a senator, most people assume, is to represent the views of his state. Ours is a federal system—a union of relatively sovereign states whose needs differ greatly—and my constitutional obligations as senator would thus appear to require me to represent the interests of my state. Who will speak for Massachusetts if her own senators do not? Her rights and even her identity become submerged. Her equal representation in Congress is lost. Her aspirations, however much they may from time to time be in the minority, are denied that equal opportunity to be heard to which all minority views are entitled.

Any senator need not look very long to realize that his colleagues are representing *their* local interests. And if such interests are ever to be abandoned in favor of the national good, let the constituents—not the senator—decide when and to what extent. For he is their agent in Washington, the protector of their rights, recognized by the vice president in the Senate Chamber as "the senator from Massachusetts" or "the senator from Texas."

But when all of this is said and admitted, we have not yet told the full story. For in Washington we are "United States senators" and members of the Senate of the United States as well as senators from Massachusetts and Texas. Our oath of office is administered by the vice president, not by the governors of our respective states; and we come to Washington, to paraphrase Edmund Burke, not as hostile ambassadors or special pleaders for our state or section, in opposition to advocates and agents of other areas, but as members of the deliberative assembly of one nation with one interest. Of course, we should not ignore the needs of our area—nor could we easily as products of that area—but none could be found to look out for the national interest if local interests wholly dominated the role of each of us.

There are other obligations in addition to those of state and region—the obligations of the party. . . . Even if I can disregard those pressures, do I not have an obligation to go along with the party that placed me in office? We

John F. Kennedy (1917–1963), thirty-fifth president of the United States, was a Democratic member of the U.S. Senate from Massachusetts from 1952 to 1960 and a member of the U.S. House of Representatives from 1947 to 1952. Selected excerpts from pp. 33–39 from *Profiles in Courage* by John F. Kennedy. Copyright © 1955, 1956, 1961 by John F. Kennedy. Copyright renewed © 1983, 1984, 1989 by Jacqueline Kennedy Onassis. Foreword copyright © 1964 by Robert F. Kennedy. Reprinted by permission of HarperCollins Publishers, Inc.

believe in this country in the principle of party responsibility, and we recognize the necessity of adhering to party platforms—if the party label is to mean anything to the voters. Only in this way can our basically two-party nation avoid the pitfalls of multiple splinter parties, whose purity and rigidity of principle, I might add—if I may suggest a sort of Gresham's Law of politics—increase inversely with the size of their membership.

And yet we cannot permit the pressures of party responsibility to submerge on every issue the call of personal responsibility. For the party which, in its drive for unity, discipline and success, ever decides to exclude new ideas, independent conduct or insurgent members, is in danger. . . .

Of course, both major parties today seek to serve the national interest. They would do so in order to obtain the broadest base of support, if for no nobler reason. But when party and officeholder differ as to how the national interest is to be served, we must place first the responsibility we owe not to our party or even to our constituents but to our individual consciences.

But it is a little easier to dismiss one's obligations to local interests and party ties to face squarely the problem of one's responsibility to the will of his constituents. A senator who avoids this responsibility would appear to be accountable to no one, and the basic safeguards of our democratic system would thus have vanished. He is no longer representative in the true sense, he has violated his public trust, he has betrayed the confidence demonstrated by those who voted for him to carry out their views. "Is the creature," as John Tyler asked the House of Representatives in his maiden speech, "to set himself in opposition to his Creator? Is the servant to disobey the wishes of his master?"

> How can he be regarded as representing the people when he speaks, not their language, but his own? He ceases to be their representative when he does so, and represents himself alone.

In short, according to this school of thought, if I am to be properly responsive to the will of my constituents, it is my duty to place their principles, not mine, above all else. This may not always be easy, but it nevertheless is the essence of democracy, faith in the wisdom of the people and their views. To be sure, the people will make mistakes—they will get no better government than they deserve—but that is far better than the representative of the people arrogating for himself the right to say he knows better than they what is good for them. Is he not chosen, the argument closes, to vote as they would vote were they in his place?

It is difficult to accept such a narrow view of the role of a United States senator—a view that assumes the people of Massachusetts sent me to Washington to serve merely as a seismograph to record shifts in popular opinion. I reject this view not because I lack faith in the "wisdom of the people," but because this concept of democracy actually puts too little faith in the people. Those who would deny the obligation of the representative to be bound by every impulse of the electorate—regardless of the conclusions his own deliberations direct—do trust in the wisdom of the people. They have faith in their ultimate sense of justice, faith in their ability to honor courage and respect judgment, and faith that in the long run they will act unselfishly for the good of the nation. It is that kind of faith on which democracy is based, not simply the often frustrated hope that public opinion will at all times under all circumstances promptly identify itself with the public interest.

The voters selected us, in short, because they had confidence in our judgment and our ability to exercise that judgment from a position where we could determine what were their own best interests, as a part of the nation's interests. This may mean that we must on occasion lead, inform, correct and sometimes even ignore constituent opinion, if we are to exercise fully that judgment for which we were elected. But acting without selfish motive or private bias, those who follow the dictates of an intelligent conscience are not aristocrats, demagogues, eccentrics, or callous politicians insensitive to the feelings of the public. They expect—and not without considerable trepidation—their constituents to be the final judges of the wisdom of their course; but they have faith that those constituents—today, tomorrow, or even in another generation—will at least respect the principles that motivated their independent stand.

If their careers are temporarily or even permanently buried under an avalanche of abusive editorials, poison-pen letters, and opposition votes at the polls—as they sometimes are, for that is the risk they take—they await the future with hope and confidence, aware of the fact that the voting public frequently suffers from what ex-Congressman T. V. Smith called the lag "between our way of thought and our way of life." . . .

Moreover, I question whether any senator, before we vote on a measure, can state with certainty exactly how the majority of his constituents feel on the issue as it is presented to the Senate. All of us in the Senate live in an iron lung—the iron lung of politics, and it is no easy task to emerge from that rarefied atmosphere in order to breathe the same fresh air our constituents breathe. It is difficult, too, to see in person an appreciable number of voters besides those professional hangers-on and vocal elements who gather about the politician on a trip home. In Washington I frequently find myself believing that forty or fifty letters, six visits from professional politicians and lobbyists, and three editorials in Massachusetts newspapers constitute public opinion on a given issue. Yet in truth I rarely know how the great majority of the voters feel, or even how much they know of the issues that seem so burning in Washington.

Today the challenge of political courage looms larger than ever before. For our everyday life is becoming so saturated with the tremendous power of mass communications that any unpopular or unorthodox course arouses a storm of protests. . . . Our political life is becoming so expensive, so mechanized, and so dominated by professional politicians and public relations men that the idealist who dreams of independent statesmanship is rudely awakened by the necessities of election and accomplishment. . . .

And thus, in the days ahead, only the very courageous will be able to take the hard and unpopular decisions necessary for our survival. . . .

The Legislator as Politico
George B. Galloway

One question which the conscientious congressman must often ask himself, especially when conflicts arise between local or regional attitudes and interests and the national welfare, is this: "As a member of Congress, am I merely a delegate from my district or state, restricted to act and vote as the majority which elected me desire, bound by the instructions of my constituents and subservient to their will? Or am I, once elected, a representative of the people of the United States, free to act as I think best for the country generally?"

In a country as large as the United States, with such diverse interests and such a heterogeneous population, the economic interests and social prejudices of particular states and regions often clash with those of other sections and with conceptions of the general interest of the whole nation. The perennial demand of the silver-mining and wool interests in certain western states for purchase and protection, the struggle over slavery, and the . . . filibuster of southern senators against the attempt to outlaw racial discrimination in employment are familiar examples of recurring conflicts between local interests and prejudices and the common welfare. These political quarrels are rooted in the varying stages of cultural development attained by the different parts of the country. It is the peculiar task of the politician to compose these differences, to reconcile conflicting national and local attitudes, and to determine when public opinion is ripe for legislative action. Some conflicts will yield in time to political adjustment; others must wait for their legal sanction upon the gradual evolution of the conscience of society. No act of Congress can abolish unemployment or barking dogs or racial prejudices. . . .

TYPES OF PRESSURES ON CONGRESS

One can sympathize with the plight of the conscientious congressman who is the focal point of all these competing pressures. The district or state he represents may need and want certain roads, post offices, courthouses, or schools. Irrigation dams or projects may be needed for the development of the area's resources.

George B. Galloway (1898–1967) was a senior specialist in American government with the Legislative Reference Service of the Library of Congress. Selected excerpts are from pp. 284–285, 301, and 319–322 from Congress at the Crossroads by George B. Galloway. Copyright 1946 by George B. Galloway. Reprinted by permission of HarperCollins Publishers, Inc.

If the representative is to prove himself successful in the eyes of the people back home, he must be able to show, at least occasionally, some visible and concrete results of his congressional activity. Or else he must be able to give good reasons why he has not been able to carry out his pledges. The local residence rule for congressmen multiplies the pressures that impinge upon him. Faithful party workers who have helped elect him will expect the congressman to pay his political debts by getting them jobs in the federal service. Constituents affected by proposed legislation may send him an avalanche of letters, telegrams, and petitions which must be acknowledged and followed up. The region from which he comes will expect him to protect and advance its interests in Washington. All the various organized groups will press their claims upon him and threaten him if he does not jump when they crack the whip. Party leaders may urge a congressman to support or oppose the administration program or to "trade" votes for the sake of party harmony or various sectional interests. He is also under pressure from his own conscience as to what he should do both to help the people who have elected him and to advance the best interests of the nation. Besieged by all these competing pressures, a congressman is often faced with the choice of compromising between various pressures, of trading votes, of resisting special interests of one sort or another, of staying off the floor when a vote is taken on some measure he prefers not to take a stand on, of getting support here and at the same time running the risk of losing support there. Dealing with pressure blocs is a problem in political psychology which involves a careful calculation of the power of the blocs, the reaction of the voters on election day, and the long-haul interests of the district, state, and nation. . . .

SHOULD CONGRESS LEAD OR FOLLOW PUBLIC OPINION?

It is axiomatic to say that in a democracy public opinion is the source of law. Unless legislation is sanctioned by the sense of right of the people, it becomes a dead letter on the statute books, like Prohibition and the Hatch Act. But public opinion is a mercurial force; now quiescent, now vociferous, it has various moods and qualities. It reacts to events and is often vague and hard to weigh.

Nor is public opinion infallible. Most people are naturally preoccupied with their personal problems and daily affairs; national problems and legislative decisions seem complex and remote to them, despite press and radio and occasional Capitol tours. Comparatively few adults understand the technicalities of foreign loans or reciprocal trade treaties, although congressional action on these aspects of our foreign economic policy may have far-reaching effects upon our standard of living. . . .

In practice, a congressman both leads and follows public opinion. The desires of his constituents, of his party, and of this or that pressure group all enter into his decisions on matters of major importance. The influence of these factors varies from member to member and measure to measure. Some congressmen consider it their duty to follow closely what they think is the majority opinion of their constituents, especially just before an election. Others feel that they should make their decisions without regard to their constituents' wishes in the first place, and then try to educate and convert them afterward. Some members are strong party men and follow more or less blindly the program of the party leaders. Except when they are very powerful in the home district, the pressure groups are more of a nuisance than a deciding influence on the average member. When a legislator is caught between the conflicting pressures of his constituents and his colleagues, he perforce compromises between them and follows his own judgment.

The average legislator discovers early in his career that certain interests or prejudices of his constituents are dangerous to trifle with. Some of these prejudices may not be of fundamental importance to the welfare of the nation, in which case he is justified in humoring them, even though he may disapprove. The difficult case occurs where the prejudice concerns some fundamental policy affecting the national welfare. A sound sense of values, the ability to discriminate between that which is of fundamental importance and that which is only superficial, is an indispensable qualification of a good legislator.

Senator Fulbright* gives an interesting example of this distinction in his stand on the poll-tax issue and isolationism. "Regardless of how persuasive my colleagues or the national press may be about the evils of the poll tax, I do not see its fundamental importance, and I shall follow the views of the people of my state. Although it may be symbolic of conditions which many deplore, it is exceedingly doubtful that its abolition will cure any of our major problems. On the other hand, regardless of how strongly opposed my constituents may prove to be to the creation of, and participation in, an ever stronger United Nations Organization, I could not follow such a policy in that field unless it becomes clearly hopeless."[1]

A TWO-WAY JOB

As believers in democracy, probably most Americans would agree that it is the duty of congressmen to follow public opinion insofar as it expresses the desires, wants, needs, aspirations, and ideals of the people. Most Americans probably would also consider it essential for their representatives to make as careful an appraisal of these needs and desires as they can, and to consider, in connection with such an appraisal, the ways and means of accomplishing them. Legislators have at hand more information about legal structures, economic problems, productive capacities, manpower possibilities, and the like, than the average citizen they represent. They can draw upon that information to inform and lead the people—by showing the extent to which their desires can be realized.

In other words, a true representative of the people would follow the people's desires and at the same time lead the people in formulating ways of accomplishing those desires. He would lead the people in the sense of calling

*At the time this article was written, J. William Fulbright was a U.S. senator from Arkansas.—*Editors.*

to their attention the difficulties of achieving those aims and the ways to overcome the difficulties. This means also that, where necessary, he would show special interest groups or even majorities how, according to his own interpretation and his own conscience, their desires need to be tempered in the common interest or for the future good of the nation.

Thus the job of a congressman is a two-way one. He represents his local area and interests in the national capital, and he also informs the people back home of the problems arising at the seat of government and how these problems affect them. It is in the nature of the congressman's job that he should determine, as far as he can, public opinion in his own constituency and in the whole nation, analyze it, measure it in terms of the practicability of turning it into public policy, and consider it in the light of his own knowledge, conscience, and convictions. Occasionally he may be obliged to go against public opinion, with the consequent task of educating or reeducating the people along lines that seem to him more sound. And finally, since he is a human being eager to succeed at his important job of statesmanship and politics, he is realistic enough to keep his eyes on the voters in terms of the next election. But he understands that a mere weather-vane following of majority public opinion is not always the path to reelection. . . .

NOTE

1. In an address on "The Legislator" delivered at the University of Chicago on February 19, 1946. *Vital Speeches*, May 15, 1946, pp. 468–472.

Legislative Process: The Filibuster

The legislative process in Congress requires the building of coalitions among its members over and over again until all legislative hurdles have been overcome. Thus, successful legislators are those who are able to shepherd legislation through various committees in both houses, then to the floors of the House and Senate, then to the conference committees, and then back to the floors. If the legislation requires an appropriation, the whole process is repeated with different committees.

Although there is much that is the same legislatively in the House of Representatives and in the Senate, there are some critical differences that, in the end, make the passage of legislation very difficult. One such difference is the filibuster *in the Senate.*

In the House of Representatives, the majority party leadership (i.e., the Speaker of the House, the majority leader, and others) control the flow of legislation. In the Senate that control is ultimately in the hands of senators themselves. Typically, if the Speaker of the House wants something, he or she can get it. In the Senate, however, a group of senators determined to block action can do so through the filibuster.

The filibuster is a legislative device to prevent action on a bill. It grows out of the necessity, under Senate custom and rules, for the Senate as a whole to determine when debate on a bill will end. Under the current rule, a three-fifths vote is required to end debate. This "supermajority"—sixty senators—is extremely difficult to achieve.

For much of the twentieth century, the filibuster was used sparingly and usually on the most critical of issues, such as civil rights bills. In recent years, however, the filibuster has been elevated to a new level, with senators from both parties either threatening or carrying out a filibuster almost as a matter of course on any manner of bills. Indeed, there have been more than thirty filibusters a year since 1993. In 2005, the minority Democrats used the filibuster to block nominees to the federal courts, thus causing the majority Republicans to threaten to take away the filibuster altogether in cases involving judicial nominations.

The central issue surrounding the filibuster is the extent to which a minority of senators should be able to block the will of the majority. Some argue, as does Senator Tom Harkin (D-Iowa) in the first selection, that whatever validity the filibuster had in history (and he thinks it was very little), it should not be allowed to continue unchanged today. The filibuster, he argues, only leads to gridlock in the legislative process, contributing to even greater cynicism and frustration among the American people.

In the second selection, a former member of the House of Representatives, Bill Frenzel (R-Minn.), makes the case for keeping the filibuster. Frenzel argues that the filibuster fits into the general scheme of limited government fashioned by the framers of the Constitution and should not be cast aside merely because it is viewed today as a major impediment to majority rule. According to Frenzel, if a majority of the people truly want the government to act, the Congress, including the Senate, will act. In the meantime, the filibuster is a useful device to filter out unneeded or unwise legislation.

167

It's Time to Change the Filibuster

Tom Harkin

Mr. Harkin. Mr. President, for the benefit of the Senators who are here and watching on the monitors, we now have before us an amendment by myself, Senator Lieberman, Senator Pell, and Senator Robb that would amend rule XXII, the so-called filibuster rule of the U.S. Senate. . . .

This amendment would change the way this Senate operates more fundamentally than anything that has been proposed thus far this year. It would fundamentally change the way we do business by changing the filibuster rule as it currently stands.

Mr. President, the last Congress showed us the destructive impact filibusters can have on the legislative process, provoking gridlock after gridlock, frustration, anger, and despondency among the American people, wondering whether we can get anything done at all here in Washington. The pattern of filibusters and delays that we saw in the last Congress is part of the rising tide of filibusters that have overwhelmed our legislative process.

While some may gloat and glory in the frustration and anger that the American people felt toward our institution which resulted in the tidal wave of dissatisfaction that struck the majority in Congress, I believe in the long run that it will harm the Senate and our Nation for this pattern to continue. . . . Mr. President, there has . . . been a rising tide in the use of the filibuster. In the last two Congresses, in 1987 to 1990, and 1991 to 1994, there have been twice as many filibusters per year as there were the last time the Republicans controlled the Senate, from 1981 to 1986, and 10 times as many as occurred between 1917 and 1960. Between 1917 and 1960, there were an average of 1.3 per session. However, in the last Congress, there were 10 times that many. This is not healthy for our legislative process and it is not healthy for our country.

I have [also] compare[d] filibusters in the entire 19th century and in the last Congress. We had twice as many filibusters in the 103d Congress as we had in the entire 100 years of the 19th century.

Clearly, this is a process that is out of control. We need to change the rules. We need to change the rules, however, without harming the long-standing Senate tradition of extended debate and deliberation, and slowing things down.

Tom Harkin is a Democratic U.S. senator from Iowa. Excerpted from a speech delivered in the U.S. Senate, *Congressional Record,* Proceedings and Debates of the 104th Congress. First Session, Senate, January 4, 1995, vol. 141, no. 1, 530–533, and January 5, 1995, vol. 141, no. 2, 5431.

I have here [also] the issues that were subject to filibusters in the last Congress. Some of these were merely delayed by filibusters. Others were killed outright, despite having the majority of both bodies and the President in favor of them. That is right. Some of these measures had a majority of support in the Senate and in the House, and by the President. Yet, they never saw the light of day. Others simply were perfunctory housekeeping types of issues.

For example, one might understand why someone would filibuster the Brady Handgun Act. There were people that felt very strongly opposed to that. I can understand that being slowed down, and having extended debate on it. Can you say that about the J. Larry Lawrence nomination? I happen to be a personal friend of Mr. Lawrence. He is now our Ambassador to Switzerland, an important post. He was nominated to be Ambassador there, and he came through the committee fine. Yet, his nomination was the subject of a filibuster. Or there was the Edward P. Berry, Jr., nomination. There was the Claude Bolton nomination. You get my point.

We had nominations that were filibustered. This was almost unheard of in our past. We filibustered the nomination of a person that actually came through the committee process and was approved by the committee, and it was filibustered here on the Senate floor.

Actually, Senators use these nominations as a lever for power. If one Senator has an issue where he or she wants something done, it is very easy. All a Senator needs to do is filibuster a nomination. Then the majority leader or the minority leader has to come to the Senator and say, "Would you release your hold on that, give up your filibuster on that?"

"OK," the Senator will reply. "What do you want in return?"

Then the deals are struck.

It is used, Mr. President, as blackmail for one Senator to get his or her way on something that they could not rightfully win through the normal processes. I am not accusing any one party of this. It happens on both sides of the aisle.

Mr. President, I believe each Senator needs to give up a little of our pride, a little of our prerogatives, and a little of our power for the good of this Senate and for the good of this country. Let me repeat that: Each Senator, I believe, has to give up a little of our pride, a little of our prerogatives, and a little of our power for the better functioning of this body and for the good of our country.

I think the voters of this country were turned off by the constant bickering, the arguing back and forth that goes on in this Senate Chamber, the gridlock that ensued here, and the pointing of fingers of blame.

Sometimes, in the fog of debate, like the fog of war, it is hard to determine who is responsible for slowing something down. It is like the shifting sand. People hide behind the filibuster. I think it is time to let the voters know that we heard their message in the last election. They did not send us here to bicker and to argue, to point fingers. They want us to get things done to address the concerns facing this country. They want us to reform this place. They want this place to operate a little better, a little more openly, and a little more decisively.

Mr. President, I believe this Senate should embrace the vision of this body that our Founding Fathers had. There is a story—I am not certain whether it is true or not, but it is a nice story—that Thomas Jefferson returned from France, where he had learned that the Constitutional Convention had set up a separate body called the U.S. Senate, with its Members appointed by the legislatures and not subject to a popular vote. Jefferson was quite upset about this. He asked George Washington why this was done. Evidently, they were sitting at a breakfast table. Washington said to him, "Well, why did you pour your coffee in the saucer?" And Jefferson replied, "Why, to cool it, of course." Washington replied, "Just so: We created the Senate to cool down the legislation that may come from the House."

I think General Washington was very wise. I think our Founding Fathers were very wise to create this body.

They had seen what had happened in Europe—violent changes, rapid changes, mob rule—so they wanted the process to slow things down, to deliberate a little more, and that is why the Senate was set up.

But George Washington did not compare the Senate to throwing the coffee pot out the window. It is just to cool it down, and slow it down.

I think that is what the Founding Fathers envisioned, and I think that is what the American people expect. That is what we ought to and should provide. The Senate should carefully consider legislation, whether it originates here, or whether it streams in like water from a fire hose from the House of Representatives, we must provide ample time for Members to speak on issues. We should not move to the limited debate that characterizes the House of Representatives. I am not suggesting that we do that. But in the end, the people of our country are entitled to know where we stand and how we vote on the merits of a bill or an amendment.

Some argue that any supermajority requirement is unconstitutional, other than those specified in the Constitution itself. I find much in this theory to agree with—and I think we should treat all the rules that would limit the ability of a majority to rule with skepticism. I think that this theory is one that we ought to examine more fully, and that is the idea that the Constitution of the United States sets up certain specified instances in which a supermajority is needed to pass the bill, and in all other cases it is silent. In fact, the Constitution provides that the President of the Senate, the Vice President of the United States, can only vote to break a tie vote—by implication, meaning that the Senate should pass legislation by a majority vote, except in those instances in which the Constitution specifically says that we need a supermajority.

The distinguished constitutional expert, Lloyd Cutler, a distinguished lawyer, has been a leading proponent of this view. I have not made up my mind on this theory, but I do believe it is something we ought to further examine. I find a lot that I agree with in that theory.

But what we are getting at here is a different procedure and process, whereby we can have the Senate as the Founding Fathers envisioned—a place to cool down, slow down, deliberate and discuss, but not as a place where a handful— yes, maybe even one Senator—can totally stop legislation or a nomination.

Over the last couple of years, I have spent a great deal of time reading the history of this cloture process. Two years ago, about this time, I first proposed this to my fellow Democratic colleagues at a retreat we had in Williamsburg, VA.

In May of that year, I proposed this to the Joint Committee on Congressional Reform. Some people said to me at that time: Senator Harkin, of course you are proposing it, you are in the majority, you want to get rid of the filibuster. Well, now I am in the minority and I am still proposing it because I think it is the right thing to do.

Let me take some time to discuss the history of cloture and the limitations on debate in the Senate. Prior to 1917 there was no mechanism to shut off debate in the Senate. There was an early version in 1789 of what was called the "previous question." It was used more like a tabling motion than as a method to close debate.

In the 19th century, Mr. President, elections were held in November and Congress met in December. This Congress was always a lame duck session, which ended in March of the next year. The newly elected members did not take office until the following December, almost 13 months later. During the entire 19th century, there were filibusters. But most of these were aimed at delaying congressional action at the end of the short session that ended March 4. A filibuster during the 19th century was used at the end of a session when the majority would try to ram something through at the end, over the objections of the minority. Extended debate was used to extend debate to March 4, when under the law at that time, it automatically died.

If the majority tried to ram something through in the closing hours, the minority would discuss it and hold it up until March 4, and that was the end of it. That process was changed. Rather than going into an automatic lame-duck session in December, we now convene a new Congress in January with the new Members. I think this is illustrative that the filibuster used in the 19th century was entirely different in concept and in form than what we now experience here in the U.S. Senate.

So those who argue that the filibuster in the U.S. Senate today is a time-honored tradition of the U.S. Senate going clear back to 1789 are mistaken, because the use of the filibuster in the 19th century was entirely different than what it is being used for today, and it was used in a different set of laws and circumstances under which Congress met.

So that brings us up to the 20th century. In 1917, the first cloture rule was introduced in response to a filibuster, again, at the end of a session that triggered a special session. This cloture rule provided for two-thirds of Members present and voting to cut off debate. It was the first time since the first Congress met that the Senate adopted a cloture rule in 1917. However, this cloture rule was found to be ineffective and was rarely used. Why? Because rulings of the chair said that the cloture rule did not apply to procedural matters. So, if someone wanted to engage in a filibuster, they could simply bring up a procedural matter and filibuster that, and the two-thirds vote did not even apply to that. For a number of years, from 1917 until 1949, we had that situation.

In 1949 an attempt was made to make the cloture motion more effective. The 1949 rule applied the cloture rule to procedural matters. It closed that loophole but did not apply to rules changes. It also raised the needed vote from two-thirds present and voting to two-thirds of the whole Senate, which at that time meant 64 votes. That rule existed for 10 years.

In 1959, Lyndon Johnson pushed through a rules change to change the needed vote back to two-thirds of those present and voting, and which also applied cloture to rules changes.

There were many attempts after that to change the filibuster. In 1975, after several years of debate here in the Senate, the current rule was adopted, as a compromise proposed by Senator Byrd of West Virginia. The present cloture rule allows cloture to be invoked by three-fifths of Senators chosen and sworn, or 60 votes, except in the case of rules changes, which still require two-thirds of those present and voting.

This change in the rule reducing the proportion of votes needed for cloture for the first time since 1917, was the culmination of many years of efforts by reformers' numerous proposals between 1959 and 1975.

Two of the proposals that were made in those intervening years I found particularly interesting. One was by Senator Hubert Humphrey in 1963, which provided for majority cloture in two stages. The other proposal I found interesting was one by Senator Dole in 1971 that moved from the then current two-thirds present and voting down to three-fifths present and voting, reducing the number of votes by one with each successive cloture vote.

We drew upon Senator Dole's proposal in developing our own proposal. Our proposal would reduce the number of votes needed to invoke cloture gradually, allowing time for debate, allowing us to slow things down, but ultimately allowing the Senate to get to the merits of a vote.

Under our proposal, the amendment now before the Senate, Senators still have to get 16 signatures to offer a cloture motion. The motion would still have to lay over 2 days. The first vote to invoke cloture would require 60 votes. If that vote did not succeed, they could file another cloture motion needing 16 signatures. They would have to wait at least 2 further days. On the next vote, they would need 57 votes to invoke cloture. If you did not get that, well, you would have to get 16 signatures, file another cloture motion, wait another couple days, and then you would have to have 54 votes. Finally, the same procedure could be repeated, and move to a cloture vote of 51. Finally, a simple majority vote could close debate, to get to the merits of the issue.

By allowing this slow ratchet down, the minority would have the opportunity to debate, focus public attention on a bill, and communicate their case to the public. In the end, though, the majority could bring the measure to a final vote, as it generally should in a democracy.

Mr. President, in the 19th century as I mentioned before, filibusters were used to delay action on a measure until the automatic expiration of the session.

Senators would then leave to go back to their States, or Congressmen back to their districts, and tell people about the legislation the majority was trying to ram through. They could get the public aroused about it, to put pressure on Senators not to support that measure or legislation.

Keep in mind that in those days, there was no television, there was no radio, and scant few newspapers. Many people could not read or write and the best means of communication was when a Senator went out and spoke directly with his constituents. So it was necessary to have several months where a

Senator could alert the public as to what the majority was trying to do, to protect the rights and interests of the minority.

That is not the case today. Every word we say here is instantaneously beamed out on C-SPAN, watched all over the United States, and picked up on news broadcasts. We have the print media sitting up in the gallery. So the public is well aware and well informed of what is happening here in the Senate on a daily basis. We do have a need to slow the process down, but we do not need the several months that was needed in the 19th century.

So as a Member of the new minority here in the Senate, I come to this issue as a clear matter of good public policy. I am pleased to say that it is a change that enjoys overwhelming support among the American people.

A recent poll conducted by Action Not Gridlock . . . found that 80 percent of Independents, 84 percent of Democrats, and 79 percent of Republicans believe that once all Senators have been able to express their views, the Senate should be permitted to vote for or against a bill. . . .

. . . [S]laying the filibuster dinosaur—and that is what I call it, a dinosaur, a relic of the ancient past—slaying the filibuster dinosaur has also been endorsed by papers around the country, including the *New York Times, USA Today,* and the *Washington Post.* . . .

* * *

But I will close my opening remarks, with this quote:

> It is one thing to provide protection against majoritarian absolutism; it is another thing again to enable a vexatious or unreasoning minority to paralyze the Senate and America's legislative process along with it.

I could not have said it better, and it was said by Senator Robert Dole, February 10, 1971.

If Senator Dole thought the filibuster was bad in 1971, certainly when we are down here, the filibuster has increased at least threefold on an annual basis since then. So it is time to get rid of this dinosaur. It is time to move ahead with the people's business in a productive manner.

Defending the Dinosaur
The Case for Not Fixing the Filibuster
Bill Frenzel

Defending the filibuster may not be quite as nasty as taking candy from a baby, but neither is it a good route to popular acclaim. Few kind words are ever spoken in defense of filibusters. Conventional wisdom and political correctness have pronounced them to be pernicious. The very word is pejorative, evoking ugly images of antidemocratic activities.

During the last biennium, filibusters became so unlovable that a group, including former senators, formed "Action, Not Gridlock!" to try to stamp them out. The public, which had tested both gridlock and action, seemed to prefer the former. The organization disappeared.

As that public reaction suggests, political correctness is a sometime thing and conventional wisdom oft goes astray. The American public may not be rushing to embrace the filibuster, but neither has it shown any inclination to root it out. The Senate's overwhelming vote . . . against changing the filibuster means that the practice won't go away soon, so it is worth examining. Despite its bad press, the story of the modern filibuster is not one-sided.

FILIBUSTERS, THE CONSTITUTION, AND THE FRAMERS

Filibuster haters claim they are contrary to the spirit of the Constitution because they require extraordinary majorities. The rationale is that the Framers, who created a majority system and rejected supermajorities, would be horrified by filibusters. Perhaps, but don't be too sure. Remember that no one has dug up a Framer lately to testify to the accuracy of this theory.

The Framers created our system based on their profound distrust of government. They loaded the system with checks and balances to make it work very slowly and with great difficulty. Their intention was to prevent swift enactment of laws and to avoid satisfying the popular whimsy of each willful majority. Maybe they would trade popular election for a filibuster rule.

Bill Frenzel is a former Republican U.S. representative from Minnesota (1971–1991). From Bill Frenzel, "Defending the Dinosaur: The Case for Not Fixing the Filibuster," *The Brookings Review* (Summer 1995), pp. 47–49. Reprinted by permission.

Without any live Framers, we can only speculate about their feelings. However, it is hard to believe that, having designed an extremely balky system, they would want to speed it up today. More likely, they would merely remind us that for more than 200 years major American policymaking has been based on "concurrent majorities" anyway.

PARLIAMENTARY COMPARISONS

Most of the parliaments of the world are copies, or variants, of Westminster [England]. With only one strong house and no separated executive branch, they can usually deliver laws swiftly. But when their actions affront public opinion, there is a political price to be paid, often very quickly. The government that offends the people soon becomes the opposition.

In our regional system, our majorities, assisted by a wide range of taxpayer-paid perks, do not usually pay any price. Our members of Congress are unbeatable (even in the earthquake of 1994, more than 90 percent of them who sought reelection were reelected). Our majorities are not eternal, but they are long-lived, unlike the Westminster forms.

It might make sense to consider trading the filibuster for congressional mortality (perhaps through term limits), but it is probably unwise to accept the blockbuster majority power of the Westminster system without accepting its balance of political turnover in return.

Actually, filibusters are not unique to the United States. Other parliaments are finding new opportunities for dilatory practices. The Japanese upper house recently presented its "ox-step," and an appointed majority in the Canadian Senate frustrated the intentions of the prime minister and his government on the ratification of the U.S.–Canada Free Trade Agreement. The strokes are different for different folks, but we are not alone. Delay is a time-honored political exercise that transcends political boundaries.

THE FILIBUSTER AND THE POPULAR WILL

The filibuster has been often indicted for denying the popular will, but over recent history, that point is hard to demonstrate. In the first place, it is not easy to get, and hold, 41 votes in the Senate under any circumstances. It is practically impossible to do so against a popular proposal. Filibusters simply do not succeed *unless* they have popular support or unless there is a lack of enthusiasm for the proposal being filibustered.

In 1993 Senator Bob Dole (R-KS) led a filibuster against the Clinton Emergency Spending Bill. It succeeded because the public liked the filibuster better than the spending. In the Bush years, Senator George Mitchell (D-ME) stopped a capital gains proposal by threat of filibuster. Senator Mitchell succeeded because the people saw no urgency in the proposal. In both cases, political reality prevailed.

If the public wants a vote, it tells its representatives. In 1994 Senate Republicans tried to filibuster the Crime Bill. Based on hot flashes from home, more than 60 senators perceived that the bill was popular, so the filibuster was broken quickly. The same thing happened to the Motor Voter Bill, the National Service Bill, and five out of six presidential appointments. If any proposal has substantial public support, a couple of cloture votes will kill the filibuster. The political reality is: frivolous filibusters do not succeed. The modern filibuster can gridlock ideas that are not popular, but it has not gridlocked the people.

THE BICAMERAL SYSTEM

In our unique system, the two houses of Congress have developed similar, but not identical, personalities and processes. The House of Representatives, with 440 orators, is harder to manage and has therefore created a set of rules to limit debate. In recent years, its majority has handled bills under rules that permitted few, if any, amendments and only an hour or two of debate.

The Senate, with only 100 orators, has stayed with free debate and an open amendment system. That is not a bad division of process. One house has been too closed, the other too open. The House operates with the relentlessness of Westminster majority, and the Senate has more time to examine, to delay, to amend, and, if necessary, to kill. All are vital functions of any legislature. . . .

There is still a relatively open pipeline for bills flowing from the House. . . . Following the Framers' wisdom, it is prudent to have a sieve in the Senate to compete with that open pipe in the House. At least some of the worst legislative lumps may be smoothed out in the finer mesh. . . .

KEY TO COMPROMISE

Many filibusters are not filibusters at all, but merely threats. Most are undertaken to notify the managers of the proposal that problems exist. They are a signal from a minority to a majority that negotiations are in order. Sometimes the majority tries a cloture vote or two before negotiating. Sometimes it negotiates. Sometimes it does not.

Most of these procedures end in a modified bill, not a dead bill. The Crime Bill noted above passed. The Dole filibuster of emergency spending did not prevent passage of many of its bits of pork in regular appropriations bills. . . .

The filibuster surely gives a minority a little more clout, but it does not prevent a majority from passing reasonably popular proposals. It gives a minority the opportunity to negotiate what it believes is an intolerable proposal into one it can live with. That compromise may serve the needs of the majority tolerably well too.

NO NEED FOR A HEAVY HAND

One political reality test for the filibuster is the congressional ingenuity in finding ways to avoid it when necessary. Trade and Reconciliation bills are considered under laws that obviate filibusters. When there is a good reason to finesse the filibuster, the Senate always seems to get the job done.

Many other Senate rules, only dimly understood by common folks, reduce the legislative pace. I do not mean to bless multiple efforts to filibuster the same proposal. Once on the bill and once on the conference report is enough. Unlimited amendment after cloture is also too much opportunity for mischief.

Former Senate Majority Leader Mitchell has left constructive proposals to speed the work of the Senate without damaging the filibuster. They ought to be considered. The minority needs rights for protection. The majority needs the ability to move its program. Both needs can be well served by the modern 60-vote cloture rule. It should not be changed.

KEEP THE FILIBUSTER

The test of the filibuster ought to be whether it is fair, appropriate, and constructive. It may have been a killer in the old days, when it slew civil rights bills, but under the new 60-vote system, it is difficult to recall a filibustered proposition that stayed dead if it was popular.

Most antifilibuster noise comes from advocates of ideas that were going to fail anyway. It is not essential for every idea that comes bouncing up or down Pennsylvania Avenue to become law. The filibuster is a useful legislative tool, consistent with the goals of the Framers, that keeps whimsical, immature, and ultimately unpopular bills out of the statute books. . . .

 **mhhe.com/**diclerico11e

Internet resources
Visit our Web site at www.mhhe.com/diclerico11e for links and resources relating to Congress.

c h a p t e r   1 1

The Presidency

*I*n 1973, the noted historian Arthur Schlesinger Jr. published his influential book The Imperial Presidency. In it he argued that the powers and prerogatives of the office had grown so extensive over the course of the twentieth century that our cherished principle of balanced government was in jeopardy. Richard Nixon, whose abuses of power ultimately forced his resignation from office, represented for Schlesinger the farthest extension of that trend.

Even before Nixon's departure, scholars, politicians, and political observers alike were calling upon Congress to rein in the power of the "imperial presidency." Legislators responded to that call, moving on the domestic and foreign policy fronts to limit and render more accountable the exercise of presidential power. These actions, in the judgment of John Yoo, author of the first selection, had the unfortunate effect of shifting the balance of power decidedly in the direction of Congress, whose size and fragmentation render it ill-suited to managing the day-to-day policies of the federal government. Accordingly, Yoo strongly endorses George W. Bush's efforts to restore the vigor of the presidency through the robust and rightful exercise of its constitutional powers on matters both foreign and domestic.

Frederick Schwarz Jr. and Aziz Huq could not disagree more. In the second selection they maintain that congressional efforts to rein in the presidency during the 1970s have given way to a more passive congressional posture. As a result, the president, taking full advantage of the 9/11 crisis, is exercising powers that go well beyond both the Constitution and the laws of our nation, and, they assert, his conception of the presidency is wholly inconsistent with what the Founders intended.

Eric Posner, in the third selection, writes from a longer perspective, suggesting that the charges of an "imperial presidency" now being leveled at George W. Bush are nothing new in American history. Nor, judging by the historical record, should we be particularly alarmed by them.

How the Presidency Regained Its Balance
John Yoo

Five years after 9/11, President Bush has taken his counterterrorism case to the American people. That's because he has had to. [In 2006], a plurality of the Supreme Court found, in *Hamdan v. Rumsfeld*, that Congress must explicitly approve military commissions to try suspected terrorists. So Mr. Bush has proposed [and Congress passed] legislation seeking to place the tribunals, and other aggressive antiterrorism measures, on a sounder footing.

But the president has broader goals than even fighting terrorism—he has long intended to make reinvigorating the presidency a priority. Vice President Dick Cheney has rightly deplored the "erosion of the powers and the ability of the president of the United States to do his job" and noted that "we are weaker today as an institution because of the unwise compromises that have been made over the last 30 to 35 years."

Thus the administration has gone to war to pre-empt foreign threats. It has data-mined communications in the United States to root out terrorism. It has detained terrorists without formal charges, interrogating some harshly. And it has formed military tribunals modeled on those of past wars, as when we tried and executed a group of Nazi saboteurs found in the United States.

To his critics, Mr. Bush is a "King George" bent on an "imperial presidency." But the inescapable fact is that war shifts power to the branch most responsible for its waging: the executive. Harry Truman sent troops to fight in Korea without Congressional authority. George H. W. Bush did not have the consent of Congress when he invaded Panama to apprehend Manuel Noriega. Nor did Bill Clinton when he initiated NATO's air war over Kosovo.

The Bush administration's decisions to terminate the 1972 antiballistic missile treaty and to withdraw from the International Criminal Court and the Kyoto accords on global warming rested on constitutional precedents going all the way back to Abraham Lincoln.

The administration has also been energetic on the domestic front. It has reclassified national security information made public in earlier administrations and declined, citing executive privilege, to disclose information to Congress or

John Yoo is professor of law at the University of California at Berkeley and a visiting scholar at the American Enterprise Institute, a policy research organization in Washington, D.C. Reprinted from "How the Presidency Regained Its Balance," *The New York Times*, September 17, 2006, p. 15, by permission of John Yoo c/o Writer's Representatives LLC. All rights reserved.

the courts about its energy policy task force. The White House has declared that the Constitution allows the president to sidestep laws that invade his executive authority. That is why Mr. Bush has issued hundreds of signing statements—more than any previous president—reserving his right not to enforce unconstitutional laws.

A reinvigorated presidency enrages President Bush's critics, who seem to believe that the Constitution created a system of judicial or congressional supremacy. Perhaps this is to be expected of the generation of legislators that views the presidency through the lens of Vietnam and Watergate. But the founders intended that wrongheaded or obsolete legislation and judicial decisions would be checked by presidential action, just as executive overreaching is to be checked by the courts and Congress.

The changes of the 1970's occurred largely because we had no serious national security threats to United States soil, but plenty of paranoia in the wake of Richard Nixon's use of national security agencies to spy on political opponents. Congress enacted the War Powers Resolution, which purports to cut off presidential uses of force abroad after 60 days. It passed the Budget and Impoundment Act to eliminate the modest presidential power to rein in wasteful spending. The Foreign Intelligence and Surveillance Act required the government to get a warrant from a special court to conduct wiretapping for national security reasons.

These statutes have produced little but dysfunction, from flouting of the war powers law, to ever-higher pork barrel spending, to the wall between intelligence and law enforcement that contributed to our failure to stop the 9/11 attacks.

The 1970s shifted power from the president to Congress, and the latter proved a far more accommodating boss to federal agencies looking for budget dollars—a fragmented legislature is obviously much easier to game than a chief executive. But 535 members of Congress cannot manage day-to-day policy. A legislature's function is to draft the laws of the land, set broad goals and spend taxpayer revenues in the national interest, not to micromanage.

The judiciary, too, has been increasingly assertive over the last three decades. It has shown far less deference to the executive in this war than in past conflicts. This energetic judiciary is partly a response to Congress's bulked-up power; the courts have had to step in to try to repair the problems created by vague laws that try to do too much, that state grandiose goals, while avoiding hard policy choices.

Congress's vague legal mandates are handed off to the states or the agencies or the courts to sort out. Our legislators rarely turn their attention to the problems created by laws that are old and obsolete, or of dubious relevance to new issues. (This is why the *Hamdan* decision was less a rebuke of the presidency than a sign of frustration with Congress's failure to update our laws to deal with the terrorist menace.)

Unfortunately, much of the public misunderstands the true role of the executive branch—in large part because today's culture transforms presidents into celebrities. On TV, a president's every move seems central to the universe, so he has the image of power that far exceeds the reality. But as the presidential scholar Richard Neustadt, a liberal icon, argued, the presidency is inherently weak, while mythic things are expected of and attributed to it—like maintaining national security and economic growth.

Today many pundits and political scientists seem to want the president's power to be the sum of his communication and political skills, his organizational ability, his cognitive style and emotional intelligence. It is almost as if any president who uses the constitutional powers allocated to his office to effect policy has failed, not succeeded.

But the presidency, unlike Congress, is the only office elected by and accountable to the nation as a whole. The president has better access to expertise from the unified executive branch—including its top secret data—than the more ad hoc information Congress develops through hearings and investigations.

That is why, while jealous of its prerogatives, Congress usually goes along with a president's policy decisions. A strong executive can accept responsibility for difficult choices that Congress wants to avoid. The Republican Congress, for instance, wanted to give President Bill Clinton a line-item veto, only to be blocked by the Supreme Court. Despite hearings and criticism of the energetic executive, Congress has yet to pass laws reining in Mr. Bush very much.

Congress has for years been avoiding its duty to revamp or repeal outmoded parts of bygone laws in the light of contemporary threats. We have needed energy in the executive branch to fill in that gap. Congress now must act to guide our counterterror policy, but it should not try to micromanage the executive branch, particularly in war, where flexibility of action is paramount.

You Go Too Far, Mr. President
The Founders Would Disapprove

Frederick A. O. Schwarz Jr. and Aziz Huq

Thirty years ago, a Senate committee headed by the late Sen. Frank Church exposed widespread abuses by law enforcement and intelligence agencies dating to the Franklin D. Roosevelt administration. In the name of "national security," the FBI, CIA and National Security Agency spied on politicians, protest groups

Frederick A. O. Schwarz Jr. is a lawyer with the Brennan Center for Justice at New York University and was chief counsel for the Church Committee in 1975–76. Aziz Huq is a Brennan Center Fellow. Reprinted from "You Go Too Far, Mr. President—The Founders Would Disapprove," *The Washington Post,* April 1, 2007, p. B1.

and civil rights activists; illegally opened mail; and sponsored scores of covert operations abroad, many of which imperiled democracy in foreign countries.

The sheer magnitude of the abuses unearthed by the committee shocked the nation, led to broad reforms and embarrassed Congress, whose feckless oversight over decades was plain for all to see. As a result, Congress required presidents to report covert operations to permanent new intelligence committees and created the Foreign Intelligence Surveillance Act, which squarely repudiated the idea of inherent executive power to spy on Americans without obtaining warrants. New guidelines were issued for FBI investigations.

For those of us involved in that effort to bring accountability and sunshine back to government, it is discouraging to read daily accounts of a new era of intelligence power abuses, growing out of a "war" on terrorism that is invoked to justify almost any secret measure.

In the past five years, we have learned that the executive branch has circumvented federal bans on torture, abandoned the Geneva Conventions, monitored Americans' phone conversations without the required warrants and "outsourced" torture through "extraordinary rendition" to several foreign governments. Recently we learned that the FBI recklessly abused its power to secure documents through emergency national security letters.

Once again, congressional oversight of the growing national security, intelligence and law enforcement establishments has fallen short. But there are now obstacles to reestablishing effective oversight that did not exist three decades ago.

For one thing, the country and Congress are far more polarized. There was a high degree of bipartisan unity on the Church Committee, and Republican President Gerald R. Ford generally cooperated in the effort to expose abuses and create remedies. The committee, formally known as the Select Committee to Study Governmental Operations with Respect to Intelligence Activities, was created in Watergate's wake and had a Democratic majority. But it focused on abuses by administrations of both parties. Indeed, its inquiries revealed that three Democratic icons, Presidents Roosevelt, John F. Kennedy and Lyndon B. Johnson, all knew about or approved questionable activities. Howard Baker Jr., a senior Senate Republican who served on the panel, disagreed with some proposals but said it had carried out its task "responsibly and thoroughly."

But Congress now faces an even bigger problem than heightened partisanship. Past presidents have never claimed that the Constitution gave them power to set aside statutes permanently. (Richard M. Nixon was no longer in office when he declared: "When the president does it, it means that it is not illegal.") The Bush administration, however, appears committed to eliminating judicial and congressional oversight of executive action at all costs. This pernicious idea, at odds with the Founders' vision of checks and balances, lies at the heart of many of today's abuses.

In some ways, the "Magna Carta" of this combative ideology was the minority report issued by eight of the Republicans on the Iran-contra committee that investigated the Reagan administration's handling of covert arms sales to Iran and the secret—and illegal—effort to finance the contra rebels fighting in Nicaragua.

Among the report's signers was then-Rep. Dick Cheney, who led the group. They rejected the idea that separation of powers would "preclude the exercise of arbitrary power" and argued that the president needed to act expeditiously and secretly to achieve American aims in a dangerous world. Their solution to executive abuse was to water down congressional and judicial oversight. The minority report referred approvingly to "monarchical notions of prerogative that will permit [presidents] to exceed the law" if Congress tried to exercise oversight on national security matters. Cheney later insisted in an interview that "you have to preserve the prerogative of the president in extraordinary circumstances," by not notifying Congress of intelligence operations.

Cheney's views have not shifted since then. In December 2005, he referred reporters to the minority report for his view of "the president's prerogatives." And for the first time in U.S. history, executive branch lawyers have argued that the president has power to "suspend" laws permanently in the name of national security. In signing statements for new laws, the chief executive has repeatedly asserted this broad power. In internal legal opinions on torture, Justice Department lawyers have proposed that the president can set aside laws that conflict with his ideas of national security. Under this logic, laws against torture, warrantless surveillance and transfers of detainees to governments that torture all buckle.

We do not know precisely which laws were turned aside, because the administration still refuses to reveal Justice Department opinions that define what laws the executive will and will not follow. Such secrecy, which has nothing to do with the legitimate protection of sources and methods of intelligence agencies, cannot be justified.

This crisis of constitutional faith did not begin with the current Republican administration. After a burst of reforms in the 1970s, Congress quickly fell back into Cold War apathy, finding it easier to let standards lapse than to hold the executive branch to account. The Iran-contra scandal was the first warning that the Church Committee's lessons had been sidelined by the executive branch. Attorney generals issued looser guidelines on FBI investigations. The White House became a keen user of unilateral executive orders that bypassed Congress.

President Bill Clinton's stint in the White House proved no exception. He broadly interpreted his war powers and aggressively used executive orders to bypass Congress—for example, ignoring a House vote opposing intervention in Kosovo. Clinton issued 107 presidential directives on policy, according to Harvard Law School Dean Elena Kagan. Reagan issued nine and George H. W. Bush just four.

Today, the argument for unchecked presidential power is starkly different from earlier invocations. While previous administrations have violated civil liberties—as in the post–World War I Palmer raids and the incarceration of Japanese Americans during World War II—such actions were public and short term. When Confederate troops neared Washington in the Civil War and mobs in Baltimore attacked Union troops, President Abraham Lincoln suspended habeas corpus—the principal legal protection against unlawful detention.

As Baltimore's mayor threatened to blow up railroad bridges used by Union troops, Lincoln acted without waiting for Congress to return from recess. Yet he subsequently sought and received congressional approval.

Unlike Lincoln and other past chief executives, President Bush asserts that he has the power to set aside fundamental laws permanently—including those that ban torture and domestic spying. The White House today argues that there will never be a day of reckoning in Congress or the courts. To the contrary, it does all it can to shield its use of unilateral detention, torture and spying powers from the review of any other branch of government. Even after five years, the lawfulness of incarcerating hundreds of detainees at Guantánamo Bay, Cuba, has not been reviewed by another branch.

Never before in U.S. history, we believe, has a president so readily exploited a crisis to amass unchecked and unreviewed power unto himself, completely at odds with the Constitution. This departure from historical practice should deeply concern those in both parties who care for the Constitution. Even in military matters, Congress has considerable authority. For instance, the Constitution specifies that Congress can "make Rules for Government and Regulation of the land and naval Forces." Military intelligence, military surveillance and military detention are all matters on which Congress can dictate the terms of how the commander-in-chief's power is exercised.

Debates at the 1787 Constitutional Convention in Philadelphia, and in the state ratifying conventions that ensued, conclusively undercut the current administration's claim to unaccountable power. Alexander Hamilton, the founding era's foremost advocate of executive vigor, disdained efforts to equate the new president's authority with the broad powers of the English monarchs. And even assuming that Hamilton was wrong in asserting that presidents have less power than English kings, the British monarchy had in fact been stripped of power to "suspend" parliamentary laws after the Glorious Revolution of 1688, about 100 years before the Constitutional Convention. The Constitution simply contains no unfettered executive authority to annul laws on a president's security-related say-so.

There is no reason to abandon the founding generation's skepticism of unchecked executive power. The Constitution rests on a profound understanding of human nature. Hamilton, James Madison and the other framers and ratifiers knew that no single individual, whether selected by birth or popular vote, could be blindly trusted to wield power wisely. They knew that both the executive and Congress would make mistakes.

The Supreme Court has repeatedly backed a strong oversight role for Congress. "The scope of [Congress's] power of inquiry . . . is as penetrating and far-reaching as the potential power to enact and appropriate under the Constitution," it wrote in 1975. Congress has repeatedly met its constitutional responsibility as a coequal branch, even in times of war, and regardless of partisan interests. Oversight is not a Republican or Democratic issue. In World War II, then-Sen. Harry S. Truman coordinated aggressive inquiries into the Democratic administration's mismanagement of war procurement. During the Civil War, Republicans in Congress drove Lincoln's first secretary of war from office by their investigations.

Today's questions about presidential power are certainly not ones that have Republican or Democratic answers. The institutional imbalance that is evident today should trouble legislators of both parties.

We believe that most Americans still would agree with the Church Committee when it stated: "The United States must not adopt the tactics of the enemy," for "each time we do so, each time the means we use are wrong, our inner strength, the strength that makes us free, is lessened."

All Hail . . . King George?

Eric A. Posner

Some say President Bush acts like an autocrat. Then again, so have most of America's greatest presidents.

President George W. Bush draws fire from many quarters. That's hardly surprising: Presidents who surround themselves with pomp and ceremony, or who claim new or controversial powers, always provoke strong criticism. But the intensity of the criticism directed at Bush is explained in part by its roots—a fear that the president sometimes exhibits monarchial or imperial tendencies. The lavish fanfare surrounding Bush's January inauguration sparked howls of protest, as did the revelation that Bush's lawyers believed that the president could, as commander in chief, unilaterally suspend U.S. treaty obligations and statutes, including one banning torture. John Dean, once a lawyer in the famously power-hungry Richard Nixon administration, has derisively said Bush's reign "may be the most imperial Presidency our history has yet seen." Bush is not, however, the first U.S. president to aggressively expand the authority of the Oval Office. Charges of presidential lawlessness date back to the first presidency.

George Washington and his contemporaries faced the vital question of how the Constitution's vague provisions on executive powers should be interpreted. James Madison argued that the president's powers were limited to those enumerated

Eric A. Posner, professor of law at the University of Chicago, is the author of *Law and Social Norms* and coauthor of the *Limits of International Law.* Reproduced with permission from www.ForeignPolicy.com (March 2005). © 2003 Carnegie Endowment for International Peace.

in the Constitution and those delegated to him by Congress. These enumerated powers included the powers of commander in chief, the power to enter into treaties (with the Senate's consent), the power to receive ambassadors, and little else. Alexander Hamilton argued that the president, as chief executive, had all the powers that an executive in those days had—and executives in those days were kings— except where the Constitution said otherwise. Although the Constitution gave some significant powers to Congress, including the power to appropriate funds and to declare war, Hamilton's formulation ensured that the president had dominant authority over foreign affairs.

Washington exercised Cincinnatus-like restraint throughout his career; nonetheless, as president he sided with Hamilton. As a result, he was not just the first president, but also the first strong president—and the first to be accused of usurping the powers of Congress. He was also the first great president. And there have been several other great presidents who also claimed (and exercised) expansive presidential powers, and were called usurpers by their critics. Abraham Lincoln won the Civil War and freed the slaves, but he also suspended the writ of habeas corpus. Theodore Roosevelt introduced the United States to the world stage, but he also asserted new presidential powers to use force and negotiate treaties without congressional involvement, especially in Panama and elsewhere in Latin America. Franklin D. Roosevelt led the United States through the Great Depression and World War II, but he also tried to pack the Supreme Court with his own nominees and broke the norm that confined presidents to two terms in office. By contrast, a dozen or more milquetoast presidents both abjured imperial power and exercised what power they acknowledged in as undistinguished a manner as possible.

So should we welcome or fear the imperial presidency? To answer this question, I conducted a very unscientific empirical study. First, I used presidential ratings compiled by Prof. James Lindgren of Northwestern Law School. I used the mean scores assigned to the presidents by a politically balanced group of political scientists, historians, and law professors, with 1 going to the worst and 5 to the best.

Second, I classified all of the presidents as either "imperial" or "republican" according to whether they, in word or deed, adopted an expansive or limited view of presidential power. (To classify presidents as imperial or republican, I focus on whether the president strained against existing constitutional understandings, and I do not try to use an absolute measure.) To minimize my own biases, I used a standard textbook on the presidency, Sidney M. Milkis and Michael Nelson's *The American Presidency*, and relied on the authors' conclusions about whether a particular president sought to expand his power, or seemed satisfied with what he had. For example, I classify Dwight D. Eisenhower as republican because he was uninterested in expanding presidential power; and I classify Andrew Johnson as imperial, even though he was perhaps the weakest president ever, because he fought hard against the efforts of an ambitious congress to curtail the powers of the presidency.

The Power and Quality of U.S. Presidents

View of Power	Low Quality (1–2)	Medium Quality (3)	High Quality (4–5)
Republican (acknowledges limited powers)	Warren Harding Franklin Pierce James Buchanan Zachary Taylor Millard Fillmore Ulysses S. Grant Jimmy Carter	James Madison Gerald Ford John Quincy Adams Bill Clinton Herbert Hoover Calvin Coolidge James Monroe William Taft Benjamin Harrison Martin Van Buren Chester Arthur John Adams George H.W. Bush	Dwight D. Eisenhower
Imperial (claims expansive powers)	Andrew Johnson John Tyler Richard Nixon	John F. Kennedy Grover Cleveland Rutherford B. Hayes William McKinley Lyndon B. Johnson Thomas Jefferson	Andrew Jackson Harry S. Truman Teddy Roosevelt Woodrow Wilson Ronald Reagan Franklin D. Roosevelt Abraham Lincoln George Washington

The table demonstrates the pattern. Imperial presidents perform better than limited-power republican presidents. Average presidents are found in both categories, but within the extremes—the great and the terrible—there are only two modern exceptions. Eisenhower was a good president who did not try to expand his power, and Nixon was a bad president who did. Indeed, Nixon alone is probably responsible for the modern view that the imperial presidency is the worst kind of presidency. But if a constitutionally weak presidency prevents another Nixon, it also prevents another FDR or Lincoln. Although once in a while an Eisenhower could come along, most of the time we would have to make do with a Jimmy Carter, a Gerald Ford, or a Millard Fillmore. Such a state of affairs would hardly be appealing.

This argument, of course, is open to several objections. First, the character of the president might explain more than the power of the presidency. Lincoln and FDR might have been great presidents even if they couldn't have exercised as much power as they did. But it seems just as likely that a limited office, with limited powers, would not have attracted a person with a powerful character; or else, such a person would have overreached and been blocked by other institutions such as Congress and the courts.

Second, the ratings themselves may reflect the scholars' emphasis on heroic traits rather than actual contributions to the welfare of the nation. A weak presidency implies more power is invested in institutions such as Congress, state governments, and courts. However, it's hard to find a single historical example in which these institutions produced great achievements during a weak presidency. In contrast, the most ambitious and successful legislation—including the Social Security Act of 1935 and the Civil Rights Act of 1964—has almost always been propelled by an imperial president.

Finally, many are concerned that the great imperial presidents set the stage for the awful ones. The familiar argument is that FDR established precedents that would be used by Nixon. But FDR also established precedents that would be used by Truman, Eisenhower, and Reagan.

None of this is to say that presidents should be unconstrained. They would then be dictators. Popular elections, a two-term limit, congressional participation in ordinary legislation, and judicial limitations are all good and necessary, and no one today would object to them. But much of the structure of the presidency—especially in foreign affairs—is hampered by 18th century restrictions that were motivated by fears of monarchy. By pushing against these restrictions, Bush is not bolstering a dangerous and all-powerful executive as much as he is further modernizing the office of the presidency and preparing it for the challenges ahead. Bush's critics should argue with the way the president is using his powers, not the fact that he is expanding them.

 **mhhe**.com/diclerico11e

Internet resources
Visit our Web site at
www.mhhe.com/diclerico11e for links and
resources relating to the Presidency.

Bureaucracy

*T*he proper role of government in society has long divided the major parties. Since the days of the New Deal, Democrats have advocated an active role for government in regulating the economy and promoting the social welfare, and Republicans have argued that government should play a much more limited role in these areas. In 1980, Republican presidential candidate Ronald Reagan declared, "Government is the problem, not the solution."

In the last several years, critics and defenders of the federal government have often focused their attention on the vast federal bureaucracy—the departments, agencies, and bureaus that are responsible for carrying out the government's daily activities. Critics, for example, have asked, "Why did the Federal Emergency Management Agency (FEMA) fail so miserably in responding to the victims of Hurricane Katrina in New Orleans in 2005?" Defenders, in contrast, have raised questions about the performance of private government contractors, who, they claim, are less accountable for their actions than civil servants and thus have less incentive to meet high standards of performance—witness the Walter Reed Army Hospital scandal in 2006.

The two selections in this chapter address the issue of government performance from the critics' and the defenders' points of view. Chris Edwards, a tax policy expert at the Cato Institute, a Washington, D.C., policy research organization devoted to the goal of reducing the role of government in society, argues that the solution to ineffective and inefficient government is to privatize many government functions or programs, such as the postal service, airports, housing programs, and loan programs. Taking the opposite position, researchers Si Kahn and Elizabeth Minnich maintain that the privatization of government not only is less efficient but also poses a threat to the foundations of our democracy and to our shared values as a people.

Downsizing the Federal Government

Chris Edwards

In recent decades governments on every continent have been busy selling off state-owned assets such as airports, railroads, and energy utilities. The privatization revolution has overthrown the belief widely held in the 20th century that governments should own the most important industries. Privatization has led to reduced production costs, higher service quality, and increased innovation in formerly moribund government industries.

In this country the federal government still owns many assets that could be moved to the private sector. The government should privatize its stand-alone businesses, such as Amtrak, and its infrastructure, such as the air traffic control system. It also has billions of dollars of loan assets and real estate that should be sold off. The budget benefits of privatization would be modest, but the economic benefits would be large as newly private industries such as postal services boosted productivity and improved performance to the benefit of American consumers.

HURDLES AND OPPORTUNITIES

In some industries, the federal government runs a monopoly and has erected barriers that prevent competition. A good example is the U.S. Postal Service's legal monopoly over first class mail. Reforms in other countries make clear that there is no good reason for this restriction. Postal services have been privatized or opened to competition in Belgium, Britain, Denmark, Finland, Germany, the Netherlands, New Zealand, and Sweden.[1] Japan is moving ahead with postal service privatization, and the European Union is taking steps to open postal services to competition in its member countries.

In other industries, the federal government needlessly duplicates services that are already available in the private sector. For example, the USPS operates parcel delivery services that compete with private parcel services. Another example is the federal government's National Zoo in Washington. There is no need for the government to be in the zoo business. Indeed, while the National

Chris Edwards is director of tax policy at the Cato Institute, a Washington, D.C., policy research organization. Excerpted from *Downsizing the Federal Government* (Washington, D.C.: Cato Institute, 2005), pp. 118–122, 125–132, 146–147. Notes were renumbered to correspond with edited text. Reprinted with author's permission.

Zoo has been rocked by scandal in recent years, some of the best zoos in the country, such as the San Diego and Bronx zoos, are private.[2]

There are also industries that businesses are dissuaded from entering because of regulations and unequal competition from the government.[3] For example, private toll highways show promise of helping to reduce congestion, but they face hurdles. One hurdle is that government regulations increase the costs of highway construction. Another is that private highways have to compete against government highways, which have free access and are funded by gas taxes that all drivers must pay.[4] Also, private companies have to pay income taxes, but government enterprises do not.

. . . In [the United States] some privatization efforts were begun in the 1980s. Ronald Reagan established a President's Commission on Privatization that proposed some reforms, and a few federal entities have been privatized. Conrail, a freight railroad in the Northeast, was privatized in 1987 for $1.7 billion. The Alaska Power Administration was privatized in 1995. The federal helium reserve was privatized in 1996, raising $1.8 billion over a number of years. The Elk Hills Petroleum Reserve was sold in 1997 for $3.7 billion. The U.S. Enrichment Corporation, which provides enriched uranium to the nuclear industry, was privatized in 1998 for $3.1 billion.

Nonetheless, there remain many federal assets that should be privatized. The Bush administration has calculated that about half of all federal employees perform tasks that are also performed in the marketplace and thus are not "inherently governmental."[5] The administration has begun contracting out some of those activities to private firms. The administration estimates that cost savings from such "competitive sourcing" average about 20 percent.[6]

However, competitive sourcing is not privatization. The administration goes astray when it supports competitive sourcing of programs that should instead be fully privatized or terminated. Privatization gets spending off the government's budget entirely, and it provides for greater dynamism, efficiency, and innovation than is possible through government contracting.

Privatization also avoids a serious pitfall of contracting: corruption. A scandal at the Pentagon in 2003 was a textbook example of contracting corruption. Two senior procurement officials were convicted of receiving sexual favors and $1 million in cash for awarding minority set-aside contracts to particular firms.[7] One of the men convicted headed the Pentagon's Office of Small and Disadvantaged Business Utilization, which helps minority firms win contracts. In this case, the best reform is not competitive sourcing but termination of this Pentagon office. In a corruption case at the USPS in 2004, a manager took $800,000 in bribes for handing out USPS printing contracts to favored businesses.[8] Privatizing the USPS would create a profit incentive to minimize such employee theft.

Privatization of federal assets makes a great deal of sense today for a number of reasons. First, sales of federal assets would cut the budget deficit. Second, privatization would reduce the responsibilities of the government so that policymakers could focus on their core responsibilities such as national security. Third, there is vast foreign privatization experience that could be drawn on in pursuing U.S. reforms. Fourth, privatization would spur economic growth by opening new markets to entrepreneurs. For example, privatization of the USPS and repeal of its monopoly would bring major innovation to the mail industry, just as the 1980s breakup of AT&T brought innovation to the telecommunications industry. . . .

STAND-ALONE BUSINESSES

The federal government operates numerous business enterprises that could be converted into publicly traded corporations, including USPS, Amtrak, and a number of electricity utilities.

- **Postal Services.** A report by a presidential commission in 2003 and other studies conclude that the outlook for the mammoth 768,000-person USPS is bleak.[9] The postal service is faced with declining mail volume and rising costs. The way ahead is to privatize the USPS and repeal the mail monopoly that it holds.[10] New Zealand and Germany have implemented bold reforms that Congress should examine. Since 1998 New Zealand's postal market has been open to private competition, with the result that postage rates have fallen and labor productivity at New Zealand Post has risen markedly.[11] Germany's Deutsche Post was partly privatized in 2000. Since then, the company has improved productivity and has expanded into new businesses.[12]
- **Passenger Rail.** Subsidies to Amtrak were supposed to be temporary when it was created in 1970. They haven't been, and Amtrak has provided second-rate rail service for 30 years while consuming about $29 billion in federal subsidies.[13] It has a poor on-time record and its infrastructure is in terrible shape. Reforms elsewhere show that private passenger rail can work. Full or partial rail privatization has occurred in Argentina, Australia, Britain, Germany, Japan, New Zealand, and other countries. Privatization would allow Amtrak greater flexibility in its finances, its capital budget, and the operation of its services—free from costly meddling by Congress.
- **Electricity Utilities.** The U.S. electricity industry is dominated by publicly traded corporations. However, the federal government owns the huge Tennessee Valley Authority and four Power Marketing Administrations, which sell power in 33 states. Those government power companies have become an anachronism as utility privatization has been pursued across the globe from Britain to Brazil and Argentina to Australia. Privatization of TVA and the PMAs would eliminate artificially low power rates that cause overconsumption and increase efficiency in utility operations and capital investment.[14] . . .

INFRASTRUCTURE

. . . Any service that can be supported by consumer fees can be privatized. A big advantage of privatized airports, air traffic control, highways, and other items is that private companies can freely tap debt and equity markets for capital expansion to meet rising demand and reduce congestion. By contrast, upgrades and modernization of government infrastructure are subject to the politics and uncertainties of the budgeting process. As a consequence, government infrastructure often uses old technology and is highly congested.

- **Air Traffic Control.** The Federal Aviation Administration has been mismanaged for decades and provides Americans with second-rate air traffic control (ATC). The FAA has struggled to modernize its technology to maintain safety and expand capacity, but those efforts have fallen behind schedule and gone overbudget. The GAO found that one FAA upgrade begun in 1983 was to be completed by 1996 for $2.5 billion.[15] But the completion date was pushed back to 2003 and the project ended up costing $7.6 billion, with $1.5 billion wasted on activities that were ultimately scrapped. . . .
- **Highways.** A number of states are experimenting with privately financed and operated highways. The Dulles Greenway in northern Virginia is a 14-mile private highway opened in 1995. It was financed through private bond and equity issues, and it uses an electronic toll system to maximize efficiency for drivers. . . . Fluor, a leading engineering company, signed a deal with Virginia in 2005 to privately fund and build High Occupancy Toll lanes on a 14-mile stretch of the Capital Beltway.[16] Drivers will pay for using the lanes with electronic tolling, which will recoup Fluor's $900 million investment in the project. The company also has a $1 billion plan to build toll lanes running 56 miles south from Washington along an existing interstate.[17] . . .
- **Airports.** Most major airports in the United States are owned by municipal governments, but the federal government helps fund airport renovation and expansion. The United States lags behind airport reforms that are taking place abroad. Airports have been fully or partially privatized in Athens, Auckland, Brussels, Copenhagen, Frankfurt, London, Melbourne, Naples, Rome, Sydney, Vienna, and other cities.[18] . . .

LOANS AND OTHER FINANCIAL SCHEMES

The federal government runs a large array of loan and loan guarantee programs for farmers, students, small businesses, utilities, shipbuilders, weapons purchasers, exporters, fishermen, and other groups. There are at least 59 federal loan programs and 70 loan guarantee programs.[19] Loan guarantees are promises to private creditors, such as banks, that the government will cover borrower defaults. At the end of 2004, there was $250 billion in outstanding federal loans and $1.2 trillion in loan guarantees.[20]

In the 1970s federal loans grew rapidly as policymakers discovered that loans could be used to aid favored special interests and that the budget impact was less visible than regular spending. Reforms were passed in 1990 to treat loans more transparently in the budget, but taxpayers are still stuck with all the loan programs that were added in prior decades. Unfortunately, an "iron triangle" of interests stands against reducing loans. Groups that oppose cuts include loan beneficiaries, financial institutions, federal administrators, and the congressional committees that oversee loans. . . .

The federal budget says that government loans are needed because markets suffer from "imperfections," such as lenders' not having perfect information about borrowers.[21] For example, banks are more hesitant to lend to start-up businesses because they do not have long credit histories. But it is appropriate that start-ups face more credit scrutiny and pay higher interest rates because of their higher risk of failure. Failure creates economic waste; thus it is good that creditors are more hesitant to lend to risky businesses. There is no market failure here. Instead, it is government intervention that is a failure when it extends loans to borrowers with excessively risky and low-value projects.

Market allocation of credit is far from perfect, but markets have developed mechanisms for funding risky endeavors. For example, venture capital and angel investment pump tens of billions of dollars into new businesses every year. There is no need for the government to compete with such private finance mechanisms. Yet the federal government runs a failing Small Business Investment Company venture capital program. . . .

Education loans also illustrate the waste and abuse of federal loan programs. The Department of Education has $7 billion in student loans that are delinquent.[22] Lax enforcement of student loan repayments has led to large losses from defaults, which cost taxpayers $28 billion during the 1990s.[23] Individuals, financial institutions, and college administrators all face incentives to make false claims to maximize student loans.[24] In 2004 it was discovered that financial institutions were swindling the taxpayer out of $1 billion per year through a loophole in student loan rules.[25] Apparently, officials knew about the problem but had ignored it until reporters starting asking questions. . . .

FEDERAL ASSETS

At the end of fiscal 2004, the federal government held $1.1 trillion in buildings and equipment, $249 billion in inventory, $601 billion in land, and $801 billion in mineral rights.[26] The federal government owns about one-fourth of the land in the United States and continues to accumulate more holdings.[27] Much of this huge treasure trove of assets is neglected and abused; it would be better cared for in the private sector. . . .

The solution is to sell federal assets that are in excess of public needs and to better manage the smaller set of remaining holdings. For example, there are widely reported maintenance backlogs on lands controlled by the Forest Service, Park Service, and Fish and Wildlife Service. The solution is not a larger maintenance budget but trimming holdings to fit limited taxpayer resources. Another part of the solution is to scrap the Davis-Bacon rules, which require that excessively high wages be paid on federal contracts, such as maintenance contracts. As the CBO has noted, Davis-Bacon rules push up maintenance costs, resulting in less maintenance being done.[28]

The ongoing process of federalizing the nation's land should be reversed and low-priority holdings sold back to the states and citizens. Unfortunately, bureaucrats do not like to give up their land holdings, even when they have no use for them. As one example, the *Washington Post* reported that the Bureau of Land Management owns 23 acres of land in southern Maryland that have sat idle since 1994 when a radio telescope installation was closed down.[29] But BLM has been vainly trying to find other government uses for the land instead of transferring it back to the private sector.

The government also owns billions of dollars' worth of excess buildings. The GAO finds that the government has "many assets it does not need," including 30 vacant Veterans Affairs buildings and 1,200 excess Department of Energy facilities.[30] The Pentagon owns excess supply depots, training facilities, medical facilities, research labs, and other installations. The agency estimates that it spends up to $4 billion each year maintaining its excess facilities.[31] . . .

DOWNSIZING AND OUR DYNAMIC SOCIETY

Surveying government growth in the 20th century, *The Economist* found that "big government is producing ever more disappointing results."[32] But we have yet to cut big government very much because of biases in the political system that create "a kind of democratic failure, akin to the market failures that government intervention is supposed to remedy."[33] The 21st century may be different, however, as globalization, technology, and other forces help to tame the overbearing state.

Globalization is reducing the power of governments to control businesses and the economy. National borders are dissolving because of rising trade, investment, and knowledge flows. As globalization advances, individuals and businesses gain greater freedom to take advantage of foreign opportunities. That increases pressure on countries to cut taxes and make governments more efficient, or capital and labor will flee abroad. Reform ideas such as privatization have spread as countries have adopted "best practices" from elsewhere to avoid falling behind. Some governments have resisted these forces, but as globalization intensifies, the economic risks of not reforming rise. . . .

The continual rise in American living standards also reduces the need for government programs and safety nets. Even modest real economic growth of 2 percent annually would result in U.S. living standards doubling in the next 35 years. As Americans become wealthier, it should be easier to wean them from government handouts for retirement, health care, education, and other items.

A final positive trend is the increasing heterogeneity of American society. Society is becoming not only more demographically diverse but also more diverse in working patterns, business activities, and cultural tastes and values. A national government that tries to impose one-size-fits-all solutions on 300 million people with very different ways of pursuing happiness makes little sense.

So let the federal downsizing begin! . . .

NOTES

1. Rick Geddes, "The Structure and Effect of International Postal Reform," American Enterprise Institute Postal Reform Papers, April 29, 2003.
2. Marc Fisher, "Privatizing Zoo Would Rescue It, for a Modest Fee," *Washington Post*, December 9, 2003, p. B1. Fisher notes that about 40 percent of U.S. zoos, including the top-notch San Diego and Bronx zoos, are run by private, nonprofit groups, and he notes that private ownership seems to have a superior record. Many private zoos, however, do receive various government subsidies. Regarding the National Zoo, the National Academy of Sciences reported in 2004 that it found failures "at all levels" in zoo management leading to animal deaths, crumbling facilities, and other problems. See Karlyn Barker and James V. Grimaldi, "National Zoo Director Quits over Lapses," *Washington Post*, February 26, 2004, p. A1.
3. A good survey of the issues is Gabriel Roth, ed., *Competing with the Government* (Stanford, CA: Hoover Institution Press, 2004).
4. Gabriel Roth, "Liberating the Roads: Reforming U.S. Highway Policy," Cato Institute Policy Analysis no. 538, March 17, 2005, pp. 10, 13.
5. *Budget of the United States Government: Fiscal Year 2003* (Washington: Government Printing Office, February 2002), p. 45.
6. Ibid.
7. Jerry Markon, "2 Pentagon Officials Get 24 Years in Fraud," *Washington Post*, December 13, 2003, p. B3.
8. Nicole Fuller, "Ex-Postal Official Admits Taking Nearly $800,000 in Bribes," *Washington Post*, October 8, 2004, p. A20.
9. For a summary of the issue, see Christopher Lee, "Postal Services Finances Bleak," *Washington Post*, March 23, 2004, p. A17.
10. For a detailed discussion of postal service reform, see Edward L. Hudgins, ed., *Mail @ the Millennium: Will the Postal Service Go Private?* (Washington: Cato Institute, 2000).
11. Geddes.
12. Ibid.
13. Joseph Vranich and Edward Hudgins, "Help Passenger Rail by Privatizing Amtrak," Cato Institute Policy Analysis no. 419, November 1, 2001. I have updated the subsidy costs listed in this report.
14. GAO, "Opportunities for Oversight and Improved Use of Taxpayer Funds: Examples from Selected GAO Work," GAO-03-1006, August 2003, p. 58. The GAO notes that the PMAs have inefficient levels of capital investment because of the unreliability of federal funding.
15. GAO, "Air Traffic Control: Evolution and Status of FAA's Automation Program," GAO/T-RCED/AIMD-98-85, March 5, 1998.
16. Steven Ginsberg, "Beltway to Get Va. Toll Lanes," *Washington Post*, April 29, 2005, p. A1.
17. Lisa Rein, "Toll Lane Proposals Pick Up Momentum," *Washington Post*, March 17, 2004, p. B1.

18. See Jerry Ellig, "The $7.7 Billion Mistake: Federal Barriers to State and Local Privatization," U.S. Congress, Joint Economic Committee, February 1996.
19. Author's count of loan programs in *Budget of the United States Government: Fiscal Year 2005, Federal Credit Supplement,* www.gpoaccess.gov/usbudget/fy05/browse.html.
20. *Budget of the United States Government: Fiscal Year 2006, Analytical Perspectives* (Washington: Government Printing Office, February 2005), p. 109. Note that the outlay amounts for loans in the federal budget are the net subsidy amounts, which are the present values of the net taxpayer costs. This treatment, established by the Federal Credit Reform Act of 1990, allows comparison between the costs of loans and other federal programs.
21. *Budget of the United States Government: Fiscal Year 2006, Analytical Perspectives,* p. 85.
22. *Budget of the United States Government: Fiscal Year 2006, Analytical Perspectives,* p. 109. See also Charles Lane, "Justices to Review Loan Offsets," *Washington Post,* April 26, 2005, p. A2.
23. GAO, "Federal Budget: Opportunities for Oversight and Improved Use of Taxpayer Funds," GAO-03-922T, June 18, 2003, p. 26.
24. Ibid., p. 16.
25. Anne Applebaum, "Student Loan Swindle," *Washington Post,* September 29, 2004, p. A29.
26. *Budget of the United States Government: Fiscal Year 2006, Analytical Perspectives,* p. 206.
27. GAO, "Federal Budget," p. 30.
28. CBO, "Budget Options," February 2001, p. 82.
29. Joshua Partlow, "Radio Telescopes' Time in the Sun Has Passed," *Washington Post,* April 12, 2004, p. B3.
30. GAO, "High-Risk Series: Federal Real Property," GAO-03-122, January 1, 2003, pp. 8, 9.
31. Ibid., p. 11.
32. "The Enigma of Acquiescence, Survey on the Future of the State," *The Economist,* September 18, 1997, www.economist.com/surveys.
33. Ibid.

The Fox in the Henhouse
How Privatization Threatens Democracy
Si Kahn and Elizabeth Minnich

Privatization may not sound to you like a threat to democracy. It's not a familiar word, and it isn't often used by people who are struggling for democracy, for freedom, for justice. People haven't usually stood up at rallies and made rousing speeches either for or against privatization.

That's because *privatization* is the kind of word economists and policymakers use. What it means in practice, its purposes and effects both internationally and in the United States, are hidden by such dry language.

We believe not only that privatization is a threat but that it is the threat to democratic commitments to the public good. It is a threat to the commonwealth that sustains us all, in the United States and around the globe.

We believe that we fail at our peril to see that the possibility of public provision for our basic human needs, safety and security, our basic human rights, and our high aspirations to liberty, justice, and equality are under concerted attack by corporate privatizers and the officials who do their bidding from inside government. We believe that efficiency in pursuit of profits is not at all the same thing as effectiveness in providing for and protecting democratic values and dreams of liberty, equality, and a decent life for all.

So, then, what is privatization?

Privatization as an agenda for the United States has been described by the *Wall Street Journal*, a generally reliable reflector of corporate thinking, as the "effort to bring the power of private markets to bear on traditional government benefits and services."[1]

Translation: Privatization is letting corporations take over and run for profit what the public sector has traditionally done.

. . . [The] following are the more obvious ways the transfer of our tax money from our government and public agencies into private pockets is already taking place.

Si Kahn is executive director of Grassroots Leadership, a policy research and advocacy organization located in Charlotte, North Carolina. Elizabeth Minnich is Senior Fellow at the Association of American Colleges and Universities. Excerpted from *The Fox in the Henhouse: How Privatization Threatens Democracy*. Copyright © 2005 by Kahn/Minnich. Berrett-Koehler Publishers, Inc., San Francisco, CA. All rights reserved. www.bkconnection.com. Notes were renumbered to correspond with edited text.

OUTSOURCING, CONTRACTING OUT

A contract to do public work is given to a nongovernmental entity, with its non-public employees. Public money is used to pay for the work done under this contract. Corporations benefit greatly, but there are also nonprofit organizations, including religious ones, that get their pieces of public funds—and profit from them (meaning that they make more money than it should cost to do the work, as evidenced, for one thing, by the corporate CEO–scale salaries some pay). . . .

Contracting out government work has a long history in the United States and has supported many small businesses that do responsible work. But it is quite another thing when public work is contracted out specifically in order to "shrink government," using privatization as a method to do so. These decisions are not made on the basis of careful assessment of real need, actual costs, and the availability of a corporation that is truly qualified in the area of work to be contracted out. The older forms of the practice were designed to support our government in doing its job of serving us. Today, privatizers seek to limit and weaken government—to make it dependent on corporations.

No matter what, though, contractors often lack knowledge in accomplishing military or other government jobs long done by public employees who have built up specialized expertise over their own years of work, and have had the benefit of a work culture that spreads and facilitates the transmission of that expertise. . . .

Contracting can also become so habitual as a way to do business that it shades into the idea that government can pay a nonpublic person or group for *anything* an administration wants, including control of the news. In 2005, the conservative newspaper columnist and commentator Armstrong Williams was exposed as having accepted $240,000 passed to him by the Department of Education and a private public relations firm—$240,000 of taxpayers' money—not to report on but *to promote* the Bush administration's agenda. This secret bribing, and perversion, of a news source has been called "checkbook journalism": You want it, you buy it—with the public's money.[2] No matter that this, shall we say, informal "contracting" is unethical, a conflict of interest, and that it is illegal to use federal money for "covert propaganda,"[3] as the General Accountability Office has ruled in this and two other such cases during the Bush administration thus far. (Four others have also been exposed, and further instances are beginning to be uncovered.)

Want it done? Don't let governmental laws, rules, and regulations stop you. Pay a nongovernmental person to do it: Make it a contracting matter.

Even the best contractors who have signed on to do honest work must be supervised, of course. You don't hire someone to mind your kids and never check on him. It's not safe for a builder to contract out electrical work and never think about it again. So contracting out, which is usually said to be done to enhance efficiency and save taxpayers money, actually requires more work and more of our money than it might seem. As an expert who has tracked privatizing by contracting out concludes, "The idea that transfer of responsibility from the public to the private sector allows government to withdraw from oversight, reduce staff, and place sole or even primary responsibility for accomplishment of public policy objectives on private service providers is an invitation to trouble."[4] . . .

LEASING

Leasing is making deals that allow profit-seeking businesses to exploit public goods, such as leasing national forests and wilderness areas to a corporation whose business is timber, natural gas, or oil. The argument here is that both the public and profit-making purses will benefit from leasing publicly owned land to a corporation that will "harvest" (read, cut down every tree in sight, a practice known in the timber industry as clear-cutting) and "extract" (read, strip-mine every inch of land) and sell what is on top of or under the land. Letting those national forests and wilderness areas *just sit there doing nothing* seems like such a waste, especially when there's this huge national debt to be reckoned with. Why not let those idle resources—the trees just standing there enjoying the wind, the oil and natural gas lying around underground doing who knows what—pay their way by sacrificing just a portion of their number for the financial good of human society?

Here's how it worked in Appalachia for decades, before the law was changed to a somewhat fairer system.[5] The United States Forest Service owns vast percentages of many mountain counties, over 40 percent of the surface land in fourteen of them. Of course, the Forest Service, being part of the federal government, doesn't pay taxes on this land as a private landowner would.

Bad news for county government? Not at all, the Forest Service said. We make payments in lieu of taxes to every county in which these lands are located.

And how was the amount determined? Well, the Forest Service gave the county 25 percent of the income it received from selling standing timber (that's trees that haven't been cut down yet) to corporations and individuals to harvest. Fine in theory. The problem was that the Forest Service sold the standing timber—a public resource—at prices way below market value. Some counties got payments in lieu of taxes as little as twenty-two cents an acre. The corporations got a steal, and the public, the people of the county, got stolen from.

Like any contract or partnership between government and corporations, leasing can go bad. Big money out to make profits and the public good rarely make for an equal marriage.

SELLING OUTRIGHT

It's obvious: What was public is turned into a resource for profit making. Once privatized, a formerly public good or service is likely to be handled differently to cut costs and increase profits. And should that turn out to make the public need to take it back, there are serious problems. It is too expensive to buy it back or start it up anew, and in any case, government expertise and provisions to run it, provide for it, care for it have been lost.

The public—particularly less wealthy, under- and uninsured people—has depended on public hospitals. Where these have been privatized, sold off to private corporations, costs were cut—and guess where the quick and easy cuts were made? Privatizers may believe in charity, but not from them. Preventive care is also likely to be cut, or cut back: Hospitals that profit from having patients do not have a stake in keeping us well by offering low-ticket wellness services. Even privatized hospitals that want, or are required under the terms of the sale, to keep up preventive and charity services may not be able to afford them. . . .

DISINVESTMENT

Divestment means pulling out public funds so that public goods and services deteriorate or even fold, and can then be taken over or bought by for-profit corporations without public protest. Or, cutting back a public commitment to fund a service so far that those who are trying to run it are forced to seek money from the private sector. Private money means greater private control. *Disinvestment* (a polite term for breaking your word and going back on a commitment of public funds, much as *disinformation* is a polite term for lying) can also force responsible public officials to make deals with private for-profits even when they do not think it a good idea.

Disinvestment in education, for example, leads to the overcrowded, undersupplied classrooms that allow privatizers to say, "See? Public education is failing," and then further undercut those schools by offering vouchers to parents to send their children to private schools. In public universities, it leads to desperate administrators putting great pressure on faculty to bring in fat grants or to work on projects under university-corporate partnership arrangements. Scholars must then look first for what might get funded, rather than to what we need and want to know.

Disinvestment can also be used against federal funding agencies. In early 2005, the Bush administration pulled back monies promised to the Fund for the Improvement of Post-Secondary Education (FIPSE), which had supported innovative programs. Authors of proposals that had already been approved for funding were suddenly told there would be no money after all. More people who might have improved education were forced to seek private funding—more private-sector control over education.

CREATING AND CONTROLLING MARKETS THAT REQUIRE PUBLIC FUNDING TO SERVE

One way privatization takes chunks out of public funds for the good of for-profit corporations is literally by creating public need and demand. This takes time and determination, and often, collusion of various more or less open sorts, but indeed it can be and has been done.

Here's a dramatic example. Most major cities in the United States used to have a trolley system that provided relatively efficient, inexpensive, and nonpolluting public transportation. But, one by one, the trolley systems disappeared.

What happened to these sensible trolleys? Were they too slow for fast-moving modern people—lumbering dinosaurs whose time had come and gone? Too expensive to maintain? Obsolete in a world of subways and airplanes? Too cute for serious cities with purposeful, high-powered people?

No, none of the above. The trolleys were doing just fine. The problem was that this public form of transportation competed directly and successfully with the emerging automotive and oil industries. Remember, the trolleys ran on electricity, not on oil or gasoline. So these corporations (including the Rockefeller oil corporations, Ford Motor Company, and Goodyear Tire and Rubber) simply bought up the public trolley systems and closed them down—wherever across the country they could.[6]

The profits made by the oil, car, and associated corporations are by now monstrously huge. Meanwhile, government has to build and maintain all those public roads we drive our cars on, provide traffic cops and all the paraphernalia, like stoplights, we need not to kill each other on the roads—and on and on, all the way to involving our government, including the military, in global struggles to keep the oil flowing. . . .

SUBSIDIES

Public monies—our tax dollars—are used to lower corporations' costs so they can continue to make, and grow, their profits. These range from so-called tax incentives to government purchases of land that are then offered to corporations that, if given sufficient incentives (that's the polite term for bribes), just might locate where jobs are needed, to tax breaks for the same reason, or to keep a corporation from moving elsewhere, to bailouts of faltering corporate giants—to military presence and actions, and today, ongoing U.S. presence and war in oil-rich regions of the world.

Subsidies are another reason corporations are interested in contracts, leasing, and partnering with the government. . . .

The reasons given for these more or less obvious bribes, collectively and politely called subsidies—or, a bit more honestly, corporate welfare—are various. Most of them, though, invoke the need for a now thoroughly corporate-dominated economy to keep growing. That these reasons have some truth to them makes a prime point about the privatizers' agenda. We and our government are being made so dependent on corporations that they call the shots, which is just what they want. . . .

APPRECIATING THE PUBLIC SECTOR

It is important to remember that the public sector has an enviable track record stretching back over many years. How many of us were born safely in public hospitals? How many of us were educated in public elementary and secondary schools? How many of us went to public community colleges, four-year colleges, and universities, both because they offered good education and because we couldn't afford the tuition at private schools, colleges, and universities? How many of us received public financial aid that got us through school?

We drive across the country on high-speed interstate highways, a public project conceived and initiated during the administration of President Dwight D. Eisenhower in the 1950s. We pitch our tents in national parks and wilderness areas that were preserved for future generations by government in response to public campaigns. We canoe down rivers that were cleaned up by government action.

We work at jobs for which some of us would never have been hired if it weren't for public laws prohibiting discrimination in hiring. Our safety on the job is protected by government regulation and inspectors. The safety of our food, medicines, water is overseen by public agencies. We can report consumer fraud to the government. We can get on the "do not call" lists of our state and federal governments to stop telemarketers from intruding into our lives whenever they want to.

If we become disabled, our income is maintained by the public Social Security disability program. If we die while working, our children under eighteen are provided with income through government Social Security survivor benefits. When we retire, we are guaranteed a certain level of income by the public Social Security insurance system.

Our community health is protected by public sewer systems, public systems of disease control, public health clinics and hospitals. Our community safety and security, that of our families and neighbors, is protected by public firefighters and police. Our national security is guarded by a public military system. (If you're feeling insecure anyway these days, would it help to know that Si learned speed-typing while in training at Fort Jackson, South Carolina, in 1967? Kept his skill honed and ready through the years, too.) Without this country's public military, who knows what would have happened in World War I and World War II?

Lord knows, none of these public services is perfect. But they were all begun to respond to real need and the collective realization that if we did not provide for them as goods for all of us, everyone would be the poorer for their lack. They were not set up for, and are not held accountable to, the making of profits. We can call them and the elected officials and public agencies responsible for them to account—while they remain in the public domain. We saw what they could do in the tragic moments of 9/11. Since then, private security firms at airports, for example, have been replaced with a federal system.

When the chips are down, we remember what we forget when times are good. We remember basic beliefs that both experience and conscience have taught and held us to.

One is a belief that when we act together, we can make all of our lives better, safer, healthier, and fuller. It is a belief in the moral, political good and power of cooperation. Together, we can refuse the injustice of discrimination. Together, we can preserve national parks so that all can share in them. Together, we can provide schooling for the generations that will inherit what we cherish of our cultures, and renew them. Together, we can ensure that the young, the dependent, the ill, the old, the disabled—among whom all of us either are now, could be at any moment, or will be at some future time in our lives—can live with safety, freedom, dignity.

Related to the belief that we can make things better when we cooperate is the belief that we are all at risk when any of us is. It is a belief in the *necessity* of cooperation. Pollution does not stay where it is caused; it spreads, it sickens and kills without regard for who caused it, who profited from it, on whom it was imposed without choice or chance. Poverty can breed sickness and crime that spreads far beyond the ghettoes into which too many are crowded, and no walls, no police, can stop that spread. Individuals and corporations that are not controlled by the rule of law turn the law-abiding into victims with no recourse. Without cooperation, the most unscrupulous win, and not only individuals but whole societies and cultures lose, and are lost. . . .

Meanwhile, *privatization* is heralded around the world as *the* political solution for public problems, and *the* way to strengthen both democracy and free markets around the globe. A global agenda that radically changes the lives of billions of people who have no say is *private?*

In the public sector, we are citizens and political actors. We make decisions together about issues of general significance. We vote for our representatives, and they are accountable to us. We have basic rights enshrined in the Constitution. Among our other rights are those to certain services that support the common good. We pay taxes to share the costs of those services and the ongoing functions of our government. We call the people who provide those services and fulfill those functions public employees, because we collectively pay them to do our shared work. We also have other public obligations and duties, such as serving on juries, and of course, obeying the laws passed by our elected representatives.

In the private sector—which does not mean the same thing as in our private lives—we are not citizens, or political actors but, rather, economic actors. We do not pool our resources for the common good but, rather, buy and sell. We are able to do so according to our income level: The rich can obviously buy things the poor cannot. The providers of what is bought are motivated by profit. That means that they charge more than it costs them to make a product, or deliver or perform a service. Exchanges between buyers and sellers that yield profits to the sellers take place in what is called the market (so the market is not a place, but rather a kind of relationship—an economic exchange).

Despite all the rhetoric, image advertising, movies, and TV shows that glorify private corporations, there is no evidence that the private sector is superior to the public. The private sector is not the source of our freedom, of all that is good about and for life. We are not most who we are as consumers. Our most important relations are not marketplace, buy-and-sell, profit-driven.

It is in the tradition of this land, of different peoples in different times and places, to refuse to be subjected to economic domination and exploitation and to value the public good. The poor in America have resisted exploitation by the more privileged. Enslaved people have resisted. Women have resisted. The Native Americans resisted the colonists before the colonists resisted the Crown.

The founders of our country learned from the Constitution of the Iroquois Confederacy[7] as well as the English Magna Carta and the ancient Greeks how to think about democratic governance for the public good.

We need to continue resisting the takeover of our government and the public sector. When the promise of democracy is twisted to justify domination, as George Orwell so famously wrote in *Animal Farm*, "all animals are equal, but some animals are more equal than others."[8] In Orwell's fable, it was the pigs who had made themselves more equal than others.

NOTES

1. John McKinnon and Christopher Cooper, "President Provides New Detail of Plan for Private Accounts," *Wall Street Journal*, Feb. 3, 2005, 1.
2. Maureen Dowd, "W's Stiletto Democracy," *New York Times*, Feb. 27, 2005, op-ed page.
3. Frank Rich, "The White House Stages Its 'Daily Show,'" *New York Times*, Feb. 20, 2005, 1.
4. James A. Krauskopf, "Privatization of Human Services in New York City: Some Examples and Lessons," presentation to the Annual Research Conference of the Association for Public Policy Analysis and Management, Oct. 1995; quoted in M. Bryna Sanger, *The Welfare Marketplace: Privatization and Welfare Reform* (Washington, D.C.: Brookings Institution Press, 2003), 106.
5. Si Kahn, *The Forest Service and Appalachia* (New York: John Hay Whitney Foundation, 1974).
6. Paul Kivel, *You Call This a Democracy? Who Benefits, Who Pays, and Who Really Decides* (New York: Apex, 2004), 84.
7. Russell Bourne, *Gods of War, Gods of Peace* (Orlando: Harcourt Brace, 2002), 91.
8. George Orwell, *Animal Farm* (New York: New American Library, 1996), 133.

mhhe.com/diclerico11e

Internet resources
Visit our Web site at www.mhhe.com/diclerico11e for links and resources relating to Bureaucracy.

chapter 13

Courts

The Supreme Court and Judicial Review

Although few Americans would question the Supreme Court's authority to interpret the Constitution, there has long been disagreement over how the nine justices should approach this awesome responsibility. This debate grew in intensity during the Reagan era as the president and his attorney general inveighed against the Supreme Court, charging that justices all too often had substituted their own values and principles for those contained in the Constitution.

In the first selection, Edwin Meese III, U.S. attorney general during part of the Reagan administration, calls upon judges to interpret the Constitution in accordance with the intent of the men who wrote and ratified it. Insisting that the Founding Fathers expected as much from the members of the Supreme Court, Meese goes on to suggest how the justices should approach this task. He remains convinced that the application of original intent—undistorted by the personal values of well-meaning judges—will best preserve the principles of democratic government.

The second selection offers a markedly different perspective from someone who has had the responsibility of interpreting the Constitution. Irving Kaufman, formerly chief judge of the U.S. Court of Appeals for the Second Circuit, maintains that ascertaining the original intent of the Founding Fathers is decidedly more difficult than Edwin Meese would lead us to believe. Nor, for that matter, is the strict application of original intent necessarily desirable in every instance. This is not to say that judges are at liberty to read whatever they choose into the wording of the Constitution, and Kaufman points to several factors that serve to restrain judges from doing so.

A Jurisprudence of Original Intention

Edwin Meese III

. . . Today I would like to discuss further the meaning of constitutional fidelity. In particular, I would like to describe in more detail this administration's approach.

Before doing so, I would like to make a few commonplace observations about the original document itself. . . .

The period surrounding the creation of the Constitution is not a dark and mythical realm. The young America of the 1780s and '90s was a vibrant place, alive with pamphlets, newspapers, and books chronicling and commenting upon the great issues of the day. We know how the Founding Fathers lived, and much of what they read, thought, and believed. The disputes and compromises of the Constitutional Convention were carefully recorded. The minutes of the convention are a matter of public record. Several of the most important participants—including James Madison, the "father" of the Constitution—wrote comprehensive accounts of the convention. Others, Federalists and Anti-Federalists alike, committed their arguments for and against ratification, as well as their understandings of the Constitution, to paper, so that their ideas and conclusions could be widely circulated, read, and understood.

In short, the Constitution is not buried in the mists of time. We know a tremendous amount of the history of its genesis. . . .

With these thoughts in mind, I would like to discuss the administration's approach to constitutional interpretation. . . .

Our approach . . . begins with the document itself. The plain fact is, it exists. It is something that has been written down. Walter Berns of the American Enterprise Institute has noted that the central object of American constitutionalism was "the effort" of the Founders "to express fundamental governmental arrangements in a legal document—to 'get it in writing.'"

Indeed, judicial review has been grounded in the fact that the Constitution is a written, as opposed to an unwritten, document. In *Marbury v. Madison* John Marshall rested his rationale for judicial review on the fact that we have a written constitution with meaning that is binding upon judges. "[I]t is apparent," he wrote, "that the framers of the Constitution contemplated that instrument as a rule for the government of *courts,* as well as of the legislature. Why otherwise does it direct the judges to take an oath to support it?"

Edwin Meese III served as U.S. attorney general under President Ronald Reagan. Excerpted from a speech by Attorney General Meese before the Washington, D.C., chapter of the Federal Society, Lawyers Division, November 15, 1985, pp. 2–14.

The presumption of a written document is that it conveys meaning. As Thomas Grey of the Stanford Law School has said, it makes "relatively definite and explicit what otherwise would be relatively indefinite and tacit."

We know that those who framed the Constitution chose their words carefully. They debated at great length the most minute points. The language they chose meant something. They proposed, they substituted, they edited, and they carefully revised. Their words were studied with equal care by state ratifying conventions.

This is not to suggest that there was unanimity among the framers and ratifiers on all points. The Constitution and the Bill of Rights, and some of the subsequent amendments, emerged after protracted debate. Nobody got everything they wanted. What's more, the framers were not clairvoyants—they could not foresee every issue that would be submitted for judicial review. Nor could they predict how all foreseeable disputes would be resolved under the Constitution. But the point is, the meaning of the Constitution can be known.

What does this written Constitution mean? In places it is exactingly specific. Where it says that Presidents of the United States must be at least 35 years of age it means exactly that. (I have not heard of any claim that 35 means 30 or 25 or 20.) Where it specifies how the House and Senate are to be organized, it means what it says.

The Constitution also expresses particular principles. One is the right to be free of an unreasonable search or seizure. Another concerns religious liberty. Another is the right to equal protection of the laws.

Those who framed these principles meant something by them. And the meanings can be found. The Constitution itself is also an expression of certain general principles. These principles reflect the deepest purpose of the Constitution—that of establishing a political system through which Americans can best govern themselves consistent with the goal of securing liberty.

The text and structure of the Constitution is instructive. It contains very little in the way of specific political solutions. It speaks volumes on how problems should be approached, and by *whom*. For example, the first three articles set out clearly the scope and limits of three distinct branches of national government. The powers of each being carefully and specifically enumerated. In this scheme it is no accident to find the legislative branch described first, as the framers had fought and sacrificed to secure the right of democratic self-governance. Naturally, this faith in republicanism was not unbounded, as the next two articles make clear.

Yet the Constitution remains a document of powers and principles. And its undergirding premise remains that democratic self government is subject only to the limits of certain constitutional principles. This respect for the political process was made explicit early on. When John Marshall upheld the act of Congress chartering a national bank in *McCulloch v. Maryland* he wrote: "The Constitution [was] intended to endure for ages to come, and, consequently, to be adapted to the various crises of human affairs." But to use McCulloch, as some have tried, as support for the idea that the Constitution is a protean, changeable thing is to stand history on its head. Marshall was keeping faith with the original intention that Congress be free to elaborate and apply constitutional powers and principles. He was not saying that the Court must invent some new constitutional value in order to keep pace with the times. In Walter Berns's words: "Marshall's meaning is not that the Constitution may be adapted to the 'various crises of human affairs,' but that the legislative powers granted by the Constitution are adaptable to meet these crises."

The approach this administration advocates is rooted in the text of the Constitution as illuminated by those who drafted, proposed, and ratified it. In his famous Commentary on the Constitution of the United States Justice Joseph Story explained that:

> The first and fundamental rule in the interpretation of all instruments is, to construe them according to the sense of the terms, and the intention of the parties.

Our approach understands the significance of a written document and seeks to discern the particular and general principles it expresses. It recognizes that there may be debate at times over the application of these principles. But it does not mean these principles cannot be identified.

Constitutional adjudication is obviously not a mechanical process. It requires an appeal to reason and discretion. The text and intention of the Constitution must be understood to constitute the banks within which constitutional interpretation must flow. As James Madison said, if "the sense in which the Constitution was accepted and ratified by the nation . . . be not the guide in expounding it, there can be no security for a consistent and stable, more than for a faithful exercise of its powers."

Thomas Jefferson, so often cited incorrectly as a framer of the Constitution, in fact shared Madison's view: "Our peculiar security is in the possession of a written Constitution. Let us not make it a blank paper by construction."

Jefferson was even more explicit in his personal correspondence:

> On every question of construction [we should] carry ourselves back to the time, when the constitution was adopted; recollect the spirit manifested in the debates; and instead of trying [to find] what meaning may be squeezed out of the text, or invented against it, conform to the probable one, in which it was passed.

In the main a jurisprudence that seeks to be faithful to our Constitution— a jurisprudence of original intention, as I have called it—is not difficult to describe. Where the language of the Constitution is specific, it must be obeyed. Where there is a demonstrable consensus among the framers and ratifiers as to a principle stated or implied by the Constitution, it should be followed. Where there is ambiguity as to the precise meaning or reach of a constitutional provision, it should be interpreted and applied in a manner so as to at least not contradict the text of the Constitution itself.

Sadly, while almost everyone participating in the current constitutional debate would give assent to these propositions, the techniques and conclusions of some of the debaters do violence to them. What is the source of this violence? In large part I believe that it is the misuse of history stemming from the neglect of the idea of a written constitution.

There is a frank proclamation by some judges and commentators that what matters most about the Constitution is not its words but its so-called "spirit." These individuals focus less on the language of specific provisions than on what they describe as the "vision" or "concepts of human dignity" they find embodied in the Constitution. This approach to jurisprudence has led to some remarkable and tragic conclusions.

In the 1850s, the Supreme Court under Chief Justice Roger B. Taney read blacks out of the Constitution in order to invalidate Congress's attempt to limit the spread of slavery. The *Dred Scott* decision, famously described as a judicial "self-inflicted wound," helped bring on civil war.

There is a lesson in this history. There is danger in seeing the Constitution as an empty vessel into which each generation may pour its passion and prejudice.

Our own time has its own fashions and passions. In recent decades many have come to view the Constitution—more accurately, part of the Constitution, provisions of the Bill of Rights and the Fourteenth Amendment—as a charter for judicial activism on behalf of various constituencies. Those who hold this view often have lacked demonstrable textual or historical support for their conclusions. Instead they have "grounded" their rulings in appeals to social theories, to moral philosophies or personal notions of human dignity, or to "penumbras," somehow emanating ghostlike from various provisions—identified and not identified—in the Bill of Rights. The problem with this approach, as John Hart Ely, Dean of the Stanford Law School, has observed with respect to one such decision, is not that it is bad constitutional law, but that it is not constitutional law in any meaningful sense, at all.

Despite this fact, the perceived popularity of some results in particular cases has encouraged some observers to believe that any critique of the methodology of those decisions is an attack on the results. This perception is sufficiently widespread that it deserves an answer. My answer is to look at history.

When the Supreme Court, in *Brown v. Board of Education*, sounded the death knell for official segregation in the country, it earned all the plaudits it received. But the Supreme Court in that case was not giving new life to old words, or adapting a "living," "flexible" Constitution to new reality. It was restoring the original principle of the Constitution to constitutional law. The *Brown* Court was correcting the damage done 50 years earlier, when in *Plessy v. Ferguson* an earlier Supreme Court had disregarded the clear intent of the framers of the Civil War amendments to eliminate the legal degradation of blacks, and had contrived a theory of the Constitution to support the charade of "separate but equal" discrimination.

Similarly, the decisions of the New Deal and beyond that freed Congress to regulate commerce and enact a plethora of social legislation were not judicial adaptations of the Constitution to new realities. They were in fact removals of encrustrations of earlier courts that had strayed from the original intent of the framers regarding the power of the legislature to make policy.

It is amazing how so much of what passes for social and political progress is really the undoing of old judicial mistakes.

Mistakes occur when the principles of specific constitutional provisions—such as those contained in the Bill of Rights—are taken by some as invitations to read into the Constitution values that contradict the clear language of other provisions.

Acceptances to this illusory invitation have proliferated in recent decades. One Supreme Court justice identified the proper judicial standard as asking "what's best for this country." Another said it is important to "keep the Court out in front" of the general society. Various academic commentators have poured rhetorical grease on this judicial fire, suggesting that constitutional interpretation appropriately be guided by such standards as whether a public policy "personifies justice" or "comports with the notion of moral evolution" or confers "an identity" upon our society or was consistent with "natural ethical law" or was consistent with some "right of equal citizenship."

Unfortunately, as I've noted, navigation by such lodestars has in the past given us questionable economics, governmental disorder, and racism—all in the guise of constitutional law. Recently one of the distinguished judges of one of our federal appeals courts got it about right when he wrote: "The truth is that the judge who looks outside the Constitution always looks inside himself and nowhere else." Or, as we recently put it before the Supreme Court in an important brief: "The further afield interpretation travels from its point of departure in the text, the greater the danger that constitutional adjudication will be like a picnic to which the framers bring the words and the judges the meaning."

In the *Osborne v. Bank of United States* decision 21 years after *Marbury,* Chief Justice Marshall further elaborated his view of the relationship between the judge and the law, be it statutory or constitutional:

> Judicial power, as contradistinguished from the power of the laws, has no existence. Courts are the mere instruments of the law, and can will nothing. When they are said to exercise a discretion, it is a mere legal discretion, a discretion to be exercised in discerning the course prescribed by law; and, when that is discerned, it is the duty of the Court to follow it.

Any true approach to constitutional interpretation must respect the document in all its parts and be faithful to the Constitution in its entirety.

What must be remembered in the current debate is that interpretation does not imply results. The framers were not trying to anticipate every answer. They were trying to create a tripartite national government, within a federal system, that would have the flexibility to adapt to face new exigencies—as it did, for example, in chartering a national bank. Their great interest was in the distribution of power and responsibility in order to secure the great goal of liberty for all.

A jurisprudence that seeks fidelity to the Constitution—a jurisprudence of original intention—is not a jurisprudence of political results. It is very much concerned with process, and it is a jurisprudence that in our day seeks to depoliticize the law. The great genius of the constitutional blueprint is found in its creation and respect for spheres of authority and the limits it places on governmental power. In this scheme the framers did not see the courts as the exclusive custodians of the Constitution. Indeed, because the document posits so few conclusions it leaves to the more political branches the matter of adapting and vivifying its principles in each generation. It also leaves to the people of the states, in the Tenth Amendment, those responsibilities and rights not committed to federal care. The power to declare acts of Congress and laws of the states null and void is truly awesome. This power must be used when the Constitution clearly speaks. It should not be used when the Constitution does not.

In *Marbury v. Madison*, at the same time he vindicated the concept of judicial review, Marshall wrote that the "principles" of the Constitution "are deemed fundamental and permanent," and except for formal amendment, "unchangeable." If we want a change in our Constitution or in our laws we must seek it through the formal mechanisms presented in that organizing document of our government.

In summary, I would emphasize that what is at issue here is not an agenda of issues or a menu of results. At issue is a way of government. A jurisprudence based on first principles is neither conservative nor liberal, neither right nor left. It is a jurisprudence that cares about committing and limiting to each organ of government the proper ambit of its responsibilities. It is a jurisprudence faithful to our Constitution.

By the same token, an activist jurisprudence, one which anchors the Constitution only in the consciences of jurists, is a chameleon jurisprudence, changing color and form in each era. The same activism hailed today may threaten the capacity for decision through democratic consensus tomorrow, as it has in many yesterdays. Ultimately, as the early democrats wrote into the Massachusetts state constitution, the best defense of our liberties is a government of laws and not men.

On this point it is helpful to recall the words of the late Justice Frankfurter. As he wrote:

> [T]here is not under our Constitution a judicial remedy for every political mischief, for every undesirable exercise of legislative power. The framers carefully and with deliberate forethought refused so to enthrone the judiciary. In this situation, as in others of like nature, appeal for relief does not belong here. Appeal must be to an informed, civically militant electorate. . . .

What Did the Founding Fathers Intend?

Irving R. Kaufman

. . . In the ongoing debate over original intent, almost all federal judges hold to the notion that judicial decisions should be based on the text of the Constitution or the structure it creates. Yet, in requiring judges to be guided solely by the expressed views of the framers, current advocates of original intent seem to call for a narrower concept. Jurists who disregard this interpretation, the argument runs, act lawlessly because they are imposing their own moral standards and political preferences on the community.

As a federal judge, I have found it often difficult to ascertain the "intent of the framers," and even more problematic to try to dispose of a constitutional question by giving great weight to the intent argument. Indeed, even if it were possible to decide hard cases on the basis of a strict interpretation of original intent, or originalism, that methodology would conflict with a judge's duty to apply the Constitution's underlying principles to changing circumstances. Furthermore, by attempting to erode the base for judicial affirmation of the freedoms guaranteed by the Bill of Rights and the 14th Amendment (no state shall "deprive any person of life, liberty, or property without due process of law; nor deny to any person . . . the equal protection of the laws"), the intent theory threatens some of the greatest achievements of the Federal judiciary.

Ultimately, the debate centers on the nature of judicial review, or the power of courts to act as the ultimate arbiters of constitutional meaning. This responsibility has been acknowledged ever since the celebrated 1803 case of *Marbury v. Madison*, in which Chief Justice John Marshall struck down a congressional grant of jurisdiction to the Supreme Court not authorized by Article III of the Constitution. But here again, originalists would accept judicial review only if it adhered to the allegedly neutral principles embalmed in historical intent.

In the course of 36 years on the federal bench, I have had to make many difficult constitutional interpretations. I have had to determine whether a teacher could wear a black armband as a protest against the Vietnam War; whether newspapers have a nonactionable right to report accusatory statements; and whether a school system might be guilty of de facto segregation. Unfortunately, the framers' intentions are not made sufficiently clear to provide easy answers.

Irving R. Kaufman (1910–1992) was a judge on the U.S. Court of Appeals for the Second Circuit. From Irving R. Kaufman, "What Did the Founding Fathers Intend?" as it appeared in *The New York Times Magazine*, February 23, 1986, pp. 59–69.

A judge must first determine what the intent was (or would have been)—a notoriously formidable task.

An initial problem is the paucity of materials. Both the official minutes of the Philadelphia Convention of 1787 and James Madison's famous notes of the proceedings, published in 1840, tend toward the terse and cursory, especially in relation to the judiciary. The congressional debates over the proposed Bill of Rights, which became effective in 1791, are scarcely better. Even Justice William Rehnquist, one of the most articulate spokesmen for original intent, admitted in a recent dissent in a case concerning school prayer that the legislative history behind the provision against the establishment of an official religion "does not seem particularly illuminating."

One source deserves special mention. *The Federalist Papers*—the series of essays written by Alexander Hamilton, James Madison and John Jay in 1787 and 1788—have long been esteemed as the earliest constitutional commentary. In 1825, for example, Thomas Jefferson noted that *The Federalist* was regularly appealed to "as evidence of the general opinion of those who framed and of those who accepted the Constitution of the United States."

The Federalist, however, did not discuss the Bill of Rights or the Civil War amendments, which were yet to be written. Moreover, the essays were part of a political campaign—the authors wrote them in support of New York's ratification of the Constitution. The essays, therefore, tended to enunciate general democratic theory or rebut anti-Federalist arguments, neither of which offers much help to modern jurists. (In light of the following passage from *The Federalist*, No. 14, I believe Madison would be surprised to find his words of 200 years ago deciding today's cases: "Is it not the glory of the people of America that . . . they have not suffered a blind veneration for antiquity . . . to overrule the suggestions of their own good sense . . . ?")

Another problem with original intent is this: Who were the framers? Generally, they are taken to be the delegates to the Philadelphia Convention and the congressional sponsors of subsequent amendments. All constitutional provisions, however, have been ratified by state conventions or legislatures on behalf of the people they represented. Is the relevant intention, then, that of the drafters, the ratifiers or the general populace?

The elusiveness of the framers' intent leads to another, more telling problem. Originalist doctrine presumes that intent can be discovered by historical sleuthing or psychological rumination. In fact, this is not possible. Judges are constantly required to resolve questions that 18th-century statesmen, no matter how prescient, simply could not or did not foresee and resolve. On most issues, to look for a collective intention held by either drafters or ratifiers is to hunt for a chimera.

A reading of the Constitution highlights this problem. The principles of our great charter are cast in grand, yet cryptic, phrases. Accordingly, judges usually confront what Justice Robert Jackson in the 1940s termed the "majestic generalities" of the Bill of Rights, or the terse commands of "due process of law," or "equal protection" contained in the 14th Amendment. The use of such open-ended provisions would indicate that the framers did not want the

Constitution to become a straitjacket on all events for all times. In contrast, when the framers held a clear intention, they did not mince words. Article II, for example, specifies a minimum Presidential age of 35 years instead of merely requiring "maturity" or "adequate age."

The First Amendment is a good example of a vaguer provision. In guaranteeing freedom of the press, some of our forefathers perhaps had specific thoughts on what publications fell within its purview. Some historians believe, in light of Colonial debates, that the main concern of the framers was to prevent governmental licensing of newspapers. If that were all the First Amendment meant today, then many important decisions protecting the press would have to be overruled. One of them would be the landmark *New York Times v. Sullivan* ruling of 1964, giving the press added protection in libel cases brought by public figures. Another would be *Near v. Minnesota,* a case involving Jay Near, a newspaper publisher who had run afoul of a Minnesota statute outlawing "malicious, scandalous and defamatory" publications. The Supreme Court struck down the statute in 1931, forbidding governmental prior restraints on publication; this ruling was the precursor of the 1971 Pentagon Papers decision.

The Founding Fathers focused not on particularities but on principles, such as the need in a democracy for people to engage in free and robust discourse. James Madison considered a popular government without popular information a "Prologue to a Farce or a Tragedy." Judges, then, must focus on underlying principles when going about their delicate duty of applying the First Amendment's precepts to today's world.

In fact, our nation's first debate over constitutional interpretation centered on grand principles. Angered at John Adams's Federalist Administration, advocates of states' rights in the late 18th century argued that original intent meant that the Constitution, like the Articles of Confederation, should be construed narrowly—as a compact among separate sovereigns. The 1798 Virginia and Kentucky Resolutions, which sought to reserve to the states the power of ultimate constitutional interpretation, were the most extreme expressions of this view. In rejecting this outlook, a nationalistic Supreme Court construed the Constitution more broadly.

The important point here is that neither side of this debate looked to the stated views of the framers to resolve the issue. Because of his leading role at the Philadelphia Convention, Madison's position is especially illuminating. "Whatever veneration might be entertained for the body of men who formed our Constitution," he declaimed on the floor of Congress in 1796, "the sense of that body could never be regarded as the oracular guide in expounding the Constitution."

Yet, I doubt if strict proponents of original intent will be deterred by such considerations. Their goal is not to venerate dead framers but to restrain living judges from imposing their own values. This restraint is most troublesome when it threatens the protection of individual rights against governmental encroachment.

According to current constitutional doctrine, the due process clause of the 14th Amendment incorporates key provisions of the Bill of Rights, which keeps in check only the Federal Government. Unless the due process clause is construed to include the most important parts of the first eight amendments in the Bill of Rights, then the states would be free, in theory, to establish an official church or inflict cruel and unusual punishments. This doctrine is called incorporation.

Aside from the late Justice Hugo Black, few have believed that history alone is a sufficient basis for applying the Bill of Rights to the states. In his Georgetown University address, Justice Brennan noted that the crucial liberties embodied in the Bill of Rights are so central to our national identity that we cannot imagine any definition of "liberty" without them.

In fact, a cramped reading of the Bill of Rights jeopardizes what I regard as the true original intent—the rationale for having a written Constitution at all. The principal reason for a charter was to restrain government. In 1787, the idea of a fundamental law set down in black and white was revolutionary. Hanoverian England in the 18th century did not have a fully written, unified constitution, having long believed in a partially written one, based on ancient custom and grants from the Crown like the Magna Carta. To this day, the British have kept their democracy alive without one. In theory, the "King-in-Parliament" was and is unlimited in sovereign might, and leading political theorists, such as Thomas Hobbes and John Locke, agreed that governments, once established by a social contract, could not then be fettered.

Although not a Bill of Rights, the Magna Carta—King John's concessions to his barons in 1215—was symbolic of the notion that even the Crown was not all-powerful. Moreover, certain judges believed that Parliament, like the king, had to respect the traditions of the common law. This staunch belief in perpetual rights, in turn, was an important spark for the Revolutionary conflagration of 1776.

In gaining independence, Americans formed the bold concept that sovereignty continually resided with the people, who cede power to governments only to achieve certain specific ends. This view dominated the Philadelphia Convention. Instead of merely improving on the Articles of Confederation, as they had been directed to do, the framers devised a government where certain powers—defined and thereby limited—flowed from the people to the Congress, the President and the Federal judiciary.

Alexander Hamilton recognized that the basic tenets of this scheme mandated judicial review. Individual rights, he observed in *The Federalist*, No. 78, "can be preserved in practice no other way than through the medium of courts of justice, whose duty it must be to declare all acts contrary to the manifest tenor of the Constitution void." Through a written constitution and judicial enforcement, the framers intended to preserve the inchoate rights they had lost as Englishmen.

The narrow interpretation of original intent is especially unfortunate because I doubt that many of its proponents are in favor of freeing the states from the constraints of the Bill of Rights. In fact, I believe the concern of many modern "intentionalists" is quite specific: outrage over the right-of-privacy cases, especially *Roe v. Wade*, the 1973 Supreme Court decision recognizing a woman's right to an abortion. (The right of privacy, of course, is not mentioned in the Constitution.) Whether one agrees with this controversial decision or not, I would submit that concern over the outcome of one difficult case is not sufficient cause to embrace a theory that calls for so many changes in existing law. . . .

. . . [I]f original intent is an uncertain guide, does some other, more functional approach to interpreting the Constitution exist?

One suggestion is to emphasize the importance of democratic "process." As John Hart Ely, dean of the Stanford Law School, forcefully advocates, this approach would direct the courts to make a distinction between "process" (the rules of the game, so to speak) and "substance" (the results of the game). Laws dealing with process include those affecting voting rights or participation in society; the Supreme Court correctly prohibited segregation, for example, because it imposed on blacks the continuing stigma of slavery. Judges, however, would not have the power to review the substantive decisions of elected officials, such as the distribution of welfare benefits.

Basically, such an approach makes courts the guardians of democracy, but a focus on process affords little help when judges decide between difficult and competing values. Judicial formulation of a democratic vision, for example, requires substantive decision-making. The dignities of human liberty enshrined in the Bill of Rights are not merely a means to an end, even so noble an end as democratic governance. For example, we cherish freedom of speech not only because it is necessary for meaningful elections, but also for its own sake.

The truth is that no litmus test exists by which judges can confidently and consistently measure the constitutionality of their decisions. Notwithstanding the clear need for judicial restraint, judges do not constitute what Prof. Raoul Berger, a retired Harvard Law School fellow, has termed an "imperial judiciary." I would argue that the judicial process itself limits the reach of a jurist's arm.

First, judges do not and cannot deliberately contravene specific constitutional rules or clear indications of original intent. No one would seriously argue or expect, for instance, that the Supreme Court could or would twist the Presidential minimum-age provision into a call for "sufficient maturity," so as to forbid the seating of a 36-year-old.

I doubt, in any event, that federal judges would ever hear such a question. The Constitution limits our power to traditional "cases" and "controversies" capable of judicial resolution. In cases like the hypothetical one regarding the presidential age, the High Court employs doctrines of standing (proving injury) and "political question" to keep citizens from suing merely out of a desire to have the government run a certain way.

Moreover, the issues properly before a judge are not presented on a *tabula rasa.* Even the vaguest constitutional provisions have received the judicial gloss of prior decisions. Precedent alone, of course, should not preserve clearly erroneous decisions; the abhorrent "separate but equal" doctrine survived for more than 50 years before the Warren Court struck it down in 1954.

The conventions of our judicial system also limit a jurist's ability to impose his or her own will. One important restraint, often overlooked, is the tradition that appellate judges issue written opinions. That is, we must support our decisions with reasons instead of whims and indicate how our constitutional rulings relate to the document. A written statement is open to the dissent of colleagues, possible review by a higher court and the judgment, sometimes scathing, of legal scholars.

In addition, the facts of a given case play a pivotal role. Facts delineate the reach of a legal decision and remind us of the "cases and controversies" requirement. Our respect for such ground rules reassures the public that, even in the most controversial case, the outcome is not just a political ruling.

Judges are also mindful that the ultimate justification for their power is public acceptance—acceptance not of every decision, but of the role they play. Without popular support, the power of judicial review would have been eviscerated by political forces long ago.

Lacking the power of the purse or the sword, the courts must rely on the elected branches to enforce their decisions. The school desegregation cases would have been a dead letter unless President Eisenhower had been willing to order out the National Guard—in support of a decision authored by a Chief Justice, Earl Warren, whose appointment the President had called "the biggest damned-fool mistake I ever made."

Instead of achieving the purple of philosopher-kings, an unprincipled judiciary would risk becoming modern King Canutes, with the cold tide of political reality and popular opprobrium lapping at their robes.

My revered predecessor on the Court of Appeals, Judge Learned Hand, remarked in a lecture at Harvard in the late 1950s that he would not want to be ruled by "a bevy of Platonic Guardians." The Constitution balances the danger of judicial abuse against the threat of a temporary majority trampling individual rights. The current debate is a continuation of an age-old, and perhaps endless, struggle to reach a balance between our commitments to democracy and to the rule of law. . . .

Judicial Selection

The U.S. *Constitution empowers presidents of the United States to appoint individuals to serve on the federal courts, provided they secure the consent of the Senate. This division of power creates the potential for conflict between the executive and legislative branches. Over the course of our history, presidents have in fact had some of their most bitter fights with the Senate over who should serve on the highest court in the land. Witness, for example, Ronald Reagan's failed attempt to appoint Robert Bork to the U.S. Supreme Court in 1987—a confrontation that left a residue of ill will between the Republican and Democratic parties—and George H. W. Bush's successful but similarly bruising battle to place Clarence Thomas there four years later.*

With the atmosphere in Washington having grown decidedly more partisan in recent years, some have voiced concern that senators' votes on federal court nominees are being determined more and more by political considerations, and less and less by qualifications for the office. In the first selection, John Eastman and Timothy Sandefur give voice to this concern, charging that liberal senators are employing an ideological litmus test for prospective court nominees, viewing favorably those who share their expansive view of the Constitution, while declining to support those espousing a more conservative and restrictive judicial philosophy. By doing so, Eastman and Sandefur maintain, these senators are not only violating the expressed intent of the Founding Fathers, but also seriously compromising the principle of separation of powers.

Erwin Chemerinsky, author of the second selection, totally disagrees. He insists that presidents and senators have always factored ideology into their decisions on nominees for the courts, and he offers a number of reasons why it is wholly appropriate for them to do so.

The Senate Is Supposed to Advise and Consent, Not Obstruct and Delay

John C. Eastman and Timothy Sandefur

I. THE FRAMERS OF THE CONSTITUTION ASSIGNED TO THE PRESIDENT THE PRE-EMINENT ROLE IN APPOINTING JUDGES

Article II of the Constitution provides that the President "shall nominate, and by and with the Advice and Consent of the Senate, shall appoint . . . Judges of the supreme Court [and such inferior courts as the Congress may from time to time ordain and establish]."[1] As the text of the provision makes explicitly clear, the power to choose nominees—to "nominate"—is vested solely in the President,[2] and the President also has the primary role to "appoint," albeit with the advice and consent of the Senate. The text of the clause itself thus demonstrates that the role envisioned for the Senate was a much more limited one than is currently being claimed.

The lengthy debates over the clause in the Constitutional Convention support this reading. According to Madison's notes, an initial proposal on July 18, 1787, to place the appointment power in the Senate was opposed because, as Massachusetts delegate Nathaniel Ghorum noted, "even that branch [was] too numerous, and too little personally responsible, to ensure a good choice."[3] Ghorum suggested instead that Judges be appointed by the President with the advice and consent of the Senate, as had long been the method successfully followed in his home state. James Wilson and Gouverneur Morris of Pennsylvania, two of the Convention's leading figures, agreed with Ghorum and moved that judges be appointed by the President.

In contrast, Luther Martin of Maryland and Roger Sherman of Connecticut argued in favor of the initial proposal, contending that the Senate should have the power because, "[b]eing taken fro[m] all the States it [would] be best informed of the characters & most capable of making a fit choice."[4] And

John C. Eastman is Henry Salvatori Professor of Law and Community Services at Chapman University School of Law and director of the Claremont Institute Center for Constitutional Jurisprudence. He formerly served as a law clerk to the Honorable Clarence Thomas, associate justice of the Supreme Court of the United States. Timothy Sandefur is staff attorney at the Pacific Legal Foundation. This article is from John C. Eastman and Timothy Sandefur, "The Senate Is Supposed to Advise and Consent, Not Obstruct and Delay," *NEXUS: A Journal of Opinion*, 7 (2002), pp. 11–25. Notes were renumbered to correspond with edited text. Reprinted by permission.

Virginia's George Mason argued that the President should not have the power to appoint judges because (among other reasons) the President "would insensibly form local & personal attachments . . . that would deprive equal merit elsewhere, of an equal chance of promotion."[5]

Ghorum replied to Mason's objection by noting that the senators were at least equally likely to "form their attachments."[6] Giving the power to the President would at least mean that he "will be responsible in point of character at least" for his choices, and would therefore "be careful to look through all the States for proper characters." For him, the problem with placing the appointment power in the Senate was that "Public bodies feel no personal responsibility, and give full play to intrigue & cabal,"[7] while if the appointment power were given to the President alone, "the Executive would certainly be more answerable for a good appointment, as the whole blame of a bad one would fall on him alone."[8]

Seeking a compromise, James Madison suggested that the power of appointment be given to the President with the Senate able to veto that choice by a 2/3 vote.[9] Another compromise was suggested by Edmund Randolph, who "thought the advantage of personal responsibility might be gained in the Senate by requiring the respective votes of the members to be entered on the Journal."[10] These compromises were defeated, however, and the vote on Ghorum's motion—that the President nominate and with the advice and consent of the Senate, should appoint—resulted in a 4–4 tie.[11] The discussion was then postponed.

When the appointment power was taken up again on July 21, the delegates returned to their previous arguments. One side argued that the President should be solely responsible for the appointments, because he would be less likely to be swayed by "partisanship"—what Madison's generation called "faction"[12]—than the Senate. The other side opposed vesting the appointment power in the President for a similar reason: he would not know as many qualified candidates as the Senate would, and might still be swayed by personal considerations or nepotism. . . .

In the end, the Convention agreed that the President would make the nominations, and the Senate would have a limited power to withhold confirmation as a check against political patronage or nepotism. Gouverneur Morris put the decision succinctly: "as the President was to nominate, there would be responsibility, and as the Senate was to concur, there would be security."[13] As the Supreme Court subsequently recognized, "the Framers anticipated that the President would be less vulnerable to interest-group pressure and personal favoritism than would a collective body."[14] No one argued that the Senate's participation in the process should include second-guessing the judicial philosophy of the President's nominees or attempting to mold that philosophy itself. Indeed, such a suggestion was routinely rejected as presenting a dangerous violation of the separation of powers, by allowing the Senate to control the President's choices and, ultimately, intrude upon the judiciary. . . .

In short, by assigning the sole power to nominate (and the primary power to appoint) judges to the President, the Convention specifically rejected a more expansive Senate role; such would undermine the President's responsibility, and

far from providing security against improper appointments, would actually lead
to the very kind of cabal-like behavior that the Convention delegates feared. . . .

II. THE CURRENT STATE OF THE CONFIRMATION POWER

Despite the original understanding of the Senate's limited role in the confirmation process . . . the Senate today appears bent on using its limited confirmation
power to impose ideological litmus on presidential nominees and even to force
the President to nominate judges preferred by individual senators, thus arrogating to itself the nomination as well as the confirmation power.

The Senate's expanded use of its confirmation power should perhaps come
as no surprise. As a result of the growing role of the judiciary—and of government in general—in the lives of Americans today, the Senate's part in the nomination process has become a powerful political tool, and, like all powerful
political tools, it is the subject of a strenuous competition among interest
groups every time the President seeks to fill a judicial vacancy. Moreover, it is
a tool that poses grave dangers to our constitutional system of government. In
its current manifestation, the Senate's ideological use of the confirmation
power threatens the separation of powers by undermining the responsibility
for appointments given to the President, by demanding of judicial nominees a
commitment to a role not appropriate to the courts, and, perhaps most importantly, by threatening the independence of the judiciary.

The reason that some senators are so intent on delving into the judicial philosophy of nominees is deeply connected to their view of the proper role of the
judiciary in American government. Viewing the Constitution as a "living document," modern-day liberals see the Court as a place where the Constitution is
stretched, shaped, cut, and rewritten in order to put in place so-called "progressive" policies that could never emerge from the legislative process. . . .

Judicial ideology is therefore critically important to modern-day liberals
because an honest reading of the Constitution reveals that it is incompatible
with their scheme of government. Senator Charles Schumer of New York, for
example, has been quite candid in acknowledging that his opposition to
President Bush's judicial nominees is based on the fact that they respect and
will enforce the Constitution's limitations on the power of Congress. "Elected
officials," Sen. Schumer told the press on May 9, 2002,

> should get the benefit of the doubt with respect to policy judgments and courts
> should not reach out to impose their will over that of elected legislatures. . . .
> Many of us on our side of the aisle are acutely concerned with the new limits
> that are now developing on our power to address the problems of those who
> elect us to serve—these decisions affect, in a fundamental way, our ability to
> address major national issues like discrimination against the disabled and the
> aged, protecting the environment, and combating gun violence.[15]

This is not to say that ideology should never play a role in the confirmation
process. Some ideologically-based views render it impossible for a nominee
who holds them to fulfill his oath of office. Consider, for instance, Judge Harry

Pregerson, who, when he was nominated to the Court of Appeals for the Ninth Circuit by President Carter, was asked whether he would follow his conscience or the law, if the two came into conflict. "I would follow my conscience," he replied.[16] That statement, grounded in Pregerson's own ideology, should easily have been grounds for disqualification, yet Pregerson was not only confirmed to the bench, but roundly praised for this statement, despite the fact that it threatens to undermine the very essence of constitutionalism and the rule of law.[17]

Contrast this with Justice Antonin Scalia, who in a recent speech said that he was glad the Pope had not declared the Catholic Church's opposition to the death penalty a matter of infallible Church doctrine, because if the Pope had done so, Justice Scalia would, as a practicing and committed Catholic, feel compelled to resign, unable to abide by his oath to enforce the law. In his view,

> the choice for the judge who believes the death penalty to be immoral is resignation, rather than simply ignoring duly enacted constitutional laws and sabotaging death penalty cases. He has, after all, taken an oath to apply the laws and has been given no power to supplant them with rules of his own. . . . This dilemma, of course, need not be confronted by a proponent of the "living Constitution," who believes that it means what it ought to mean. If the death penalty is (in his view) immoral, then it is (hey, presto!) automatically unconstitutional, and he can continue to sit while nullifying a sanction that has been imposed, with no suggestion of its unconstitutionality, since the beginning of the Republic. (You can see why the "living Constitution" has such attraction for us judges.)[18]

Ideology understood in this light is of course relevant in selecting a judicial nominee. Broadly understood, "ideology" would encompass a nominee's honor and character, which are necessary to fulfill the oath of office.[19] A nominee who for ideological reasons cannot "support and defend the Constitution of the United States"—say, an agent working for the Taliban—would be unfit for office because he would lack the *qualifications* necessary for the position. In fact, although we tend to take the concept of an oath lightly today, James Madison wrote that under the Constitution, *"the concurrence of the Senate* chosen by the State Legislatures, in appointing the Judges, *and the oaths* and official tenures of these, with the surveillance of public Opinion, [would be] relied on as *guarantying their impartiality. . . ."*[20] This is very different than demanding of a nominee that he toe the line of leftist jurisprudence.

Today, senators inquire into a nominee's ideology for precisely the opposite reason: to ensure that the nominee will *not* abide by the Constitution—to ensure that he will stretch and bend the Constitution in the directions that the senator prefers.

On top of the danger that this presents to the fair resolution of controversies in Constitutional law, it presents a great danger to another vital principle of American government: separation of powers. In *Federalist 78*, Alexander Hamilton declared the judiciary the "least dangerous branch" of the new federal government. "[T]he general liberty of the people can never be endangered" by the judiciary, he wrote, "so long as the judiciary remains truly distinct from both the legislature and the Executive. . . . [L]iberty can have nothing to fear from the judiciary alone, but would have every thing to fear from its union with either of the other departments," and "all the effects of such a union must ensue from a dependence of the former on the latter, notwithstanding a nominal and apparent separation."[21] The enforcement of political orthodoxy on the bench is creating precisely this dependence, strengthened even more by judicial "deference" to Congressional acts that exceed the limited scope of the federal government's Constitutional powers.

"The complete independence of the courts of justice is peculiarly essential in a limited Constitution," wrote Hamilton. The courts alone could "declare all acts contrary to the manifest tenor of the Constitution void."[22] But the current attempt to block judges who believe in limited government is not motivated by a desire to maintain inviolate the "exceptions to the legislative authority." It is motivated by a desire to ensure that the judiciary will interpret the Constitution in a way most suited to *extend* that legislative authority as far as possible.

What that essentially means is that the current attempt to use the Senate's confirmation power to regulate the ideology of judges is part of an overall trend which is turning the *judiciary* into a second *legislative* branch. The fundamental differences between the legislative and the judicial branch is that in the former, parties lobby, contend, vote, and decide on procedures that may infringe on the private rights of individuals. The courts are supposed to act as a "countermajoritarian" mechanism to ensure that the legislature does not engage in "the invasion of private rights . . . from acts in which the Government is the mere instrument of the major number of the constituents."[23] The very existence of the judiciary is premised on the fact that the majority is not always right. Allowing the Senate—elected by the majority—too great a hand in regulating the federal bench risks eroding the judiciary's power to perform this most crucial task. . . .

CONCLUSION

In June of 2001, President Clinton's White House Counsel, Lloyd Cutler, told the Senate Judiciary Committee that "it would be a tragic development if ideology became an increasingly important consideration in the future. To make ideology an issue in the confirmation process is to suggest that the legal process is and should be a political one. That is not only wrong as a matter of political science; it also serves to weaken public confidence in the courts."[24]

Today the Senate is doing precisely what one delegate to the North Carolina ratification convention warned against: it is taking over the nomination power which the Constitution vested in the President alone. "[T]he President may nominate, but they have a negative upon his nomination, till he has exhausted the number of those he wishes to be appointed: He will be obliged finally to acquiesce in the appointment of those which the Senate shall nominate, or else no appointment will take place."[25] The dangers posed by such a system are as real today as they were to the founding generation. It is time to rid ourselves of all ideological litmus tests save one: "Mr. Nominee, are you prepared to honor your oath to support the Constitution as written and not as you would like it to be, if we confirm you to this important office?"[26] Any nominee who answers that question in the negative deserves to be rejected. Unfortunately, the Senate is today refusing a hearing to several nominees precisely because the current leadership knows that those nominees would honestly answer that question in the affirmative.

NOTES

1. U.S. Const. art. II § 2 cl. 2; art. III § 1.
2. See also *Weiss v. United States,* 510 U.S. 163, 185 n. 1 (1994) (Souter, J., concurring) ("the President was . . . rightly given the sole power to nominate").
3. 2 M. Farrand, Records of the Federal Convention 41 (1911).
4. *Id.*
5. *Id.* at 42. Mason's objections were actually more complicated. He argued that the President should not appoint judges because the judges might try impeachments of the President. This problem was later avoided by having the Senate try impeachments with the Chief Justice of the Supreme Court merely presiding. *See* U.S. Const. art. I § 3 cl. 6. Gouverneur Morris, in replying to Mason, argued that impeachments should not be "tried before the Judges." Farrand, *supra* note 3 at 41–42. Mason also worried that "the Seat of Govt must be in some state,"and the President would form personal attachments to people in that state, which might exclude citizens of other states from the federal bench—an understandable objection from an antifederalist like Mason. This problem was at least partly obviated by placing the capital in a federal district which would not be subject to the jurisdiction of any state. *See* U.S. Const. art. I § 8 cl. 17.
6. Farrand, *supra* note 3 at 42.
7. *Id.*
8. *Id.* at 43.
9. *Id.* at 42.
10. *Id.* at 43.
11. The Convention voted by state. Georgia abstained from this vote, and Rhode Island never sent a delegate. Other states' delegates were sometimes absent for various reasons—for instance, although the Convention had been under way for more than a month, New Hampshire's delegates had still not arrived. In addition, this debate came during one of the lowest points of the Convention, when the differences between the delegates was at its severest. New York delegates, Robert Yates and John Lansing, had left the Convention on July 10, opposed to all its proceedings. New York's third delegate, Alexander Hamilton, had left ten days earlier. *See* Catherine Drinker Bowen, *Miracle at Philadelphia* 140 (Book of the Month Club, 1986) (1966). The day Lansing and Yates left the Convention, Washington wrote to Hamilton that he "almost despaired" of the Convention's success. *Id.* at 185–186.

(Hamilton returned to the Convention in September and was New York's only signer.) Thus the vote on July 18 was Massachusetts, Pennsylvania, Maryland and Virginia in favor of Ghorum's motion, and Connecticut, Delaware, North Carolina and South Carolina against.

12. See *The Federalist* Nos. 10 & 51 (C. Rossiter ed. 1961).
13. Farrand, *supra* note 3 at 539.
14. *Edmond v. United States*, 520 U.S. 651, 659 (1997).
15. Statement at Courts Subcommittee hearing, May 9, 2002 (visited May 26, 2002) <http://schumer.senate.gov/SchumerWebsite/pressroom/pressreleases/PR00978.html>.
16. John Johnson, "Judge Harry Pregerson, Choosing Between Law and His Conscience," *Los Angeles Times*, May 3, 1992 at B5.
17. In 1992, Judge Pregerson ordered a stay to the execution of the serial killer Robert Alton Harris, the *fourth* such stay that was issued on the night of Harris' scheduled execution. The result was an unprecedented decision from the Supreme Court of the United States, ordering that "no further stays of Robert Alton Harris' execution shall be entered by the federal courts except upon order of this Court." *Vasquez v. Harris*, 503 U.S. 1000 (1992). See further Charles Fried, *Impudence*, 1992 Sup. Ct. Rev. 155, 188–92.
18. Antonin Scalia, "God's Justice and Ours," *First Things*, May 1, 2002 at 17.
19. The oath of office is prescribed in U.S. Const. art. VI § 3.
20. Letter to Thomas Jefferson (June 27, 1798), in Rakove, *supra* note 23 at 801 (emphasis added).
21. *The Federalist* No. 78 at 466 (C. Rossiter ed. 1961).
22. *Id.*
23. Letter from James Madison to Thomas Jefferson (Oct. 17, 1788) in Madison: *Writings* (J. Rakove ed. 1999) at 418, 421.
24. Statement to Administrative Oversight and the Courts Subcommittee (June 26, 2001) 2001 WL 21756493.
25. Samuel Spencer, *Speech at the North Carolina Ratification Convention*, July 28, 1788, reprinted in 2 Bailyn, *Debate on the Constitution*, at 879.
26. In this view, the qualifications of judges are similar to the qualifications of jurors as explained in *Wainwright v. Witt*, 469 U.S. 412 (1985). There the Court held that "the proper standard for determining when a prospective juror may be excluded for cause because of his or her views on capital punishment. That standard is whether the juror's views would 'prevent or substantially impair the performance of his duties as a juror in accordance with his instructions and his oath.'" *Id.* at 424 (quoting *Adams v. Texas*, 448 U.S. 38, 45 (1980)).

Of Course Ideology Should Matter in Judicial Selection

Erwin Chemerinsky

I. IDEOLOGY ALWAYS HAS MATTERED IN JUDICIAL SELECTION

The debate over the place of ideology in the judicial selection process has so far been framed in terms of whether it is appropriate for the United States Senate to consider the views of the prospective judge during the confirmation process. No one seems to deny that it is completely appropriate for the President to consider ideology when making appointments. In fact, they always have done so. Every President has appointed primarily, if not almost exclusively, individuals from the President's political party. Ever since George Washington, Presidents have looked to ideology when making judicial picks. Some Presidents are more ideological than others; not surprisingly, these Presidents focus more on ideology in their judicial nominations. President Franklin Roosevelt, for example, wanted judges who would uphold his "New Deal" programs and President Ronald Reagan emphasized selecting conservative jurists.

Senates always have done the same, using ideology as a basis for evaluating presidential nominees for the federal bench. Early in American history, President George Washington appointed John Rutledge to be the second Chief Justice of the United States.[1] Rutledge was impeccably qualified; he already had been confirmed by the Senate as an Associate Justice (although he never actually sat in that capacity) and had even been a delegate to the Constitutional Convention. But the Senate rejected Rutledge for the position as Chief Justice, because of its disagreement with Rutledge's views on a United States treaty with Great Britain.

During the nineteenth century, the Senate rejected twenty-one presidential nominations for the United States Supreme Court.[2] The vast majority of these individuals were defeated because of Senate disagreement with their ideology.[3] Professor Grover Rees explains that "during the nineteenth century only four Supreme Court Justices were rejected on the ground that they lacked the

Erwin Chemerinsky is Alston and Bird Professor of Law and professor of political science at Duke University. This article is from Erwin Chemerinsky, "Of Course Ideology Should Matter in Judicial Selection," *NEXUS: A Journal of Opinion*, 7 (2002), pp. 3–10. Notes were renumbered to correspond with edited text. Reprinted by permission.

requisite credentials, whereas seventeen were rejected for political or philo-
sophical reasons."[4]

During the twentieth century, too, nominees for the Supreme Court were
rejected solely because of their ideology. In 1930, a federal court of appeals
judge, John Parker, was denied a seat on the high Court because of his anti-labor,
anti–civil rights views.[5] In 1969, the Senate rejected United States Court of
Appeals judge Clement Haynsworth largely because of his anti-union views.[6]
The Senate then rejected President Nixon's next pick for the Supreme Court,
Federal Court of Appeals Judge Harold Carswell.[7]

In 1987, the Senate rejected Robert Bork, even though he had impeccable
professional qualifications and unquestioned ability. Bork was rejected because
of his unduly restrictive views of Constitutional law; for instance, he rejected
constitutional protection for a right to privacy,[8] believed freedom of speech was
limited only to political expression,[9] and denied protection for women under
the Equal Protection Clause. The defeat of Robert Bork was in line with a tradition as old as the republic itself.[10]

Those who contend that ideology should play no role in judicial selection
are arguing for a radical change from how the process has worked from the earliest days of the nation. Never has the selection or confirmation process focused
solely on whether the candidate has sufficient professional credentials.

There is a widespread sense that the focus on ideology has increased in
recent years. . . . There are several explanations for why there is such intense
focus on ideology at this point in American history. First, the demise of the general public's belief in formalism encourages a focus on ideology. People have
come to recognize that law is not mechanical, that judges often have great discretion in deciding cases. They realize that how judges rule on questions like
abortion, affirmative action, the death penalty, and countless other issues is a
reflection of the individual jurist's views. *Bush v. Gore*[11] simply reinforced the
widespread belief that judges' political views often determine how they vote in
important cases. Thus, Democratic voters want Democratic Senators to block
conservative nominees and Republican voters want Republican Senators to
block liberal nominees. This creates a political incentive for Senators to do so,
and means that they will certainly not risk alienating their core constituency by
using ideology in evaluating nominees.

Second, the lack of "party government" in recent years explains the
increased focus on ideology. During the last six years of the Clinton presidency,
the Senate was controlled by Republicans. During at least the first two years
of the current Bush presidency, the Senate has been controlled by Democrats. If
the Senate is of the same political party as the President, there will obviously be
far fewer fights over judicial nominations. Certainly, confirmation battles are
still possible, for instance through filibusters, or if the President lacks support
from a faction of his own party. But in general confirmation fights are a product of the Senate and the President being from different political parties.

Finally, confirmation fights occur when there is the perception of deep ideological divisions over issues likely to be decided by the courts. Now, for example, conservatives and liberals deeply disagree over countless issues: the

appropriate method of constitutional interpretation; the desirable scope of Congress's power and the judicial role in limiting it; the content of individual rights, such as privacy. It is widely recognized that the outcome of cases concerning these questions will be determined by who is on the bench. Therefore, Senators know, and voters recognize, that the confirmation process is enormously important in deciding the content of the law. Interest groups on both sides of the ideological divide have strong reasons for making judicial confirmation a high priority, because they know what is at stake in who occupies the federal bench.

II. IDEOLOGY SHOULD BE CONSIDERED IN THE JUDICIAL SELECTION AND CONFIRMATION PROCESS

There are many reasons why ideology should be considered in the judicial selection process.

First, most simply and most importantly, ideology should be considered because ideology matters. Judges are not fungible; a person's ideology influences how he or she will vote on important issues. It is appropriate for an evaluator—be it the President, the Senate, or the voters in states with judicial elections[12]—to pay careful attention to the likely consequences of an individual's presence on the court.

This seems so obvious as to hardly require elaboration. Imagine that the President appoints someone who turns out to be an active member of the Ku Klux Klan or the American Nazi Party and repeatedly has expressed racist or anti-semitic views.[13] Assume that the individual has impeccable professional qualifications: a degree from a prestigious university, years of experience in high level legal practice, and a strong record of bar service. Notwithstanding these credentials, I think virtually everyone would agree that the nominee should be rejected. If I am correct in this assumption, then everyone agrees that ideology *should* matter and the only issue is *what* views should be a basis for excluding a person from holding judicial office.

On the Supreme Court, the decisions in a large proportion of cases are a product of the judges' views. The federalism decisions of recent years—limiting the scope of Congress's power under the commerce clause and section five of the Fourteenth Amendment, reviving the Tenth Amendment as a limit on federal power, and the expansion of sovereign immunity—have almost all been 5–4 rulings reflecting the ideology of the Justices.[14] Beyond the obviously controversial issues like abortion, affirmative action, and the death penalty, virtually all cases about individual liberties and civil rights are a product of who sits on the bench. Criminal procedure cases often require balancing the government's interests in law enforcement against the rights of individuals; this balancing will reflect the individual Justice's views. Decisions in statutory cases, too, are a result of the ideology of the Justices. Frequently in statutory civil rights cases, the Court is split exactly along ideological lines.[15]

Obviously this is not limited to the Supreme Court. Every case before the Supreme Court was first decided by the lower federal courts, and ideology matters there just as much. There may be more cases in the lower courts where ideology does not matter in determining outcomes—that is, where regardless of ideology any judge would come to the same conclusion—but that does not deny the large number of cases in which the judge's views matter greatly. When I talk to a lawyer who is about to have an argument before a federal court of appeals, the first question I always ask is: *who is your panel?* That is because ideology matters so much in determining the result in so many cases.

Second, the Senate should use ideology precisely because the President uses it. Republicans who today are arguing for the Senate to approve nominations without regard to their views are being disingenuous when the President—from their party—is basing his picks so much on ideology. Under the Constitution, the Senate should not be a rubber-stamp and should not treat judicial selection as a presidential prerogative. The Senate owes no duty of deference to the President and, as explained above, never has shown such deference through American history.

Finally, ideology should be considered because the judicial selection process is the key majoritarian check on an anti-majoritarian institution. Once confirmed, federal judges have life tenure. A crucial democratic check is the process of determining who will hold these appointments. A great deal of constitutional scholarship in the last quarter-century has focused on what Professor Alexander Bickel termed the "counter-majoritarian difficulty"— the exercise of substantial power by unelected judges who can invalidate the decisions of elected officials.[16] The most significant majoritarian check is at the nomination and confirmation stage. Selection by the President and confirmation by the Senate is a legitimate mechanism of majoritarian control over the composition of the federal courts.

Those who oppose the use of ideology in the judicial selection process must sustain one of two arguments: either that an individual's ideology is unlikely to affect his or her decisions on the bench, or that, even if ideology will influence decisions, it should not be examined because the disadvantages to such consideration will outweigh the benefits.

The former argument—that a person's ideology is unlikely to affect performance in office—is impossible to sustain. Unless one believes in truly mechanistic judging,[17] it is clear that judges possess discretion and that the exercise of discretion is strongly influenced by that judge's preexisting ideological beliefs. In cases involving questions of constitutional or statutory interpretation, the language of the document and the intent of the drafters often will be unclear. Judges will have to decide the meaning, and this is going to be a product of their views. Many cases, especially in Constitutional law, require a balancing of interests. The relative weight assigned to the respective claims often turns on the judge's own values. Given the reality of judicial decision making, it is impossible to claim that a judge's ideology will not affect his or her decisions.

So opposition to considering ideology must be based on the latter argument: that even though ideology matters, it is undesirable for the Senate to consider it. One argument is that considering ideology will undermine judicial independence. Professor Stephen Carter makes this argument: "if a nominee's ideas fall within the very broad range of judicial views that are not radical in any non-trivial sense—and Robert Bork has as much right to that middle ground as any other nominee in recent decades—the Senate enacts a terrible threat to the independence of the judiciary if a substantive review of the nominee's legal theories brings about a rejection."[18]

But Professor Carter never explains why judicial independence requires blindness to ideology during the confirmation or selection of a federal judge. Judicial independence means that a judge should feel free to decide cases according to his or her view of the law and not in response to popular pressure. This is why Article III's assurance of life tenure, and its protection against a reduction in salaries, provide independence.[19] Judges are free to decide each case according to their consciences and best judgment; they need not worry that their rulings will cause them to be ousted from office. Professor Carter never justifies why this is insufficient to protect judicial independence. He subtly shifts the definition of independence from autonomy while in office to autonomy from scrutiny before taking office. But he does not explain why the latter, freedom from evaluation before ascending to the bench, is a prerequisite for judicial independence in the former, far more meaningful sense. In fact, the opposite order makes more sense. It is precisely because the framers of the Constitution's protections for judicial independence *understood* that judges would be subject to great ideological pressures, that they saw fit to insulate them from expressions of popular resentment. Judicial independence was therefore created by people who understood that judicial ideology matters.[20]

Another argument against considering ideology is that it will deadlock the selection process, with liberals blocking conservatives and vice versa. The reality is that this is a risk only when the Senate and the President are from different political parties. Even then, every Senate—including the Republican Senate during the Clinton years and the Democratic Senate today—has approved a large number of presidential nominations for the federal bench. There have been times when a number of nominations have been rejected—for instance, the Senate refused to confirm *any* of President John Tyler's picks for the Supreme Court,[21] and rejected two nominations in a row by President Nixon.[22] But in over 200 years of history, deadlocks have been rare.

Most importantly . . . the solution to deadlocks is in the President's hands: nominate individuals who are acceptable to the Senate. Presidents will have to select more moderate individuals than if the Senate was controlled by their political party. President Clinton undoubtedly was forced to select more moderate judges because the Senate was controlled by Republicans for the last six years of his presidency. President Bush would be far more successful in getting his nominations through the Senate if he chose less conservative individuals. The President has the prerogative to pick conservatives like Pickering, McConnell, Kuhl, or Estrada, but he should expect resistance in a Democratic Senate that would not be there if Bush selected more moderate nominees.

Finally, some suggest that using ideology is undesirable because it will encourage judges to base their rulings on ideology. The argument is that ideology must be hidden from the process so as to limit the likelihood that once on the bench judges will base their decisions on ideology. This argument is based on numerous unsupportable assumptions: it assumes that it is possible for judges to decide cases apart from their views and ideology; that judges don't already often decide cases because of their views and ideology; that considering ideology in the selection process will somehow increase this tendency. All of these are simply false. Long ago, the Legal Realists exploded the myth of formalistic value-neutral judging.[23] Having the judicial confirmation process recognize the demise of formalism won't change a thing in how judges behave on the bench.

The argument for considering ideology in judicial selection is simple: people should care about the decisions of the Supreme Court and other federal courts; they affect millions of people's lives in subtle but profound ways. The ideological composition of the court will determine those decisions, and the appropriate place for majoritarian influences in the judicial process is at the selection stage.

CONCLUSION

I bring some personal experience to this topic. Twice during the Clinton years, I was under serious consideration for a federal judgeship. Once, the press reported that I was on a list of three names being considered to fill two vacancies on the federal bench.[24] The other two individuals were picked. Another time, I received a call from the White House Counsel's office that I was being considered for the Ninth Circuit.

In each instance, I was told that I was not selected because the Republican-controlled Senate would find me too liberal and not confirm me. In the latter instance, I was informed that my opposition to Proposition 209, which eliminated affirmative action in California, would likely prevent Republicans from confirming me.

I confess to being disappointed, but not at all surprised; I knew from the outset that ideology always has been a key part of the confirmation process. But now I feel outrage when I hear Republicans say that it is wrong for a Democratic-controlled Senate to look at ideology, when that is exactly what Republicans did for the last six years of the Clinton presidency. . . .

Ultimately, disputes over confirmations are battles over the proper content of the law. This is as it should be, and attention should not be diverted by claims that it is improper to consider a nominee's ideological orientation. Of course, ideology should and must be considered in the judicial selection process.

NOTES

1. Laurence Tribe, *God Save This Honorable Court* 87, 90–91 (1985).
2. Grover Rees, *Questions for Supreme Court Nominees at Confirmation Hearings: Excluding the Constitution,* 17 Ga. L. Rev. 913, 944 (1983).
3. *See also* Jeffrey K. Tulis, *Constitutional Abdication: The Senate, The President, and Appointments to the Supreme Court,* 47 Case W. Res. 1331 (Summer 1997).

4. Rees, *supra* note 2.
5. See Gail Fruchtman, *et al.*, *Questions and Answers*, 84 Law Libr. J. 627, 637 (Summer, 1992); "Background Paper," in *Twentieth Century Fund, Judicial Roulette: Report of the Task Force on Judicial Selection* 77 (1988).
6. *Id.* at 77. See also Bob Woodward & Scott Armstrong, *The Brethren* 56–57 (1979).
7. *See id.* at 74–75.
8. *See* Robert Bork, *The Tempting of America: The Political Seduction of the Law* (1990) 95–100.
9. *See* Robert Bork, *Neutral Principles and Some First Amendment Problems*, 47 Ind. L.J. 1 (1971).
10. *See further* Mark Gitenstein, *Matters of Principle: An Insider's Account of America's Rejection of Robert Bork's Nomination to the Supreme Court* (1992).
11. 121 S.Ct. 545 (2000).
12. It is ironic that those opposed to the use of ideology in the judicial nomination process rarely comment on the fact that *state* judges are elected in almost all the states of the union.
13. This is not so ridiculous a proposition. Justice Hugo Black was a member of the KKK. *See* Gerald T. Dunne, *Hugo Black and the Judicial Revolution* 71–75 (1977).
14. *See, e.g., United States v. Lopez*, 514 U.S. 549 (1995); *United States v. Morrison*, 529 U.S. 598 (2000); *University of Alabama v. Garrett*, 531 U.S. 356 (2001).
15. *See, e.g., Alexander v. Sandoval*, 532 U.S. 275 (2001) (5–4 decision finding no private cause of action under Title VI of 1964 Civil Rights Act against recipients of federal funds for practices that have discriminatory impact in violation of regulations promulgated under that provision); *Circuit City v. Adams*, 532 U.S. 105 (2001) (5–4 decision that Federal Arbitration Act requires arbitration of state law employment discrimination claims); *Buckhannon Board v. West Virginia Department of Health and Human Services*, 532 U.S. 598 (2001) (5–4 decision holding that to be "prevailing party" under attorney fees statute, it is insufficient that plaintiff is catalyst for legislative action).
16. Alexander Bickel, *The Least Dangerous Branch* 16 (1962).
17. This is a difficult proposition to swallow. If judicial decisions could be made so algorithmically, there would be little reason to have a court, let alone any nomination and confirmation process, to begin with! The decision could be made merely according to a set of written equations, or even by a computer. Moreover, if a judge's own values did not affect his or her decisions, there would be no reason for judges to recuse themselves from cases giving rise to conflicts of interest.
18. Stephen Carter, *The Confirmation Mess*, 101 Harv. L. Rev. 1185, 1198 (1988).
19. U.S. Const. art. III § 1 ("The Judges, both of the supreme and inferior Courts, shall hold their Offices during good Behaviour, and shall, at stated Times, receive for their Services, a Compensation, which shall not be diminished during their Continuance in Office").
20. This is a very old principle. Lord Edward Coke, for instance, one of the most important figures in English legal history, wrote, "Honorable and

reverend judges and justices, that do or shall sit in high tribunals and courts or seats of justice . . . fear not to do right to all, and to deliver your opinions justly according to the laws; for feare is nothing but a betraying of the succors that reason should afford. And if you shall sincerely execute justice, be assured . . . that though thereby you may offend a great many favourites, yet you shall have the favourable kindnesse of the Almighty. . . ." Quoted in Catherine Drinker Bowen, The *Lion and The Throne: The Life of Edward Coke* 523 (Atlantic Monthly 1957) (1956). King James I fired Coke as Chief Justice of King's Bench because of Coke's rulings in cases like Dr. Bonham's Case, 8 Co. Rep 113b, 77 Eng. Rep 646 (K.B. 1610), which famously declared that the Court had the power to strike down laws which violated the common law. See Bowen at 314–317, 384–388.

21. Tulis, *supra* note 3 at 1350.
22. *Id.* at 1336; Woodward & Armstrong, *supra* note 6 at 15–16.
23. "Legal realism" refers to a school of thought which sees law as developing not by the discovery of internally operating logical or natural laws, but according to political pressures, experiences, and experiments which result in social structures designed to perpetuate (or to alter) existing sociological or class lines. *See* Karl N. Llewellyn, *A Realistic Jurisprudence—The Next Step*, 30 Harv. L. Rev. 431 (1930). *See further* N. E. H. Hull, *Reconstructing The Origins of Realistic Jurisprudence: A Prequel to The Llewellyn-Pound Exchange over Legal Realism*, 1989 Duke L.J. 1302.
24. Henry Weinstein, "Boxer Recommends L.A. Jurist to Be Nominated for Federal Judgeship," *Los Angeles Times*, Jan. 28, 1995 at B1.

mhhe.com/diclerico11e

Internet resources
Visit our Web site at www.mhhe.com/diclerico11e for links and resources relating to Courts.

 chapter 14

Civil Liberties

Free Speech

*F*reedom of speech is one of the most important freedoms accorded citizens of the United States. Nowhere is that freedom more highly prized than in American universities, whose central mission—the generation and transmission of knowledge—is predicated upon the free expression of ideas. Thus, it should occasion no surprise that considerable debate erupts on campuses from time to time over the extent to which universities are fostering an environment conducive to free expression.

The most recent debate on this question centers on student fees—mandatory fees that the university imposes on students for the purpose of supporting various student organizations and activities on campus. Five students at the University of Wisconsin took strong exception to the fact that their student fees were going to support campus organizations whose views and purposes they did not share. They were so offended that they decided to challenge this practice in court.

The first selection consists of portions of an amicus curiae brief submitted to the U.S. Supreme Court by the American Council on Education on behalf of the University of Wisconsin. It insists that universities have a responsibility to create an environment that fosters a free marketplace of ideas. One of the ways to do so is to support with student fees a host of different campus organizations. Such support, in the view of the American Council on Education, in no way diminishes the free speech of students paying those fees.

The second selection also contains portions of an amicus curiae brief submitted to the U.S. Supreme Court—this one by the Pacific Legal Foundation on behalf of the five students. It argues that by requiring students to support, through their fees, organizations with which they disagree, the University of Wisconsin is in fact abridging their right to freedom of speech.

Mandatory Student Fees Do Not Abridge Freedom of Speech

American Council on Education

I. A UNIVERSITY'S USE OF COMPULSORY FEES TO CREATE A STUDENT ACTIVITY FUND SHOULD BE ANALYZED AS THE CREATION OF A FORUM, RATHER THAN AS COMPELLED SPEECH AND ASSOCIATION

A. A University, as a Marketplace of Ideas, Has a Compelling Interest in Promoting the Presence of a Diversity of Viewpoints

"It is the business of a university to provide that atmosphere which is most conducive to speculation, experiment and creation."[1] A university can provide this atmosphere only by offering an environment in which a rich diversity of ideas, values, and perspectives is championed and challenged. In this sense, "[t]he college classroom with its surrounding environs is peculiarly the 'marketplace of ideas.'"[2]

This marketplace trains future citizens and leaders by providing "wide exposure to that robust exchange of ideas which discovers truth 'out of a multitude of tongues.'"[3] If a university is to provide such training, some members of the academic community will inevitably encounter speech that they find unfamiliar, even abhorrent. Furthermore, learning to tolerate and respond to such speech is an important part of the educational process. "To endure the speech of false ideas or offensive content and then to counter it is part of learning how to live in a pluralistic society, a society which insists upon open discourse towards the end of a tolerant citizenry."[4]

The marketplace extends beyond the classroom to extracurricular activities, which are "a critical aspect of campus life."[5] Education involves more than tests, textbooks, lectures, and libraries. Fundamentally, it is about the development of character.[6] Consequently, education does not end at the classroom door, but permeates campus and university life. As this Court recognizes, a "great deal of learning occurs informally."[7] Indeed, since the nineteenth century,

From the *amicus curiae* brief filed by the American Council on Education in support of the University of Wisconsin in the U.S. Supreme Court case of *Board of Regents, University of Wisconsin v. Scott Southworth* (1999), 5–21.

extracurricular activities have played an increasingly significant role in advancing the core mission of universities:

> Over time . . . extracurricular programs have come to be seen not merely as useful services but as an integral part of the educational process itself. Educators point to the dangers of a college that stresses only learning and cognitive skills while ignoring opportunities for students to engage in cooperative activities in which each relies on the efforts of others and is relied upon by others in return. . . . More and more, [extracurricular activities] are regarded not only as a source of enjoyment but as ideal experiences for learning to cooperate and take responsibility for the welfare of one's peers.
>
> . . . The contemporary college or university does not concentrate only on formal education; it assumes the larger responsibility of promoting human development in all its forms.[8]

. . . In sum, colleges and universities hold a unique position in our society and pursue a correspondingly unique mission. Their business is to provide "that atmosphere which is most conducive to speculation, experiment and creation."[9] This mission can be achieved only by fostering a marketplace of ideas on campus and by ensuring that the resultant diversity of thoughts and perspectives informs the full range of experiences—from course selections to lecture series to student organizations. If a university is barred from this essential business, it cannot prepare its students "to live in a pluralistic society, a society which insists upon open discourse towards the end of a tolerant citizenry."[10]

B. Consistent with the First Amendment, a University Can Use Mandatory Fees to Fund a Neutral Forum That Helps Support a Diverse Variety of Organizations

. . . [T]he University of Wisconsin (and many other colleges and universities) pay fees not to particular groups but to the student government, which then uses the money to fund a wide array of organizations in a viewpoint-neutral manner.[11] "The speech of the offending groups can hardly be attributed to the student government, which funds groups of radically different views."[12] . . .

The University of Wisconsin simply requires its students to support a neutral forum, just as if it "built a large auditorium and held it open for everyone."[13] The fact that this case concerns a fund, rather than a physical space like an auditorium or an amphitheater, does not mean that forum analysis does not apply. . . .

Application of these principles makes clear that a critical difference exists between (a) supporting a forum and (b) supporting the speakers that ultimately use that forum. Thus, in *Widmar v. Vincent,*[14] this Court rejected a university's argument that if it were to allow religious groups to use its buildings it would create an impression that it endorsed religion in violation of the Establishment Clause: "[B]y creating a forum the University does not thereby endorse or promote any of the particular ideas aired there."[15] A student compelled to pay a restoration fee for a university amphitheater can hardly complain that her First Amendment rights are violated because she disagrees with some of the speakers who appear there. She has no greater constitutional cause to complain of a content-neutral student activity fund because she disagrees with some of the organizations it ultimately supports.

If a forum supports organizations in a truly neutral fashion, as is stipulated here, . . . and thereby funds groups that take radically differing positions on the same issues, it cannot be said to endorse or promote any particular group or any specific position.[16] . . .

II. EVEN IF A UNIVERSITY'S USE OF MANDATORY FEES TO FUND STUDENT GOVERNMENT AND ORGANIZATIONS IS ANALYZED UNDER *ABOOD-KELLER* AS COMPELLED SPEECH AND ASSOCIATION, RATHER THAN AS THE CREATION OF A NEUTRAL FORUM, SUCH A USE OF FEES DOES NOT VIOLATE THE FIRST AMENDMENT

A. The Challenged Use of Mandatory Fees Is Germane to a University's Broad Educational Mission, Including Its Interests in Promoting Diverse Expression and in Providing a Market-place of Ideas

Abood and *Keller* involve contexts very different from colleges and universities. *Keller* holds that compulsory state bar dues cannot be used to finance ideological activities unrelated to the purposes of the compelled association—regulation of the legal profession and improvement of legal services. Similarly, *Abood* holds that a union may not use a dissenting individual's dues to fund ideological activities not germane to collective bargaining. The purposes of the State Bar in *Keller*, to supervise attorney conduct, and of the union shop in *Abood*, to negotiate contracts, are relatively narrow and definable. The educational mission of a university is substantially broader.[17] ("The goals of the university are much broader than the goals of a labor union or a state bar, and they are inextricably connected with the underlying policies of the First Amendment."[18])

It is the business of a university to create a marketplace of ideas, exposing its students to a broad range of viewpoints on many issues, including the political and the ideological. This happens in classrooms—in courses in history, literature, political science, sociology, philosophy, and many other disciplines. It happens in auditoriums—when guest lecturers speak on ethics, contemporary problems, civil rights, and the like. And it happens in extracurricular activities—in connection with student government, student newspapers, and student organizations identical to those at issue here. Neither state bars nor unions—nor perhaps any institutions other than American colleges and universities—have this broad mission and mandate.

As a result, numerous courts recognize that a university's mission unquestionably reaches the funding of student organizations. Thus, the Second Circuit holds that a university may allocate student activity fees to a group with whose speech some students disagree.[19] *Carroll* recognizes three distinct university interests served by the compulsory fee: "the promotion of extracurricular life, the transmission of skills and civic duty, and the stimulation of energetic campus debate."[20] . . .

B. Courts Should Afford Universities Wide Latitude to Determine Whether the Use of Student Fees Is Germane to Their Educational Mission

Amici respectfully submit that the court below failed to give proper deference to the University of Wisconsin's decision that the use of mandatory fees advances its educational mission. Universities have interests in academic freedom that are a special concern of the First Amendment. This freedom is lost if courts do not afford universities discretion to define the contours of their educational mission and to determine the most effective means of achieving it. Judicial intervention in academic decision making affects not only the academic freedom of the university, but it results as well in a loss of the freedom of the students, faculty, and other members of the academic community, all of whom participate in and help to create the marketplace of ideas.

For these reasons, this Court has recognized that government intervention in the intellectual life of a university is to be avoided.[21] Universities are "characterized by the spirit of free inquiry," and academic freedom gives the university the ability "to determine for itself on academic grounds who may teach, what may be taught, how it shall be taught, and who may be admitted to study."[22] . . .

In this case, the University of Wisconsin—a campus with a rich history of the "robust exchange of ideas"[23]—made a judgment that funding a forum that supports a wide variety of student groups, including some engaged in political and ideological activities, plays an important role in its educational mission. This decision deserves respect, "breathing room," and some significant measure of deference. . . .

III. FORCING THE UNIVERSITY TO DISTINGUISH BETWEEN "EDUCATIONAL" ORGANIZATIONS AND "POLITICAL" OR "IDEOLOGICAL" ORGANIZATIONS RISKS VIOLATING STUDENTS' FIRST AMENDMENT RIGHTS

The court below effectively requires universities to distinguish political from non-political, and ideological from non-ideological organizations, and then to grant or withhold funding based upon these distinctions. Such distinctions may be constitutionally workable in the context of the activities of a union or a state bar, where the government has a narrower interest and where that interest does not include exposure to a diverse marketplace of ideas. Such distinctions emphatically do not work in the context of a university, however, where the government has a broad interest, and where that interest includes exposure to various political and ideological perspectives. Further, in the context of university campus activities, such distinctions not only fail to work, but they actually create significant constitutional mischief.

Consider a student debate club that sponsors a public forum on presidential impeachment; or a student economic society that hosts a series of speakers on tax reform; or a student group that distributes leaflets asserting that a university discriminates because it hires too few minority professors; or a film society that sponsors a film concerning the events at Tiananmen Square; or an environmental organization that presents a series of lectures on the impact of logging; or a literary studies club that funds a panel discussion of alternative theories of literary criticism, including Marxist, feminist, deconstructionist, and Freudian approaches. At some point it simply becomes impossible to separate the ideological and political from the educational and informative.[24]

Furthermore, a university that attempts to make such distinctions, and then to make funding decisions based upon them, may run afoul of First Amendment prohibitions against content- and viewpoint-based discrimination. In other words, forcing universities to draw these lines does not avoid constitutional difficulties; it compounds them. The University of Wisconsin uses the mandatory activity fee to create a public forum that distributes fees on a content-neutral basis. . . . By supporting groups without regard to the content or viewpoint of their speech, the forum detaches funding decisions from endorsement or condemnation of the political or ideological positions of the different organizations. In contrast, the holding of the *Southworth I* court, which would require the University to refuse funding for groups that are too ideological or political, violates the rule against content and viewpoint discrimination in a public forum. . . .

Faced with a project that calls upon them to do the impossible, with the knowledge that in the effort they might also do the unconstitutional, many universities will respond by funding no student organizations at all or only those that seem to pose no risk whatsoever.[25] As the dissenting judges in *Southworth II* cautioned, such a requirement may "spell the end, as a practical matter, to the long tradition of student-managed activities on these campuses."[26] As funding fails, and as organizations disband, some voices—including, in all likelihood, the most provocative and stimulating, if also the least popular voices—will no longer be heard at our universities. The marketplace of ideas on our campuses will suffer immeasurably.

NOTES

1. *Sweezy v. New Hampshire,* 354 U.S. 234, 263 (1957) (Frankfurter, J., concurring).
2. *Healy v. James,* 408 U.S. 169, 180 (1972) (quoting *Keyishian v. Board of Regents of Univ. of N.Y.,* 385 U.S. 589, 603 (1967)).
3. Keyishian, 385 U.S. at 603 (quoting *United States v. Associated Press,* 52 F. Supp. 362, 372 (D.N.Y., 1943)).
4. *Lee v. Weisman,* 505 U.S. 577, 590 (1992).
5. *Widmar v. Vincent,* 454 U.S. 263, 279 n. 2 (1981) (Stevens, J., concurring).
6. See Higher Education Amendments of 1998, Pub. L. No. 105-244, §863, 112 Stat. 1581, 1826 (Congress recognizes that "the development of virtue

and moral character, those habits of mind, heart, and spirit that help young people to know, desire, and do what is right, has historically been a primary mission of colleges and universities. . . .").

7. *Regents of the Univ. of Cal. v. Bakke,* 438 U.S. 265, 313 n. 48 (1978) (opinion of Powell, J.) (quoting William J. Bowen, "Admissions and the Relevance of Race," *Princeton Alumni Weekly* 7, 9 (Sept. 26, 1977)).
8. Derek C. Bok, *Higher Learning* 51–52 (1986). . . .
9. *Sweezy,* 354 U.S. at 263 (Frankfurter, J., concurring).
10. *Lee,* 505 U.S. at 590.
11. The only exception to this procedure may be Wisconsin PIRG, for which funding is authorized by direct student referendum. This brief does not address the separate and different issue raised by this direct funding, although the "germaneness" analysis discussed below would apply to this funding as well.
12. *Southworth II,* 157 F. 3d at 1125.
13. Id. at 1129 (Wood, J., dissenting).
14. 454 U.S. 263 (1981).
15. See also Carolyn Wiggin, Note, *A Funny Thing Happens When You Pay for a Forum: Mandatory Student Fees to Support Political Speech at Public Universities,* 103 Yale L.J. 2009, 2017 (1994) ("[T]he lack of content-based standards . . . enables the system to support a legitimate campus forum, and this in turn creates a distance between those who fund the forum and any particular view expressed within it, thus avoiding unconstitutional forced speech").
16. See Robert M. O'Neil, "Student Fees and Student Rights: Evolving Constitutional Principles," 15 J.C. & U.L. 569, 574 (1999). . . .
17. See *Rounds,* 166 F. 3d at 1039.
18. See also William Walsh, Comment, *Smith v. Regents of the University of California: The Marketplace Is Closed,* 21 J.C. & U.L. 405, 423 (1994) ("[T]he organizations' purposes in *Keller* and *Abood* were much narrower than the university's purpose. It is much easier to see something as 'political or ideological,' and therefore ineligible for funding, because it is unrelated to collective bargaining than it is to distinguish the same from an 'educational mission'").
19. See *Carroll v. Blinken,* 957 F. 2d 991, 992 (2d Cir. 1992).
20. Id. at 1001. . . .
21. See, e.g., *Sweezy,* 354 U.S. at 262 (Frankfurter, J. concurring).
22. Id. at 262–63.
23. *Keyishian,* 385 U.S. at 603.
24. See *Smith,* 844 P. 2d at 524–25 (Arabian, J., dissenting).
25. An "opt-out refund" procedure might address certain constitutional concerns, see O'Neil, supra, 575, 578, and use of such a procedure certainly should not be foreclosed by this Court. For the reasons set forth in this brief, however, such a procedure should not be required to save the constitutionality of mandatory fees.
26. 157 F. 3d at 1127 (Wood, J., dissenting).

Mandatory Student Fees Violate Students' Right to Free Speech

Pacific Legal Foundation

THE UNIVERSITY HAS NO CONSTITUTIONAL JUSTIFICATION TO COMPEL PAYMENT OF FEES TO PROMOTE STUDENT EXPRESSIVE ACTIVITIES

A. The University Has No Compelling Interest in Coercing Students to Subsidize Voluntary Organizations' Political and Ideological Activities

While a university may well have a compelling interest in *exposing* students to various conflicting viewpoints, it does not have a compelling interest in coercing *support* for those viewpoints.

> [T]he freedom to keep silent as well as to speak is grounded in something broader than a national fear of the state. It is equally the product of our view of personhood, which encompasses what the Supreme Court later referred to as "freedom of thought," "freedom of mind" and a "sphere of intellect and spirit." Were there no state at all, or were it inalterably benign, our conception of what it means to be human would still lead us to respect the individual autonomy of intellect and will enshrined in the First Amendment.[1]

By coercing support for political groups, the university sends a troubling message to students: If students want to advance a political position for which they cannot find support, the government will give them money to propagate their unpopular views. This is an illegitimate lesson for a public university to teach its students. The defendants in *Abood* and *Keller* understood that mandating support for an organization smothers, rather than stokes, contrary speech.[*2] Moreover, the university, let alone the political groups themselves, does not create a free marketplace or forum for the expression of ideas. Rather it requires students to be the financial sponsors of someone else's speech. Indeed, the notion that a free marketplace of ideas can be created and encouraged by involuntary contributions

From the *amicus curiae* brief filed by the Pacific Legal Foundation in support of the plaintiff, Scott Southworth, in the U.S. Supreme Court case of *Board of Regents, University of Wisconsin v. Scott Southworth* (1999), 24–27.

*Two previous cases in which the Supreme Court ruled that non-union teachers and members of a bar association did not have to support the political activities of their groups.—*Editors.*

is an oxymoron. The strength of an idea (i.e., its acceptance in the marketplace) is best measured by how many people will volunteer to spread the idea or to help finance its propagation.

The university's position also implies that the First Amendment has only limited application within the confines of a public university campus. As the court below noted,

> far from *serving* the school's interest in education, forcing objecting students to fund objectionable organizations undermines that interest. In some courses students are likely taught the values of individualism and dissent. Yet despite the objecting students' dissent they must fund organizations promoting opposing views or they don't graduate.[3]

If the university really wants students to learn practical civics lessons, it should encourage politically active groups to learn the art of fund-raising. In real political campaigns, opponents of the message do not give money to the cause.

B. A State University May Permit Voluntary Funding of Student Groups as a Less Intrusive Method of Promoting Such Groups on Campus

Universities are free to adopt any system of funding student activities that avoids constitutional defects. The best system, however, is the "positive check-off" voluntary system. Such a check-off could be designed in a number of ways. For example, it could list each recognized student group eligible for funding and permit students to choose which particular groups they wish to subsidize. Alternatively, it could simply provide a single box which, if checked, would mean that the student assents to funding all eligible student groups. By requiring students to designate affirmatively that they wish to fund particular groups, either individually or as a whole, the university advances several compelling goals. First, it requires thought on the part of the student, rather than mindless contributions to groups the student may not even be able to identify. Second, it encourages student groups to organize and articulate their messages clearly so as to attract as much financial support as possible.[4] Third, and most importantly, it sends a strong message to the entire student body that the university respects the constitutional rights of *all* students and has taken the strongest measures possible to protect those rights.[5]

Supporters of compelled funding have derided such a method, complaining that

> funding will soon devolve into a political *popularity* contest. Thus, in a setting where provocative ideas should receive the most support and encouragement, precisely the opposite will occur; student groups will be subject to an ideological referendum, and the most marginal groups will receive the least financial assistance. This is truly Orwellian.[6]

Justice Arabian's reasoning is backwards. What is Orwellian is a situation in which marginal groups are presented to the community as having support where there is none and presented as mainstream rather than extreme. Giving these ideas the cover of legitimacy and acceptability because of coerced subsidization from students who oppose the message perpetrates a great disservice. Students who wish to attract adherents to unconventional ideas must do so by convincing others of the soundness of their theories. Giving these unconventional thinkers the unwilling financial support of their dissenters grants them the means to speak more loudly than their actual support would permit.

CONCLUSION

The students in *West Virginia State Board of Education v. Barnette,* by being forced to salute the flag, were more than exposed to patriotism; they were forced to support it with a raised hand. Like them, the students at UW–Madison were not simply exposed to divergent views, they were forced to reach into their pockets to finance their opponents' views. Ideas that could not win adherence through persuasion and reason were thus kept alive by the state by imposing fees on those who do not support the idea in question. The First Amendment was designed to prevent just such an exercise of state power.

Attempts by the government, whether through a public agency, a legislature, or a court, to force individuals to financially support political and ideological activities with which they disagree have been rejected from the time of Thomas Jefferson to the present. This Court has on numerous occasions protected the rights of teachers, attorneys, and nonunion agency shop fee payers to refrain from supporting speech which they oppose. Students are entitled to no less protection.

NOTES

1. *Carroll v. Blinken,* 957 F. 2d 991, 996 (2d Cir.) cert. denied, 506 U.S. 906 (1992).
2. *Abood v. Detroit Board of Education* 431 U.S. 209 (1977) and *Keller v. State Bar of California* 496 U.S. 1 (1990).
3. *Southworth v. Grebe* 151 F. 3d 728 (1998).
4. The groups benefit in another way: if they suffer a funding shortfall when their opponents are no longer forced to subsidize their activities, the groups will likely turn to their own members to make up the difference. A person who pays a membership fee to belong to one of these groups will have a more personal stake in the group's successful attainment of its objectives. Bevilacqua, *Public Universities, Mandatory Student Activity Fees, and the First Amendment,* 24 J.L. & Educ. 1, 29–30 (1995).
5. La Fetra, "Recent Developments in Mandatory Student Fee Cases," 10 J.L. & Pol. 579, 612–13 (1994).
6. *Smith v. Regents of the University of California,* 4 Cal. 4th 843, 881 (1993) (Arabian, J., dissenting).

Freedom of Religion

*T*he place of religion in the public space has long been a matter of controversy in American society and nowhere more so than in the public schools. The issue was joined again in 2002 when Michael Newdow, an atheist, brought suit in federal court on behalf of his son on grounds that the Elk County School District in California was violating his son's First Amendment rights. Specifically, he contended that the daily recitation of the Pledge of Allegiance with the phrase "under God" included, constituted an endorsement of religion by the state and thus violated the establishment clause of the First Amendment. A federal district court agreed, as did the U.S. Court of Appeals for the Ninth Circuit. The case was ultimately appealed to the U.S. Supreme Court, which declined to rule on the substance, instead dismissing the case on the ground that Michael Newdow lacked standing to sue on behalf of his son.

The first selection is an amicus curiae brief submitted to the U.S. Supreme Court by Senator George Allen et al. in support of the Elk County School District. In it the authors argue that acknowledgment of a deity is steeped in our traditions, that the lower court ruling is inconsistent with previous Supreme Court opinions on both the Pledge and prayer in schools, and finally that acceptance of the reasoning of the lower court carries with it implications that go far beyond excluding a reference to the deity in the Pledge of Allegiance.

The second selection is a statement issued by the American Civil Liberties Union (ACLU) of Northern California. The ACLU calls for the removal of "under God" from the Pledge, in part because the purpose behind inserting it was religious. Moreover, in the ACLU's judgment, the contention that "under God" is merely a "ceremonial" acknowledgment of the deity does not stand up to close scrutiny. The ACLU also insists that students cannot help but feel pressured to recite the Pledge, even though its current form may be offensive not only to those students who do not recognize a deity but to members of minority faiths who may believe in more than one god or in a god different from that of the Judeo-Christian tradition.

Keep "Under God" in the Pledge of Allegiance

George Allen et al.

. . . Amici urge this Court to reverse the Court of Appeals for the Ninth Circuit in this case because they are convinced that the Ninth Circuit's decision holding the phrase "under God" in the Pledge of Allegiance unconstitutional is profoundly wrong. . . .

I. THE PHRASE "UNDER GOD" IN THE PLEDGE OF ALLEGIANCE ACCURATELY REFLECTS THE HISTORICAL FACT THAT THIS NATION WAS FOUNDED UPON A BELIEF IN GOD

The Founders of this Nation based a national philosophy on a belief in Deity. The Declaration of Independence[1] and the Bill of Rights locate inalienable rights in a Creator rather than in government, precisely so that such rights cannot be stripped away by government. In 1782, Thomas Jefferson wrote, "Can the liberties of a nation be thought secure when we have removed their only firm basis, a conviction in the minds of the people that these liberties are the gift of God? That they are not to be violated but with His wrath?" Thomas Jefferson, *Notes on Virginia* Q.XVIII (1782).

The Father of the Country, George Washington, acknowledged on many occasions the role of Divine Providence in the Nation's affairs. His first inaugural address is replete with references to God, including thanksgivings and supplications.[2] In Washington's Proclamation of a Day of National Thanksgiving, he wrote that it is the "duty of all nations to acknowledge the providence of Almighty God, to obey His will, to be grateful for His benefits, and humbly

George Allen is a former U.S. senator from Virginia. He is joined in this court brief by sixty-seven other U.S. senators and representatives and by the Committee to Protect the Pledge. Excerpted from Brief Amici Curiae of U.S. Senator George Allen et al. in the case *Elk Grove USD v. Newdow,* 542 U.S. 1 (2004), accessed at http://supreme.1p.findlaw.com/supreme_court/briefs/02-1624/02-1624.meri.ami.allen.pdf. Notes were renumbered to correspond with edited text.

to implore His protection and favor." Jared Sparks, *The Writings of George Washington,* Vol. XII, p. T19 (1833–1837). George Washington used the phrase "under God" in several of his orders to the Continental Army. On one occasion he wrote that "The fate of unborn millions will now depend, under God, on the courage and conduct of this army."[3] The Founders may have differed over the contours of the relationship between religion and government, but they never deviated from the conviction that "there was a necessary and valuable moral connection between the two." Philip Hamburger, *Separation of Church and State* 480 (2002).

Thus, the phrase "one nation under God" in the Pledge of Allegiance simply describes an indisputable historical fact. As one commentator has observed,

> The Pledge [of Allegiance] accurately reflects how the founding generation viewed the separation of powers as the surest security of civil right. Anchoring basic rights upon a metaphysical source is very much part of that structural separation, for without God, the law is invited to become god. This was well known to Rousseau and Marx who both complained that acknowledging God creates a competition or check upon the secular state.

Douglas W. Kmiec, *Symposium on Religion in the Public Square: Oh God! Can I Say That in Public?,* 17 Notre Dame J.L. Ethics & Public Pol'y 307, 313 (2003).

[The Supreme] Court recognized the primacy of religion in the Nation's heritage in *Zorach v. Clauson,* 343 U.S. 306 (1952), when it stated:

> We are a religious people whose institutions presuppose a Supreme Being. We guarantee the freedom to worship as one chooses. We make room for as wide a variety of beliefs and creeds as the spiritual needs of man deem necessary. We sponsor an attitude on the part of government that shows no partiality to any one group and that lets each flourish according to the zeal of its adherents and the appeal of its dogma. When the state encourages religious instruction or cooperates with religious authorities by adjusting the schedule of public events to sectarian needs, it follows the best of our traditions. For it then respects the religious nature of our people and accommodates the public service to their spiritual needs. To hold that it may not would be to find in the Constitution a requirement that the government show a callous indifference to religious groups. *That would be preferring those who believe in no religion over those who do believe. . . .*

The Ninth Circuit's decision does exactly what this Court warned against in *Zorach.* It prefers atheism over religion even to the extent of censoring the historical fact that the United States was founded upon a belief in God.

In *Zorach,* this Court rejected reasoning strikingly similar to that used by the Ninth Circuit. Upholding the constitutionality of New York's released time program permitting children who so desired to be released from school grounds for religious instruction, this Court rejected the argument that those children not choosing to attend such religious instruction would nevertheless feel coerced by the fact that other children attended. . . .

II. THE NINTH CIRCUIT'S DECISION CONTRADICTS THIS COURT'S MANY PRONOUNCEMENTS THAT PATRIOTIC EXERCISES WITH RELIGIOUS REFERENCES ARE CONSISTENT WITH THE ESTABLISHMENT CLAUSE

Although purporting to give "due deference," *United States v. Newdow*, 328 F.3d 466, 489 (9th Cir. 2003), to [the Supreme] Court's numerous statements about the constitutionality of the Pledge of Allegiance, the Ninth Circuit's decision is patently inconsistent with those statements. In every instance in which the Court or individual Justices have addressed patriotic exercises with religious references, including the Pledge of Allegiance, they have concluded unequivocally that those references pose no Establishment Clause problems. No Member of the Court, past or current, has suggested otherwise. To the contrary, recognizing that certain of its precedents may create the impression that patriotic exercises with religious references would be constitutionally suspect, the Court has taken pains to assure that such is not the case.

A. The Ninth Circuit Misconstrued the Court's School Prayer Cases, . . . When It Lumped Together for Constitutional Analysis Religious Exercises and Patriotic Exercises

The Ninth Circuit's analysis was flawed from the start. . . . In every school prayer case, . . . [the Supreme] Court consistently has distinguished between religious exercises, such as prayer and Bible reading, and patriotic exercises with religious references. In *Engel v. Vitale*, 370 U.S. 421 (1962), which struck down New York State's law requiring school officials to open the school day with prayer, this Court explained:

> There is of course nothing in the decision reached here that is inconsistent with the fact that school children and others are officially encouraged to express love for our country by reciting historical documents such as the Declaration of Independence which contain references to the Deity or by singing officially espoused anthems which include the composer's professions of faith in a Supreme Being, or with the fact that there are many manifestations in our public life of belief in God. Such patriotic or ceremonial occasions bear no true resemblance to the unquestioned *religious exercise* that the State of New York has sponsored in this instance. . . .

In *Lee v. Weisman*, 505 U.S. 577 (1992), a decision built in large part on *Engel*, . . . the Court reaffirmed the distinction it drew in Engel between religious exercises such as state-composed prayers and patriotic exercises with religious references:

> We do not hold that every state action implicating religion is invalid if one or a few citizens find it offensive. People may take offense at all manner of religious as well as nonreligious messages, but offense alone does not in every case show a violation. We know too that sometimes to endure social isolation or even anger may be the price of conscience or nonconformity. But, by any

reading of our cases, the conformity required of the student in this case was too high an exaction to withstand the test of the Establishment Clause. The *prayer exercises* in this case are especially improper because the State has in every practical sense compelled attendance and participation in an explicit *religious exercise* at an event of singular importance to every student, one the objecting student had no real alternative to avoid. . . .

Our society would be less than true to its heritage if it lacked abiding concern for the values of its young people, and we acknowledge the profound belief of adherents to many faiths that there must be a place in the student's life for precepts of a morality higher even than the law we today enforce. We express no hostility to those aspirations, nor would our oath permit us to do so. *A relentless and all-pervasive attempt to exclude religion from every aspect of public life could itself become inconsistent with the Constitution.* We recognize that, at graduation time and *throughout the course of the educational process, there will be instances when religious values, religious practices, and religious persons will have some interaction with the public schools and their students.* . . .

As in *Engel,* . . . the deciding factor in *Lee* was that school officials sponsored a religious exercise—prayer. *Lee* gives no support to the Ninth Circuit's conclusion that the voluntary recitation of the Pledge of Allegiance violates the Establishment Clause because it contains the phrase "One Nation Under God." . . .

B. Every Member of the Court Who Has Addressed the Constitutionality of Patriotic Exercises with Religious References, Including the Pledge of Allegiance, Has Concluded That Those References Are Constitutional Acknowledgments of the Nation's Religious Heritage

In addition to misreading the Court's school prayer cases, the Ninth Circuit also refused to heed the unequivocal import of Supreme Court statements addressing the Pledge of Allegiance in other contexts. Every time the Court or an individual Justice has mentioned the Pledge of Allegiance, whether in majority, concurring, or dissenting opinions, the conclusion has been that it poses no Establishment Clause problems.

In *Lynch v. Donnelly,* 465 U.S. 668 (1984), the Court recognized the "unbroken history of official acknowledgment by all three branches of government of the role of religion in American life." . . . "Our history is replete with official references to the value and invocation of Divine guidance in deliberations and pronouncements of the Founding Fathers and contemporary leaders." . . . The Court listed many examples of our "government's acknowledgment of our religious heritage," and included among those examples Congress' addition of the words "under God" in the Pledge of Allegiance in 1954. . . .

[E]xamples of reference to our religious heritage are found in the statutorily prescribed national motto "In God We Trust," . . . which Congress and the President mandated for our currency, . . . and in the language "one nation under God," as part of the Pledge of Allegiance to the American flag. That pledge is recited by many thousands of public school children—and adults—every year. . . .

In a concurring opinion, Justice O'Connor stated that governmental acknowl-
edgments of religion such as the National Motto "In God We Trust" "serve, in the
only ways reasonably possible in our culture, the legitimate secular purposes of
solemnizing public occasions, expressing confidence in the future, and encourag-
ing the recognition of what is worthy of appreciation in society." . . .

A year later in *Wallace v. Jaffree,* 472 U.S. 38 (1985), Justice O'Connor stated
explicitly that the words "under God" in the Pledge do not violate the Constitution because they "serve as an acknowledgment of religion with 'the legitimate secular purpose of solemnizing public occasions, and expressing
confidence in the future.'" . . .

In *Allegheny County v. American Civil Liberties Union,* 492 U.S. 573 (1989),
Justices Blackmun, Marshall, Brennan and Stevens stated:

> Our previous opinions have considered in dicta the motto and the pledge, char-
> acterizing them as consistent with the proposition that government may not
> communicate an endorsement of religious belief. We need not return to the sub-
> ject of "ceremonial deism," . . . because there is an obvious distinction between
> creche displays and references to God in the motto and the pledge. . . .

In sum, every Member of the current Court that has expressed any opinion
about the constitutionality of the Pledge of Allegiance has stated that it poses
no Establishment Clause problems. The Ninth Circuit's insistence, therefore,
that the Pledge of Allegiance becomes unconstitutional when school children
recite it is insupportable.

III. THE FIRST AMENDMENT DOES NOT COMPEL THE REDACTION OF ALL REFERENCES TO GOD IN THE PLEDGE OF ALLEGIANCE, PATRIOTIC MUSIC, AND FOUNDATIONAL DOCUMENTS JUST TO SUIT ATHEISTIC PREFERENCES, EVEN WHEN SUCH MATERIALS ARE TAUGHT IN THE PUBLIC SCHOOLS

Although the primary issue is whether the Establishment Clause prohibits public schools from leading students in the voluntary recitation of the Pledge of
Allegiance, far more is at stake in this case. A decision affirming the Ninth Circuit would render constitutionally suspect a number of public school practices
that traditionally have been considered an important part of American public
education.

The first casualty of such a holding would be the practice of requiring students to learn and recite passages from many historical documents reflecting
the Nation's religious heritage and character. If a public school district violates
the Establishment Clause by requiring teachers to lead students in the voluntary recitation of the Pledge of Allegiance, it is difficult to conceive of a rationale by which compelled study or recitation from the Nation's founding
documents would not also violate the Constitution. The Mayflower Compact[4]
and the Declaration of Independence contain religious references substantiating

the fact that America's "institutions presuppose a Supreme Being." *Zorach v. Clauson.* . . . Similarly, the Gettysburg Address, though not a founding document, contains religious language and, historically, has been the subject of required recitations in public schools. President Lincoln declared "that this Nation, *under God,* shall have a new birth of freedom—and that Government of the people, by the people, for the people, shall not perish from the earth." President Abraham Lincoln, *The Gettysburg Address* (Nov. 19, 1863).[5]

Indeed, the references to deity in these historical documents are presumably even more problematic according to the Ninth Circuit's reasoning because they proclaim not only God's existence but specific dogma about God—He is involved in the affairs of men; He holds men accountable for their actions; and He is the Author of human liberty. Additionally, while students may be exempted from reciting the Pledge of Allegiance, *see Bd. of Educ. v. Barnette,* 319 U.S. 624 (1943), student recitations of passages from historical documents are often treated as a mandatory part of an American history or civics class, not subject to individual exemptions.

Equally disturbing is the likelihood that a decision affirming the Ninth Circuit will eventually foreclose the Nation's school districts from teaching students to sing and appreciate the Nation's patriotic music as well as a vast universe of classical music with religious themes. Students might learn about the Nation's founding documents without being required to recite them. Public school music programs cannot exist, however, without student performance. Thus, patriotic anthems, such as *"America the Beautiful"* and *"God Bless America,"* will become taboo because they cannot realistically be learned unless they are sung. Such musical treasures as Bach's choral arrangements and African-American spirituals will also become constitutionally suspect, at least as a part of public school music curricula.[6] According to the Ninth Circuit's logic, if a group of students sings *"God Bless America,"* the Establishment Clause is violated because an atheistic student might *feel coerced* to sing along (and indeed may well be coerced inasmuch as music teachers are not constitutionally compelled to exempt students from singing with the class).

The Ninth Circuit's effort to distinguish the Pledge of Allegiance from religious references in historical documents and music fails. The court reasoned that the Pledge of Allegiance is "performative," whereas the Declaration of Independence and patriotic music are not. . . . But, the court's logic ignores completely the fact that students may refuse to "perform" the Pledge of Allegiance. Moreover, students do not have the same constitutional right to refuse to sing *"America the Beautiful"* in music class.

An affirmance of the Ninth Circuit's decision will threaten a sort of Orwellian reformation of public school curricula by censoring American history and excluding much that is valuable in the world of choral music. Additionally, an affirmance would call into question the continued validity of two federal appellate court decisions upholding the constitutionality of the performance of religious choral music in public schools. *See Bauchman v. West High Sch.,* 132 F.3d 542 (10th Cir. 1997); *Doe v. Duncanville Indep. Sch. Dist.,* 70 F.3d 402 (5th Cir. 1995). . . .

For the foregoing reasons, and those expressed in Appellants' brief, this Court should reverse the judgment below.

NOTES

1. The Declaration of Independence recognizes that human liberties are a gift from God: "All men are created equal, that they are endowed by *their Creator* with certain unalienable Rights." *The Declaration of Independence* para. 2 (U.S. 1776). Jefferson wrote further that the right to "dissolve the political lands" connecting the Colonies to England derives from Natural Law and *"Nature's God." Id.* para. 1. The founders also believed that God holds man accountable for his actions as the signers of the Declaration "appeal [] to the *Supreme Judge of the world* to rectify their intentions." *Id.* para. 32. In 1774, Jefferson wrote that "The God who gave us life gave us liberty at the same time; the hand of force may destroy, but cannot disjoin them." Thomas Jefferson, *Rights of British America,* 1774. ME 1:211, Papers 1: 135.

2. "Such being the impressions under which I have, in obedience to the public summons, repaired to the present station, it would be peculiarly improper to omit in this first official act my fervent supplications to that Almighty Being who rules over the universe, who presides in the councils of nations, and whose providential aids can supply every human defect, that His benediction may consecrate to the liberties and happiness of the people of the United States a Government instituted by themselves for these essential purposes, and may enable every instrument employed in its administration to execute with success the functions allotted to his charge. In tendering this homage to the Great Author of every public and private good, I assure myself that it expresses your sentiments not less than my own, nor those of my fellow-citizens at large less than either. No people can be bound to acknowledge and adore the Invisible Hand which conducts the affairs of men more than those of the United States." George Washington's First Inaugural Address, *available at* http://www.archives.gov/exhibit_hall/american_originals/inaugtxt.html.

3. Kerby Anderson, *Pledge of Allegiance, available at* http://www.pointofview .net/ar_pledge1111.htm. On another occasion, Washington encouraged his army, declaring that "the peace and safety of this country depends, under God, solely on the success of our arms." Edwin S. Davis, *The Religion of George Washington: A Bicentennial Report,* Air Univ. Rev. July–Aug. 1976, *available at* http://www.airpower.maxwell.af.mil/airchronicles/aureview/ 1976/jul-aug/edavis.html (quoting 3 *The Writings of George Washington* 301 (John C. Fitzpatrick ed., 1931–1944)).

4. The Mayflower Compact, written by William Bradford in 1620, provides:

   > We whose names are underwritten, the loyal subjects of our dread sovereign Lord, King James, by *the grace of God,* of Great Britain, France and Ireland king, defender of the faith, etc., having undertaken, *for the glory of God, and advancement of the Christian faith,* and honor of our king and country, a voyage to plant the first colony in the Northern parts of Virginia, do by these

presents solemnly and mutually *in the presence of God,* and one of another, covenant and combine ourselves together into a civil body politic, for our better ordering and preservation and furtherance of the ends aforesaid; and by virtue hereof to enact, constitute, and frame such just and equal laws, ordinances, acts, constitutions, and offices, from time to time, as shall be thought most meet and convenient for the general good of the colony, unto which we promise all due submission and obedience.

Mayflower Compact, *available at* http://www.pointofview.net/ar_pledge1111 .htm (emphasis added).

5. Transcriptions of the address, as given, include the phrase "under God," while earlier written drafts omit the phrase. *See* Allan Nevins, *Lincoln and the Gettysburg Address* (1964); William E. Barton & Edward Everett, *Lincoln at Gettysburg* (reprint 1971) (1930). Lincoln's inclusion of the phrase in his address is thoroughly consistent with his conviction, shared with Washington and Jefferson, that Divine Providence played an essential role in the rise of the Nation.

6. Two federal appellate courts have upheld the constitutionality of religious choral music in public schools. Significantly, both courts found that a substantial percentage of serious choral music is based on religious themes or text. *See Bauchman v. West High Sch.,* 132 F.3d 542, 554 (10th Cir. 1997). . . .

Remove "Under God" from the Pledge

Margaret Crosby and ACLU of Northern California

In striking down the McCarthy-era law that rewrote the Pledge of Allegiance to insert the words "under God," . . . the Ninth Circuit breathed life into the Pledge's stirring ideal of a country "with liberty and justice for all." The decision secured liberty for children of minority faiths who have quietly been denied religious freedom for nearly 50 years, when pressured in public school to pledge allegiance to a God they do not worship. By enforcing the First Amendment, the Ninth Circuit provided justice for all children in the United States.

The firestorm of protest sparked by the *Newdow* ruling is reminiscent of the public's reaction in 1962 to the original United States Supreme Court decision banning prayer in public school. (*Engel v. Vitale*, 370 U.S. 421 (1962)). Then, however, President John F. Kennedy stepped forward to support the court decision and the constitutional separation of church and state. He reminded Americans that the Supreme Court had not prevented anyone from worship. Families remained free to pray at home and in church, where, he pointed out, religious expression may be robust in ways it never can be when the government composes watered-down religious scripts for schoolchildren to recite.

Today's political leaders are no John Kennedys. Across the political spectrum, politicians leaped to microphones to denounce the *Newdow* decision. "Just nuts" (Majority Leader Tom Daschle's comment) and "embarrassing at best" (Senator Feinstein's comment) illustrate the analytical acuity of the attacks on the Court. President Bush announced that the decision proved that the country needs federal judges who have "common sense" (apparently a synonym for majoritarian supporters) and, chillingly, federal judges who "recognize that our rights come from God."

In our system of government, fundamental rights come from the Constitution. The Ninth Circuit took those rights seriously in *Newdow*.

In adding "under God" to the Pledge of Allegiance in 1954, Congress intended to put religion in public school. As President Eisenhower said in signing the law, from "this day forward, the millions of our schoolchildren will

The American Civil Liberties Union (ACLU) is an organization whose primary mission is to protect rights guaranteed by the Bill of Rights and the Fourteenth Amendment to the U.S. Constitution. Reprinted from ACLU of Northern California, "The Values of the Pledge of Allegiance," by Margaret Crosby, *The Daily Journal*, Sept. 3, 2002. This article can be accessed at http://www.aclunc.org/news/opinions/the_values_of_the_pledge_of_allegiance.shtml. Reprinted with permission of *The Daily Journal*. The title of the original was changed for this reprint in *Points of View*.

daily proclaim, in every city and town, every village and rural schoolhouse, the dedication of our nation and our people to the Almighty." Since students were praying daily in many public schools, the new Pledge language was not subject to an immediate constitutional challenge. Courts had not yet recognized the rights of minority faiths to be free of religious coercion in public schools.

But 50 years later, a law requiring school children to pledge allegiance to a nation "under God" cannot be reconciled with the Supreme Court's strict constitutional precedents on religion in public school. The Court has disallowed far less coercive practices, such as laws creating a moment of silence "for meditation or prayer" (*Wallace v. Jaffree,* 472 U.S. 38 (1985) and far less official practices (such as policies allowing students to broadcast any message, including prayer, before school sporting events (*Santa Fe Independent School District v. Doe,* 530 U.S. 290 (2000)). The Court has insisted that government not make students of minority faiths feel like second-class citizens in public schools that exist to serve children of all religions.

How then can Congress write a religious reference into the Pledge of Allegiance that many states and local school districts require to be recited daily? Supporters of the Cold War Pledge offer justifications. They are wholly unpersuasive:

The phrase "under God" is inclusive, because everyone believes in some kind of god. No, they don't. The hallmark of the McCarthy era was its pressure to conform in politics and religion, in speech and belief. The prevailing assumption was that all good (non-Communist) Americans believed in a monotheistic God. Untrue in the 50s, this assumption is more strikingly untrue today. Many Americans subscribe to no religion. And even people who do worship a monotheistic God show great variation in their definition of the deity; many do not subscribe to the idea that God's role is to organize the affairs of humans and countries, as embodied in the phrase "one nation under God."

Moreover, immigration patterns and the growth of new indigenous faith communities have altered the religious geography of the United States greatly from the 1950s. Today's pluralistic America contains adherents to nontheistic religions (for example, Buddhism) and pantheistic religions (for example, Santeria). Other members of spiritual groups do not worship a Judeo-Christian deity (for example, Native Americans). On a national level, these minority faiths are apparently invisible to many people, but they are important members of local communities—certainly here in California—and, under the Constitution, have equal rights with the religious mainstream religions.

The silence of religious minorities—their reluctance to take on the combined power of government and majority by challenging the law rewriting the Pledge—is understandable. They simply feel too vulnerable to invite the kind of vituperative response that greeted the *Newdow* ruling. However, many people of minority faith vividly remember feeling shamed, isolated, confused and coerced as children in American public schools by the daily recitation of the Pledge of Allegiance to a God foreign to the faith of their families.

Students may decline to participate in the Pledge of Allegiance. True, and irrelevant. All of the school prayer cases have involved religious exercises that students are free not to join. As the Supreme Court has recognized, it is callous for the government to force schoolchildren of minority faiths to isolate themselves from their classmates to avoid participating in a religious exercise in violation of their conscience.

The phrase "under God" has never been religious or has lost any religious meaning by rote repetition, and it's a trivial matter. Why, then, did *Newdow* provoke such an angry reaction? Plainly, because many people felt that the court had attacked their religion by restoring the Pledge of Allegiance to its original form. Pretending that the phrase is purely secular is both untrue and devalues religion.

The claim of secularization is central to the constitutional defense to "under God." Most frequently, the defense is phrased as "ceremonial deism," a category of permissible references to a deity that simply acknowledge this country's historically religious roots. But ceremonial deism is itself a doctrinally problematic rationale: courts invoke it to justify government endorsement of religion inconsistent with the First Amendment, reasoning, for example, that a city-owned Nativity Scene may be part of an official Christmas display. Moreover, the Pledge of Allegiance is inherently different from other mottoes or references to a Deity. The Pledge is not simply a passive reference to religion; it calls upon children in public school to promise loyalty to the concept of their country as under God.

The final variant of the secularization rationale is the claim that the term "under God" has lost, through rote repetition, any true meaning. But why? Have the phrases in the original Pledge—say, the parts about "liberty and justice for all"—also lost their meaning through repetition over time?

The Ninth Circuit didn't think so. And when we think with pride of a country founded on the ideals of liberty and justice for all, we should also be proud of the Court that made those ideals real.

Criminal Rights

Courts have a special role to play in our society. Unlike the two political branches of our government—Congress and the Executive—which are most sensitive to majority public opinion, courts must protect and defend minorities. Indeed, courts most often are called upon to ensure that the government acts in a fair and reasonable manner and to make certain that individual rights are protected.

Courts have a particularly important role to play in the protection of criminal rights; they must see that no injustice is done to the person accused of a crime. In the last thirty years, the U.S. Supreme Court has taken great care in enforcing the constitutional rights of persons accused of crimes. These include such protections as the right to remain silent and the right to counsel. Some of these criminal procedural safeguards have sparked controversy among law-enforcement officials, political leaders, commentators, and the general public. Typically, critics of the criminal justice system point to its failures—failures that either put criminals back on the streets or penalize innocent and unsuspecting people.

The next two selections examine the role of the courts in the criminal justice system. In the first, journalist Bernard Gavzer reports on the views of New York State judge Harold Rothwax, an outspoken critic and the author of Guilty: The Collapse of Criminal Justice. According to Judge Rothwax, the criminal justice system, with all its procedural guarantees, is tilted too much in favor of criminal suspects, so much so that he believes "We're in the fight of our lives" to preserve a law-abiding society.

In the second selection, John Kilwein, professor of political science at West Virginia University, challenges Rothwax's views. While conceding that crime continues to be a major problem in the United States, Kilwein argues that it would be unwise to adopt Rothwax's "reforms" of the criminal justice system. Kilwein contends that the real issue is whether the criminal justice system fully protects all citizens from the possible abuses and excesses of law-enforcement officials. The many procedural guarantees of the Constitution and the courts, he argues, are merely the means to ensure a "fair fight" between a criminal defendant and a criminal justice system that is stacked heavily in favor of the government. Without these guarantees, Kilwein contends, there exists the very real possibility that innocent persons might be accused, tried, convicted, and punished without adequate protection of the law.

"We're in the Fight of Our Lives"

Bernard Gavzer

At 2 A.M. on November 20, 1990, Leonardo Turriago was pulled over for speeding by two state troopers. They asked if they could look into his van, and Turriago said they could. Inside, the troopers saw a trunk and asked Turriago about it. He sprang open its lock, then ran away. Opening the trunk, the troopers found the body of a man shot five times.

Turriago was quickly caught. In his apartment, police found 11 pounds of cocaine and guns. The suspect told them where to look for the murder weapon, and it was recovered. Turriago was convicted of second-degree murder and sentenced to 45 years to life.

The defense appealed, saying the troopers had no right to search the van. On June 6, 1996, Turriago's conviction was overturned. A New York appellate court ruled that the police search was not justified and had been coerced.

"Criminal justice in America is in a state of collapse," says Judge Harold J. Rothwax, who has spent 25 years presiding over criminal cases in New York City. "We have formalism and technicalities but little common sense. It's about time America wakes up to the fact that we're in the fight of our lives."

Rothwax believes cases such as Turriago's illustrate that the procedural dotting of every "i" and crossing of every "t" has become more important than the crime's substance. "The bottom line is that criminals are going free," he says. "There is no respect for the truth, and without truth, there can be no justice."

While the search for truth should be the guiding principle of our courts, instead, the judge says, "our system is a carefully crafted maze, constructed of elaborate and impenetrable barriers to the truth." . . .

Practices we have taken for granted—such as the *Miranda* warning, the right to counsel, even unanimous jury verdicts—need to be reconsidered, says the judge. "You know," Rothwax confides, "more than 80 percent of the people who appear before me are probably guilty of some crime."

Rothwax insists there is a fundamental difference between the investigative and the trial stages of a case. The investigative stage is marked by the notion of probable guilt, he asserts, not the presumption of innocence. "Until a defendant goes on trial, he is probably guilty," the judge says, noting that by the time a person reaches trial he has been deemed "probably guilty" several times.

Bernard Gavzer is a contributing editor for *Parade* magazine. From Bernard Gavzer, "We're in the Fight of Our Lives," *Parade*, July 28, 1996, pp. 4–6. Reprinted with permission from *Parade*. Copyright © 1996.

"When a person is arrested, indicted by a grand jury, held in detention or released on bail, it is all based on probable guilt." Rothwax adds, "Once *on trial*, he is presumed innocent." . . .

The positions the judge has staked out in what he regards as his crusade to bring sense to the criminal justice system have shocked those who long associated him with strong liberal causes. A lifelong Democrat, Rothwax was a senior defense trial attorney for the Legal Aid Society in New York and a stalwart of the New York Civil Liberties Union early in his career.

"I represented Lenny Bruce and Abbie Hoffman, the Black Panthers and the Vietnam war protesters," he says, "I am today as much a civil libertarian as ever. But that does not mean I must close my eyes to the devastation that has occurred in criminal justice. We have the crime, but where is the justice? It is all tilted in favor of the criminal, and it is time to bring this into balance."

The interests of the victim weigh solidly in Rothwax's courtroom in the Criminal Court Building in Manhattan. However, he is troubled by some decisions of the U.S. Supreme Court, saying: "Its rulings over the last 35 years have made the criminal justice system incomprehensible and unworkable."

Although neither the Supreme Court nor the Courts of Appeals decide the guilt or innocence of a defendant, they do make rulings on the constitutionality of acts by the police and lower courts and thus have a significant impact on our justice system. Key practices of our current system—which have come about as a result of Supreme Court rulings in recent decades—need to be changed, Rothwax believes. Among them are:

The Miranda *Warning.*   In New York, Alfio Ferro was arrested in 1975 in connection with a fur robbery that turned into a murder. In the lockup, a detective—without saying a word—dropped some of the stolen furs in front of Ferro's cell. Ferro then made incriminating statements that led to his conviction for second-degree murder.

In 1984, an appellate court overturned the conviction, saying that the detective's action amounted to interrogation and violated Ferro's *Miranda* rights. The *Miranda* warning requires that the suspect be told he has a right to remain silent, that any statement he makes might be used against him and that he has the right to have a lawyer present.

"*Miranda* came about because of abuses such as prolonged custodial interrogation, beatings and starving in order to get a confession," says Rothwax. "I think those abuses have been largely dealt with. Now the police officer is put in the position of telling a suspect in a murder or rape, 'Look, you don't have to tell us anything, and that may be the best thing for you.' And it produces a situation in which a proper confession is thrown out because of the way in which it was read or that it wasn't read at the right time."

Rothwax believes *Miranda* can be replaced by the recording of an arrest and interrogation through videotapes, tape recorders and other technology. This would probably show whether a confession or statement was coerced.

The Exclusionary Rule.   [In the winter of 1996] Federal Judge Harold Baer Jr. refused to admit as evidence 80 pounds of cocaine and heroin obtained in the arrest of a drug courier in the Washington Heights neighborhood of New York City.

The evidence was excluded because, said Baer, the police had violated the Fourth Amendment protection against unreasonable search and seizure when they searched the car in which the drugs were found.

The police said their search was proper in view of the fact that they saw men hastily loading bags into an out-of-state car in a high drug area in the middle of the night, and the men ran away when the police approached. Judge Baer, however, said just because the men ran off was no reason to suspect them of a crime. In Washington Heights, the judge said, it was not unusual for even innocent people to flee, because police there were regarded as "corrupt, violent and abusive."

Under a growing chorus of criticism, Judge Baer first reversed himself and then asked that the case be assigned to another judge. It was. Rothwax says this is the sort of muddled episode which arises from the exclusionary rule, producing "truth and justice denied on a technicality."

"The Supreme Court has consistently ruled that evidence seized in violation of the Fourth Amendment *should* be excluded from a criminal trial. But if you read the Fourth Amendment, nowhere does it say that *illegally* obtained evidence *must* be excluded," says Rothwax. "In my view, when you exclude or suppress evidence, you suppress the truth."

Judge Rothwax has a remedy: "Make the exclusionary rule *discretionary* instead of mandatory. If it was at the discretion of the judge, there could be a test of reasonableness. A judge could consider factors such as whether a police officer acted with objective reasonableness and subjective good faith. As it is now, the exclusionary rule is irrational, arbitrary and lacks proportion. No wonder that in 90 percent of exclusionary cases, the police don't know what the law is."

The Right to Counsel.   In 1982, Kenneth West of New York, an alleged drug dealer, was suspected of being involved in killing a man who had taken his parking place. His lawyer, at a police lineup, told the police not to question West in his absence. Nothing came of the case for three years. Then police arrested a former cohort of West who said West had been one of the shooters. The informer secretly taped West talking about the killing. West was convicted, but in 1993 the New York Court of Appeals reversed the conviction, saying the secret taping amounted to questioning him without the presence of counsel.

The right to counsel is provided by the Sixth Amendment. "It is essential there be a right to counsel," Judge Rothwax says. "But the amendment doesn't say it has to be during police questioning and investigation. As a result of technicalities over this issue of counsel, I have seen murderers go free. Make it clear that the right to a lawyer shouldn't be a factor in the *investigative* stage but only in pre-trial and trial stages."

Instructions to the Jury.   After closing arguments in the O. J. Simpson murder trial, Judge Ito took great care in telling jurors that Simpson's failure to take the stand in his own defense should in no way be taken to mean anything negative or to draw any other adverse conclusion.

This instruction to the jury occurs in all cases in which the defense asks for it, because of a Supreme Court ruling in 1981 that said not to do so amounted to a violation of the Fifth Amendment. [The Fifth Amendment states that no person shall be forced to testify against himself.] "The Fifth Amendment does not say that one might not draw reasonable inferences from the silence of a defendant," Judge Rothwax says. "I think we must find a way to return to the standard that existed before, that the judge could tell the jury that the failure to explain could amount to an inability to explain."

The judge would like to see other changes made to the jury system. Among them:

1. *Unanimous jury verdicts should no longer be required.* Why? Rothwax cites a murder case he presided over. "It was an overwhelming case of clear guilt. Yet there was a hung jury. One juror was convinced the defendant was not guilty. How did she know? Well, as she explained it, 'Someone that good-looking could not commit such a crime.' We had to retry the case, and the man was quickly found guilty."

   By allowing verdicts to be decided by a vote of 11–1 or 10–2, Rothwax says, there could be a reduced risk that a single juror could cause a retrial or force a compromise in the face of overwhelming evidence of guilt.

2. *Peremptory challenges to prospective jurors should be strictly limited or abolished.* Peremptory challenges allow lawyers to knock someone off the jury without giving any reason. "As we saw in the Simpson case," Rothwax says, "it makes it possible to stack a jury so that the most educated juror is excused, and you end up with a jury that can be manipulated to accept innuendo as evidence."

Judge Rothwax regards the entire conduct of the Simpson trial as an unspeakable insult to the American people, one that left them "feeling wounded and deeply distrustful of the system." He adds: "There was an opportunity to show a vast audience the potential vitality of justice at work. Instead we are assaulted by an obscene circus. We saw proof that the American courtroom is dangerously out of order." . . .

To sit with Rothwax in court, as this writer did, is to get a sense of his urgency for reform. In three hours, there was a procession of men and women charged with felonies from murder to drug dealing. Rothwax was all business, and he was tough with everyone. After 47 cases had been considered and dealt with, the judge turned to me and asked, with irony, about the defendants we had seen: "Did you notice the huge display of remorse?" There hadn't been any. "That's why" he said, "we are in the fight of our lives."

Just Make It a Fair Fight

John C. Kilwein

Crime is a significant problem in this country. In 2000, 15,517 Americans became victims of homicide.[1] Property loss and medical expenses related to crime approach $20 billion per year. Responding to these and other troubling statistics, Congress has "federalized" dozens of crimes that were formerly only state offenses, and state legislatures have passed mandatory-minimum sentence laws that require convicted criminals to spend more time in prison. The U.S. Bureau of Justice Statistics reports that as a result of these changes the number of people incarcerated in federal and state prisons more than quadrupled, increasing from 319,600 in 1980 to 1,406,031 in 2001. In addition, Congress has made it much more difficult for prisoners to use the federal courts, the Constitution, and writ of *habeas corpus* to appeal their convictions. All of this is evidence of a concerted national effort, some might argue excessive effort, to deal with the crime problem.

But efforts such as these are not enough for New York Judge Harold Rothwax. He wants to shock us into taking action in the criminal courts, and in so doing he uses arguments that are based on fear.[2] Judge Rothwax warns Americans, as they read their Sunday papers, of the ominous threats of such dark predators as Leonardo Turriago, who cart murder victims around in the trunks of their automobiles, and who walk the streets thanks to legal "technicalities." But as Judge Rothwax spins his frightening yarn, he fails to tell the reader that the crime rate is actually dropping, in spite of the alleged flaws of the criminal justice system. Violent crime, for example, dropped 10 percent in 2000–2001. Why the paradox?: A *reduction* in crime, while Judge Rothwax thinks we are in "the fight of our lives"!

Judge Rothwax offers us a new system of criminal justice that assumes that all police officers and prosecutors do their jobs in a fair and objective manner, free of any systematic bias against groups or individuals in society. The Rothwax system assumes that prosecutors will base their prosecutorial decisions strictly on legal grounds, ignoring other factors such as political gain or racial animus. Judge Rothwax believes that as a society we have largely solved the problem of police brutality; that American law enforcement officials no longer use uncomfortable detention, physical violence, or psychological coercion to secure convictions.

John C. Kilwein is professor of political science at West Virginia University. He wrote this article especially for *Points of View* in 1997 and revised it in 2000 and again in 2003.

The Rothwax system assumes that criminal defendants in the United States have more legal representation than they deserve, and that the system would benefit from reducing the formal rules that lawyers bring to the pre-trial process. Unfortunately, the real world of American criminal justice is far more complex than the "good vs. evil" morality play suggested by Judge Rothwax.

THE GOVERNMENT VS. THE CRIMINAL DEFENDANT: A FAIR FIGHT?

The legal system in the United States is based on the belief that the best way for a court to discover the truth in a legal dispute is to allow the parties to battle it out in the courtroom before a jury or judge. The judge acts as an independent and objective arbiter or referee who makes sure that the disputants battle fairly by following the rules of law. The disputants are responsible for developing the case they will bring into the courtroom, and they understandably have a strong incentive to seek out any evidence or witnesses that might assist them. The disputants also have the right to challenge the veracity of their opponents' presentations. The confrontation in court between these two competing sides, each presenting a very different version of a contested dispute, will, in theory, maximize the likelihood that the truth will come out.[3] Of course, the difficult job for the judge or the jury is sifting through the two accounts to arrive at a sense of what actually took place and what justice should be.

When applied to disputes involving a crime, the disputants in the adversarial system are the defendant, or the person charged with committing the crime, and the state. The state, rather than the victim, is the litigant in criminal cases because, by definition, crimes not only harm victims, they also harm and threaten society as a whole. In a criminal case, therefore, the battle to be played out in the courtroom is between a person charged with a crime and a prosecutor who represents the interests of society—a battle that strains the notion of a fair fight. The government clearly has a lot more advantages than the criminal defendant. The extent of this mismatch is underscored by the fact that prosecutors have available to them the machinery of government, including the vast investigative powers of law enforcement, whereas defendants must do it on their own.

The American justice system takes into account this disparity, however, by providing the defendant with certain procedural rights and advantages that are intended to equalize the courtroom battle in criminal cases. This system assumes that when a powerful litigant, the state, faces a weaker litigant, the defendant, there is a high probability of a wrongful conviction of an innocent person unless the state follows procedures designed to make it a fair fight. And in our criminal legal tradition, there is no greater miscarriage of justice than sending innocent individuals to prison or to their death. Modern-day criminal procedure protections seek to prevent such an outcome.

Among the equalizers built into the American legal system are the presumption of innocence, the beyond-a-reasonable-doubt standard of proof; the prohibitions against unreasonable search and seizure, forced self-incrimination, excessive bail, excessive fines, double jeopardy, and cruel and unusual punishment; and the right to counsel, to a trial by jury, to a public and speedy trial, to speak at trial, to confront and cross-examine hostile witnesses, to present favorable witnesses, and to access the writ of *habeas corpus*. Some of these "equalizers" have been incorporated into our system as part of formal documents, or constitutions, that act as the blueprints for our American governments, while others were added as our criminal justice system evolved and became part of our legal tradition.

For Judge Rothwax the balance between the state and the criminally accused is fundamentally flawed. Criminal defendants are not the "weak sisters" in a criminal trial; the state is. For Judge Rothwax, a "liberal" judiciary led by the U.S. Supreme Court has conspired to create new and extreme rights for the defendant. These extravagant rights, moreover, make it extremely difficult for the prosecutor and the police to do their jobs. Seemingly guilty defendants are released from custody because their defense lawyers exploited some constitutional technicality. The murder trial of O. J. Simpson is given as a case in point. Overworked, underpaid, and inept prosecutors fumbled before a group of highly paid "dream team" defense lawyers, who exploited every procedural technicality to achieve a verdict of innocence.

Judge Rothwax offers up an alternative system of criminal justice that tips the balance in the courtroom battle toward the side of the prosecution by limiting a defendant's right to counsel, altering the presumption of innocence, increasing the power of police to search for proof of criminality and to interrogate defendants, allowing more evidence favoring the prosecution's case to be admitted in court, and altering the nature of jury deliberations in criminal trials. In short, the Rothwax system makes it easier for the prosecution to prove to a jury that a criminal defendant is guilty as charged and deserving of punishment.

THE "SUSPECT RIGHTS" OF SUSPECTS

The Presumption of Innocence

Our legal system recognizes that a criminal dispute is more serious than a civil dispute. In criminal law, society has the capacity to publicly punish the convicted criminal, using several forms of punishment. First, the defendant faces the shame and consequences associated with being declared a convicted criminal, including the loss of certain freedoms and rights as, for example, access to a variety of licenses or the freedom to perform certain jobs. Second, criminal conviction can bring with it the possibility of substantial monetary fines, often in the thousands of dollars. Third, criminal conviction can result in a complete loss of freedom through incarceration, with all the unintended consequences of life behind bars, a violent world often filled with physical assault, rape, and other indignities. Finally, in thirty-eight states and at the federal level, defendants charged with capital crimes face the ultimate punishment of being put to death by the state.

Given the seriousness of being charged with a crime, the American legal system confers on the defendant an important protection: the presumption of innocence. The primary purpose of this rule is to prevent a wrongful conviction that sends an innocent person to prison or to death. There is a simple yet profound logic behind this rule. When a criminal victimizes an individual, society intervenes to find, try, and punish the criminal. The harm suffered by the victim can never be undone, but some solace comes from the fact that the state takes a direct interest in resolving the criminal dispute. On the other hand, when the state wrongfully punishes an innocent defendant, the victimization is absolute. There is no solace available to the innocent person since the perpetrator is the state. This perspective gives rise to the old saw that it is better to let ten guilty persons go free, than to send one innocent individual to prison or death. For Judge Rothwax, however, that old saw is apparently a bit rusty and should be replaced by a new motto: The criminal justice system almost never convicts the wrong person; and those guilty individuals who are set free are threatening us all.

Judge Rothwax makes a distinction between the investigative (pre-trial) and trial stages of the criminal process. Rothwax argues that, during the investigative stage, defendants are assumed to be guilty by the police and the prosecutor or they would not have been arrested and indicted in the first place. He concludes that when defendants appear before his bench, they are probably guilty of the charges or their cases would never have reached his court. In short, Judge Rothwax gives the state the benefit of the doubt that it only prosecutes clearly guilty people. This perspective is troubling because it ignores the basic idea behind adversarial justice: Legal conflicts are not pre-judged but decided through the courtroom battle.

While it is true that the great majority of police officers and prosecutors are honest people who play by the rules and who have no desire to harm innocent people, Rothwax's position ignores a number of very real problems. The most obvious problem of the proposed system is that it fails to take into account that justice officials can and do make mistakes, and the importance of the trial process in detecting these honest errors. Second, Judge Rothwax ignores the fact that a minority of justice officials, however small, are lazy, dishonest, corrupt, racist, or some combination of these. Examples of these troubling behaviors abound in our criminal justice system. In 2003, the Republican governor of Illinois, George Ryan, took the unprecedented action of commuting the death sentences of all men and women on death row, 167 prisoners, to life imprisonment. Governor Ryan based his decision on his research into the machinery of Illinois' capital justice system, which left him with serious questions about its inherent fairness.[4] Ryan cited misconduct by prosecutors and police officers as factors that can lead to unjust capital sentences. A year earlier in Los Angeles, police officers admitted to systematically committing crimes to convict innocent individuals.[5] The Los Angeles District Attorney's Office took the unprecedented action of seeking the reversal of forty felony convictions, because it had clear evidence that those convictions were based on the false testimony of the errant officers.

In 1997, an internal U.S. Department of Justice investigation revealed that agents of the highly respected F.B.I. crime laboratory altered evidence and skewed testimony to assist prosecutors.[6] In Texas and West Virginia false testimony given by an incompetent and dishonest medical examiner sent at least six innocent men to prison.[7] To avoid the embarrassment and political fallout of being unable to convict the perpetrators of an arson fire with multiple deaths in New York[8] and the killing of a police officer in Houston,[9] prosecutors in both cities tenaciously pursued capital murder charges against apparently innocent individuals, while ignoring or concealing exculpatory evidence in the prosecution's possession. And evidence that some police officers and prosecutors target young black and Hispanic men for questionable arrest and prosecution comes to light with alarming clarity, as in the case of Carlton Brown.[10]

The case of Carlton Brown is particularly enlightening. Mr. Brown, who is black, is paralyzed from the chest down following injuries he sustained while under arrest in New York City's 63rd Precinct. Charged with driving with a suspended license, Mr. Brown contended that the arresting officers, after becoming irritated with his demands for information on his arrest, smashed his head, while he was handcuffed, into a bulletproof, double-plate glass window and severely injured his spine. The two police officers involved with his arrest countered that Mr. Brown had hurt himself falling down in the police station. The police officers were charged, tried before a judge, and acquitted. In a subsequent civil proceeding, however, the city of New York agreed to pay Mr. Brown $4.5 million in civil damages, a record-setting pre-trial settlement. Needless to say, such a settlement calls into question Judge Rothwax's confidence in the criminal justice system's ability to function in an unbiased manner. Our system of justice assumes that people, including law enforcement officials, are not angels[11] or saints; nor are they infallible; and it builds in protections, like the presumption of innocence, accordingly. The Rothwax system depends on an angelic conversion among these officials, an unlikely occurrence now or ever.

Miranda, the Right to Remain Silent and the Right to Counsel

Judge Rothwax reserves some of his harshest criticism for the U.S. Supreme Court's 1966 decision in *Miranda v. Arizona*.[12] In that decision the Court ruled that a confession made by Ernest Miranda, who was charged with kidnapping and raping an eighteen-year-old woman, was unconstitutionally obtained by police interrogators.[13] Extending its ruling beyond the immediate circumstances of the arrest and interrogation of Miranda, the Court required that henceforth all police officers and prosecutors must inform defendants of their rights to remain silent and to have counsel.[14] Commenting on state law enforcement officials, the Court observed,

> The use of physical brutality and violence is not, unfortunately, relegated to the past or to any part of the country. Only recently in Kings County [Brooklyn Borough], New York, the police brutally beat, kicked and placed lighted cigarette butts on the back of a potential witness under interrogation for the purpose of securing a statement incriminating a third party.[15]

The Court added that, although not using physical violence, other police inter-rogators use psychological abuse and lies to trick defendants into confessing to crimes.

Seen as an indictment against all police officers and prosecutors, the decision in *Miranda* was, and, as highlighted by Judge Rothwax, still is very unpopular within the law enforcement community.[16] This is unfortunate because, as Chief Justice Warren argued in the opinion, the *Miranda* requirements do not prevent good law enforcement officers from doing their job. Indeed, as pointed out by Warren, agents of the F.B.I. had already been using the warnings and were still able to investigate and assist in the conviction of federal defendants. What the warnings were designed to do was prevent an innocent defendant from confess-ing in order to bring an end to an abusive interrogation. The fact of the matter is that police officers who do not abuse defendants have nothing to fear from the *Miranda* requirements.

The *Miranda* decision also sought to make effective two important equaliz-ers in the Bill of Rights: the prohibition against self-incrimination and the right to counsel. The right against self-incrimination, or the right to remain silent, is based on an old common law principle that the state cannot force defendants to testify against themselves. Rather, the state makes the charges and must prove its case. Although the right to counsel came later in the Anglo-American legal tradition, it is based on the belief that it is unreasonable to expect ordinary persons to understand the legal implications of statements they might make or actions they might take in the pre-trial stage, actions that might again lead to their wrongful conviction. The *Miranda* requirement was based on the reason-able assumption that illiterate or uninformed defendants probably are not aware of these protections and therefore the state has a responsibility to inform them.

Judge Rothwax argues against this necessity, contending that, because defense attorneys step in and convince their clients to do otherwise, *Miranda* prevents the police from securing confessions from cooperative defendants. Apparently Judge Rothwax is opposed to the general principle of informed consent; that is, that defendants should know what they are doing before they say anything or confess. Judge Rothwax also seems to believe that the abuse of defendants while in police custody, cited by Chief Justice Warren in *Miranda*, is no longer a problem. Unfortunately, evidence suggests that, in his zeal to get tougher on crime and criminals, Judge Rothwax is ignoring the fact that abuses continue in the interrogation stage of the pre-trial process. An example from Rothwax's own hometown underscores this conclusion.[17] Police officers in New York's 24th Precinct arrested a seventeen-year-old white male for a mis-demeanor. He refused to confess. The defendant was held in a jail cell for two nights. At one point, he was placed in a van and chained in the sweltering heat. At another point a police officer waved his gun in front of the defendant and threatened to "shoot his dick off." One wonders if the cameras in the precinct, called for by Judge Rothwax to protect against such abuse, would have cap-tured this particular "Kodak moment"! The evidence suggests that this incident is not a random occurrence, in New York or nationally. Amnesty International has cited ninety cases of police brutality allegedly perpetrated by officers of the New York Police Department alone. Similar charges by other watchdog groups have been leveled at other departments around the country.[18]

Sometimes law enforcement officers use less violent forms of coercion in the interrogation room. For example, in 1999, F.B.I. agents lied to Wen Ho Lee, a Department of Energy employee suspected of spying for China, by informing him that he had failed a lie detector test, when, in fact, he had registered a score indicating he was telling the truth.[19] Building on this lie, the agents then told Mr. Lee that if he did not provide them with a confession, he would likely die in the electric chair.

For most first-time defendants the pre-trial process can be a very frightening experience. Defendants, innocent or guilty, who cannot post bail are held in jail until their trial. The pace of some criminal justice systems can be glacial, taking up to two years for a case to make it to trial. This delay, moreover, can be used to entice or coerce a defendant into making a confession, even a false one. For example, a prosecutor can offer defendants awaiting trial a plea bargain that gives them credit for time served while awaiting trial in exchange for a guilty plea. Given this offer, an innocent defendant might make a false confession, assuming that the conviction is a small price to pay for immediate release from prison.[20] The deal may be especially appealing if the defendant considers that a guilty verdict by jury at trial could yield an even stiffer sentence. Interrogations are also daunting for a defendant unfamiliar with the law. And although the great majority of questionings are conducted by professional officers observing all relevant constitutional requirements, the fact remains that police officers have substantially more experience in the process than do defendants, thereby increasing the probability that defendants will unwittingly damage their own case. In these and every other pre-trial situation, defendants would be at a severe disadvantage without legal representation.

In the end, the Rothwax system would punish the ignorant, the weak, and the poor. Wealthy or more highly educated defendants, who have a basic understanding of the legal system, are more likely to know they have the right to remain silent and to make informed choices about its use. Likewise, sophisticated defendants who are not intimidated by pre-trial detention and rough treatment are also more likely to refuse to assist the police in developing the state's case against them. Moreover, defendants with long-standing criminal records are also likely to be especially cognizant of their right to remain silent. In addition, multiple offenders who have experienced the daily violence of the corrections system are probably less likely to be frightened into confessing as the result of a difficult interrogation.

The most troubling aspect of Rothwax's system, however, from the point of view of equal justice for all, is that it rewards wealthier criminal defendants. Individuals who can afford to hire a lawyer and post bail are able to avoid the various forms of pre-trial pressure since they can await trial in the comfort of their own homes; and, with the advice of counsel, they are more likely to remain silent, thereby putting the government to its full task of convicting them without their assistance. It is quite possible, therefore, that the system proposed by Judge Rothwax will have the unintended consequence of convicting more innocent, first-time criminal defendants, while releasing those defendants with experience and/or money. These potential biases do not seem to concern Judge Rothwax. Like some American generals in Vietnam, Judge Rothwax seems to be singularly concerned only with body counts: So what if these new convictions are gained at the expense of fairness? They're convictions; and that's what counts! A justice system that operates in this manner has abandoned any pretense of being blind to a defendant's wealth or social status. It is a justice system more likely to convict an innocent defendant whose real crime is that he or she lives in the South Bronx rather than on Long Island.

The Exclusionary Rule

The exclusionary rule is an American invention, created by the U.S. Supreme Court in 1914.[21] It was designed to resolve the question of what should be done when a police officer or prosecutor violates the constitutional protections of defendants who have been the targets of illegal searches or interrogations. By making this ruling, the Supreme Court, using a classic American "free-market" approach, has ruled that such evidence is tainted and must therefore be excluded from trial. The exclusionary rule, the Court has argued, removes any incentive for law enforcement officials to engage in unconstitutional and illegal activities, since ill-gotten gains cannot be used in court.

Since the Bill of Rights makes no mention of this rule in the Fourth Amendment's prohibition against unreasonable searches and seizures, Judge Rothwax contends that the rule is an illegitimate hindrance to the criminal justice system's operation. He argues that excluded evidence prevents the court from getting the total truth surrounding a case. To accept this logic, however, one must, again, accept, as Rothwax clearly does, that in the rule's absence, police officers or prosecutors are unlikely to violate the Fourth or Fifth Amendments in their search for evidence or confessions. Given the examples of illegal police conduct cited, it is difficult to share Justice Rothwax's views of the motives and actions of the police.

Judge Rothwax is also upset because the exclusionary rule has, in his view, been used by judges in an overly technical and picky manner, with good cases being thrown out because investigating officers forgot to "dot the i's and cross the t's." He blames the "liberal" U.S. Supreme Court for decisions that favor criminal defendants. The Supreme Court of 2003, however, is, in fact, a very conservative one, particularly in its decisions dealing with the rights of criminal defendants. Since the mid-1970s, the U.S. Supreme Court has consistently shifted the constitutional advantage in criminal matters away from criminal defendants toward the police and prosecution. Specifically, in terms of the exclusionary rule, the Court has ruled in ways that enable prosecutors to use more questionable evidence and confessions against criminal defendants. Two examples highlight this shift. In *U.S. v. Havens,*[22] the Court allowed illegally obtained evidence to be used in trial to discredit testimony during cross-examination. And in *Nix v. Williams,*[23] the Court ruled that tainted evidence can be used against the defendant if the trial court judge concludes that evidence would inevitably have been discovered. Still, this very pro-police U.S. Supreme Court drew the line by refusing to over-turn Miranda when given the opportunity in *Dickerson v. U.S.*[24]

Peremptory Challenges and Unanimous Jury Verdicts

Judge Rothwax's remaining indictments of the present criminal justice system deal with criminal juries. Responding to the controversy surrounding the O. J. Simpson murder trial, he criticizes the defense team's use of peremptory challenges to eliminate prospective jurors.[25] He argues that the Simpson defense team used such challenges to seat a jury that could easily be fooled by court-room pyrotechnics. Whether this is true or not is a matter of conjecture, but it should be noted that Judge Rothwax ignores the fact that the prosecution had the same opportunity to affect the makeup of the jury. In reality, peremptory challenges help both sides in the courtroom battle, and thus we can assume that their removal would potentially hurt both sides as well. In 1997, for example, a videotape surfaced that was used as a training device for assistant prosecutors in Philadelphia.[26] The tape shows a senior prosecutor counseling his trainees to exclude black citizens from serving on criminal juries because they are dis-trustful of the police and therefore less likely to convict. The tape tells the trainees they should especially avoid placing young black women on their juries, because they are very bad for the prosecution's case. Although this episode remains to be investigated, and the attorney featured in the video vehe-mently denies having done anything illegal or morally wrong, the advice pre-sented on this tape would appear to violate a Supreme Court ruling prohibiting race from being used as a factor in selecting jurors. More fundamentally, this example calls into question Judge Rothwax's contention that the justice system has solved the problem of systemic racism.

Judge Rothwax also opposes the requirement that a criminal jury reach a verdict of guilt unanimously, suggesting instead that we should allow a jury to convict a defendant with a substantial majority, such as a vote of 11–1 or 10–2. In fact, the practice of jury unanimity[27] is merely a legal custom and not an explicit constitutional right, and the U.S. Supreme Court has established that, if states choose, they can allow juries to reach their decision with a clear, non-unanimous verdict.[28] Given the Supreme Court's view on this issue, Judge Rothwax's gripe, then, is with the legal system of the state of New York, which apparently has decided to continue the practice of jury unanimity, and not with the rulings of the so-called "liberal" U.S. Supreme Court in Washington.

WE FACE THE CHOICE OF OUR LIVES

The late Senator Sam Ervin once said, "In a free society you have to take some risks. If you lock everybody up, or even if you lock up everybody you think might commit a crime, you'll be pretty safe, but you won't be free."[29] To this one might add, "And you might end up getting locked up yourself!"

This country was shaped in part by a healthy concern for the potential abuses of governments. The U.S. Bill of Rights and the civil liberty protections of the state constitutions were created to ensure certain fundamental protections for all citizens. These guarantees were designed to withstand the shifting winds created by agitated majorities. Judge Rothwax is not the first American, nor will he likely be the last, to tell his fellow citizens that we live in a particularly dangerous time and that to survive we must forgo the "luxury" of our civil liberties.

Judge Rothwax is wrong. The guarantees created by James Madison and the Constitution are not luxuries. Rather, they make up a very battered constitutional firewall that barely protects us from the police state that he, cynical politicians, and a very conservative U.S. Supreme Court seem to be inching toward. These civil liberties are not excessive; if anything, they provide too little protection for the realities of daily life in an increasingly urban, multicultural society facing the twenty-first century.

Of course, many Americans share Judge Rothwax's concern over criminal predators like Leonardo Turriago who prey on their fellow citizens. These violent criminals should be punished severely. But the same level of concern ought to be expressed in regard to how today's criminal justice system treats black, Hispanic, American Indian, poor, and uneducated Americans. Americans ought to be concerned about the rights of innocent, hardworking Americans who are harassed, injured, maimed, or killed every day by abusive police officers for being in the "wrong" neighborhood or driving too "nice" a car. Judge Rothwax's system will not win the war against the Leonardo Turriagos of the world; it will likely create more Carlton Browns.

NOTES

1. Federal Bureau of Investigation, *Uniform Crime Report*, 2000.
2. Bernard Gavzer, "We're in the Fight of Our Lives." *Parade* (July 28, 1996): 4–6.
3. In other countries, such as most of the nations of continental Europe, an inquisitorial system of justice is used. In this system, it is the judge who determines the direction of the trial by calling witnesses, examining evidence and drawing final conclusions of fact. When compared to an adversarial justice system, inquisitorial disputants and, more importantly, their lawyers play a much less active role in affecting the composition of the case. Instead of a courtroom battle, the inquisitorial trial might be likened to a trip to the principal's office to determine who did what to whom and what should be done about it.
4. Jodi Wilgoren, "Citing Issue of Fairness, Gov. Clears Out Death Row in Ill." *The New York Times* (January 12, 2003).
5. James Sterngold, "Los Angeles Police's Report Cites Vast Command Lapses." *The New York Times* (March 2, 2000): A14.
6. David Johnston, "Report Criticizes Scientific Testing at FBI Crime Lab." *The New York Times* (April 16, 1997): A1.

7. Mark S. Warnick, "A Matter of Conviction." *Pittsburgh Post-Gazette* (September 24, 1995): A1.
8. Bob Herbert, "Brooklyn's Obsessive Pursuit." *The New York Times* (August 21, 1994): E15.
9. "Mexican Once Nearly Executed Wins Freedom in Texas." *The New York Times* (April 17, 1997): A8.
10. Bob Herbert, "Savagery Beyond Sense." *The New York Times* (October 18, 1996): A12.
11. James Madison, the leading figure in the development of the U.S. Constitution and Bill of Rights, commented on the need for checks on human behavior associated with the affairs of the state in *Federalist* No. 51: "If men were angels, no government would be necessary. If angels were to govern men, neither external nor internal controls on government would be necessary."
12. 384 U.S. 436.
13. Both sides conceded that, during the interrogation, the police did not use any force, threats, or promises of leniency if Miranda would confess. Both sides also conceded that at no point did the police inform Miranda that he had a constitutional right to refuse to talk to the police and that he could have counsel if he so desired.
14. Thus yielding the famous *Miranda* warnings:
    - You have the right to remain silent.
    - Anything you say can and will be used against you in a court of law.
    - You have a right to a lawyer.
    - If you can't afford a lawyer one will be provided to you.
    - If you say at any point that you do not want to talk to the police the interrogation must cease.
15. 384 U.S. 446.
16. It is worth noting that critics of the Miranda decision often ignore the fact that Ernesto Miranda did not go unpunished as a result of the Court's action. Instead, he was prosecuted by the State of Arizona in a second trial, without the use of his confession, and was convicted and sentenced to prison.
17. *Economist* (July 13, 1996): 29.
18. Ibid.
19. David Ignatius, "Tricks, Lies and Criminal Confessions." *The Washington Post National Weekly Edition* (January 24, 2000): 26.
20. It is important to note that only about 10 percent of criminal cases are resolved through the formal trial process. Most criminal convictions in this country are the result of plea bargaining between the defendant and the prosecutor.
21. *Weeks v. U.S.*, 232 U.S. 383 (1914).
22. 446 U.S. 620 (1980).
23. 467 U.S. 431 (1984).
24. 530 U.S. 428 (2000).
25. When a jury is used as the fact finder in a criminal case, the defense and prosecution have a significant role in determining who will sit on the jury.

In the jury selection process both sides can challenge a prospective juror in two ways. A challenge for cause is used when an attorney can show the court that there are tangible characteristics of the prospective jurors that make them biased and warrant their removal from consideration; lawyers have an unlimited ability to challenge for cause. A peremptory challenge allows a lawyer to remove a potential juror without giving a reason; each lawyer in a case gets a limited number of these. But peremptory challenges are not as peremptory as their name implies. The Supreme Court has ruled that lawyers cannot use them to systematically exclude all blacks or women from consideration for jury service.

26. Michael Janofsky, "Under Siege, Philadelphia's Criminal Justice System Suffers Another Blow." *The New York Times* (April 10, 1997): A9.
27. Jury unanimity is another balancer. It is based on the notion that the prosecutor should be required to present a case that convinces all jurors that the defendant is guilty beyond a reasonable doubt.
28. *Johnson v. Louisiana,* 406 U.S. 356 (1972), and *Apodaco v. Oregon,* 406 U.S. 404 (1972).
29. Quoted in Richard Harris, *Justice.* New York: Avon, 1969, p. 162.

 **mhhe.com/**diclerico11e

Internet resources
Visit our Web site at www.mhhe.com/diclerico11e for links and resources relating to Civil Liberties.

chapter 15

Civil Rights

Affirmative Action

For at least four decades, the federal government and many state governments have pursued a policy of "affirmative action," which requires government agencies and many public and private groups to take positive steps to guarantee nondiscrimination and a fair share of jobs, contracts, and college admissions for racial minorities and women. The underlying assumption of affirmative action is that because racial minorities, particularly African Americans, were historically discriminated against, special efforts must be made to make amends for past discriminatory policies and practices and to ensure equal opportunity in the future.

In recent years, affirmative action has become a hot-button issue, generating intense debate focused on these fundamental questions: Should minorities and women, because of past discrimination, be given special consideration in employment, admission to colleges and universities, government contracts, and the like? Or should race and gender be ignored, even if the result leads to a lack of diversity and limits opportunity in many fields?

To balance the competing interests in affirmative action and discrimination cases, the Supreme Court has set forth certain principles for judging the legitimacy of actions designed to guarantee equal opportunity. Affirmative action programs must serve a "compelling state interest" and must be "narrowly tailored" to accomplish their goal.

In 2003, the Court sought to apply these principles in two cases involving the University of Michigan. In Gratz v. Bollinger, *the justices reviewed the affirmative action process in the context of undergraduate admissions at the university. The Court ruled that the university's undergraduate admissions procedure did not meet the requirements of either compelling interest or narrowly tailored remedy and invalidaed it. However, in* Grutter v. Bollinger, *involving affirmative action in the University of Michigan Law School's admission process, the Court accepted the school's underlying rationale of accomplishing "diversity" as a legitimate state interest, thereby upholding the affirmative action program.*

The two selections in this section are from the Grutter case. The first, from the majority opinion, was written by Associate Justice Sandra Day O'Connor, at that time one of the more senior members of the Court and a supporter of affirmative action. The second selection is a dissenting opinion written by Associate Justice Clarence Thomas, at that time one of the newest members of the Court and its only African American.

Law School Admissions
The Case for Affirmative Action
Sandra Day O'Connor

This case requires us to decide whether the use of race as a factor in student admissions by the University of Michigan Law School is unlawful. . . .

Before this Court, as they have throughout this litigation, respondents assert only one justification for their use of race in the admissions process: obtaining "the educational benefits that flow from a diverse student body." . . . In other words, the Law School asks us to recognize, in the context of higher education, a compelling state interest in student body diversity. . . .

The Law School's educational judgment that such diversity is essential to its educational mission is one to which we defer. The Law School's assessment that diversity will, in fact, yield educational benefits is substantiated by respondents and their *amici*. Our scrutiny of the interest asserted by the Law School is no less strict for taking into account complex educational judgments in an area that lies primarily within the expertise of the university. Our holding today is in keeping with our tradition of giving a degree of deference to a university's academic decisions, within constitutionally prescribed limits. . . .

We have long recognized that, given the important purpose of public education and the expansive freedoms of speech and thought associated with the university environment, universities occupy a special niche in our constitutional tradition. . . . In announcing the principle of student body diversity as a compelling state interest, Justice Powell invoked our cases recognizing a constitutional dimension, grounded in the First Amendment, of educational autonomy: "The freedom of a university to make its own judgments as to education includes the selection of its student body." *Bakke*, 438 U.S. at 312. From this premise, Justice Powell reasoned that by claiming "the right to select those students who will contribute the most to the 'robust exchange of ideas,'" a university "seek[s] to achieve a goal that is of paramount importance in the fulfillment of its mission." Our conclusion that the Law School has a compelling interest in a diverse student body is informed by our view that attaining a diverse student body is at the heart of the Law School's proper institutional mission, and that "good faith" on the part of a university is "presumed" absent "a showing to the contrary." 438 U.S., at 318–319.

Sandra Day O'Connor was associate justice of the U.S. Supreme Court (1981–2006). Excerpted from the majority opinion in *Grutter v. Bollinger*, 539 U.S. 306 (2003). Some notes and references were deleted to maintain continuity in the text.

As part of its goal of "assembling a class that is both exceptionally academically qualified and broadly diverse," the Law School seeks to "enroll a 'critical mass' of minority students." . . . The Law School's interest is not simply "to assure within its student body some specified percentage of a particular group merely because of its race or ethnic origin." *Bakke,* 438 U.S., at 307 (opinion of Powell, J.). That would amount to outright racial balancing, which is patently unconstitutional. . . . Rather, the Law School's concept of critical mass is defined by reference to the educational benefits that diversity is designed to produce.

These benefits are substantial. As the District Court emphasized, the Law School's admissions policy promotes "cross-racial understanding," helps to break down racial stereotypes, and "enables [students] to better understand persons of different races." . . . These benefits are "important and laudable," because "classroom discussion is livelier, more spirited, and simply more enlightening and interesting" when the students have "the greatest possible variety of backgrounds." . . .

The Law School's claim of a compelling interest is further bolstered by its *amici,* who point to the educational benefits that flow from student body diversity. In addition to the expert studies and reports entered into evidence at trial, numerous studies show that student body diversity promotes learning outcomes, and "better prepares students for an increasingly diverse workforce and society, and better prepares them as professionals." Brief for American Educational Research Association et al. as *Amici Curiae* 3. . . .

These benefits are not theoretical but real, as major American businesses have made clear that the skills needed in today's increasingly global marketplace can only be developed through exposure to widely diverse people, cultures, ideas, and viewpoints. Brief for 3M et al. as *Amici Curiae* 5; Brief for General Motors Corp. as *Amicus Curiae* 3-4. What is more, high-ranking retired officers and civilian leaders of the United States military assert that, "[b]ased on [their] decades of experience," a "highly qualified, racially diverse officer corps . . . is essential to the military's ability to fulfill its principle mission to provide national security." Brief for Julius W. Becton, Jr. et al. as *Amici Curiae* 27. . . .

We have repeatedly acknowledged the overriding importance of preparing students for work and citizenship, describing education as pivotal to "sustaining our political and cultural heritage" with a fundamental role in maintaining the fabric of society. *Plyler v. Doe,* 457 U.S. 202, 221 (1982). This Court has long recognized that "education . . . is the very foundation of good citizenship." *Brown v. Board of Education,* 347 U.S. 483, 493 (1954). For this reason, the diffusion of knowledge and opportunity through public institutions of higher education must be accessible to all individuals regardless of race or ethnicity. The United States, as *amicus curiae,* affirms that "[e]nsuring that public institutions are open and available to all segments of American society, including people of all races and ethnicities, represents a paramount government objective." Brief for United States as *Amicus Curiae* 13. And, "[n]owhere is the importance of such openness more acute than in the context of higher education." *Ibid.* Effective participation by members of all racial and ethnic groups in the civic life of our Nation is essential if the dream of one Nation, indivisible, is to be realized.

Moreover, universities, and in particular, law schools, represent the training ground for a large number of our Nation's leaders. . . . Individuals with law degrees occupy roughly half the state governorships, more than half the seats in the United States Senate, and more than a third of the seats in the United States House of Representatives. . . . The pattern is even more striking when it comes to highly selective law schools. A handful of these schools accounts for 25 of the 100 United States Senators, 74 United States Courts of Appeals judges, and nearly 200 of the more than 600 United States District Court judges.

In order to cultivate a set of leaders with legitimacy in the eyes of the citizenry, it is necessary that the path to leadership be visibly open to talented and qualified individuals of every race and ethnicity. All members of our heterogeneous society must have confidence in the openness and integrity of the educational institutions that provide this training. As we have recognized, law schools "cannot be effective in isolation from the individuals and institutions with which the law interacts." . . . Access to legal education (and thus the legal profession) must be inclusive of talented and qualified individuals of every race and ethnicity, so that all members of our heterogeneous society may participate in the educational institutions that provide the training and education necessary to succeed in America.

The Law School does not premise its need for critical mass on "any belief that minority students always (or even consistently) express some characteristic minority viewpoint on any issue." . . . To the contrary, diminishing the force of such stereotypes is both a crucial part of the Law School's mission, and one that it cannot accomplish with only token numbers of minority students. Just as growing up in a particular region or having particular professional experiences is likely to affect an individual's views, so too is one's own, unique experience of being a racial minority in a society, like our own, in which race unfortunately still matters. The Law School has determined, based on its experience and expertise, that a "critical mass" of underrepresented minorities is necessary to further its compelling interest in securing the educational benefits of a diverse student body. . . .

We find that the Law School's admissions program bears the hallmarks of a narrowly tailored plan. As Justice Powell made clear in *Bakke*, truly individualized consideration demands that race be used in a flexible, nonmechanical way. It follows from this mandate that universities cannot establish quotas for members of certain racial groups or put members of those groups on separate admissions tracks. . . . Nor can universities insulate applicants who belong to certain racial or ethnic groups from the competition for admission. *Ibid*. Universities can, however, consider race or ethnicity more flexibly as a "plus" factor in the context of individualized consideration of each and every applicant. . . .

We are satisfied that the Law School's admissions program, like the Harvard plan described by Justice Powell, does not operate as a quota. Properly understood, a "quota" is a program in which a certain fixed number or proportion of opportunities are "reserved exclusively for certain minority groups." . . . Quotas "'impose a fixed number or percentage which must be attained, or which cannot be exceeded,'" . . . and "insulate the individual from comparison with all other candidates for the available seats." *Bakke, supra*, at 317 (opinion of

Powell, J.). In contrast, "a permissible goal . . . require[s] only a good-faith effort . . . to come within a range demarcated by the goal itself," *Sheet Metal Workers v. EEOC, supra,* at 495, and permits consideration of race as a "plus" factor in any given case while still ensuring that each candidate "compete[s] with all other qualified applicants," . . .

That a race-conscious admissions program does not operate as a quota does not, by itself, satisfy the requirement of individualized consideration. When using race as a "plus" factor in university admissions, a university's admissions program must remain flexible enough to ensure that each applicant is evaluated as an individual and not in a way that makes an applicant's race or ethnicity the defining feature of his or her application. The importance of this individualized consideration in the context of a race-conscious admissions program is paramount. See *Bakke, supra,* at 318, n. 52 (opinion of Powell, J). . . .

Here, the Law School engages in a highly individualized, holistic review of each applicant's file, giving serious consideration to all the ways an applicant might contribute to a diverse educational environment. The Law School affords this individualized consideration to applicants of all races. There is no policy, either *de jure* or *de facto,* of automatic acceptance or rejection based on any single "soft" variable. . . . [T]he Law School awards no mechanical, predetermined diversity "bonuses" based on race or ethnicity. . . . Like the Harvard plan, the Law School's admissions policy "is flexible enough to consider all pertinent elements of diversity in light of the particular qualifications of each applicant, and to place them on the same footing for consideration, although not necessarily according them the same weight," *Bakke, supra,* at 317 (opinion of Powell, J.).

We also find that, like the Harvard plan Justice Powell referenced in *Bakke,* the Law School's race-conscious admissions program adequately ensures that all factors that may contribute to student body diversity are meaningfully considered alongside race in admissions decisions. With respect to the use of race itself, all underrepresented minority students admitted by the Law School have been deemed qualified. By virtue of our Nation's struggle with racial inequality, such students are both likely to have experiences of particular importance to the Law School's mission, and less likely to be admitted in meaningful numbers on criteria that ignore those experiences. . . .

The Law School does not, however, limit in any way the broad range of qualities and experiences that may be considered valuable contributions to student body diversity. To the contrary, the 1992 policy makes clear "[t]here are many possible bases for diversity admission," and provides examples of admittees who have lived or traveled widely abroad, are fluent in several languages, have overcome personal adversity and family hardship, have exceptional records of extensive community service, and have had successful careers in other fields. . . . The Law School seriously considers each "applicant's promise of making a notable contribution to the class by way of a particular strength, attainment, or characteristic—e.g., an unusual intellectual achievement, employment experience, nonacademic performance, or personal background," . . . All applicants have the opportunity to highlight their own potential diversity contributions through the submission of a personal statement, letters of recommendation, and an essay describing the ways in which the applicant will contribute to the life and diversity of the Law School.

What is more, the Law School actually gives substantial weight to diversity factors besides race. The Law School frequently accepts nonminority applicants with grades and test scores lower than underrepresented minority applicants (and other nonminority applicants) who are rejected. . . . This shows that the Law School seriously weighs many other diversity factors besides race that can make a real and dispositive difference for nonminority applicants as well. By this flexible approach, the Law School sufficiently takes into account, in practice as well as in theory, a wide variety of characteristics besides race and ethnicity that contribute to a diverse student body . . . .

We are mindful . . ., that "[a] core purpose of the Fourteenth Amendment was to do away with all governmentally imposed discrimination based on race," *Palmore v. Sidoti,* 466 U.S. 429, 432 (1984). Accordingly, race-conscious admissions policies must be limited in time. This requirement reflects that racial classifications, however compelling their goals, are potentially so dangerous that they may be employed no more broadly than the interest demands. Enshrining a permanent justification for racial preferences would offend this fundamental equal protection principle. We see no reason to exempt race-conscious admissions programs from the requirement that all governmental use of race must have a logical end point. The Law School, too, concedes that all "race-conscious programs must have reasonable durational limits." . . .

In the context of higher education, the durational requirement can be met by sunset provisions in race-conscious admissions policies and periodic reviews to determine whether racial preferences are still necessary to achieve student body diversity. Universities in California, Florida, and Washington State, where racial preferences in admissions are prohibited by state law, are currently engaged in experimenting with a wide variety of alternative approaches. Universities in other States can and should draw on the most promising aspects of these race-neutral alternatives as they develop. . . .

The requirement that all race-conscious admissions programs have a termination point "assure[s] all citizen that the deviation from the norm of equal treatment of all racial and ethnic groups is a temporary matter, a measure taken in the service of the goal of equality itself." *Richmond v. J.A. Croson Co.,* 488 U.S., at 510 (plurality opinion). . . .

We take the Law School at its word that it would "like nothing better than to find a race-neutral admissions formula" and will terminate its race-conscious admissions program as soon as practicable. See Brief for Respondents Bollinger et al. 34; *Bakke, supra,* at 317–318 (opinion of Powell, J.) (presuming good faith of university officials in the absence of a showing to the contrary). It has been 25 years since Justice Powell first approved the use of race to further an interest in student body diversity in the context of public higher education. Since that time, the number of minority applicants with high grades and test scores has indeed increased. . . . We expect that 25 years from now, the use of racial preferences will no longer be necessary to further the interest approved today.

Law School Admissions
The Case Against Affirmative Action
Clarence Thomas

Frederick Douglass, speaking to a group of abolitionists almost 140 years ago, delivered a message lost on today's majority:

> "[I]n regard to the colored people, there is always more that is benevolent, I perceive, than just, manifested towards us. What I ask for the negro is not benevolence, not pity, not sympathy, but simply *justice.* The American people have always been anxious to know what they shall do with us. . . . I have had but one answer from the beginning. Do nothing with us! Your doing with us has already played the mischief with us. Do nothing with us! If the apples will not remain on the tree of their own strength, if they are worm-eaten at the core, if they are early ripe and disposed to fall, let them fall! . . . And if the negro cannot stand on his own legs, let him fall also. All I ask is, give him a chance to stand on his own legs! Let him alone! . . . [Y]our interference is doing him positive injury. . . .

Like Douglass, I believe blacks can achieve in every avenue of American life without the meddling of university administrators. Because I wish to see all students succeed whatever their color, I share, in some respect, the sympathies of those who sponsor the type of discrimination advanced by the University of Michigan Law School (Law School). The Constitution does not, however, tolerate institutional devotion to the status quo in admissions policies when such devotion ripens into racial discrimination. . . .

The Constitution abhors classifications based on race, not only because those classifications can harm favored races or are based on illegitimate motives, but also because every time the government places citizens on racial registers and makes race relevant to the provision of burdens or benefits, it demeans us all. . . .

. . . I believe what lies beneath the Court's decision today are the benighted notions that one can tell when racial discrimination benefits (rather than hurts) minority groups, . . . and that racial discrimination is necessary to remedy general societal ills. This Court's precedents supposedly settled both issues, but clearly the majority still cannot commit to the principle that racial classifications

Clarence Thomas is associate justice of the U.S. Supreme Court. Excerpted from a dissenting opinion in *Grutter v. Bollinger,* 539 U.S. 306 (2003). Some notes and references were deleted to maintain continuity in the text.

are *per se* harmful and that almost no amount of benefit in the eye of the beholder can justify such classifications.

. . . I must contest the notion that the Law School's discrimination benefits those admitted as a result of it. The Court spends considerable time discussing the impressive display of *amicus* support for the Law School in this case from all corners of society. But nowhere in any of the filings in this Court is any evidence that the purported "beneficiaries" of this racial discrimination prove themselves by performing at (or even near) the same level as those students who receive no preferences. . . .

The silence in this case is deafening to those of us who view higher education's purpose as imparting knowledge and skills to students, rather than a communal, rubber-stamp, credentialing process. The Law School is not looking for those students who, despite a lower LSAT score or undergraduate grade point average, will succeed in the study of law. The Law School seeks only a facade— it is sufficient that the class looks right, even if it does not perform right.

The Law School tantalizes unprepared students with the promise of a University of Michigan degree and all of the opportunities that it offers. These overmatched students take the bait, only to find that they cannot succeed in the cauldron of competition. And this mismatch crisis is not restricted to elite institutions. . . . Indeed, to cover the tracks of the aestheticists, this cruel farce of racial discrimination must continue—in selection for the *Michigan Law Review*, . . . and in hiring at law firms and for judicial clerkships—until the "beneficiaries" are no longer tolerated. While these students may graduate with law degrees, there is no evidence that they have received a qualitatively better legal education (or become better lawyers) than if they had gone to a less "elite" law school for which they were better prepared. And the aestheticists will never address the real problems facing "underrepresented minorities," instead continuing their social experiments on other people's children.

Beyond the harm the Law School's racial discrimination visits upon its test subjects, no social science has disproved the notion that this discrimination "engender[s] attitudes of superiority or, alternatively, provoke[s] resentment among those who believe that they have been wronged by the government's use of race." *Adarand*, 515 U.S., at 241 (Thomas, J., concurring in part and concurring in judgment). "These programs stamp minorities with a badge of inferiority and may cause them to develop dependencies or to adopt an attitude that they are 'entitled' to preferences." *Ibid.*

It is uncontested that each year, the Law School admits a handful of blacks who would be admitted in the absence of racial discrimination. . . . Who can differentiate between those who belong and those who do not? The majority of blacks are admitted to the Law School because of discrimination, and because of this policy all are tarred as undeserving. This problem of stigma does not depend on determinacy as to whether those stigmatized are actually the "beneficiaries" of racial discrimination. When blacks take positions in the highest places of government, industry, or academia, it is an open question today whether their skin color played a part in their advancement. The question itself is the stigma—because either racial discrimination did play a role, in which case the person may be deemed "otherwise unqualified," or it did not, in which case asking the question itself unfairly marks those blacks who would succeed without discrimination. Is this what the Court means by "visibly open"?

Finally, the Court's disturbing reference to the importance of the country's law schools as training grounds meant to cultivate "a set of leaders with legitimacy in the eyes of the citizenry" through the use of racial discrimination deserves discussion. As noted earlier, the Court has soundly rejected the remedying of societal discrimination as a justification for governmental use of race. . . . For those who believe that every racial disproportionality in our society is caused by some kind of racial discrimination, there can be no distinction between remedying societal discrimination and erasing racial disproportionalities in the country's leadership caste. And if the lack of proportional racial representation among our leaders is not caused by societal discrimination, then "fixing" it is even less of a pressing public necessity.

The Court's civics lesson presents yet another example of judicial selection of a theory of political representation based on skin color—an endeavor I have previously rejected. . . . The majority appears to believe that broader utopian goals justify the Law School's use of race, but "[t]he Equal Protection Clause commands the elimination of racial barriers, not their creation in order to satisfy our theory as to how society ought to be organized." *DeFunis*, 416 U.S., at 342 (Douglas, J., dissenting). . . .

The Court also holds that racial discrimination in admissions should be given another 25 years before it is deemed no longer narrowly tailored to the Law School's fabricated compelling state interest. While I agree that in 25 years the practices of the Law School will be illegal, they are, for the reasons I have given, illegal now. The majority does not and cannot rest its time limitation on any evidence that the gap in credentials between black and white students is shrinking or will be gone in that timeframe. In recent years there has been virtually no change, for example, in the proportion of law school applicants with LSAT scores of 165 and higher who are black. In 1993 blacks constituted 1.1% of law school applicants in that score range, though they represented 11.1% of all applicants. Law School Admission Council, National Statistical Report (1994) (hereinafter LSAC Statistical Report). In 2000 the comparable numbers were 1.0% and 11.3%. LSAC Statistical Report (2001). No one can seriously contend, and the Court does not, that the racial gap in academic credentials will disappear in 25 years. Nor is the Court's holding that racial discrimination will be unconstitutional in 25 years made contingent on the gap closing in that time.

Indeed, the very existence of racial discrimination of the type practiced by the Law School may impede the narrowing of the LSAT testing gap. An applicant's LSAT score can improve dramatically with preparation, but such preparation is a cost, and there must be sufficient benefits attached to an improved score to justify additional study. Whites scoring between 163 and 167 on the LSAT are routinely rejected by the Law School, and thus whites aspiring to admission at the Law School have every incentive to improve their score to levels above that range. . . . [I]n 2000, 209 out of 422 white applicants were rejected in this scoring range). Blacks, on the other hand, are nearly guaranteed admission if they score above 155 . . . (63 out of 77 black applicants are accepted with LSAT scores above 155). As admission prospects approach certainty, there is no incentive for the black applicant to continue to prepare for the LSAT once he is reasonably assured of achieving the requisite score. It is far from certain that the LSAT test-taker's behavior is responsive to the Law School's admissions policies. Nevertheless, the possibility remains that this racial discrimination will help fulfill the bigot's prophecy about black underperformance—just as it confirms the conspiracy theorist's belief that "institutional racism" is at fault for every racial disparity in our society.

I therefore can understand the imposition of a 25-year time limit only as a holding that the deference the Court pays to the Law School's educational judgments and refusal to change its admissions policies will itself expire. At that point these policies will clearly have failed to "'eliminat[e] the [perceived] need for any racial or ethnic'" discrimination because the academic credentials gap will still be there. . . .

For the immediate future, however, the majority has placed its imprimatur on a practice that can only weaken the principle of equality embodied in the Declaration of Independence and the Equal Protection Clause. "Our Constitution is color-blind, and neither knows nor tolerates classes among citizens." *Plessy v. Ferguson,* 163 U.S. 537,559 (1896) (Harlan, J., dissenting). It has been nearly 140 years since Frederick Douglass asked the intellectual ancestors of the Law School to "[d]o nothing with us!" and the Nation adopted the Fourteenth Amendment. Now we must wait another 25 years to see this principle of equality vindicated. I therefore respectfully dissent from the remainder of the Court's opinion and the judgment.

Gender Equity

*T*he modern era has been unprecedented in the advancement of civil rights for minorities and women: elimination of racial segregation; removal of racial, gender, and disability discrimination in employment, school admissions, and other areas; and the extension of the vote to millions of Americans. Yet, in the face of much progress, there are areas in civil rights policy where opinion is strongly divided. One such area is gender equity in sports.

In 1972, Congress passed the Education Act Amendment. Title IX of this law prohibits discrimination against women on college campuses in housing, financial assistance, faculty and staff hiring and pay, and, most contentious of all, athletics. It is the last area— gender equity in sports—that is the subject of the two essays in this section.

The main issue in Title IX is the requirement that women be given athletic opportunities in proportion to their numbers at particular colleges and universities. Thus, according to current interpretations of Title IX, on a college campus that is 50 percent male and 50 percent female, the male-to-female ratio in sponsored sports must also be 50-50. This proportionality requirement has led some schools to eliminate athletic opportunities for men, as in the case of men's wrestling, to make room for more women.

In 2005, the regulations regarding implementation of Title IX were changed to permit colleges and universities to determine, via the Internet, students' degree of "interest" in sports as a means of meeting the proportionality requirement. Critics, including the NCAA (the National Collegiate Athletic Association), complain that this action reduces the impact of Title IX. Regardless of the outcome of this new controversy, the fundamental issue remains: Does Title IX provide a fair way to achieve equality in sports?

The authors of the essays that follow discuss the merits of eliminating or changing Title IX rules. John Irving, a prominent writer and a part-time wrestling coach, concedes the value of Title IX but argues that it is simply unfair in application. According to Irving, men's teams should not have to suffer in order to meet a proportionality test that is, at best, unreasonable. Law professor Joanna Grossman disagrees, insisting that Title IX has permitted women to make unprecedented gains in sports—gains that they would likely not have obtained without it—and that the critics of Title IX are setting up a smoke screen to hide the real problem in providing equity for both men and women in sports: the favored position of college football.

Wrestling with Title IX

John Irving

Title IX, the federal law that prohibits sex discrimination in educational programs receiving federal assistance, may be in for an overhaul. This week
[January 27, 2003] a committee appointed by the Bush administration will hold
its final meetings before submitting its recommendations for changing the law
to Secretary of Education Rod Paige. Since Title IX was enacted in 1972, it has
been the subject of debate—much of it misguided—about its application to college athletics. At issue now is how to alter the law—or not—so that, as Secretary
Paige has put it, we can find ways of "expanding opportunities to ensure fairness for all college athletes."

I hope the commission will realize that what's wrong with Title IX isn't
Title IX. What's wrong is that, in practice, there are two Title IX's. The first Title
IX was the one passed by Congress in 1972 to put an end to sex discrimination
in schools—good for the original Title IX! The second Title IX, the one currently
enforced, is the product of a policy interpretation in 1979 by the Department
of Education's Office for Civil Rights (but never debated or approved by
Congress)—and which is functioning as a gender quota law.

In its prohibition against sex discrimination, the 1972 law expressly states
as "exceptions" any "preferential or disparate treatment because of imbalance
in participation" or any "statistical evidence of imbalance." In English, this
means that Congress recognized that the intent of Title IX was not to establish
gender quotas or require preferential treatment as reparation for past discrimination. Smart thinking—after all, the legislation was intended to prohibit discrimination against either sex.

But what happened in 1979—and in subsequent re-evaluations of the law—
has invited discrimination against male athletes. The 1979 interpretation required
colleges to meet at least one of the following three criteria: that the number of athletes from each sex be roughly equivalent to the number of students enrolled; that
colleges demonstrate a commitment to adding women's sports; and that they
prove that the athletic interests of female students are effectively accommodated.
The problems lie in complying with the first criterion. In order to achieve gender
proportionality, men's collegiate sports are being undermined and eliminated.
This was never the intention of Title IX.

John Irving is a novelist and former wrestler. "Wrestling with Title IX," by John Irving from
The New York Times, January 28, 2003. Reprinted with the author's permission.

The proportionality rule stipulates that the ratio of male to female athletes be proportionate to the ratio of male to female students at a particular college. On average, females make up about 56 percent of college enrollment, males 44 percent; for most colleges to be in compliance with proportionality, more than half the athletes on team rosters must be women. Can you imagine this rule being applied to all educational programs—classes in science, engineering, accounting, medicine or law? What about dance, drama or music—not to mention women's studies?

In 1996, the Department of Education further bolstered the proportionality zealots by requiring colleges to count every name on a team's roster—scholarship and nonscholarship athletes, starters and nonstarters. It is this ruling that has prompted a lawsuit by the National Wrestling Coaches Association, the Committee to Save Bucknell Wrestling, the Marquette Wrestling Club, the Yale Wrestling Association, and the National Coalition for Athletics Equity, all of whom argue that the 1996 rules exceed the Department of Education's statutory authority "by effectively mandating the very discrimination that Title IX prohibits."

Why are wrestlers so upset about this? The number of collegiate wrestling programs lost to Title IX compliance is staggering; this is especially alarming because, since 1993, wrestling has been a rapidly growing sport at the high-school level. Data compiled by Gary Abbott, director of special projects at USA Wrestling, indicates that in 2001, there were 244,984 athletes wrestling in high school; only 5,966 got to wrestle in the National Collegiate Athletic Association. Not to put too fine a point on it: there is only one N.C.A.A. spot for every 41 high-school wrestlers. The numbers have been going downhill for a while. In 1982, there were 363 N.C.A.A. wrestling teams with 7,914 wrestlers competing; in 2001, there were only 229 teams with fewer than 6,000 wrestlers. Yet, in that same period, the number of N.C.A.A. institutions has increased from 787 to 1,049. No wonder wrestlers are unhappy.

As for the virtual elimination of walk-ons (nonscholarship athletes) in many men's sports, and the unrealistic capping of male team rosters—again, to make the number of male athletes proportional to the number of females—the problem is that athletic programs are going to absurd lengths to fill the unfilled rosters for women's teams. But women, statistically, aren't interested in participating in intercollegiate athletics to the degree that men are. J. Robinson, wrestling coach at the University of Minnesota, cites intramural sports, which are wholly interest driven, as an example. In a column about Title IX published in the *Chronicle of Higher Education,* Robinson wrote that "men outnumber women 3–1 or 4–1 on the intramural field."

Don't we need to know the exact numbers for how many women are interested in playing college sports now? But the Women's Sports Foundation, an advocacy group that favors maintaining proportionality, opposes conducting surveys of incoming students—that is, expressly to gauge interest in athletics. These surveys, they say, would force "female athletes to prove their interest in sports in order to obtain the right to participate and be treated fairly." But men would fill out the same surveys.

One suggestion that the presidential commission is considering is counting the available spots on teams, rather than the actual participants. The Women's Sports Foundation rejects this idea, arguing that it counts "ghost female participants." However, the foundation has no objection to counting interest that isn't there.

In fact, those women's groups opposed to tampering with either the 1979 interpretation or the 1996 ruling, which endorses the proportionality arm of Title IX, often argue that there are three ways (at least on paper) for an institution to comply with Title IX—not just proportionality. But only proportionality can be measured concretely. A 1996 clarification letter from the Department of Education refers to the proportionality test as a "safe harbor"—meaning that this simple-to-apply numerical formula can assure an athletic director and a university president that their institution is in compliance and not subject to legal action. In other words, proportionality is not only wrong—it's lazy.

Some women's advocates argue that it is not proportionality that forces athletic directors to cut men's teams; they blame the budget excesses of Division I football and men's basketball. But there are countless examples where money was not the issue in the case of the sport that was dropped. Marquette University had a wrestling team that was completely financed by alumni and supporters; yet the sport was dropped in 2001, to comply with gender equity. (Marquette has no football team.)

Boston College dropped three sports that had only part-time coaches and offered no scholarships; these sports could easily have been sponsored by fundraising. Keep in mind, too, that the majority of male college teams dropped in the 1990s were from Division II and Division III programs, which don't have big-time football or men's basketball.

Furthermore, many Division I football and basketball programs earn millions of dollars a year, enough to support all the other sports programs—men's and women's. Moreover, most schools with high-profile football programs are schools where women's teams have thrived. (Witness the Big 10, the S.E.C., the Big 12 and other Division I athletic conferences, which have produced both winning football teams as well as great women's teams in other sports.)

While eliminating men's sports like wrestling, where the interest in participation is increasing, athletic programs go begging to find women athletes to fill the vacancies on an ever-expanding number of women's teams.

One of the most ludicrous examples of this was the attempt by Arizona State University in Tempe—a cactus-studded campus in the middle of the Sonoran Desert—to add a competitive women's rowing team. There's not a lot of water in Arizona. But the school asked the city to create a body of water (by flooding a dry gulch) on which the team could practice. Because of a lack of funds, the school had to drop the plan. This is probably just as well; taxpayer dollars would have financed scholarships either to rowers from out of state or to teach Arizona women (most of whom have never held an oar) how to row. But Arizona State is to be commended. It not only worked to meet the numerical demands of proportionality, it tried to adhere to the original spirit of Title IX by adding opportunities for women, not by cutting opportunities for men.

To apply the rule of proportionality to men's and women's collegiate athletics amounts to a feminist form of sex discrimination. And I won't be dismissed by that other argument I've heard (ad nauseam) from those women's advocates unwilling to let proportionality go—namely, that to oppose proportionality, or even the crudest enforcement of Title IX to eliminate men's sports programs, is tantamount to being antifeminist and hostile to women in sports. Don't try to lay that on me.

I *am* a women's advocate. I have long been active in the pro-choice movement; my principal political commitment is my long-standing and continuing role as an abortion-rights advocate. But I'm also an advocate of fairness. What is unfair is not Title IX—it is Title IX's enforcement of proportionality, which discriminates against men.

In 1992, Brian Picklo, a walk-on, asked the Michigan State Wrestling coach, Tom Minkel, if he could try out for the team. Picklo had wrestled for only two years in high school and never qualified for state tournaments. Minkel thought Picklo's chances of wrestling in the Big 10 were "slim to none." But Picklo became a two-time Division I All-American, and he won the Big 10 title at 190 pounds. In most wrestling programs across the country today, Brian Picklo wouldn't be allowed to be a walk-on.

Title IX, the original legislation, was conceived as a fairness-for-all law; it has been reinvented as a tool to treat men unfairly. Advocates of proportionality claim that universities that are not "proportional" are breaking the law, but they're not breaking the original law.

The Women's Sports Foundation has accused the presidential commission of politicizing Title IX. But Title IX was politicized by the Department of Education in 1979 and 1996—during Democratic administrations. Is it only now political because a Republican administration is taking a closer look at the way Title IX is applied? (I make this criticism, by the way, as a Democrat. I'd have a hard time being an abortion rights advocate in the Bush administration, wouldn't I?)

Based on 2001 membership data—raw data from the National Federation of State High Schools, and from the N.C.A.A.—for every single N.C.A.A. sports opportunity for a woman, there are 17 high school athletes available to fill the spot; for a man, there are 18. Isn't that equal enough? In fact, women have more opportunity to compete in college than men do. Yet the attitude represented by the Women's Sports Foundation, and other women's groups, is that women are far from achieving gender equity; by their continuing endorsement of proportionality in collegiate athletics, these women's advocates are being purely vindictive.

Years ago, I was playing in a Little League baseball game when an umpire made what I thought was a memorable mistake. Later, in another game, he made it again. I realized it was no mistake at all—he meant to say it. Instead of hollering "Play ball!" at the start of the game, this umpire shouted "Play fair!"

Keep Title IX; eliminate proportionality. Play fair.

We Must Preserve Equity
for Women in College Athletics

Joanna Grossman

The year 2003 marked the thirtieth anniversary of the passage of Title IX of the Education Amendments of 1972. . . . Title IX is a federal statute banning sex discrimination in educational programs receiving federal financial assistance. . . .

Title IX has been used to challenge gender inequity in a variety of contexts: sexual harassment; pregnancy; school admissions, testing, and scholarships; and, most controversially, school athletics. It is the statute's impact on collegiate athletics that has garnered it its highest praise, as well as its harshest criticism.

Critics have called for amendments of Title IX and its regulations that would make its demand for gender equity—particularly in the realm of college athletics—less strict. Among those critics is the Bush Administration, whose lackluster defense of the statute in a recent lawsuit reveals its utter lack of commitment to gender equity in athletics. (On this issue, the President is perhaps continuing the legacy of his father—who made headlines as vice-president for suggesting in a 1981 speech that Title IX had simply gone too far in the field of athletics.)

The Administration and other critics of Title IX, however, are wrong, and should be opposed. Title IX has turned out to be one of the most important pieces of protection for women against sex discrimination—and in particular, a crucial way to ensure women's equality in college athletics. Rather than going too far, it has held an important line—a line that should not now be moved backwards.

THE HISTORY OF TITLE IX AND ITS REGULATIONS RELEVANT TO COLLEGE ATHLETICS

In 1975, it was made clear that Title IX applied to athletics, as well as to other aspects of education—and the controversy that has plagued this application of the statute began.

That year, the Department of Health, Education, and Welfare (the predecessor to today's Department of Education) issued regulations to implement

Joanna Grossman is associate professor of law at Hofstra University. From Joanna Grossman, "On the Thirtieth Anniversary of Title IX, We Need to Preserve, Not Reverse, Its Guarantee of Equity for Women in College Athletics." This column originally appeared on www.FindLaw.com on June 18, 2002, pp. 1–6. Reprinted with permission.

Title IX. The regulations required institutions to provide "equal athletic opportunity for members of both sexes."

This general standard was supplemented by ten factors to be considered in determining whether equal opportunity was in fact being provided. The first of these factors—and the one most frequently at issue in litigation—asks "whether the selection of sports and levels of competition effectively accommodate the interests and abilities of both sexes."

In a 1979 Policy Interpretation, HEW broke down this factor further, into a three-prong test. Under that test, an institution can show effective accommodation by proving one of three things: First, it can show that it provides athletic opportunities to men and women substantially proportionate to their overall enrollment. Second, it can show that it is engaged in a continuing practice of program expansion with respect to the underrepresented sex (almost always women). Third, it can show that it has fully and effectively accommodated the interests and abilities of the members of the underrepresented sex.

In 1995, the Department of Education sent a "clarification" of the Policy Interpretation to thousands of interested parties. The clarification explained, among other things, that although proportionality alone can provide a "safe harbor" for institutions able to demonstrate it, they are also free to comply with the other prongs of the test instead.

The new clarification also said that institutions were authorized, though not required, to eliminate teams, or cap team size, as a way of achieving gender proportionality. (For example, eliminating the men's lacrosse team could be a way to address the fact that there was no women's lacrosse team.)

Finally, the clarification said that participation opportunities should be measured based on actual athletes rather than "slots"—a healthy dose of realism that meant schools had to focus on women athletes, not theoretical possibilities that there could be women athletes.

TITLE IX'S IMPACT ON WOMEN'S SPORTS: OVERWHELMINGLY POSITIVE

There has been a dramatic increase in athletic participation of girls and women since Title IX was enacted. Every available statistic bears this out.

For instance, participation by high school girls in varsity sports has risen from one in twenty-seven to one in two-and-a-half. Meanwhile, participation by college female athletes has risen from under 30,000 to more than 150,000. Interestingly, during the same thirty years, participation by male athletes, at both the high school and college levels, has risen as well, though not nearly as dramatically.

While cause and effect are hard to pinpoint, Title IX litigation and administrative enforcement have clearly been important to these developments. However, there are still important areas of inequity.

For instance, an estimated 80 percent of high schools and colleges run athletic programs that do not comply with Title IX. And, of course, men's athletic programs continue to receive much more money for athletic scholarships, recruiting, coaching, and general operations than women's athletic programs do. In addition, female coaches get paid a fraction of what male coaches earn, and only two percent of the head coaching jobs for men's teams. . . .

MORE THAN PROPORTIONALITY ALONE: OTHER WAYS TO SATISFY TITLE IX

In the popular media, the three-prong test of the Title IX regulations has been reduced to a single idea—a requirement of proportionality. The media also suggests that the only way schools achieve proportionality is by cutting men's "minor" sports—like wrestling, swimming, and gymnastics—in order to bring the overall opportunities for men down to the level of women's.

As noted above, the "clarification" does allow men's programs to be cut in order to achieve equality. But in fact, the reality is quite different—as the fact that male athletes have prospered, rather than being harmed, over the last thirty years can attest.

As the clarification also notes, proportionality is only one way to comply with Title IX. Schools can also comply by showing a good-faith effort to expand opportunities for women. Alternatively, they can show that women's interests and abilities are fully accommodated, even though that means they have significantly fewer actual roster spots or teams. More than two-thirds of the schools involved in Title IX cases before the Department of Education during a recent five-year period chose to comply with one of these alternative prongs, rather than by instituting gender proportionality.

Moreover, for schools who do try to achieve proportionality, only some of them accomplish it by cutting men's teams or capping team size. Two-thirds of colleges and universities have not cut any men's teams at all in their efforts to achieve gender equity. (And many schools have cut both women's and men's teams in certain sports, like gymnastics, wrestling, and field hockey, and replaced them with more popular sports like soccer and track.)

But where schools have cut men's teams purportedly to comply with Title IX, those decisions have often been the target of litigation. Male athletes on teams that have been cut have alleged reverse discrimination, claiming that the decision to eliminate their particular team was made solely on the basis of sex.

However, every case bringing a reverse discrimination claim has ultimately been unsuccessful. As the relevant courts have often noted, when a school reallocates resources to remedy past inequity against women, it does not commit a new act of reverse discrimination. Thus, the school does not violate either Title IX or the Equal Protection Clause.

After all, if the remedy for discrimination were called "reverse discrimination" and forbidden, Title IX would be effectively unenforceable. If cutting men's teams were not sometimes an option, then it would be impossible for schools to cure past discrimination without dramatically expanding their budget for athletics, an option not available to most schools.

This conclusion may sound harsh, but consider the situation. A school has a men's lacrosse team and a men's hockey team, and no women's teams in either sport. It can't afford new teams, so it cuts men's lacrosse and creates women's hockey. Although the male lacrosse players will be understandably aggrieved (and so will would-be women's lacrosse players, who never had and never will have a team), the outcome is more fair than the status quo—and that is because of Title IX.

THE CURRENT ASSAULT ON TITLE IX, AND THE ADMINISTRATION'S FAILURE TO DEFEND IT

In February 2002, the National Wrestling Coaches' Association filed a lawsuit against the Department of Education. The Association alleges that the interpretation of Title IX embodied in the Policy Guidance and its subsequent clarification—and still currently in use—is unlawful.

More specifically, the Association argues that this interpretation of the statute authorizes intentional discrimination against male athletes. (Thus, the Association is making the same "reverse discrimination" argument that has failed every time it has been raised before.) Based on this argument, the Association is seeking an order declaring that the Policy Interpretation—and the three-part test it propounded—is invalid and unenforceable.

The Bush Administration had the opportunity in this lawsuit to mount a strong defense of Title IX and its regulations regarding athletics. The argument could have been based on law—consider the many suits dismissing similar "reverse discrimination" claims—not just on policy preferences. Yet instead, the Administration filed a motion to dismiss that cited only narrow technical defects in the lawsuit as a basis for throwing it out of court.

The government's brief is carefully worded to avoid any defense of Title IX on the merits. In fact, the implicit message is to the contrary—that the plaintiffs are wrong only in their choice of defendant (they have sued the government, not the schools), rather than on the merits.

That this Administration will not fight to protect Title IX is clear. So those who support the statute—and more generally, who support equality in women's high school and college athletics—will have to fight for it instead, and fight against the Administration if necessary.

THE RHETORICAL BATTLE OVER TITLE IX

Title IX's critics have tried to score rhetorical points by convincing the public, first, that Title IX's insistence on gender equity is misplaced. They make several arguments, but none are convincing.

First, they claim that women are naturally less interested in sports than men. But in fact, the evidence shows that women's interest in sport is not innately fixed, but dynamic and affected by tangible factors such as playing opportunities and available resources—as well as intangible factors like public opinion and culture.

Watching senior women soccer stars triumph, for example, can motivate a freshman high school girl to follow up on her athletic ambitions. If all the seniors had been cheerleaders and homecoming queens, she might have sacrificed the same ambitions to the ever-present urge to fit in. Are women "naturally" less interested in sports, or "socially" less interested? If the phenomenon is social, it can change.

And it has. Consider the eight-fold rise in female athletic participation at the high school level and the five-fold increase at the college level over the last 30 years—the lifetime of Title IX. It is pretty good—indeed, overwhelming—evidence that opportunities create athletes as much as biology does.

Second, critics often claim that greedy female athletes are responsible for the downfall of men's minor sports. (In our previous scenario, for instance, the men's lacrosse team has been sacrificed so the women's hockey team could be created.)

This argument, too, is unfair and inaccurate. It is unfair for the equality reason given above; women's hockey and lacrosse players should not both have to suffer so men's lacrosse players can prosper. It is inaccurate because of, in a word, football.

The greed and excess, both in terms of participation opportunities and resource allocation, endemic to men's collegiate football programs is by far the greatest reason that other men's sports get the sack. Football, with its unnecessarily large number of players and scholarships (an average of 94 per NCAA Division I team, compared with only 53 per NFL team), eats up the lion's share of athletic resources, which adversely impacts both men's minor sports and women's sports.

And when football is the culprit, there is no equality justification for the loss. The men's lacrosse team loses out simply because the brawnier sport wins out. A man who loses his lacrosse team due to emphasis on football should be upset about the gender-policing of his institution, which prefers more "masculine" sports. In contrast, a man who loses his lacrosse team due to Title IX can at least see that it was unfair that women never had such a team in the first place. But schools themselves feed these misperceptions, often expressly citing Title IX as the reason for cutting a particular men's team.

The reason men's teams must sometimes be cut is because for decades they have received more resources than they should have. Men had almost unlimited opportunities to participate in sports *because* women were denied them, and this denial freed up money the men's teams could use. This artificially inflated allocation of resources—due in large part to stereotypes about women and their lack of interest and ability in sports—does not create an entitlement to have such resources continue.

Ideally, men and women should both have a team in every sport and if the behemoth of football did not consume such huge resources, that might be possible. But if a new women's team must be created at the expense of an old male team, that is only fair. Women are not saying that years of men-only sports should be compensated with the same number of years of women-only sports. Rather, they are only asking for equality today.

Passage of the Nineteenth Amendment (granting women the right to vote) diluted the male vote by half, but nonetheless did not constitute an act of "reverse discrimination." Neither does a reallocation of resources for collegiate sports away from the sex that has historically had plentiful opportunities, and toward the sex that has had few.

Abortion

During the last thirty years, probably no domestic issue has polarized the nation more than abortion. It has been a hotly contested subject in state and national elections and the occasion for repeated mass demonstrations in our nation's capital. That abortion arouses such strong feelings is not surprising, for some see the right to privacy at stake even as others insist that the real issue is the taking of human life.

In the first selection, Susan Estrich and Kathleen Sullivan argue that, if the decision on abortion is taken out of the hands of the mother, then she will necessarily be forced to surrender autonomy over her own body and over family decisions. Government intrusion into these spheres, they insist, would constitute an intolerable infringement on the fundamental right to privacy—a view shared by the Supreme Court when it upheld a woman's right to an abortion in Roe v. Wade *(1973).*

In the second selection, James Bopp and Richard Coleson contend that the Roe v. Wade *decision is a glaring example of judicial power gone wild, with the justices manufacturing a right to privacy in the Constitution where it is nowhere to be found. In doing so, they say, the Court not only violated its own stated criteria for determining what qualifies as a fundamental right, but also arrogated to itself a power that the people alone may exercise. Bopp and Coleson further argue that the right to abortion should be rejected on moral as well as legal grounds, and they challenge pro-choice claims that the outlawing of abortions would have harmful social consequences for women.*

Abortion Politics
The Case for the Right to Privacy

Susan R. Estrich and Kathleen M. Sullivan

I. THE EXISTENCE OF A LIBERTY INTEREST

A. Reproductive Choice Is Essential to a Woman's Control of Her Destiny and Family Life

Notwithstanding the abortion controversy, the Supreme Court has long acknowledged an unenumerated right to privacy as a species of "liberty" that the due process clauses protect.[1] The principle is as ancient as *Meyer v. Nebraska*[2] and *Pierce v. Society of Sisters*,[3] which protected parents' freedom to educate their children free of the state's controlling hand. In its modern elaboration, this right continues to protect child rearing and family life from the overly intrusive reach of government.[4] The modern privacy cases have also plainly established that decisions whether to bear children are no less fundamental than decisions about how to raise them. The Court has consistently held since *Griswold v. Connecticut*[5] that the Constitution accords special protection to "matters so fundamentally affecting a person as the decision whether to bear or beget a child," and has therefore strictly scrutinized laws restricting contraception.[6] Roe held that these principles extend no less to abortion than to contraception.

The privacy cases rest, as Justice Stevens recognized in *Thornburgh*, centrally on "'the moral fact that a person belongs to himself [or herself] and not others nor to society as a whole.' "[7] Extending this principle to the abortion decision follows from the fact that "[f]ew decisions are . . . more basic to individual dignity and autonomy" or more appropriate to the "private sphere of individual liberty" than the uniquely personal, intimate, and self-defining decision whether or not to continue a pregnancy.[8]

Susan R. Estrich is Robert Kingsley Professor of Law at the University of Southern California, and Kathleen M. Sullivan is Richard E. Lang Professor of Law and dean of Stanford University Law School. This selection is from Susan R. Estrich and Kathleen M. Sullivan, "Abortion Politics: Writing for an Audience of One," *University of Pennsylvania Law Review*, 138:125–132, pp. 150–155 (1989). Copyright © 1989 by the University of Pennsylvania. Reprinted by permission. Notes were renumbered to correspond with edited text.

In two senses, abortion restrictions keep a woman from "belonging to herself." First and most obviously, they deprive her of bodily self-possession. As Chief Justice Rehnquist observed in another context, pregnancy entails "profound physical, emotional, and psychological consequences."[9] To name a few, pregnancy increases a woman's uterine size 500–1,000 times, her pulse rate by 10 to 15 beats a minute, and her body weight by 25 pounds or more.[10] Even the healthiest pregnancy can entail nausea, vomiting, more frequent urination, fatigue, back pain, labored breathing, or water retention.[11] There are also numerous medical risks involved in carrying pregnancy to term: of every 10 women who experience pregnancy and childbirth, 6 need treatment for some medical complication, and 3 need treatment for major complications.[12] In addition, labor and delivery impose extraordinary physical demands, whether over the 6-to-12 hour or longer course of vaginal delivery, or during the highly invasive surgery involved in a cesarean section, which accounts for one out of four deliveries.[13]

By compelling pregnancy to term and delivery even where they are unwanted, abortion restrictions thus exert far more profound intrusions into bodily integrity than the stomach-pumping the Court invalidated in *Rochin v. California*,[14] or the surgical removal of a bullet from a shoulder that the Court invalidated in *Winston v. Lee*.[15] "The integrity of an individual's person is a cherished value of our society"[16] because it is so essential to identity: as former Solicitor General Charles Fried, who argued for the United States in *Webster*, recognized in another context: "[to say] that my body can be used is [to say] that I can be used."[17]

These points would be too obvious to require restatement if the state attempted to compel abortions rather than to restrict them. Indeed, in colloquy with Justice O'Connor during the *Webster* oral argument, former Solicitor General Fried conceded that in such a case, liberty principles, although unenumerated, would compel the strictest view. To be sure, as Mr. Fried suggested, restrictive abortion laws do not literally involve "laying hands on a woman."[18] But this distinction should make no difference: the state would plainly infringe its citizens' bodily integrity whether its agents inflicted knife wounds or its laws forbade surgery or restricted blood transfusions in cases of private knifings.[19]

Apart from this impact on bodily integrity, abortion restrictions infringe a woman's autonomy in a second sense as well; they invade the autonomy in family affairs that the Supreme Court has long deemed central to the right of privacy. Liberty requires independence in making the most important decisions in life.[20] "The decision whether or not to beget or bear a child" lies at "the very heart of this cluster of constitutionally protected choices,"[21] because few decisions can more importantly alter the course of one's life than the decision to bring a child into the world. Bearing a child dramatically affects "'what a person is, what [s]he wants, the determination of [her] life plan, of [her] concept of the good'" and every other aspect of the "'self-determination . . . [that] give[s] substance to the concept of liberty.'"[22] Becoming a parent dramatically alters a woman's educational prospects,[23] employment opportunities,[24] and sense of self.[25] In light of these elemental facts, it is no surprise that the freedom to choose one's own family formation is "deeply rooted in this Nation's history and tradition."[26]

Today, virtually no one disputes that these principles require heightened scrutiny of laws restricting access to contraception.[27] But critics of *Roe* sometimes argue that abortion is "different in kind from the decision not to conceive in the first place."[28] Justice White, for example, has asserted that, while the liberty interest is fundamental in the contraception context,[29] that interest falls to minimal after conception.[30]

Such a distinction cannot stand, however, because no bright line can be drawn between contraception and abortion in light of modern scientific and medical advances. Contraception and abortion are points on a continuum. Even "conception" itself is a complex process of which fertilization is simply the first stage. According to contemporary medical authorities, conception begins not with fertilization, but rather six to seven days later when the fertilized egg becomes implanted in the uterine wall, itself a complex process.[31] Many medically accepted contraceptives operate after fertilization. For example, both oral contraceptives and the intra-uterine device (IUD) not only prevent fertilization but in some instances prevent implantation.[32] Moreover, the most significant new developments in contraceptive technology, such as RU486, act by foiling implantation.[33] All such contraceptives blur the line between contraception and abortion.

In the absence of a bright physiological line, there can be no bright constitutional line between the moments before and after conception. A woman's fundamental liberty does not simply evaporate when sperm meets ovum. Indeed, as Justice Stevens has recognized, "if one decision is more 'fundamental' to the individual's freedom than the other, surely it is the postconception decision that is the more serious."[34] Saying this much does not deny that profound evolutionary changes occur between fertilization and birth. Clearly, there is some difference between "the freshly fertilized egg and . . . the 9-month-gestated . . . fetus on the eve of birth."[35] But as *Roe v. Wade* fully recognized, such differences go at most to the weight of the state's justification for interfering with a pregnancy; they do not extinguish the underlying fundamental liberty.

Thus *Roe* is not a mere "thread" that the Court could pull without "unravel[ing]" the now elaborately woven "fabric" of the privacy decisions.[36] Rather, *Roe* is integral to the principle that childbearing decisions come to "th[e] Court with a momentum for respect that is lacking when appeal is made to liberties which derive merely from shifting economic arrangements."[37] The decision to become a mother is too fundamental to be equated with the decision to buy a car, choose optometry over ophthalmology, take early retirement, or any other merely economic decision that the government may regulate by showing only a minimally rational basis.

B. Keeping Reproductive Choice in Private Hands Is Essential to a Free Society

Even if there were any disagreement about the degree of bodily or decisional autonomy that is essential to personhood, there is a separate, alternative rationale for the privacy cases: keeping the state out of the business of reproductive decision making. Regimentation of reproduction is a hallmark of the totalitarian state, from Plato's Republic to Hitler's Germany, from Huxley's *Brave New World* to Atwood's *A Handmaid's Tale*. Whether the state compels reproduction or prevents it, "totalitarian limitation of family size . . . is at complete variance with our constitutional concepts."[38] The state's monopoly of force cautions against any official reproductive orthodoxy.

For these reasons, the Supreme Court has long recognized that the privacy right protects not only the individual but also our society. As early as *Meyer*[39] and *Pierce*,[40] the Court acknowledged that "[t]he fundamental theory of liberty" on which a free society rests "excludes any general power of the State to standardize" its citizens.[41] As Justice Powell likewise recognized for the Moore plurality, "a free society" is one that avoids the homogenization of family life.[42]

The right of privacy, like freedoms of speech and religion, protects conscience and spirit from the encroachment of overbearing government. "Struggles to coerce uniformity of sentiment," Justice Jackson recognized in *West Virginia State Board of Education v. Barnett*,[43] are the inevitably futile province of "our totalitarian enemies."[44] Preserving a private sphere for childbearing and childbearing decisions not only liberates the individual; it desirably constrains the state.[45]

Those who would relegate all control over abortion to the state legislatures ignore these fundamental, systematic values. It is a red herring to focus on the question of judicial versus legislative control of reproductive decisions, as so many of *Roe's* critics do. The real distinction is that between private and public control of the decision: the private control that the courts protect through *Griswold* and *Roe*, and the public control that the popular branches could well usurp in a world without those decisions.

Precisely because of the importance of a private sphere for family, spirit, and conscience, the framers never intended to commit all moral disagreements to the political arena. Quite the contrary:

> The very purpose of a Bill of Rights was to withdraw certain subjects from the vicissitudes of political controversy, to place them beyond the reach of majorities and officials and to establish them as legal principles to be applied by the courts. One's right to life, liberty, and property, to free speech, a free press, freedom of worship and assembly, and other fundamental rights may not be submitted to vote; they depend on the outcome of no elections.[46]

Such "withdrawal" of fundamental liberties from the political arena is basic to constitutional democracy as opposed to rank majoritarianism, and nowhere is such "withdrawal" more important than in controversies where moral convictions and passions run deepest. The inclusion of the free exercise clause attests to this point.[47]

The framers also never intended that toleration on matters of family, conscience, and spirit would vary from state to state. The value of the states and localities as "laborator[ies for] . . . social and economic experiments"[48] has never extended to "'experiments at the expense of the dignity and personality of the individual.'"[49] Rather as Madison once warned, "'it is proper to take alarm at the first experiment on our liberties. We hold this prudent jealousy to be the first duty of citizens, and one of [the] noblest characteristics of the late Revolution.'"[50]

Roe v. Wade thus properly withdrew the abortion decision, like other decisions on matters of conscience, "from the vicissitudes of political controversy." It did not withdraw that decision from the vicissitudes of moral argument or social suasion by persuasive rather than coercive means.[51] In withdrawing the abortion decision from the hot lights of politics, Roe protected not only persons but the processes of constitutional democracy. . . .

II. THE POLITICAL PROCESS: NOT TO BE TRUSTED

On October 13, 1989, the *New York Times* declared that the tide had turned in the political process on abortion.[52] The Florida legislature, in special session, rejected a series of proposals to restrict abortion, and Congress voted to expand abortion funding for poor women to cases of rape and incest. And most stunningly of all, the Attorney General of Illinois on November 2, 1989, settled a pending challenge to Illinois' abortion clinic regulation rather than risk winning his case in the United States Supreme Court. These events have triggered the assessment that the post-*Webster* pro-choice mobilization has succeeded. Which raises the question: why not leave these matters to the political process?

The short answer, of course, is that we don't leave freedom of speech or religion or association to the political process, even on good days when the polls suggest they might stand a chance, at least in some states. The very essence of a fundamental right is that it "depend[s] on the outcome of no elections."[53]

The long answer is, as always, that fundamental liberties are not occasions for the experimentation that federalism invites. The right to abortion should not depend on where you live and how much money you have for travel.[54] And, regardless of our recent, at-long-last successes, the reality remains that the political process is to be trusted the least where, as here, it imposes burdens unequally.

The direct impact of abortion restrictions falls exclusively on a class of people that consists entirely of women. Only women get pregnant. Only women have abortions. Only women will endure unwanted pregnancies and adverse health consequences if states restrict abortions. Only women will suffer dangerous, illegal abortions where legal ones are unavailable. And only women will bear children if they cannot obtain abortions.[55] Yet every restrictive abortion law has been passed by a legislature in which men constitute a numerical majority. And every restrictive abortion law, by definition, contains an unwritten clause exempting all men from its strictures.

As Justice Jackson wrote, legislators threaten liberty when they pass laws that exempt themselves or people like them: "The framers of the Constitution knew, and we should not forget today, that there is no more effective practical guaranty against arbitrary and unreasonable government than to require that the principles of law which officials would impose upon a minority must be imposed generally."[56] The Supreme Court has long interpreted the equal protection clause to require even-handedness in legislation, lest the powerful few too casually trade away for others key liberties that they are careful to reserve for themselves.

For example, in striking down a law permitting castration of recidivist chicken thieves but sparing white collar embezzlers the knife, the Court implied that, put to an all-or-nothing choice, legislators would rather sterilize no one than jeopardize a politically potent class.[57] In the words of Justice Jackson: "There are limits to the extent to which a legislatively represented majority may conduct biological experiments at the expense of the dignity and personality and natural powers of a minority—even those who are guilty of what the majority defines as crimes."[58]

At least there should be. Relying on state legislatures, as Chief Justice Rehnquist would, to protect women against "abortion regulation reminiscent of the dark ages,"[59] ignores the fact that the overwhelming majority of "those who serve in such bodies"[60] are biologically exempt from the penalties they are imposing.

The danger is greater still when the subject is abortion. The lessons of history are disquieting. Abortion restrictions, like the most classic restrictions on women seeking to participate in the worlds of work and ideas, have historically rested on archaic stereotypes portraying women as persons whose "paramount destiny and mission . . . [is] to fulfill the noble and benign office of wife and mother."[61] Legislation prohibiting abortion, largely a product of the years between 1860 and 1880, reflected *precisely* the same ideas about women's natural and proper roles as other legislation from the same period, long since discredited, that prohibited women from serving on juries or participating in the professions, including the practice of law.[62] And modern studies have found that support for laws banning abortion continues to be an outgrowth of the same stereotypical notions that women's only appropriate roles are those of mother and housewife. In many cases, abortion laws are a direct reaction to the increasing number of women who work outside of the home.[63] Those involved in anti-abortion activities tend to echo the well-known views of Justice Bradley in *Bradwell:*

> Men and women, as a result of . . . intrinsic differences, have different roles to play. Men are best suited to the public world of work, whereas women are best suited to rearing children, managing homes, and loving and caring for husbands. . . . Mothering, in their view, is itself a full-time job, and any woman who cannot commit herself fully to mothering should eschew it entirely.[64]

But the lessons of history are not limited to the powers of enduring stereotypes. History also makes clear that a world without *Roe* will not be a world without abortion but a world in which abortion is accessible according to one's constitutional case. While affluent women will travel to jurisdictions where safe and legal abortions are available, paying whatever is necessary, restrictive abortion laws and with them, the life-threatening prospect of back-alley abortion, will disproportionately descend upon "those without . . . adequate resources" to avoid them.[65] Those for whom the burdens of an unwanted pregnancy may be the most crushing—the young, the poor, women whose color already renders them victims of discrimination—will be the ones least able to secure a safe abortion.

In the years before *Roe*, "[p]oor and minority women were virtually precluded from obtaining safe, legal procedures, the overwhelming majority of which were obtained by white women in the private hospital services on psychiatric indications."[66] Women without access to safe and legal abortions often had dangerous and illegal ones. According to one study, mishandled criminal abortions were the leading cause of maternal deaths in the 1960s,[67] and mortality rates for African-American women were as much as nine times the rate for white women.[68] To trust the political process to protect these women is to ignore the lessons of history and the realities of power and powerlessness in America today.

In the face of such lessons, those who would have us put our faith in the political process might first want to look a little more closely at the victories which are said to support such a choice. The Florida legislature's rejection of proposed abortion restrictions came days *after* the state's highest court held that the State Constitution protects the right to choose abortion, rendering the entire session, by the press's verdict before it began, symbolic at best. The session was still a triumph, but hardly one in which the courts were beside the point. And while extending funding to cases of rape and incest would have been a step forward, the narrowness of the victory and the veto of the resulting legislation should give pause, at least.[69]

We believe that energizing and mobilizing pro-choice voters, and women in particular, is vitally important on its own terms. We hope, frankly, that with apportionment approaching in 2000, that mobilization will affect issues well beyond abortion. We hope more women will find themselves running for office and winning. We hope pro-choice voters and the legislators they elect will attack a range of issues of particular importance to women, including the attention that children receive after they are born.

But we have no illusions. We will lose some along the way. Young and poor and minority women will pay most dearly when we do. That's the way it is in politics. That's why politics should not dictate constitutional rights. . . .

NOTES

1. The right of privacy is only one among many instances in which the Court has recognized rights that are not expressly named in the Constitution's text. To name just a few other examples, the Court has recognized unenumerated rights to freedom of association, see *National Association for the Advancement of Colored People v. Alabama,* 357 U.S. 449, 466 (1958); to equal protection under the Fifth Amendment due process clause, see *Bolling v. Sharpe,* 347 U.S. 497, 500 (1954); to travel between the states, see *Shapiro v. Thompson,* 394 U.S. 618, 638 (1966); to vote, see *Harper v. Virginia Bd. of Elections,* 383 U.S. 663, 665–66 (1966); *Reynolds v. Sims,* 377 U.S. 533, 554 (1964); and to attend criminal trials, see *Richmond Newspapers Inc. v. Virginia,* 448 U.S. 555, 579–80 (1980).
2. 262 U.S. 390 (1923).

3. 268 U.S. 510 (1925).
4. See, e.g., *Moore v. City of East Cleveland*, 431 U.S. 494, 503–06 (1977) (plurality opinion) (noting a constitutional right to live with one's grandchildren); *Loving v. Virginia*, 388 U.S. 1, 12 (1967) (affirming a right to interracial marriage).
5. 381 U.S. 479 (1965).
6. *Eisenstadt v. Baird*, 405 U.S. 438, 453 (1972).
7. *Thornburgh v. American College of Obstetricians & Gynecologists*, 476 U.S. 747, 777 n.5 (1985) (Stevens, J., concurring) (quoting former Solicitor General Fried, "Correspondence," 6 *Phil. & Pub. Aff.* 288–89 (1977)).
8. *Thornburgh*, 476 U.S. at 772.
9. *Michael M. v. Sonoma County Superior Court*, 480 U.S. 464, 471 (1981).
10. See J. Pritchard, P. McDonald & N. Gant, *Williams Obstetrics*, 181–210, 260–63 (17th ed. 1985) [hereinafter *Williams Obstetrics*].
11. See *Id.*
12. See R. Gold, A. Kenney & S. Singh, *Blessed Events and the Bottom Line: Financing Maternity Care in the United States*, 10 (1987).
13. See D. Danforth, M. Hughey & A. Wagner, The *Complete Guide to Pregnancy*, 228–31 (1983); S. Romney, M. J. Gray, A. B. Little, J. Merrill, E. J. Quilligan & R. Stander, *Gynecology and Obstetrics: The Health Care of Women*, 626–37 (2d ed. 1981).
14. 342 U.S. 165 (1952).
15. 470 U.S. 753 (1985).
16. *Id.* at 760.
17. C. Fried, *Right and Wrong*, 121 n.* (1978).
18. "Transcript of Oral Argument in Abortion Case," *N.Y. Times*, Apr. 27, 1989, at B12, col. 5.
19. Likewise, a state would surely infringe reproductive freedom by compelling abortions even if it became technologically possible to do so without "laying hands on a woman."
20. See *Whalen v. Roe*, 429 U.S. 589, 599–600 (1977).
21. *Carey v. Population Serv. Int'l*, 431 U.S. 678, 685 (1977).
22. *Thornburgh v. American College of Obstetricians & Gynecologists*, 476 U.S. 747, 777 n.5 (1985) (Stevens, J., concurring) (quoting C. Fried, *Right and Wrong*, 146–47 (1978)).
23. Teenage mothers have high dropout rates: 8 out of 10 who become mothers at age 17 or younger do not finish high school. See Fielding, *Adolescent Pregnancy Revisited*, 299 Mass. Dep't Pub. Health, 893, 894 (1978).
24. Control over the rate of childbirth is a key factor in explaining recent gains in women's wages relative to men's. See Fuchs, "Women's Quest for Economic Equality," 3 *J. Econ. Persp.* 25, 33–37 (1989).
25. This fact is evident even if the biological mother does not raise her child. Relinquishing a child for adoption may alleviate material hardship, but it is psychologically traumatic. See Winkler & VanKeppel, *Relinquishing Mothers in Adoption: Their Long-Term Adjustment*, Monograph No. 3, Institute of Family Studies (1984).

26. *Moore v. City of East Cleveland,* 431 U.S. 494, 503 (1977) (plurality opinion).
27. The United States has conceded before the Supreme Court that the *Griswold* line of cases was correctly decided. See *Brief for the United States as Amicus Curiae Supporting Appellants,* 11–13; *Webster v. Reproductive Health Serv.,* 1109 S.Ct. 3040 (1989) (No. 88-605); "Transcript of Oral Argument in Abortion Case," *N.Y. Times,* Apr. 27, 1989, at B13, col. 1 (Argument of former Solicitor General Fried on behalf of the United States).
28. *Thornburgh,* 476 U.S. at 792 n.2 (White, J., dissenting).
29. See *Eisenstadt v. Baird,* 405 U.S. 438, 463–64 (1972) (White, J., concurring in result); *Griswold v. Connecticut,* 381 U.S. 479, 502–03 (1965) (White, J., concurring in judgment).
30. See *Thornburgh,* 476 U.S. at 792 n.2 (White, J., dissenting) (arguing that the fetus's presence after conception changes not merely the state justification but "the characterization of the liberty interest itself").
31. See *Williams Obstetrics, supra* note 10, at 88–91; Milby, "The New Biology and the Question of Personhood: Implications for Abortion," *9 Am. J.L. & Med.* 31, 39–41 (1983). Indeed, the American College of Obstetricians & Gynecologists, the preeminent authority on such matters, has adopted the following official definition of conception: conception consists of "the implantation of the blastocyst [fertilized ovum]" in the uterus, and thus is "not synonymous with fertilization." *Obstetric-Gynecologic Terminology* 229, 327 (E. Hughes ed. 1972). Such a definition is not surprising in view of the fact that less than half of fertilized ova ever successfully become implanted. See "Post-Coital Contraception," 1 *The Lancet* 855, 856 (1983).
32. See R. Hatcher, E. Guest, F. Stewart, G. Stewart, J. Trussell, S. Bowen & W. Gates, *Contraceptive Technology,* 252–53, 377 (14th rev. ed. 1988) [hereinafter *Contraceptive Technology*]; *United States Department of Health and Human Services, IUDs: Guidelines for Informed Decision-Making and Use* (1987).
33. See *Contraceptive Technology, supra* note 32, at 378; Nieman, Choate, Chrousas, Healy, Morin, Renquist, Merriam, Spitz, Bardin, Balieu & Loriaux, "The Progesterone Antagonist RU486: A Potential New Contraceptive Agent," 316 *N. Eng. J. Med.* 187 (1987). RU486 is approved for use in France but not in the United States.
34. *Thornburgh,* 476 U.S. at 776 (Stevens, J., concurring).
35. *Id.* at 779.
36. "Transcript of Oral Argument in Abortion Case," *N.Y. Times,* April 27, 1989, at B12, col. 5 (former Solicitor General Fried, arguing on behalf of the United States). Counsel for Appellees gave the following complete reply: "It has always been my personal experience that when I pull a thread, my sleeve falls off." *Id.* at B13, col. 1 (argument of Mr. Susman).
37. *Thornburgh,* 476 U.S. at 775 (Stevens, J., concurring) (citing *Griswold v. Connecticut,* 381 U.S. 479, 502–03 (1965) (White, J., dissenting)).
38. *Griswold,* 381 U.S. at 497 (Goldberg, J., concurring).
39. *Meyer v. Nebraska,* 262 U.S. 390 (1923).
40. *Pierce v. Society of Sisters,* 268 U.S. 510 (1925).
41. *Id.* at 535.

42. See *Moore v. City of East Cleveland*, 431 U.S. 494, 503 n.11 (1977) (quoting from a discussion of *Griswold* in Pollak, "Thomas I. Emerson, Lawyer and Scholar: *Ipse Custodiet Custodes*," 84 Yale L.J. 638, 653 (1975)).
43. 319 U.S. 624 (1943).
44. *Id*. at 640–41.
45. See generally Rubenfeld, "The Right of Privacy," 102 *Harv. L. Rev.* 737, 804–07 (1989) (arguing that the constitutional right of privacy protects individuals from being turned into instrumentalities of the regimenting state, or being forced into a state-chosen identity).
46. *Barnette*, 319 U.S. at 638.
47. Justice Douglas wrote:

    > The Fathers of the Constitution were not unaware of the varied and extreme views of religious sects, of the violence of disagreement among them, and of the lack of any one religious creed on which all men would agree. They fashioned a charter of government which envisaged the widest possible toleration of conflicting views.

    United States v. Ballard, 322 U.S. 78, 87 (1944). See also *Webster*, 109 S. Ct. at 3085 & n.16 (Stevens, J., concurring in part and dissenting in part) (noting that "the intensely divisive character of much of the national debate over the abortion issue reflects the deeply held religious convictions of many participants in the debate").
48. *New State Ice Co. v. Liebmann*, 285 U.S. 262, 311 (1932) (Brandeis, J., dissenting).
49. *Poe v. Ullman*, 367 U.S. 497, 555 (1961) (Harlan, J., dissenting) (quoting *Skinner v. Oklahoma*, 316 U.S. 535, 546 (1942) (Jackson, J., concurring)).
50. *Everson v. Board of Educ.*, 330 U.S. 1, 65 (1947) (Appendix, Rutledge, J., dissenting) (quoting Madison, *Memorial and Remonstrance Against Religious Assessments*).
51. Nor, of course, did it bar political efforts to reduce the abortion rate through noncoercive means, such as funding sex education and contraception, or providing economic security to indigent mothers.
52. See Apple, "An Altered Political Climate Suddenly Surrounds Abortion," *N.Y. Times*, Oct. 13, 1989, at A1, col. 4; see also Berke, "The Abortion-Rights Movement Has Its Day," *N.Y. Times*, Oct. 15, 1989, § 4 at 1, col. 1.
53. *West Virginia Bd. of Educ. v. Barnette*, 319 U.S. 624, 638 (1943).
54. Even if only 10 or 11 states were to preclude abortion within their borders, many women would be held hostage there by the combination of geography, poverty, and youth. This situation would be no more tolerable than the enforcement of racial segregation in a "mere" ten or eleven states in the 1950s.
55. See *Michael M. v. Sonoma County Superior Court*, 450 U.S. 464, 473 (1981) ("[V]irtually all of the significant harmful and inescapably identifiable consequences of teenage pregnancy fall on the young female").
56. *Railway Express Agency v. New York*, 336 U.S. 106, 112 (1949) (Jackson, J., concurring).
57. See *Skinner v. Oklahoma*, 316 U.S. 535 (1942). Cf. Epstein, "The Supreme Court, 1987 Term: Foreword: Unconstitutional Conditions, State Power,

and the Limits of Consent," 102 *Harv. L. Rev.* 4 (1988) (arguing that enforcement of unconstitutional conditions doctrine similarly functions to put
legislatures to an all-or-nothing choice).

58. *Skinner,* 316 U.S. at 546 (Jackson, J., concurring).
59. *Webster,* 109 S. Ct. at 3045.
60. *Id.*
61. *Bradwell v. Illinois,* 83 U.S. (16 Wall.) 130, 142 (1873) (Bradley, J., concurring).
62. See J. Mohr, *Abortion in America: The Origins and Evolution of National Policy.
    1800–1900,* at 168–72 (1978). To many of the doctors who were largely
    responsible for abortion restrictions, "the chief purpose of women was to
    produce children; anything that interfered with that purpose, or allowed
    women to 'indulge' themselves in less important activities, threatened . . .
    the future of society itself." *Id.* at 169. The view of one such 19th-century
    doctor drew the parallel even more explicitly: he complained that "the ten-
    dency to force women into men's places" was creating the insidious new
    idea that a woman's "ministrations . . . as a mother should be abandoned
    for the sterner rights of voting and law making." *Id.* at 105; see also
    L. Gordon, *Woman's Body, Woman's Right: A Social History of Birth Control in
    America* (1976) (chronicling the social and political history of reproductive
    rights in the United States).
63. See generally K. Luker, *Abortion and the Politics of Motherhood,* 192–215 (1984)
    (describing how the abortion debate, among women, represents a "war"
    between the feminist vision of women in society and the homemaker's world
    view); Luker, "Abortion and the Meaning of Life," in *Abortion: Understanding
    Differences* 25, 31–33 (S. Callahan & D. Callahan eds. 1984) (concluding that
    "[b]ecause many prolife people see sex as literally sacred, *and because, for
    women, procreative sex is a fundamental part of their career* . . . abortion is, from
    their [the prolife] point of view, to turn the world upside down").
64. Luker, *supra* note 63, at 31. It is, of course, precisely such stereotypes, as
    they are reflected in legislation, which have over and over again been the
    focus of this Court's modern equal protection cases. See, e.g., *Califano v.
    Goldfarb,* 430 U.S. 199, 206–07 (1977) ("Gender-based differentiation . . . is
    forbidden by the Constitution, at least when supported by no more sub-
    stantial justification than 'archaic and overbroad' generalizations.");
    Weinberger v. Wiesenfeld, 420 U.S. 636, 645 (1975) ("Gender-based general-
    izations" that men are more likely than women to support their families
    "cannot suffice to justify the denigration of the effects of women who do
    work. . . ."); *Stanton v. Stanton,* 421 U.S. 7, 14 (1975) ("A child, male or
    female, is still a child. No longer is the female destined solely for the home
    and the rearing of the family, and only the male for the marketplace and the
    world of ideas."); *Frontiero v. Richardson,* 441 U.S. 677, 684 (1973) ("[O]ur
    Nation has had a long and unfortunate history of sex discrimination . . .
    which in practical effect put women, not on a pedestal, but in a cage.").
65. *Griswold v. Connecticut,* 318 U.S. 479, 503 (1965) (White, J., concurring).
66. *Polgar & Fried,* "The Bad Old Days: Clandestine Abortions Among the Poor
    in New York City Before Liberalization of the Abortion Law," 8 *Fam. Plan.*

Persp. 125 (1976); see also Gold, "Therapeutic Abortions in New York: A 20-Year Review," 55 *Am J. Pub. Health* 964, 66 (1965) (noting that the ratio of legal hospital abortions per live birth was 5 times more for white women than for women of color, and 26 times more for white women than for Puerto Rican women in New York City from 1951–62); Pilpel, "The Abortion Crisis," in *The Case for Legalized Abortion Now* 97, 101 (Guttmacher ed. 1967) (noting that 93% of in-hospital abortions in New York State were performed on white women who were able to afford private rooms).

67. See Niswander, "Medical Abortion Practice in the United States," in *Abortion and the Law,* 37, 37 (D. Smith ed. 1967).
68. See Gold, *supra* note 66, at 964–65.
69. Requiring prompt reporting of cases of rape and incest to criminal authorities, measured in terms of days if not hours, as the White House has suggested, is to ignore study after study that has found precisely such cases among the least often reported to the police. Yet late reporting, which should be encouraged, becomes grounds to deny funding, and excludes altogether those who fear, often with reasons, to report at all. The pain and suffering of brutal victimization and of an unwanted pregnancy are in no way affected by the speed of the initial criminal report. A small victory, indeed.

President Bush vetoed the legislation on October 21, 1989. The House vote to override was 231–191, short of the necessary two-thirds majority. See 135 *Cong. Rec.* H7482-95 (daily ed. Oct. 25, 1989).

Abortion on Demand Has No Constitutional or Moral Justification

James Bopp Jr. and Richard E. Coleson

I. THE ABSENCE OF A CONSTITUTIONAL RIGHT TO ABORTION

Abortion is not mentioned in the United States Constitution. Yet, in *Roe v. Wade*,[1] the United States Supreme Court held that there is a constitutional right to abortion.

How could the Court justify such a decision? Actually, it never did. The Court simply *asserted* that the "right of privacy . . . is broad enough to encompass a woman's decision whether or not to terminate her pregnancy."[2] Leading constitutional scholars were outraged at the Court's action in *Roe* and vigorously argued that the Court had no constitutional power to create new constitutional rights in this fashion.[3] And, of course, many people were incensed that a whole class of innocent human beings—those awaiting birth—was stripped of all rights, including the right to life itself.

Why does it matter whether abortion is found in the Constitution? Why shouldn't the United States Supreme Court be free to create new constitutional rights whenever it chooses? The answers lie in the carefully designed structure of our democracy, whose blueprints were drawn over two centuries ago by the framers of the Constitution and ratified by the People. This design is explained below as the foundation for rejecting abortion on demand on a constitutional basis.

But what of abortion on demand as a legislative issue? Even if there is no constitutional right to abortion, how much should state legislatures restrict abortion? The answer lies in the states' compelling interest in protecting innocent human life, born or preborn. This interest is given scant attention by abortion rights advocates. Rather, they envision an extreme abortion-on-demand regime; but their societal vision is overwhelmingly rejected by public opinion. As shown below, the states constitutionally may and morally should limit abortion on demand.

James Bopp Jr. is an attorney in the law firm Bopp, Coleson, & Bostrom (Terre Haute, Indiana) and general counsel to the National Right to Life Committee Inc. Richard E. Coleson is an associate with Bopp, Coleson, & Bostrom and general counsel to Indiana Citizens for Life Inc. This article was written especially for *Points of View* in 1992.

A. The People Have Created a Constitutional Democracy with Certain Matters Reserved to Democratic Control and Other Matters Constitutionally Protected

The United States Constitution begins with the words "We the People of the United States . . . do ordain and establish this Constitution for the United States of America."[4] Thus, our Republic is founded on the cornerstone of democratic self-governance—all authority to govern is granted by the People.[5] The only legitimate form of government is that authorized by the People; the only rightful authority is that which the People have granted to the institutions of government.[6]

The People have chosen to authorize a regime governed by the rule of law, rather than rule by persons.[7] The supreme law of the land is the Constitution,[8] the charter by which the People conferred authority to govern and created the governing institutions. Thus, the only legitimate form and authority for governance are found in the Constitution.

The constitutional grant of governing authority was not a general grant but one carefully measured, balanced, and limited. Three fundamental principles underlie the Constitution: (1) the People have removed certain matters from simple majority rule by making them constitutional rights but have retained other matters to be democratically controlled through their elected representatives[9]; (2) the People have distributed governmental powers among three branches of government, with each limited to its own sphere of power[10]; and (3) the People have established a federal system in which the power to regulate certain matters is granted to the national government and all remaining power is retained by the states or by the People themselves.[11]

Because these fundamental principles were violated by the Supreme Court in *Roe v. Wade*,[12] leading constitutional scholars condemned the decision. Law professors and dissenting Supreme Court Justices declared that the Court had seized power not granted to it in the Constitution, because (1) it had created new constitutional rights, which power only the People have,[13] (2) it had acted as a legislature rather than as a court,[14] and (3) it had trespassed into an area governed by the states for over two centuries.[15] The scholarly rejection of *Roe v. Wade* continues to the present.[16]

Although the Court's power grab in *Roe* was a seizure less obvious to the public than tanks in the street, it has nevertheless been rightly characterized as a "limited *coup d'état*."[17] The Court seized from the People a matter they had left to their own democratic governance by declaring a constitutional right to abortion without establishing any connection between the Constitution and a right to abortion. Richard Epstein attacked the Court's *Roe* decision thus, "*Roe* . . . is symptomatic of the analytical poverty possible in constitutional litigation."[18] He concluded: "[W]e must criticize both Mr. Justice Blackmun in *Roe v. Wade* . . . and the entire method of constitutional interpretation that allows the Supreme Court . . . both to 'define' and to 'balance' interests on the major social and political issues of our time."[19]

B. To Determine Which Matters Are Constitutionally Removed from Democratic Control, the Supreme Court Has Developed Tests to Determine Fundamental Rights

The Court did not violate the Constitution in *Roe* simply because there is no *express* mention of abortion in the Constitution. There are matters which the Constitution does not *expressly* mention which the Supreme Court has legitimately found to be within some express constitutional protection. But where the Court employs such constitutional analysis, it must clearly demonstrate that the newly recognized constitutional right properly falls within the scope of an express right. This requires a careful examination and explanation of what the People intended when they ratified the particular constitutional provision in question. It was the *Roe* Court's failure to provide this logical connection between the Constitution and a claimed right to abortion which elicited scholarly outrage.

Under the Supreme Court's own tests, the Court had to find that the claimed right to abortion was a "fundamental" right in order to extend constitutional protection to it under the Fourteenth Amendment, the constitutional provision in which the Court claimed to have found a right to abortion.[20] The Fourteenth Amendment guarantees that no "State [shall] deprive any person of life, liberty, or property, without due process of law."[21] While the provision on its face seems to guarantee only proper legal proceedings before a state may impose capital punishment, imprisonment, or a fine, the Court has assumed the authority to examine activities asserted as constitutional rights to determine whether—in the Court's opinion—they fall within the concept of "liberty."[22] The notion that the Court may create new constitutional rights at will by reading them into the "liberty" clause of the Fourteenth Amendment could readily lead to a rejection of the foundational constitutional premise of the rule of law, not of persons. If a handful of Justices can place whatever matters they wish under the umbrella of the Constitution—totally bypassing the People and their elected representatives—then these Justices have constituted themselves as Platonic guardians,[23] thereby rejecting the rule of law for the rule of persons. What would prevent a majority of the Supreme Court from declaring that there is a constitutional right to practice, e.g., infanticide or polygamy (matters which the states have historically governed)?

This danger has caused many scholars to reject the sort of analysis which allows five Justices (a majority of the Court) to read new constitutional rights into the "liberty" clause.[24] It led the Court in earlier years to forcefully repudiate the sort of analysis the Court used in *Roe v. Wade.*[25] This danger has caused the current Court to establish more rigorous tests for what constitutes a constitutional right to prevent the Supreme Court from "roaming at large in the constitutional field."[26] These tests had been established at the time of *Roe,* but were ignored in that case.[27]

The Court has developed two tests for determining whether a new constitutional right should be recognized. The first test asks whether an asserted fundamental right is "implicit in the concept of ordered liberty."[28] The second test—a historical test—is whether the right asserted as "fundamental" is "so rooted in the traditions and conscience of our people as to be ranked as fundamental."[29] The historical test is the one now primarily relied upon by the Court.

C. Applying the Proper Test for Determining Constitutional Rights Reveals That Abortion Is Not a Constitutional Right

In *Roe*, the Court should have determined whether or not there is a constitutional right to abortion by asking whether it has historically been treated as "implicit in the concept of ordered liberty" in this nation or whether it has been "deeply rooted [as a right] in this Nation's history and tradition."

The *Roe* opinion itself recounted how abortion had been regulated by the states by statutory law for over a century and before that it had been regulated by the judge-made common law inherited from England.[30] In fact, the period from 1860 to 1880—the Fourteenth Amendment was ratified in 1868[31]—saw "the most important burst of anti-abortion legislation in the nation's history."[32] Therefore, the framers of the Fourteenth Amendment and the People who ratified it clearly did not intend for the Amendment to protect the right to abortion, which was considered a crime at the time.

Now Chief Justice Rehnquist stated well the case against *Roe*'s right to abortion in his 1973 dissent to that decision:

> To reach its result, the Court necessarily has had to find within the scope of the Fourteenth Amendment a right that was apparently completely unknown to the drafters of the Amendment. As early as 1821, the first state law dealing directly with abortion was enacted by the Connecticut Legislature. By the time of the adoption of the Fourteenth Amendment in 1868, there were at least 36 laws enacted by state or territorial legislatures limiting abortion. While many states have amended or updated their laws, 21 of the laws on the books in 1968 remain in effect today. Indeed, the Texas statute struck down today was, as the majority notes, first enacted in 1857 and has remained substantially unchanged to the present time.
>
> There apparently was no question concerning the validity of this provision or of any of the other state statutes when the Fourteenth Amendment was adopted. The only conclusion possible from this history is that the drafters did not intend to have the Fourteenth Amendment withdraw from the states the power to legislate with respect to this matter.[33]

Thus, applying the Court's own tests, it is clear that there is no constitutional right to abortion. As a result, the Supreme Court has simply arbitrarily declared one by saying that the right of privacy—previously found by the Court in the "liberty" clause—"is broad enough to encompass a woman's decision whether or not to terminate her pregnancy."[34] In so doing, the Court brushed aside the restraints placed on it by the Constitution, seized power from the People, and placed within the protections of the Constitution an abortion right that does not properly belong there.

One thing is clear from this nation's abortion debate: abortion advocates do not trust the People to decide how abortion should be regulated.[35] However, in rejecting the voice of the People, abortion partisans also reject the very foundation of our democratic Republic and seek to install an oligarchy—with the Court governing the nation—a system of government rejected by our Constitution.

II. THE INTEREST IN PROTECTING INNOCENT HUMAN LIFE

Abortion rights advocates generally ignore one key fact about abortion: abortion requires the willful taking of innocent human life. Abortion involves not merely the issue of what a woman may do with her body. Rather, abortion also involves the question of what may the woman do with the body of another, the unborn child.

A. The People Have an Interest in Protecting Preborn Human Life

The fact that human life begins at conception was well-known at the time the Fourteenth Amendment was ratified in 1868. In fact it was precisely during the time when this Amendment was adopted that the medical profession was carrying the news of the discovery of cell biology and its implications into the legislatures of the states and territories. Prior to that time, science had followed the view of Aristotle that the unborn child became a human being (i.e., received a human soul) at some point after conception (40 days for males and 80–90 days for females).[36] This flawed scientific view became the basis for the "quickening" (greater legal protection was provided to the unborn from abortion after the mother felt movement in the womb than before) distinction in the common law received from England, which imposed lesser penalties for abortions performed prior to "quickening." With the scientific discovery of cell biology, however, the legislatures acted promptly to alter abortion laws to reflect the newly established scientific fact that individual human life begins at conception.

Victor Rosenblum summarized the history well:

> Only in the second quarter of the nineteenth century did biological research advance to the extent of understanding the actual mechanism of human reproduction and of what truly comprised the onset of gestational development. The nineteenth century saw a gradual but profoundly influential revolution in the scientific understanding of the beginning of individual mammalian life. Although sperm had been discovered in 1677, the mammalian egg was not identified until 1827. The cell was first recognized as the structural unit of organisms in 1839, and the egg and sperm were recognized as cells in the next two decades. These developments were brought to the attention of the American state legislatures and public by those professionals most familiar with their unfolding import—physicians. It was the new research findings which persuaded doctors that the old "quickening" distinction embodied in the common and some statutory law was unscientific and indefensible.[37]

About 1857, the American Medical Association led the "physicians' crusade," a successful campaign to push the legal protection provided for the unborn by abortion laws from quickening to conception.[38]

What science discovered over a century before *Roe v. Wade* was true in 1973 (when *Roe* was decided) and still holds true today. For example, a recent textbook on human embryology declared:

> It is the penetration of the ovum by a spermatozoon and the resultant mingling of the nuclear material each brings to the union that constitutes the culmination of the process of *fertilization* and *marks the initiation of the life of a new individual.*[39]

However, abortion rights advocates attempt to obscure the scientific evidence that individual human life begins at conception by the claiming that conception is a "complex" process and by confusing contraception with abortion.[40]

The complexity of the process of conception does not change the fact that it marks the certain beginning of individual human life.[41] Moreover, the complex process of conception occurs in a very brief time at the beginning of pregnancy.[42]

Furthermore, the fact that some so-called "contraceptives" actually act after conception and would be more correctly termed "abortifacients" (substances or devices causing abortion, i.e., acting to abort a pregnancy already begun at conception) does nothing to blur the line at which individual human life begins. It only indicates that some so-called "contraceptives" have been mislabelled.[43] Such mislabelling misleads women, who have a right to know whether they are receiving a contraceptive or are having an abortion.

The "spin"[44] which abortion advocates place on the redefinition of "contraception" is deceptive in two respects. First, there is a clear distinction between devices and substances which act before conception and those which act after conception. This was admitted by Planned Parenthood itself (before it became involved in advocating, referring for, and performing abortions) in a 1963 pamphlet entitled *Plan Your Children*: "An abortion kills the life of a baby after it has begun. . . . Birth control merely postpones the beginning of life."[45]

Second, even if there were no "bright physiological line . . . between the moments before and after conception"[46] this does not mean there can be no constitutional line.[47] At *some point* early in pregnancy, scientific truth compels the conclusion that individual human life has begun. If the indistinction is the real problem, then abortion advocates should be joining prolife supporters in protecting unborn life from a time when there is certitude.[48] However, abortion partisans are not really interested in protecting unborn human life from the time when it may be certain that it exists. They are seeking to justify absolute, on-demand abortion throughout pregnancy.

B. Abortion Rights Advocates Envision an Abortion-on-Demand Regime Unsupported by the People

Abortion rights proponents often argue that our democratic Republic must sanction abortion on demand lest women resort to dangerous "back-alley" abortions. The claims of abortion advocates that thousands of women died each year when abortion was illegal are groundless fabrications created for polemical purposes.[49] In reality, the Surgeon General of the United States has estimated that only a handful of deaths occurred each year in the United States due to illegal abortions.[50] Even since *Roe*, there are still maternal deaths from legal abortions.[51] As tragic as the death of any person is, it must be acknowledged that women who obtain illegal abortions do so by choice and most women will choose to abide by the law. In contrast, preborn human beings are destroyed—without having a choice—at the rate of about 1.5 million per year in the United States alone.[52]

Abortion supporters also resort to the practice of personally attacking prolifers and making false charges about them.[53] A founding member of what is now called the National Abortion Rights Action League (NARAL) chronicles how prolifers were purposely portrayed as Catholics whenever possible, in an attempt to appeal to latent (and sometimes overt) anti-Catholic sentiment in certain communities.[54] It is also routinely claimed that opposition to abortion is really an attempt to "keep women in their place"[55]—to subjugate them—as if requiring fathers to support their children subjugates them. And prolifers are depicted as forcing what are merely their religious views upon society,[56] despite the fact that the United States Supreme Court has held that opposition to abortion "is as much a reflection of 'traditionalist' values towards abortion, as it is an embodiment of the views of any particular religion."[57] Those attempting so to "poison the well," by attacking prolife supporters with untruthful allegations, ignore the fact that polls consistently show that abortion opinion is rather evenly divided in our country within all major demographic groups. For example, women are roughly equally divided on the subject, as are whites, non-whites, Republicans and Democrats.[58] Abortion advocates also ignore the fact that most prolifers simply are opposed to the taking of what they consider (and science demonstrates) to be innocent human life.

Of even greater risk than the risk to a few women who might choose to obtain illegal abortions is the effect of abortion on demand—for any or no reason—on society. Abortion cheapens the value of human life, promotes the idea that it is permissible to solve one's problems at the expense of another, even to the taking of the other's life, legitimizes violence (which abortion is against the unborn) as an appropriate solution for problems, and exposes a whole class of human beings (those preborn) to discrimination on the basis of their age or place of residence (or sometimes their race, gender, or disability).

The regime which abortion-on-demand advocates envision for our society is a radical one. Their ideal society is one where abortions may be obtained for any reason, including simply because the child is the wrong sex; where a husband need not be given any consideration in (or even notice of) an abortion decision involving a child which he fathered; where fathers are shut out even when the child to be aborted might be the only one a man could ever have; where parents could remain ignorant of their daughter's abortion, even when she is persuaded to abort by counselors at an abortion mill whose practitioners care only about financial gain, practice their trade dangerously, and never bother to follow up with their patients; where abortion may be used as a means of birth control; where abortionists do not offer neutral, scientific information about fetal development (and about resources for choosing alternatives to

abortion) to women considering abortion; where women are not given adequate time to consider whether they really want an abortion; where abortion is
available right up to the time of birth; and where our taxes are used to pay for
abortion on demand.[59]

The American People reject such a regime. In fact, polls show that an overwhelming majority would ban well over 90 percent of all abortions that are performed.[60] For example a Boston Globe national poll . . . revealed that:

> Most Americans would ban the vast majority of abortions performed in this
> country. . . .
>
> While 78 percent of the nation would keep abortion legal in limited circum-
> stances, according to the poll, those circumstances account for a tiny percent-
> age of the reasons cited by women having abortions.
>
> When pregnancy results from rape or incest, when the mother's physical
> health is endangered and when there is likely to be a genetic deformity in the
> fetus, those queried strongly approve of legal abortion.
>
> But when pregnancy poses financial or emotional strain, or when the woman
> is alone or a teen-ager—the reasons given by most women seeking abortions—
> an overwhelming majority of Americans believes abortion should be illegal,
> the poll shows.[61]

Yet *Family Planning Perspectives*, a publication of the Alan Guttmacher
Institute, which is a research arm of the Planned Parenthood Federation,
reveals that these are precisely the reasons why over 90 percent of abortions
are performed.[62]

Thus, it is little wonder that the Supreme Court's effort to settle the abortion question with its decision in *Roe v. Wade* has utterly failed. That there is not
an even greater groundswell of public opposition to abortion must be attributed to the fact that many Americans are not aware that *Roe* requires virtual
abortion on demand for the full nine months of pregnancy.[63] Many people still
believe that abortion is only available in the earliest weeks of pregnancy and
that abortions are usually obtained for grave reasons, such as rape and incest,
which abortion rights advocates always talk about in abortion debates. Of
course, such "hard" cases make up only a tiny fraction of all abortions, and
many state abortion laws, even before *Roe*, allowed abortions for such grave
reasons. It is clear, therefore, that the People reject the radical abortion-on-
demand regime promoted by abortion rights advocates.

III. CONCLUSION: STATES CONSTITUTIONALLY MAY AND MORALLY SHOULD LIMIT ABORTION ON DEMAND

One of the principles underlying our liberal democratic Republic is that we as a
People choose to give the maximum freedom possible to members of our society.
John Stuart Mill's essay *On Liberty*,[64] a ubiquitous source on the subject, is often
cited for the principle that people ought to be granted maximum liberty—almost
to the degree of license. Yet, Mill himself set limits on liberty relevant to the

abortion debate. Mill wrote his essay *On Liberty* to assert "one very simple princi- ple," namely, "[t]hat the only purpose for which power can be rightfully exercised over any member of a civilized community, against his will, is to prevent harm to others."[65] Thus, under Mill's principles, abortion should go unrestricted only if it does no harm to another. But that, of course, is precisely the core of the abortion debate. If a fetus is not really an individual human being until he or she is born, then the moral issue is reduced to what duty is owed to potential life (which is still a significant moral issue). If however, a fetus is an individual human being from the moment of conception (or at least some time shortly thereafter), then the unborn are entitled to legal protection. Ironically, the United States Supreme Court neglected this key determination—when human life begins—in its *Roe* decision.[66]

Science, of course, has provided the answer to us for well over a hundred years. Indeed, modern science and technological advances have impressed upon us more fully the humanity and individuality of each unborn person. As Dr. Liley has said:

> Another fallacy that modern obstetrics discards is the idea that the pregnant woman can be treated as a patient alone. No problem in fetal health or disease can any longer be considered in isolation. At the very least two people are involved, the mother and her child.[67]

In fact, since *Roe*, the technology for improving fetal therapy is advancing expo- nentially.[68] In sum, modern science has shown us that:

> The fetus as patient is becoming more of a reality each year. New medical ther- apies and surgical technology increasingly offer parents a new choice when a fetus has a particular disorder. Recently, the only choices were abortion, early delivery, vaginal versus a cesarean delivery, or no intervention. We are now able to offer medical and/or surgical intervention as a viable alternative to a number of infants. With advancing technologies, it is clearly evident that many new and exciting therapies lie just ahead for the fetus.[69]

Because all civilized moral codes limit the liberty of individuals where the exercise of liberty would result in the taking of innocent human life, arguments that abortion is necessary to prevent the subjugation of women must also be rejected.[70] It cannot logically be considered the subjugation of anyone to prevent him or her from taking innocent human life; otherwise, society could not pre- vent infanticide, homicide, or involuntary euthanasia. No civilized society could exist if the unjustified killing of one citizen by another could not be prosecuted.

Nor do abortion restrictions deny women equality by denying them the same freedom which men have. Men do not have the right to kill their children, nor may they force women to do so. Thus, abortion rights advocates are really arguing for a right that men don't have, and, indeed, no one should have— the right to take innocent human life.

Society has recognized that in some situations men and women should be treated differently, because they are biologically different and are, therefore, not similarly situated for constitutional purposes. For example, the Supreme Court decided in 1981 that a statute that permitted only men to be drafted was not unconstitutional because "[m]en and women . . . are simply not similarly situated for purposes of a draft or registration for a draft."[71] The same principle, however, made constitutional a Navy policy which allowed women a longer period of time for promotion prior to mandatory discharge than was allowed for men.[72] The Supreme Court in this case found that "the different treatment of men and women naval officers . . . reflects, not archaic and overbroad generalizations, but, instead, the demonstrable fact that male and female line officers . . . are not similarly situated."[73] Because men and women are not similarly situated—by the dictates of nature rather than by society or the law—with respect to pregnancy, it is neither a denial of equality to women nor the subjugation of women to provide legal protection for unborn human beings.[74]

It is essential to a civilized society to limit liberties where reasonably necessary to protect others. Thus, government has required involuntary vaccination to prevent a plague from decimating the community,[75] military conscription to prevent annihilation of the populace by enemies,[76] and the imposition of child support—for 18 years—upon fathers unwilling to support their children.[77] These and other limits on freedom are not the subjugation of citizens, but are the essence of life in a community.

In sum, the states constitutionally may and morally should limit abortion on demand.

NOTES

1. 410 U.S. 113 (1973).
2. *Id.* at 153.
3. See *infra*, notes 13–19 and accompanying text.
4. U.S. Const., preamble.
5. In the landmark case of *Marbury v. Madison*, 1 Cranch 137, 176 (1803), the United States Supreme Court explained, "That the people have an original right to establish, for their future government, such principles, as, in their own opinion, shall most conduce to their own happiness is the basis on which the whole American fabric has been erected. See also The Declaration of Independence, para. 2 (U.S. 1776); *The Federalist*, No. 49 (J. Madison).
6. *Marbury*, 1 Cranch at 176 ("The original and supreme will [of the People] organizes the government, and assigns to different departments their respective powers. It may either stop here, or establish certain limits not to be transcended by those departments. The government of the United States is of the latter description.").
7. See, e.g., *id.* at 163 ("The government of the United States has been emphatically termed a government of laws, and not of men."); *Akron v. Akron Center for Reproductive Health*, 462 U.S. 416, 419–20 (1983) (We are a "society governed by the rule of law.").
8. *Marbury*, 1 Cranch at 177 ("Certainly all those who have framed written constitutions contemplate them as forming the fundamental and paramount law of the nation. . . ."); *id.* at 179 ("[T]he constitution of the United

States confirms and strengthens the principle, supposed to be essential to all written constitutions, that a law repugnant to the constitution is void; and that courts, as well as other departments, are bound by that instrument.").

9. The Constitution enumerates certain rights; the creation of additional constitutionally protected rights is through amending the Constitution, which depends upon establishing public support for such a right by a supermajority of the People acting through their elected representatives. U.S. Const., art. V. *Cf.* Bork, "Neutral Principles and Some First Amendment Problems," 47 *Ind. L. J.* 1, 3 (1971).

10. U.S. Const., art. I, § 1, art. II, § 1, art. III, § 1.

11. U.S. Const., amend. IX ("The enumeration in the Constitution, of certain rights, shall not be construed to deny or disparage others retained by the people."), amend. X ("The powers not delegated to the United States by the Constitution, nor prohibited by it to the States, are reserved to the States respectively, or to the people.").

12. 410 U.S. 113.

13. Ely, "The Wages of Crying Wolf: A Comment on *Roe v. Wade,*" 82 *Yale L.J.* 920, 947 (1973) (*Roe* was "a very bad decision. Not because it [would] perceptibly weaken the Court . . . and not because it conflict[ed] with [his] idea of progress. . . . It [was] bad because it [was] bad constitutional law, or rather because it [was] not constitutional law and [gave] almost no sense of an obligation to try to be.") (emphasis in the original). *Doe v. Bolton,* 410 U.S. 179, 222 (1973) (White, J., dissenting in this companion case to *Roe*) (The Court's action is "an exercise of raw judicial power. . . . This issue, for the most part, should be left with the people and to the political processes the people have devised to govern their affairs.").

14. The *Michigan Law Review,* in an edition devoted to abortion jurisprudence, contained two passages which summarize the scholarly critiques well. In the first, Richard Morgan wrote:

> Rarely does the Supreme Court invite critical outrage as it did in *Roe* by offering so little explanation for a decision that requires so much. The stark inadequacy of the Court's attempt to justify its conclusions . . . suggests to some scholars that the Court, finding no justification at all in the Constitution, unabashedly usurped the legislative function.

Morgan, "*Roe v. Wade* and the Lesson of the Pre-*Roe* Case Law," 77 *Mich. L. Rev.* 1724, 1724 (1979). The editors of the journal concluded from their survey of the literature on *Roe,* "[T]he consensus among legal academics seems to be that, whatever one thinks of the holding, the opinion is unsatisfying." "Editor's Preface," 77 *Mich. L. Rev.* (no number) (1979).

15. *Roe,* 400 U.S. at 174–77 (Rehnquist, J., dissenting).

16. See, e.g., Wardle, " 'Time Enough': *Webster v. Reproductive Health Services* and the Prudent Pace of Justice," 41 *Fla. L. Rev.* 881, 927–49 (1989); Bopp & Coleson, "The Right to Abortion: Anomalous, Absolute, and Ripe for Reversal," 3 *B.Y.U. J. Pub. L.* 181, 185–92 (1989) (cataloging critiques of *Roe* in yet another critique of *Roe*).

17. Bork, *supra* note 9, at 6.
18. Epstein, "Substantive Due Process by Any Other Name: The Abortion Cases," 1973 *Sup. Ct. Rv.* 159, 184.
19. *Id.* at 185.
20. The Court acknowledged this duty in *Roe* itself, but failed to apply the usual tests for determining what rights are rightfully deemed "fundamental." *Roe*, 410 U.S. at 152.
21. U.S. Const., amend. XIV, § 1, cl. 3.
22. *Roe v. Wade*, 410 U.S. 113, revived this sort of "substantive due process" analysis in recent years.
23. The Greek philosopher Plato advocated rule by a class of philosopher-guardians as the ideal form of government. A. Bloom, *The Republic of Plato*, 376c, lines 4–5, 412b–427d (1968).
24. See, e.g., Ely, *supra* note 13; Bork, *supra* note 9.
25. In repudiating an earlier line of "substantive due process" (i.e., finding new rights in the "liberty" clause of the Fourteenth Amendment) cases symbolized by *Lochner v. New York*, 198 U.S. 45 (1905), the Supreme Court declared that the doctrine "that due process authorizes courts to hold laws unconstitutional when they believe the legislature has acted unwisely, has been discarded." *Ferguson v. Skrupa*, 372 U.S. 726, 730 (1963). The Court concluded in *Ferguson*, "We have returned to the original constitutional proposition that courts do not substitute their social and economic beliefs for the judgment of legislative bodies, who are elected to pass laws." *Id.*
26. *Griswold v. Connecticut*, 381 U.S. 479, 502 (1965) (Harlan, J., concurring.)
27. Cf. *Duncan v. Louisiana*, 391 U.S. 145, 149–50 n.14 (1968), with *Roe v. Wade*, 410 U.S. at 152, and *Moore v. City of East Cleveland*, 431 U.S. 494, 503–04 n.12 (1977). See also Ely, *supra* note 13, at 931 n.79 (The *Palko* test was of "questionable contemporary vitality" when *Roe* was decided).
28. *Roe*, 410 U.S. at 152 (quoting *Palko v. Connecticut*, 302 U.S. 319, 325 (1937)) (quotation marks omitted).
29. *Palko*, 302 U.S., at 325 (quoting *Snyder v. Massachusetts*, 291 U.S. 97, 105 (1934)) (quotation marks omitted).
30. *Roe*, 410 U.S. at 139.
31. *Black's Law Dictionary*, 1500 (5th ed. 1979).
32. J. Mohr, *Abortion in America: The Origins and Evolution of National Policy 1800–1900*, 200 (1978). These laws were clearly aimed at protecting preborn human beings and not just maternal health, *id.* at 35–36, so that medical improvements bringing more maternal safety to abortions do not undercut the foundations of these laws, as *Roe* alleged. *Roe*, 410 U.S. at 151–52.
33. *Roe*, 410 U.S. at 174–77 (Rehnquist, J., dissenting) (citations and quotation marks omitted).
34. *Id.* at 153.
35. Cf. Estrich & Sullivan, "Abortion Politics: Writing for an Audience of One," 138 *U. Pa. L. Rev.* 119, 150–55 (1989), with *Webster v. Reproductive Health Services*, 109 S. Ct. 3040, 3058 (1989) (plurality opinion). In *Webster*, the plurality opinion declared:

> The goal of constitutional adjudication is to hold true the balance between that which the Constitution puts beyond the reach of the democratic process and that which it does not. We think we have done that today. The dissent's suggestion that legislative bodies, in a Nation where more than half of our population is women, will treat our decision today as an invitation to enact abortion regulation reminiscent of the dark ages not only misreads our views but does scant justice to those who serve in such bodies and the people who elect them.

    Id. (citation omitted).

36. *Roe,* 410 U.S. at 133 n.22.
37. *The Human Life Bill: Hearings on S. 158 Before the Subcomm. on Separation of Powers of the Senate Comm. on the Judiciary,* 97th Cong., 1st Sess. 474 (statement of Victor Rosenblum). See also Dellapenna, "The History of Abortion: Technology, Morality, and Law," 40 *U. Pitt. L. Rev.* 359, 402–04 (1979).
38. J. Mohr, *supra* note 32, at 147–70. This 19th-century legislation was designed to protect the unborn as stated explicitly by 11 state court decisions interpreting these statutes and implicitly by 9 others. Gorby, "The 'Right' to an Abortion, the Scope of Fourteenth Amendment 'Personhood,' and the Supreme Court's Birth Requirement," 1979 S. *Ill, U.L.J.* 1, 16–17. Twenty-six of the 36 states had laws against abortion as early as 1865, the end of the Civil War, as did six of the ten territories. Dellapenna, *supra* note 37, at 429.
39. B. Patten, *Human Embryology,* 43 (3rd ed. 1969) (emphasis added). See also L. Arey, *Developmental Anatomy,* 55 (7th ed. 1974); W. Hamilton & H. Mossman, *Human Embryology,* 1, 14 (4th ed. 1972); K. Moore, *The Developing Human: Clinically Oriented Embryology,* 1, 12, 24 (2nd ed. 1977); *Human Reproduction, Conception and Contraception,* 461 (Hafez ed., 2nd ed. 1980); J. Greenhill & E. Friedman, *Biological Principles and Modern Practice of Obstetrics,* 17, 23 (1974); D. Reid, K. Ryan & K. Benirschke, *Principles and Management of Human Reproduction,* 176 (1972).
40. See, e.g., Estrich & Sullivan, *supra* note 35, at 128–29. While a complete discussion of cell biology, genetics and fetology is beyond the scope of this brief writing, the standard reference works cited by Estrich & Sullivan verify the fact that individual human life begins at conception.
41. *Supra,* note 39.
42. *Id.*
43. By its etymology (*contra* + *conception,* i.e., against conception) and traditional and common usage, the term *"contraception"* properly refers to "[t]he prevention of conception or impregnation," Dorland's *Illustrated Medical Dictionary,* 339 (24th ed. 1965), or a "deliberate prevention of conception or impregnation," *Webster's Ninth New Collegiate Dictionary,* 284 (1985).
44. Estrich & Sullivan, *supra* note 35, at 1.
45. Planned Parenthood International, *Plan Your Children* (1963).
46. Estrich & Sullivan, *supra* note 35, at 129.
47. At oral arguments in *Webster v. Reproductive Health Services,* 109 S. Ct. 3040 (1989), Justice Antonin Scalia could see a distinction between contraception and abortion, remarking, "I don't see why a court that can draw that line

[between the first, second, and third trimesters of pregnancy] cannot separate abortion from birth control quite readily."

48. For example, the West German Constitutional Court in 1975 set aside a federal abortion statute which was too permissive, for it "did not sufficiently protect unborn life." M. Glendon, *Abortion and Divorce in Western Law*, 33 (1987). The West German court began with the presumption that "at least after the fourteenth day, developing human life is at stake." *Id.* at 34.

49. B. Nathanson, *Aborting America*, 193 (1979). Nathanson, a former abortionist and early, organizing member of the National Association for the Repeal of Abortion Laws (NARAL, now known as the National Abortion Rights Action League), says:

> In N.A.R.A.L. . . . . it was always "5,000 to 10,000 deaths a year [from illegal abortion]." I confess that I knew the figures were totally false. . . . In 1967, with moderate A.L.I.-type laws in three states, the federal government listed only 160 deaths from illegal abortion. In the last year before the [*Roe*] era began, 1972, the total was only 39 deaths. Christopher Tietze estimated 1,000 maternal deaths as the outside possibility in an average year before legalization; the actual total was probably closer to 500.

Id. at 193. Nathanson adds that even this limited "carnage" argument must now be dismissed "because technology has eliminated it." *Id.* at 194 (referring to the fact that even abortions made illegal by more restrictive abortion laws will generally be performed with modern techniques providing greater safety, and antibiotics now resolve most complications).

50. U.S. Dept. of Health and Human Services, *Centers for Disease Control Abortion Surveillance*, 61 (annual summary 1978, issued Nov. 1980) (finding that there were 39 maternal deaths due to illegal abortion in 1972, the last year before *Roe*).

51. Deaths from legally induced abortions were as follows: 1972 = 24, 1973 = 26, 1974 = 26, 1975 = 31, 1976 = 11, 1977 = 17, 1978 = 11. *Id.* During the same period, deaths from illegal abortions continued as follows: 1972 = 39, 1973 = 19, 1974 = 6, 1975 = 4, 1976 = 2, 1977 = 4, 1978 = 7. *Id.*

52. See, e.g., Henshaw, Forrest & Van Vort, "Abortion Services in the United States, 1984 and 1985," 19 *Fam. Plan. Persps.* 64, table 1 (1987) (at the rate of roughly 1.5 million abortions per year for the 18 years from 1973 to 1990, there have been about 27 million abortions in the U.S.A.).

53. Estrich & Sullivan, *supra* note 35, at 152–54.

54. B. Nathanson, *The Abortion Papers: Inside the Abortion Mentality*, 177–209 (1983).

55. Estrich & Sullivan, *supra* note 35, at 152–54.

56. See, e.g., *id.* at 153 n.132.

57. *Harris v. McRae*, 448 U.S. 297, 319 (1980).

58. See generally R. Adamek, *Abortion and Public Opinion in the United States* (1989).

59. These are some of the radical positions urged by abortion rights partisans in cases such as *Roe v. Wade*, 410 U.S. 113, *Planned Parenthood of Central Missouri v. Danforth*, 428 U.S. 52 (1976), and *Thornburgh v. American College of Obstetricians and Gynecologists*, 476 U.S. 747 (1986).

60. "Most in US favor ban on majority of abortions, poll finds," *Boston Globe,* March 31, 1989, at 1, col. 2–4.

61. *Id.*

62. Torres & Forrest, "Why Do Women Have Abortions?" 20 *Fam. Plan. Persps.,* 169 (1988). Table 1 of this article reveals the following reasons and percentages of women giving their most important reason for choosing abortion: 16% said they were concerned about how having a baby would change their life; 21% said they couldn't afford a baby now; 12% said they had problems with a relationship and wanted to avoid single parenthood; 21% said they were unready for responsibility; 1% said they didn't want others to know they had sex or were pregnant; 11% said they were not mature enough or were too young to have a child; 8% said they had all the children they wanted or had all grown-up children; 1% said their husband wanted them to have an abortion; 3% said the fetus had possible health problems; 3% said they had a health problem; less than .5% said their parents wanted them to have an abortion; 1% said they were a victim of rape or incest; and 3% gave another, unspecified reason. (Figures total more than 100% due to rounding off of numbers.) It is significant to note, also, that 39% of all abortions are repeat abortions. Henshaw, "Characteristics of U.S. Women Having Abortions, 1982–1983," 19 *Fam. Plan. Persps.* 1, 6 (1987).

63. *Roe* held that a state may prohibit abortion after fetal viability, but that it may not do so where the mother's "life or health" would be at risk. 410 U.S. at 165. In the companion case to *Roe, Doe v. Bolton,* the Supreme Court construed "health" in an extremely broad fashion to include "all factors—physical, emotional, psychological, familial, and the woman's age—relevant to the well-being of the patient." 410 U.S. 179, 195 (1973). The breadth of these factors makes a "health" reason for an abortion extremely easy to establish, so that we have virtual abortion on demand for all nine months of pregnancy in America. Moreover, there are physicians who declare that if a woman simply seeks an abortion she *ipso facto* has a "health" reason and the abortion may be performed. *McRae v. Califano,* No. 76-C-1804 (E.D.N.Y. Transcript, August 3, 1977, pp. 99–101) (Testimony of Dr. Jane Hodgson) (Dr. Hodgson testified that she felt that there was a medical indication to abort a pregnancy if it "is not wanted by the patient.").

64. J. Mill, *On Liberty* (Atlantic Monthly Press edition 1921).

65. *Id.* at 13. It should be noted that Mill's contention that society should never use its power to protect the individual from the actions of himself or herself is hotly disputed. See, e.g., J. Stephen, *Liberty, Equality, Fraternity* (R. White ed. 1967) (the 1873 classic response to Mill); P. Devlin, *The Enforcement of Morals* (1974).

66. *Roe,* 410 U.S. at 159 ("We need not resolve the difficult question of when life begins.").

67. H. Liley, *Modern Motherhood* 207 (1969).

68. "Technology for Improving Fetal Therapy Advancing Exponentially," *Ob. Gyn. News,* Aug. 1–14, 1987, at 31.

69. P. Williams, "Medical and Surgical Treatment for the Unborn Child," in *Human Life and Health Care Ethics,* 77 (J. Bopp ed. 1985).

70. Estrich & Sullivan, *supra* note 35, at 152–54. In legal terms, this argument is an equal protection one. See *id.* at 124 n.10. However, equal protection of the laws is only constitutionally guaranteed to those who are equally situated, and the Supreme Court has held that treating pregnancy differently from other matters does not constitute gender-based discrimination. *Geduldig v. Aiello*, 417 U.S. 484, 496–97 n.20 (1974). For a further discussion of this point, see Bopp, "Will There Be a Constitutional Right to Abortion After the Reconsideration of *Roe v. Wade*?" 15 *J. Contemp. L.* 131, 136–41 (1989). See also Smolin, "Why Abortion Rights Are Not Justified by Reference to Gender Equality: A Response to Professor Tribe," 23 *John Marshall L. Rev.* 621 (1990).
71. *Rostker v. Goldberg*, 453 U.S. 57 (1981).
72. *Schlesinger v. Ballard*, 419 U.S. 498 (1975).
73. *Id.* at 508.
74. Bopp, "Is Equal Protection a Shelter for the Right to Abortion?" in *Abortion, Medicine and the Law* (4th ed. 1991).
75. *Jacobson v. Massachusetts*, 197 U.S. 11 (1905).
76. *The Selective Service Draft Law Cases*, 245 U.S. 366 (1918).
77. See, e.g., *Sistare v. Sistare*, 218 U.S. 1 (1910). All states have recognized this obligation by passage of the Uniform Reciprocal Enforcement of Support Act. See Fox, "The Uniform Reciprocal Enforcement of Support Act," 12 *Fam. L.Q.* 113, 113–14 (1978).

Internet resources
Visit our Web site at www.mhhe.com/diclerico11e for links and resources relating to Civil Rights.